Pt. Jawaharlal Nehru

Pandit Jawaharlal Nehru

Series Editor
Dr. M.H. Syed

Editor
Anil Kathuria **Bharat Singh**

Himalaya Books Pvt. Ltd.
'Ramdoot', Dr. Bhalerao Marg, Girgaon, Mumbai - 400 004
Tel : (022) 23863863, Fax : (022) 23877178
Email : himpub@vsnl.com

Edition : 2017

Published by : **H.B.P.L.**
"Pooja Apartments", 4-B, Murari Lal Street, Ansari Road,
Darya Ganj, New Delhi-110 002
Phones : 23270392, 23278631
Fax : 011-23256286 Email : hphdel@vsnl.com

Sole Distributers : HIMALAYA PUBLISHING HOUSE PVT. LTD.

Branch Offices

Mumbai : "Ramdoot", Dr. Bhalerao Marg, Girgaon, Mumbai-400 004.
Phones : 23860170/23863863 Fax : 022-23877178
Email : himpub@vsnl.com
Website : www.himpub.com

Nagpur : Kundanlal Chandak Industrial Estate, Ghat Road, **Nagpur - 440 018.**
Phone: 2738731, 3296733 Telefax : 0712-2721215

Bengaluru : No. 16/1 (Old 12/1), 1st Floor, Next to Hotel Highlands, Madhava Nagar, Race Course Road, **Bengaluru - 560 001.**
Phone : 22281541, 22385461, Telefax: 080-22286611

Hyderabad : No. 3-4-184, Lingampally, Besides Raghavendra Swamy Matham, Kachiguda, **Hyderabad - 500 027.** Phone: 040-27560041, 27550139,
Mobile:- 09848130433 Telefax: 040-27560041

Chennai : No. 85/50, Bazullah Road, T. Nagar, **Chennai - 600 017.**
Phone: 044-28344020, 32463737, 42124860

Pune : No. 527, "Laksha" Apartment, First Floor, Mehunpura, Shaniwarpeth, (Near Prabhat Theatre), **Pune - 411 030.**
Phone: 020-24496323/24496333/32326733

Lucknow : Jai Baba Bhawan, Near Manas Complex, Church Road, Aliganj, **Lucknow - 226 024.** Phone: 0522-2339329, 9305302158, 9415349385

Ahmedabad : No. 114, "SHAIL", 1st Floor, Opp. Madhu Sudan House, C.G.Road, Navrang Pura, **Ahmedabad – 380 009.**
Phone: 079-26560126, Mobiles: 09327324149, 09314679413

Ernakulam : No. 39/104 A, Lakshmi Apartment, Karikkamuri Cross Rd., Ernakulam, **Cochin – 682011**, Kerala. Phone: 0484-2378012, 2378016,
Mob.: 09344199799

Bhubaneswar : 5 Station Square, **Bhubaneswar (Orissa) - 751 001.**
Mobile: 9861046007, E-mail:- orissa@himpub.com

Indore : Kesardeep Avenue Extension, 73, Narayan Bagh.Flat No. 302, IIIrd Floor, Near Humpty Dumpty School, Narayan Bagh, **Indore (M.P.) 452 007**
Mobile: 09301386468

Kolkata : 108/4, Beliaghata, Main Road, Near ID Hospital, Opp. SBI Bank **Kolkata - 700 010.** Mobile: 09910440956, E-mail:- nkmitra@himpub.com

Guwahati : House No. 15, Behind Prajjyotish College, Near Sharma Printing Press, P.O. Bharalumukh, Guwahati - 781009 (Assam
Mobile: 07439040301; 07439040302

Printed by : Infinity Imaging Systems, New Delhi.

Preface

Biography, is now a form of literature, very much in vogue. In fact, biography is a description or account of someone's life and the times, which is usually published in the form of a book. A biography is more than a mention of personal facts (life, education, work, relationships and death), it also portrays the subject's experience of events. Technically speaking, a work is biographical, if it covers, all of a person's life. Biography writing has a long history. A biography is real. Ancient Greeks developed the biographical tradition, which we have inherited, although until the 5th century AD, when the word 'biographia' first appeared, in Damascius' "Life of Isodorus," biographical pieces were called simply "lives". It is quite likely that the Greeks were drawing on a pre-existing eastern tradition. Certainly Herodotus' "Histories" contains more detailed biographical information on Persian kings and subjects. The earliest surviving pieces, which we would identify as biographical are Isocrates' "Life of Evagoras" and Xenophon's "Life of Agesilaos," both from the fifth century BC. "Parallel Lives" by Plutarch, a Greek writing under the Roman empire, is a series of short biographies of eminent men.

The Golden Age of English biography emerged in late eighteenth century, the century in which the terms "biography" and "autobiography" entered English lexicon. The classic works of the period were Samuel Johnson's "Critical Lives of the Poets" and James Boswell's "Massive Life of Johnson". Generally American biography followed English model. By World War I, cheap hardcover reprints had become popular. The decade of the

1920s witnessed a biographical 'boom'. Later, biographical writings developed a lot and today biographies are written and compiled in the finest form of the genre. In India too, biography, as a form of literature has been evolved, cultivated and polished over the years. Here is an effort to promote this tradition further.

This series of biographies of great men, great women and celebrities in all walks of life is an adventurous academic endeavour, in its own right. A team of researchers and compilers has worked for a good period of time to accomplish the project. For this purpose, hundreds of books by eminent authors and editors have been consulted and referred to. We have benefited from various works, liberally, in order to illustrate and enrich this effort of ours. Present book is devoted to the great personality of Pt. Jawaharlal Nehru.

Jawaharlal Nehru (14 November 1889–27 May 1964) was a great statesman, who was the first (and to date the longest-serving) prime minister of India, from 1947 until 1964. A leading figure in the Indian independence movement, Nehru was elected by the Congress Party to assume office as independent India's first Prime Minister, and re-elected when the Congress Party won India's first general election in 1952. As one of the founders of the Non-aligned Movement, he was also an important figure in the international politics of the post-war era. The son of a wealthy barrister and politician, Motilal Nehru, he became a leader of the left wing of the Indian National Congress, when still fairly young. Rising to become Congress President, under the mentorship of Mahatma Gandhi, Nehru was a charismatic and radical leader, advocating complete independence from the British Empire. In the long struggle for Indian independence, in which he was a key player, Nehru was eventually recognised as Gandhi's political heir.

This is a compact and comprehensive account of the above mentioned great life, which is bound to attract the attention of scholars, researchers, students and the general readers alike. Let's hope this humble effort would receive a warm welcome and due applause.

— ***Editors***

Contents

1

An Illustrious Life

The great statesman and world leader, Jawaharlal Nehru (14 November 1889 - 27 May 1964) was the first (and to date the longest-serving) Prime Minister of India, from 1947 until 1964. A leading figure in the Indian independence movement, Nehru was elected by the Congress Party to assume office as independent India's first Prime Minister, and re-elected when the Congress Party won India's first general election in 1952. As one of the founders of the Non-aligned Movement, he was also an important figure in the international politics of the post-war era. He is frequently referred to as Pandit Nehru ("pandit" being a Sanskrit and Hindi honorific meaning "scholar" or "teacher") and, specifically in India, as Panditji (with "-ji" being a suffix to the honorific).

The son of a wealthy Indian barrister and politician, Motilal Nehru, Nehru became a leader of the left wing of the Indian National Congress when still fairly young. Rising to become Congress President, under the mentorship of Mahatma Gandhi, Nehru was a charismatic and radical leader, advocating complete independence from the British Empire. In the long struggle for Indian independence, in which he was a key player, Nehru was eventually recognised as Gandhi's political heir. Throughout his life, Nehru was also an advocate for Fabian socialism and the public sector as the means by which long-standing challenges of economic development could be addressed by poorer nations.

Family Background

Jawaharlal Nehru, the first Prime Minister of India, had a strong and influential lineage. Born on the 14th of November, 1889 at Allahabad, Jawaharlal Nehru was the eldest child of Motilal Nehru and Swarup Rani. His family was from Kashmiri heritage and belonged to a high Hindu caste. They were Saraswat Brahmins, who were revered greatly in Allahabad in those days. Originally part of the Kashmiri Pandit community, the Nehrus had to shift to what was called United Provinces. But the family gelled well with the people there and Motilal Nehru, Jawaharlal's father, started practicing law in Allahabad. He was also a highly influential man, both socially as well as politically. He was a learned scholar too. He excelled in several languages that included Persian, Urdu, Arabic, English and many more.

Jawaharlal Nehru and his entire family lived in a large house called 'Anand Bhawan' in Allahabad. The house is still there. Motilal Nehru was a successful man, who was also well known in the society. He was a barrister by profession and won several accolades for his legal works from different spheres. All these brought him lot of name and fame. As a result, he could give his children the best of everything in life. Jawaharlal Nehru was his only son, while he also had two beautiful daughters named Vijaya Lakshmi Pandit and Krishna Pandit. No discrimination was made between the son and daughters in the family. All of them were provided quality education and privileges. All the children were brought amidst immense luxury and comfort. With a swimming pool and a tennis court in the house premises, Jawaharlal Nehru led a lavish life.

Motilal Nehru never compromised on the education and other facilities that are required to make a happy upbringing for children. He emphasised on English and western education for his children. Jawaharlal Nehru received his initial education at home under an English governess. Hindi and Sanskrit were also taught to the children at the Nehru House. Training was also provided to converse in English fluently. Apart from formal education, various

English mannerisms and customs were also taught to Jawaharlal Nehru in his childhood days. The dresses that were adorned by the Nehru family also reflected English style. After some formal education at home, Jawaharlal Nehru also went to a local convent school in Allahabad. At the age of fifteen, he went to England to study at Harrow.

The illustrious family of the Nehrus had a deep impact on the life and childhood of Jawaharlal Nehru. At home, his mother practiced several staunch Hindu customs and even tried to influence young Nehru by them. But she was not much successful in it. Motilal was not a very strong follower of religion, but he was not an absolute atheist too. Motilal Nehru was concerned about very minute details regarding his son. He corresponded with his son, even when he was abroad and enquired about every small detail regarding his stay, studies and all the other curricular activities. Even after coming back from abroad, Jawaharlal Nehru began a firm and solid career with the help of his father. He attained instant fame and glory in his profession and made himself and his family proud.

Motilal Nehru was an active member of the Indian National Congress, which had also influenced and helped in shaping the political life of Jawaharlal Nehru. Motilal Nehru shared extremely good and cordial relation with the British officials. He had a strong belief on British justice and British promises. Several incidents have been sited when Motilal Nehru had been in support of the British officers. His home was also open to various British officers. British officers also respected him and his family and welcomed them to their homes. As a result of this intermingling, Jawaharlal Nehru and his two sisters also got opportunities to have a glimpse of British lifestyle. Some of the British officers could also fluently speak Urdu and Hindi.

Motilal Nehru was a stylish man and he loved to live life luxuriously. He was a follower of beauty and beautiful things. He had the passion of collecting various beautiful articles from various parts of India as well as from foreign countries. He had made a huge collection of artifacts that were considered as masterpieces and rare articles. One of the most important facts that were seen in the family of Jawaharlal Nehru was that, there were no class restrictions or class distinctions. People of all castes and religions were accepted and welcomed in 'Anand Bhawan'. There were many servants in the Nehru household, who belonged to different castes and religions. The doors of 'Anand Bhawan' remained open for all people irrespective of differences in caste and religion.

Another important part of the family of Jawaharlal Nehru was the active participation of his two sisters, Vijaya Lakshmi Pandit and Krishna Pandit in various matters of the family as well as in politics. They supported him and he had a great influence on their lives. Vijaya Lakshmi Pandit mentioned in one of her lectures about the childhood they had spent together. She also emphasised on the influence that Jawaharlal Nehru had on her political career and personal life.

Jawaharlal Nehru did not have a blissful married life. He was married at a young age in the year 1916. When he was at Harrow, Motilal Nehru and his wife decided to find a perfect match for Jawaharlal Nehru. They started their search and found Kamala Kaul, a girl from a middle-class Kashmiri Brahmin family in 1912. She was a thirteen year old girl, well-educated at home and knew Hindu and Urdu. They waited till 1916, when Kamala attained the age of seventeen years. Kamala was finally married to Jawaharlal Nehru in February, 1916.

The initial years of marriage were not very happy for Kamala as Nehru was then basking in glory and paid little importance to the home front. Kamala Nehru was a strong woman and she endured all this without any protest. She also had to endure several blunt remarks from her husband's relatives regarding her inferior social origins. But she did not retaliate to any of these. She began to involve herself in the Indian freedom struggle and even went to the prison. This event also helped her to come closer to her husband. Jawaharlal Nehru and Kamala Nehru also had a beautiful daughter in 1917, who was called Indira Priyadarshini Gandhi. Kamala Nehru also gave birth to a pre-matured baby boy, who died in 1924. After that she underwent a miscarriage after three years.

Kamala Nehru could not bear this trauma and fell seriously ill. She was diagnosed of tuberculosis and underwent treatment in various hospitals in the country as well as abroad. It was during this time that Jawaharlal Nehru realised his love and passion for her. He used to visit her regularly and even took her abroad for treatment. They also spent few days in Switzerland. Finally she breathed her last in 1936.

To summarise, it has been observed that childhood of Jawaharlal Nehru had a great influence on the later life of this great Indian personality. Though he was brought up amidst immense luxury and glory, it did not restrict him from mingling with general masses and feeling their pulse. His family also had a great influence on his social and political career.

Education

Jawaharlal Nehru was educated in Britain at the independent boy's school, Harrow School and Trinity College, Cambridge. During his time in Britain, Nehru was known as Joe Nehru.

Life and Career

Nehru was given the singular honour of raising the flag of independent India in New Delhi on 15 August 1947, the day India gained Independence. Nehru's appreciation of the virtues of parliamentary democracy, secularism and liberalism, coupled with his concerns for the poor and underprivileged, are recognised to have guided him in formulating policies that influence India to this day. They also reflect the socialist origins of his worldview. His long tenure was instrumental in shaping the traditions and structures of independent India. He is sometimes referred to as the "Architect of Modern India". His daughter, Indira Gandhi, and grandson, Rajiv Gandhi, also served as Prime Ministers of India.

Gita Sahgal — a writer and journalist who addresses issues of feminism, fundamentalism, and racism, director of prize-winning documentary films, and human rights activist — is his grand-niece.

Successor to Gandhi

On 15 January 1941 Gandhiji said, "Some say Pandit Nehru and I were estranged. It will require much more than difference of opinion to estrange us. We had differences from the time we became co-workers and yet I have said for some years and say now that not Rajaji (Chakravarti Rajagopalachari) but Nehru will be my successor."

Towards Freedom

Written in 1936, it ran nine editions in the first year alone. "Towards Freedom" is also known as "An Autobiography."

India's first Prime Minister

Nehru and his colleagues had been released as the British Cabinet Mission arrived to propose plans for transfer of power. Once elected, Nehru headed an interim government, which was impaired by outbreaks of communal violence and political disorder, and the opposition of the Muslim League led by Muhammad Ali Jinnah, who were demanding a separate Muslim state of Pakistan. After failed bids to form coalitions, Nehru reluctantly supported the partition of India, according to a plan released by the British on 3 June 1947. He took office as the Prime Minister of India on 15 August, and delivered his inaugural address titled "A Tryst With Destiny":

> "Long years ago we made a tryst with destiny, and now the time comes when we shall redeem our pledge, not wholly or in full measure, but very substantially. At the stroke of the midnight hour, when the world sleeps, India will awake to life and freedom. A moment comes, which comes but rarely in history, when we step out from the old to the new, when an age ends, and when the soul of a nation, long suppressed, finds utterance. It is fitting that at this solemn moment we take the pledge of dedication to the service of India and her people and to the still larger cause of humanity."

However, this period was marked with intense communal violence. This violence swept across the Punjab region, Delhi, Bengal and other parts of India. Nehru conducted joint tours with Pakistani leaders to encourage peace and calm angry and disillusioned refugees. Nehru would work with Maulana Azad and other Muslim leaders to safeguard and encourage Muslims to remain in India. The violence of the time deeply affected Nehru, who called for a ceasefire and UN intervention to stop the Indo-Pak War of 1947. Fearing communal reprisals, Nehru also hesitated in supporting the annexation of Hyderabad State.

In the years following independence, Nehru frequently turned to his daughter Indira to look after him and manage his personal affairs. Under his leadership, the Congress won an overwhelming majority in the elections of 1952. Indira moved into Nehru's official residence to attend to him and became his constant companion in his travels across India and the world. Indira would virtually become Nehru's chief of staff.

Economic Policies

Nehru presided over the introduction of a modified, Indian version of state planning and control over the economy. Creating the Planning commission of India, Nehru drew up the first Five-Year Plan in 1951, which charted the government's investments in industries and agriculture. Increasing business and income taxes, Nehru envisaged a mixed economy in which the government would manage strategic industries such as mining, electricity and heavy industries, serving public interest and a check to private enterprise. Nehru pursued land redistribution and launched programmes to build irrigation canals, dams and spread the use of fertilizers to increase agricultural production. He also pioneered a series of community development programmes aimed at spreading diverse cottage industries and increasing efficiency into rural India. While encouraging the construction of large dams (which Nehru called the "new temples of India"), irrigation works and the generation of hydroelectricity, Nehru also launched India's programme to harness nuclear energy.

For most of Nehru's term as Prime Minister, India would continue to face serious food shortages despite progress and increases in agricultural production. Nehru's industrial policies, summarised in the Industrial Policy Resolution of 1956, encouraged the growth of diverse manufacturing and heavy industries, yet state planning, controls and regulations began to impair productivity, quality and profitability. Although the Indian economy enjoyed a steady rate of growth, chronic unemployment amidst widespread poverty continued to plague the population.

Education and Social Reforms

Jawaharlal Nehru was a passionate advocate of education for India's children and youth, believing it essential for India's future progress. His government oversaw the establishment of many institutions of higher learning, including the All India Institute of Medical Sciences, the Indian Institutes of Technology and the Indian Institutes of Management. Nehru also outlined a commitment in his five-year plans to guarantee free and compulsory primary education to all of India's children. For this purpose, Nehru oversaw the creation of mass village enrolment programmes and the construction of thousands of schools. Nehru also launched initiatives such as the provision of free milk and meals to children in order to fight malnutrition. Adult education centres, vocational and technical schools were also organised for adults, especially in the rural areas.

Under Nehru, the Indian Parliament enacted many changes to Hindu law to criminalise caste discrimination and increase the legal rights and social freedoms of women. A system of reservations in government services and educational institutions was created to eradicate the social inequalities and disadvantages faced by peoples of the scheduled castes and scheduled tribes. Nehru also championed secularism and religious harmony, increasing the representation of minorities in government.

National Security and Foreign Policy

Nehru led newly independent India from 1947 to 1964, during its first years of freedom from British rule. Both the United States and the Union Soviet Socialist Republic competed to make India an ally throughout the Cold War.

On the international scene, Nehru was a champion of pacifism and a strong supporter of the United Nations. He pioneered the policy of non-alignment and co-founded the Non-aligned Movement of nations professing neutrality between the rival blocs of nations led by the US and the USSR. Recognising the People's Republic of China soon after its founding (while most of the Western bloc continued relations with the Republic of China), Nehru argued for its inclusion in the United Nations and refused to brand the Chinese as the aggressors in their conflict with Korea.

He sought to establish warm and friendly relations with China despite the invasion of Tibet in 1950, and hoped to act as an intermediary to bridge the gulf and tensions between the communist states and the Western bloc.

Meanwhile, Nehru had promised in 1948 to hold a plebiscite in Kashmir under the auspices of the UN but, as Pakistan failed to pull back troops in accordance with the UN resolution and as Nehru grew increasingly wary of the UN, he declined to hold a plebiscite in 1953. He ordered the arrest of the Kashmiri politician Sheikh Abdullah, whom he had previously supported but now suspected of harbouring separatist ambitions; Bakshi Ghulam Muhammad replaced him.

His policy of pacifism and appeasement with respect to China also came unravelled when China annexed Aksai Chin, the region of Kashmir adjoining Tibet in 1962 that led to the Sino-Indian war.

Nehru was hailed by many for working to defuse global tensions and the threat of nuclear weapons. He commissioned the first study of the human effects of nuclear explosions, and campaigned ceaselessly for the abolition of what he called "these frightful engines of destruction." He also had pragmatic reasons for promoting denuclearisation, fearing that a nuclear arms race would lead to over-militarisation that would be unaffordable for developing countries such as his own.

In 1956 he had criticised the joint invasion of the Suez Canal by the British, French and Israelis. Suspicion and distrust cooled relations between India and the US, which suspected Nehru of tacitly supporting the Soviet Union. Accepting the arbitration of the UK and World Bank, Nehru signed the Indus Water Treaty in 1960 with Pakistani ruler Ayyub Khan to resolve long-standing disputes about sharing the resources of the major rivers of the Punjab region.

Last Days and Demise

Nehru had led the Congress to a major victory in the 1957 elections, but his government was facing rising problems and criticism. Disillusioned by intra-party corruption and bickering, Nehru contemplated resigning but continued to serve. The election of his daughter Indira as Congress President in 1959 aroused criticism for alleged nepotism, although actually Nehru had disapproved of her election, partly because he considered it smacked of "dynastism"; he said, indeed it was "wholly undemocratic and an undesirable thing", and refused her a position in his Cabinet. Indira herself was at loggerheads with her father over policy; most notably, she used his oft-stated personal deference to the Congress Working Committee to push through the dismissal of the Communist Party of India government in the state of Kerala, over his own objections. Nehru began to be frequently embarrassed by her ruthlessness and disregard for parliamentary tradition, and was "hurt" by what he saw as an assertiveness with no purpose other than to stake out an identity independent of her father.

Although the Panchsheel (Five Principles of Peaceful Coexistence) was the basis of the 1954 Sino-Indian treaty over Tibet, in later years, Nehru's foreign policy suffered through increasing Chinese antagonism over border disputes and Nehru's decision to grant asylum to the Dalai Lama. After years of failed negotiations, Nehru authorised the Indian Army to annex Goa from Portugal in 1961. While increasing his popularity, Nehru received criticism for opting for military action.

In the 1962 elections, Nehru led the Congress to victory yet with a diminished majority. Opposition parties ranging from the right-wing Bharatiya Jana Sangh and Swatantra Party, socialists and the Communist Party of India performed well.

In a matter of months, the border disputes with China turned into open conflict. Nehru assumed that as former victims of imperialism (India being a colony itself) they shared a sense of solidarity, as expressed in the phrase "Hindi-Chini bhai bhai" (Indians and Chinese are brothers). He was dedicated to the ideals of brotherhood and solidarity among developing nations. Nehru, credulously, did not believe that one fellow Socialist country would attack another; and in any event, he felt secure behind the impregnable wall of ice that is the Himalayas. Both proved to be severe miscalculations of China's intentions and military capabilities. Following reports of his intention to confront Chinese occupation of the disputed areas-summarised in a memorable statement that he had asked the Army to "throw them (Chinese) out" — China launched a pre-emptive attack.

In a matter of days, a Chinese invasion of northeastern India exposed the weaknesses of India's military as Chinese forces came as far as Assam. Widely criticised for his government's insufficient attention to defence, Nehru was forced to sack the defence minister Krishna Menon and seek US military aid. Nehru's health began declining steadily, and he was forced to spend months recuperating in Kashmir through 1963. Some historians attribute this dramatic decline to his surprise and chagrin over the invasion of India by the Chinese, which he perceived as a betrayal of trust. Upon his return from Kashmir in May 1964, Nehru suffered a stroke and later a heart attack. He died in the early hours of 27 May 1964. Nehru was cremated in accordance with Hindu rites at the Shantivana on the banks of the Yamuna River, witnessed by hundreds of thousands of mourners who had flocked into the streets of Delhi and the cremation grounds.

The Legacy

As India's first Prime minister and external affairs minister, Jawaharlal Nehru played a major role in shaping modern India's government and political culture along with sound foreign policy. He is praised for creating a system providing universal primary education, reaching children in the farthest corners of rural India. Nehru's education policy is also credited for the development of world-class educational institutions such as the All India Institute of Medical Sciences, Indian Institutes of Technology, and the Indian Institutes of Management.

> "Nehru was a great man... Nehru gave to Indians an image of themselves that I don't think others might have succeeded in doing." — Sir Isaiah Berlin

Nehru is credited for establishing a widespread system of affirmative action to provide equal opportunities and rights for India's ethnic groups, minorities, women, scheduled castes and scheduled tribes. Nehru's passion for egalitarianism meant that he put the state to work to try and end widespread practices of discrimination against women and depressed classes, though with limited success in his lifetime.

Nevertheless, Nehru's stance as a unfailing nationalist led him to also implement policies which stressed commonality among

Indians while still appreciating regional diversities. This proved particularly important as post-Independence differences surfaced since British withdrawal from the subcontinent prompted regional leaders to no longer relate to one another as allies against a common adversary. While differences of culture and, especially, language threatened the unity of the new nation, Nehru established programmes such as the National Book Trust and the National Literary Academy which promoted the translation of regional literatures between languages and also organised the transfer of materials between regions. In pursuit of a single, unified India, Nehru warned, "Integrate or perish."

Commemoration

In his lifetime, Jawaharlal Nehru enjoyed an iconic status in India and was widely admired across the world for his idealism and statesmanship. His birthday, 14 November, is celebrated in India as Baal Divas (Children's Day) in recognition of his lifelong passion and work for the welfare, education and development of children and young people. Children across India remember him as Chacha Nehru (Uncle Nehru). Nehru remains a popular symbol of the Congress party which frequently celebrates his memory. Congress leaders and activists often emulate his style of clothing, especially the Gandhi cap, and his mannerisms. Nehru's ideals and policies continue to shape the Congress party's manifesto and core political philosophy. An emotional attachment to his legacy was instrumental in the rise of his daughter Indira to leadership of the Congress party and the national government.

Many documentaries about Nehru's life have been produced. He has also been portrayed in fictionalised films. The canonical performance is probably that of Roshan Seth, who played him three times: in Richard Attenborough's 1982 film Gandhi, Shyam Benegal's 1988 television series Bharat Ek Khoj, based on Nehru's The Discovery of India, and in a 2007 TV film entitled The Last Days of the Raj. In Ketan Mehta's film Sardar, Nehru was portrayed by Benjamin Gilani. Nehru's personal preference for the sherwani ensured that it continues to be considered formal wear in North India today; aside from lending his name to a kind of cap, the Nehru jacket is named in his honour due to his preference for that style.

Numerous public institutions and memorials across India are dedicated to Nehru's memory. The Jawaharlal Nehru University in Delhi is among the most prestigious universities in India. The Jawaharlal Nehru Port near the city of Mumbai is a modern port and dock designed to handle a huge cargo and traffic load. Nehru's residence in Delhi is preserved as the Nehru Memorial Museum and Library. The Nehru family homes at Anand Bhavan and Swaraj Bhavan are also preserved to commemorate Nehru and his family's legacy.

Writings

Nehru was a prolific writer in English and wrote a number of books, such as The Discovery of India, Glimpses of World History, and his autobiography, Towards Freedom.

2

Journey of Life

Early Childhood

Even in his birth which took place at Allahabad near the Chowk, in quarters known as Mirganj, on November 14, 1889, Jawaharlal was most fortunate. His father was Motilal, a Kashmiri Brahmin with a Roman appearance, and his mother, Swaruprani, a gentle and noble lady steeped in the best Hindu traditions. They gave him not only their affection in plenty — he was "Nanhe" or the "little one" to them — but also an aristocratic training with the latest Western stamp. As a leader of the Bar, Motilal had all the wealth at his command; as a friend of the British officials, he was familiar with their style of living. In the result, he was anxious to bring up his son as a gentleman in the then accepted sense of the word. He was so particular about it that he did not like to spoil Jawaharlal by sending him to a local school. He, therefore, entrusted his training exclusively to the care of European governesses and later to European tutors. From his childhood, therefore, Jawaharlal had the best of both riches and the new culture. He was born in luxury and bred in affluence.

When Jawaharlal was about ten, Motilal moved into a palatial house on Church Road near the University which he named "Anand Bhawan"; it had a huge garden, two beautiful swimming pools and all the amenities and comforts of modern life. In its luxurious settings Jawaharlal found amusement; his pastimes were swimming, horse-riding, cricket, etc. However, being the only child — his sister, Vijayalakshmi was born when he was eleven — the new residence did not diminish his loneliness. There were no companions of his age to play with him and therefore the bigness of the house made him feel still more lonely. Then there was the patriarchal shadow of his father, affectionate but domineering, awe-inspiring but still grand to look at, which enveloped his life. He did not have to ask for anything. He was a spoilt child. Nor was he ever required to decide anything; decisions for him were made by his father and he had no reason to complain against them. That is why even in later years when Jawaharlal became a leader and almost lived with millions of his people he could not shed his loneliness, or his vacillation. Today also he remains a lonely man, often hesitant and rather indecisive.

Of his many friends who used to visit their house frequently in those days the nearest to the family was the late Tej Bahadur Sapru; he was like a little uncle to him and though both of them later plunged into politics taking different paths, their affection for each other remained unchanged. From his deathbed on December 2, 1948 Sapru wrote to Nehru:"..... I must be prepared for the end soon. I must bless my stars that I have seen the freedom of India with you at the helm."

Of the early confidants of his father, Munshi Mubarak A. H. was closest to Jawaharlal. He was, to use Nehru's own words, a "sure haven of refuge whenever I was unhappy or in trouble. The Munshi amused the boy by telling him stories and playing pranks with him; he, however, had no hold over him. The real influence on Jawaharlal during this very formative period was of his Irish tutor, the youthful Ferdinand T. Brooks who was a theosophist and a disciple of Annie Besant who had recommended him for the job to Motilal. For nearly three years until Jawaharlal sailed for England with his father, Brooks taught him at "Anand Bhawan" and laid the foundation of his future make-up. In his outlook on life, however, the teacher was more a Hindu than a Westerner; he believed in plain living and high thinking, was a strict vegetarian and rarely touched alcohol.

In particular Brooks inculcated in Jawaharlal love of reading; the young disciple found great delight in books by Scott, Dickens, Thackeray, Wells and Mark Twain, and also the Kipling and Sherlock Holmes stories and the fables of Lewis Carrol. Brooks also developed in him a love for poetry. Furthermore, Jawaharlal used to be thrilled by the mysteries of science and spent many hours with Brooks in a laboratory that they had managed to set up in "Anand Bhawan".

Because of Brooks, Jawaharlal also became interested in theosophy and made some study of religion including Hindu mythological tales and their inner significance. He was initiated into the Theosophical Society by Mrs. Besant personally, but Jawaharlal was more attracted to her by her silver-tongued oratory than her theosophical mission. He loved to hear her at public meetings and became almost enamoured of her charm aid brilliance. Intellectually, she exercised — perhaps more than his father — a most domineering influence on Jawaharlal. Otherwise it was under the grand umbrella of Motilal with all his pride, imperiousness, grandeur and even ferocious temper that Jawaharlal grew up. His mother, who was a poem in self-effacement, provided a feminine and consequently a softer touch, but the hand that cast the boy was that of the father with the result that the attachment between the two was always deep and strong, and survived all the political differences that later arose between them.

Harrow, Cambridge and London

For Motilal who almost doted on Jawaharlal, his son's future was of great concern; he had made up his mind to put him in an exclusive British public school and after long deliberation, he decided upon Harrow and through his influential English friends was able to get his son admitted there. Accordingly, when Jawaharlal was hardly-fifteen, his father took him to England and personally put him at Harrow. For two years the boy remained in the school, but made no particular mark there. Quiet and reserved by nature, he took little part in extra-curricular activities except for sports and enlisting in the volunteer corps. Sometimes he indulged in rowing and occasionally went mountaineering. Otherwise by his own admission "he was never an exact fit" at

Harrow. In his studies, however, he did not lag behind and once or twice even topped his form, for which he received prizes. One such prize was Trevelyan's biography of Garibaldi. He read it and was much impressed by the Italian hero's deeds. As he later wrote in his *Autobiography* "visions of similar deeds in India came before me, of a gallant fight for freedom".

In Harrow he took some interest in British politics, but was more interested in aviation, which had just then caught the world's imagination. In fact, he was so thrilled by it that he dreamt of paying soon a weekend visit to India by air. Perhaps his love of air journeys, which he has made so often and so widely throughout the worlds dates back from that time. Though at Harrow his contemporaries included scions of many distinguished English fancies, he did not develop any personal friendship with them. He remained aloof and confined himself to his own work. Though Jawaharlal retains some love for the institution, it is doubtful whether he really imbibed the so-called Harrow spirit or cared much about it in later life.

In the autumn of 1907 Jawaharlal went to Trinity College, Cambridge, which in the 19th century and earlier was regarded as the training ground of British Prime Ministers. He took natural science tripos, though in second class, and studied chemistry, geology and botany. In Cambridge, however, he came out of his shell a little and read books on literature and politics. He was particularly impressed by the Fabians and took pains to understand modern economic theories. He became familiar with socialism, but was not particularly drawn to it then. His political thinking, if any, was essentially of a nationalist type — more Tilakite than Gandhian in its approach. Racialism created far greater resentment in him than the plight of the underdog.

From Cambridge Jawaharlal moved to London and joined the Inner Temple to qualify for the Bar. At first there was some talk of his competing for the Indian Civil Service, but it was soon abandoned. Motilal wanted his son to be a barrister and to succeed to his lucrative practice; he did not like the idea of employment, even if it were of the imperial kind.

In London Jawaharlal found enough leisure; the law studies did not entail much work; and there were so many attractions to occupy his time. He had ample allowances; he could always get more if he wanted. He ate well; he dressed well; his clothes were tailored in Bond Street; he frequented the best of places; he moved in aristocratic circles; he visited social clubs and saw plays and ballets. To quote his own words, "I enjoyed life and I refused to see why I should consider it a thing of sin."

He was attracted by a kind of cyrenaicism — "the desire for a soft life and pleasant experiences" — partly because of his youth and partly, as he has revealed, because of "the influence of Oscar Wilde and Walter Pater".

Hence; by the time Nehru had qualified for the Bar in the summer of 1912, he had become a typical British public school product — handsome and elegant to look at, gay and carefree in his attitude, polished and urbane in his manner albeit a little snobbish towards those whom he considered socially his inferiors. As at Cambridge so also in London he participated neither in debates nor in other student activities; even from the Indian Majlis he kept himself aloof. The summer holidays he spent in touring other parts of Europe, where he moved like a Prince, from place to place, motoring, skiing, sightseeing and wandering. Life to him — then as now, though in a different context — was an adventure of absorbing interest, where there was so much to be done, so much to be seen.

At last after a stay of seven long years Jawaharlal returned to India in August, 1912. In between he had no doubt visited his parents twice — once in 1906 and again in 1908. Even while returning finally he did not entertain the idea of either entering politics or leading the kind of life the future held for him. As he himself disclosed during his first trial in 1922: "Less than ten years ago, I returned from England after a lengthy stay there. I had passed through the usual course of public school and university. I had imbibed most of the prejudices of Harrow and Cambridge and in my likes and dislikes I was perhaps more an Englishman than an Indian. I looked upon the world almost from an Englishman's stand-point. And so I returned to India as much prejudiced in favour of England and the English as it was possible for an Indian to be."

At the Bar and Marriage

The India to which Nehru returned was somewhat different from the one he had left behind seven years earlier. There was the aftermath of the Bengal "anti-partition" agitation and the fight between the moderates and extremists in the Congress. Then there was the excitement among the rich and educated about the Minto-Morley Reforms. These developments, however trivial they may look in retrospect, were important enough then and must have made some impact on Jawaharlal's mind.

Though brought up in the British tradition or rather because of it he hated the racial superiority displayed by the British in India. Their overlordship created a sense of resentment in him. Also, his father had begun to take part in politics by joining the moderates with the result that Jawaharlal could not keep himself completely aloof from it. Nevertheless he took the legal profession seriously and devoted much time to it so that he could make his mark at the bar. He joined his father's chambers and studied his cases, ransacking the law for him, and going through all the plodding, which is the lot of a junior.

Somehow he was not able to make much of an impression; whether it was due to his own deficiencies or the overpowering personality of Motilal who was then the unchallenged leader of the bar or whether he found the atmosphere as he put it "not intellectually stimulating", the bar did not satisfy him. He found it dull, drab and almost lifeless. Gradually he began to find an outlet in politics and like most educated Indians of those days indulged in armchair discussions on current affairs. He had already attended the Bankipore session of the Congress as a delegate but he found nothing interesting or invigorating in its deliberations. The following year he joined the U.P. Congress Committee, but in its activities also he hardly took any part.

For some time he was attracted to Gokhale's Servants of India Society, but he hesitated to join it, because it specialised more in a kind of missionary work which did not have much attraction for him. Because of his father, Jawaharlal received public attention wherever he went, but he was still so shy and reserved that he kept to himself. In fact, it was in 1915 at a public meeting in

Allahabad that he made his maiden speech. This came as a pleasant surprise to Sapru, who was present at the meeting; immediately after the speech he rushed to the platform and kissed Jawaharlal openly. In 1917, however, more because of the Home Rule agitation unleashed by Tilak and Mrs. Besant, Jawaharlal was awakened to the realities of the Indian situation and started thinking seriously about them. Moreover, Mrs. Besant always exercised almost a hypnotic influence on Jawaharlal. He admired her bold and fearless revolt against the British; in particular, her arrest in 1917 moved him greatly.

Meanwhile, life at "Anand Bhawan" went on in the usual luxurious manner. Apart from his father there was his mother, ever proud of her young son; and his two sisters — Vijayalakshmi and Krishna, growing ever more fond of their elder brother, who was an embodiment of grace and charm. For some years his parents had been on the lookout for a suitable bride for Jawaharlal, but it was not until he was twenty-six that they finally decided upon Kamala Kaul, the daughter of a well-known Kashmiri business man belonging to the same Brahmin sub-caste. The girl was hardly seventeen then and like a doll — demure, slim and tender. The parents were much impressed by her; and so they selected her for their son and on February 26, 1916, Jawaharlal was married at Delhi in lavish and grand manner, the like of which even the capital had not seen before.

Plunge into Politics

Though interested in politics, Nehru's plunge into it was a rather reluctant one; it was more the circumstance than any personal urge that brought him into public life. True, as a member of the bar he indulged in political discussions; as a sensitive Indian he resented the rule of the British and did not like the idea of being considered a slave to them. But action rather than talk appealed to him; that was why Gandhiji's struggle in South Africa evoked more interest in him, than the Congress proceedings.

It was for the first time in 1915, as a result of the formation of a Kisan Sabha by Madan Mohan Malaviya with the object of ameliorating the plight of the peasantry in the U.P., that he became somewhat active and started thinking seriously of political work.

The same year, in the last week of December, he met Mahatma Gandhi at the Lucknow Congress, but their meeting was casual and did not produce any particular effect on Jawaharlal's mind though even at that time he had developed some respect for the Mahatma's sincerity and boldness, if not for his orthodox approach or appearance. It was the kisan movement which Began to engage more and more Jawaharlal's attention as he slowly took to public activities. In 1918 he became the Vice-President of the Kisan Sabha and toured Oudh exhorting peasants to fight for their rights and for the betterment of their lot.

As a result of his contacts with them his outlook on life as also his whole mode of living changed. He discarded wearing suits and started putting on *achkan*. He gave up moving in cars and went walking to villages, sometimes even barefooted. He gave up European food and ate with the farmers whatever they cooked and gave him. He spent several nights in their huts and did not mind sharing his life with them. This was too sudden and too much of a transformation in Jawaharlal for the liking of his father who was still too attached to the Western style of living.

He did not mind his son's participation in the kisan movement, but he was opposed to such a complete identification with their rustic lot. He, therefore, argued with his son and tried to persuade him to take a more constitutional attitude, but the son had seen too much poverty and misery to be satisfied with that kind of an approach. He wanted action. He had, therefore, no interest in the controversies between the moderates and the extremists or the differences between the Hindus and the Muslims. At the Lucknow session of the Congress in 1916 he was, no doubt, a witness to a *rapprochement* between the Congress and the League, but it made no impress on his mind.

It was then that Gandhiji entered the political scene and gave a new call to his people. He did not talk of submission or loyalty, but of assertion of people's rights. Jawaharlal liked his politics. There was a call for action in it, an emphasis on shedding of fear and braving troubles. Gandhiji wanted to fight first for the vital needs of the poor and said that all the graces and ornaments of life would follow thereafter. For India's toiling millions his message was one of "eternal vigil"; he declared that his mission was to wipe away every tear from every eye. To such a message Jawaharlal could not fail to respond and hence in spite of the initial opposition of his father who dreaded the idea of his son languishing in a British jail, Jawaharlal plunged heart and soul into the non-cooperation movement launched by Gandhiji. Those were the days of protest against the Rowlatt Acts; and Nehru took full part in organising India-wide *hartals* on April 6, 1919. These resulted, however, in the notorious Jalianwala Bagh massacres in Amritsar a week later and horrors of martial law administration in the Punjab. Nehru was horrified at these developments and began to identify himself more and more with the movement. Under his pressure, even Motilal relented and gave up his lucrative practice. In the enquiry committee that the Congress set up into these tragedies not only Jawaharlal but Motilal and C. R. Das took active part.

On account of what Jawaharlal had seen in the Punjab and heard from the people, he was determined to fight the British and to end the slavery and disgrace of his people. He was young; he was sensitive; and he had become politically alive. To him the fight represented an ideal; and he was prepared to die for it. Moreover, he was attracted by the method of that fight. As he put it, "The idea of non-cooperation is simple enough, clear to the meanest intellect, but none the less few of us had realised it, excepting partly during the Bengal partition days, till the Mahatma issued his call to action. Evil flourishes only because we tolerate and assist it; the most despotic and tyrannical government can only carry on because the people it governs themselves submit to it. England holds India in bondage because Indians cooperate with the Englishmen and thereby strengthen British rule. Withdraw that cooperation and the fabric of foreign rule collapses.

In the result Nehru went the whole hog in making a success of Gandhiji's new movement which consisted primarily in shedding fear of the British by picketing at liquor shops, giving up the use of foreign goods specially cloth, and by renouncing British titles and awards and even by boycotting courts, colleges and schools. It was a novel method of non-cooperation. But to Nehru's mind, it was more than a plan for action; there was a touch of romantic dynamism about it. However, as the movement was in full swing an incident occurred in Chauri Chaura in the district of Gorakhpur in Nehru's home province in February, 1922 when an infuriated mob set fire to some police chowkies and burnt twenty-one policemen including an inspector; this upset the apostle of non-violence so much that he called of the struggle. For Jawaharlal it was too much. He became not only angry with Gandhiji but almost furious.

He was in jail at that time having been arrested earlier and imprisoned for six months. He did not know what to do. Frustrated and depressed, he wrote to Gandhiji and gave him a piece of his mind. Gandhiji, however, was unrepentant. To him, non-violence was a creed; he, therefore, could not countenance any exhibition of violence by his people. For Nehru it was a matter of expediency. He used non-violence because it suited the peculiar conditions in India; he was not prepared to sacrifice freedom at its altar.

On his release Nehru found awaiting him a different world than what he had left behind. There was frustration and dissatisfaction everywhere. More than 3,000 people languished in jails, and many more had braved lathi charges and given up their schools, colleges and professions. But what was the result? The British grip on the people had become tighter and there was little hope of an immediate revolt. Early in 1924, Mahatma Gandhi took seriously ill and was convalescing at Juhu. Nehru accompanied by his father had several talks with him. He, however, returned more hopeless and despaired of the future.

Hindu-Muslim Tension

There was another development which troubled him greatly at this time: the worsening of Hindu-Muslim relations. Against the background of unity that was brought about by Gandhiji and the Ali Brothers during the non-cooperation and Khilafat movements, it was heart-breaking to see communal riots sully different parts of the country. First came the tragic Moplah riots of 1920 and then similar outbreaks in such towns as Delhi, Nagpur, Lucknow, Shahjahanpur, Allahabad and Jabalpur — most of them in Nehru's home province of the U.P. In 1924 the tragedy reached its peak at Kohat in the North-West Frontier Province, where more than a hundred persons were killed. In a desperate effort to stem the tide of communal hatred Gandhiji embarked on an almost perilous fast of twenty-one days. It resulted in a unity conference and eased the tension to some extent, but Jawaharlal was not much impressed by these sentimental efforts. He looked at the problem rationally and in its economic context; he was anxious that the Congress leadership should also tackle it accordingly. His proved to be a voice in the wilderness and found little support even among his colleagues.

The communal situation did not necessarily deteriorate but it never really improved; in fact, until the British left, Hindu-Muslim conflict became a regular feature of Indian life. In a letter to his friend, Syed Mahmud, who later became a minister in his Cabinet, Nehru poured out his heart, "I do not attach much importance to political squabbles, but the communal frenzy is awful to contemplate. We seem to have been caught in a whirlpool of mutual hatred and we go round and round and down and down this abyss." Nehru developed a hatred for religion and declared that religion had become like "the old man of the sea for us"; it had not only "broken our backs but stultified and almost killed all originality of thought and mind". He was convinced that unless India got rid of "this terrible burden", it could not "breathe freely or do anything useful". In this he made no distinction between the "legitimate" and "illegitimate" offspring of religion. To Lenin religion might have been "the opium of people"; to Nehru it was just poison.

Depressed and frustrated at the turn of events Nehru found some solace in municipal affairs. In 1923 he was elected Chairman of the Allahabad Municipality and he approached his work with vigour and enthusiasm. He became the General Secretary of the Congress and busied himself with organisational matters; he continued in that position until the end of the presidentship of Gandhiji in 1925. After a two-year recess, he was again persuaded to take it up in 1927 and remained as the General Secretary until 1929 when he was elected the Congress President for the first time. The municipal experience was not pleasant, but it proved instructive and gave Nehru a peep into the working of administration; it was there that the foundation of his future role as an administrator was laid.

Though the relations between Nehru and Gandhiji at that time were rather strained because of the difference in their outlook and approach, it did not bring him politically nearer to his father and C. R. Das, who advocated constitutional agitation. The fight between the "pro-changers" and "no-changers", as the cooperators and non-cooperators were called,, was at its height then, but the younger Nehru found no interest in it, nor was he enamoured of fighting the British in the council chambers as his father was. He kept aloof from these controversies. His father also never pressed him to take any part in the Swaraj Party which he along with Das had organised as a group within the Congress.

For his part, Jawaharlal had enough organisational work on hand; and he occupied himself with it. In 1924, Mohammed Ali became the President of the Kakinada session and though Jawaharlal was not eager to continue as the General Secretary, the President-elect forced him to do so. The Maulana remarked, "It is just because some members of the Working Committee distrust and dislike your presence as Secretary that I like it." The two got on very well despite their difference in approach, particularly to religious beliefs.

As Jawaharlal became less involved in political activity, he found a little more time to devote to his family affairs. Twenty months after his marriage, his only child Indira was born, but Kamala became weak and developed an infection of tuberculosis which troubled her greatly in the following years and eventually took her life. In 1925, Kamala's condition suddenly became serious and she had to be kept for months in a hospital in Lucknow. Jawaharlal was much disturbed and spent many an hour with his ailing wife. Her health did not improve and ultimately on the advice of his friend Dr. M. A. Ansari, who later became Congress President, Jawaharlal decided to take her to Switzerland for treatment. In March, 1926 Jawaharlal with Kamala and their eight-year-old daughter, Indira, sailed from Bombay for Switzerland via Venice.

Trip to Europe

Accompanying them during their trip to Europe, were his sister Vijayalakshmi and her husband, Ranjit Pandit. Later,

Jawaharlal's second sister, Krishna, also joined them. Nehru intended to stay in Europe for six or seven months, but as there was little improvement in Kamala's health he had to delay his return until December, 1927. However, this long sojourn in the West had a tremendous effect on his mind. It widened his horizon and broadened his vision. As the late Narendra Deva had testified, ".... it is definite that he came decisively under the impact of socialism during his sojourn in Europe in 1926-27". Though holidaying, he utilised the period for a serious study of political and economic problems. Mostly, he remained in Switzerland because of Kamala, but he visited France, England, Belgium, Holland, Germany and lastly the Soviet Union as well. In Brussels he represented the Congress at the anti-imperialist Congress of Oppressed Nationalities held in February, 1927 and made valuable contacts there; these were of great benefit to him. In their company he found a new vigour and hope. In one of her letters to Nehru in Europe, Sarojini Naidu rejoiced "that your soul has found its chance to renew its youth and glory'.

Of the interesting people he met in Europe, two stood out: one was Romain Rolland, the biographer of Gandhiji, and the other was Earnest Toller, with whom Nehru developed almost personal attachment. For the Moscow visit Jawaharlal persuaded his father, who had by then joined the family in Europe, to accompany them. They participated as official guests in the tenth anniversary celebrations of the Bolshevik Revolution. On their arrival in the Soviet Union they were given a great welcome; they missed the mammoth parade in the Red Square but, otherwise, they had a full programme. Though Nehru and his father visited only Moscow and were there for about four days, the visit had a great impact on Jawaharlal. He became more sympathetic to the Soviet Union, more understanding of the role of the communists and keen on developing Indo-Soviet friendship.

On his return he wrote articles in the form of "random sketches and impressions" of the Soviet society for the Indian press, which showed his deep sympathy and even affection for the Russians. As he told his countrymen, "the contrasts between extreme luxury and poverty are not visible, nor does one notice the hierarchy of class or caste" in the Soviet Union. In particular, he was impressed by the simplicity of the life of Soviet officials and members of the Communist Party and by their campaign to eradicate illiteracy and poverty and their jail reforms. He also admired the manner in which they had tried to solve their minorities problem. As he put it, "It is difficult to draw any final conclusions about anything Russian at this stage but it would certainly appear from the progress made in the last five years that the problem of minorities has been largely solved there." He applauded their efforts to establish equality between the sexes. Lenin was no more but in the well-known mausoleum he found in his remains "a strange beauty", even his eyebrow looked "peaceful and unclouded".

Nehru's tribute to the Soviet leader was unequivocal. To quote his words, "By an amazing power of will he hypnotised a nation and filled a disunited and demoralised people with energy and determination and the strength to endure and suffer for a cause." He was also clear about Indo-Soviet relations. He emphasised, "Russia again cannot be ignored by us because she is our neighbour, a powerful neighbour, which may be friendly to us and cooperate with us or may be a thorn in our side. In either event we have to know her and understand her to shape our policy accordingly."

As Kamala's health improved, Jawaharlal was anxious to return. He sailed for India, but this time he came back not so much a nationalist as a socialist determined to give a new content and meaning to Indian nationalism, as much economic as political.

Socialist Trend

From Europe Nehru returned via Colombo and from there arrived straight in Madras to attend the Congress session. In its deliberations he took full part and sponsored many resolutions, particularly on foreign affairs; from then on, he emerged as the Congress spokesman on international developments and in his voice there was a new direction. Moreover, he committed the Congress to the goal of "complete national independence", by making it pass a resolution to that effect. Gandhiji was not present when this happened, but when he came to know of it, he rebuked Nehru. He thought that "the Congress stultified itself by repeating year after year resolutions of this character when it knows that it is not capable of carrying them into effect. By passing such resolutions we make an exhibition of our impotence. We have almost sunk to the level of a school boys' debating society." Gandhiji was also disturbed by the violent tone of Nehru's radicalism; he told him so in several letters, and sometimes even publicly.

Jawaharlal, however, did not give in easily. He was too full of the new ideas that he had imbibed during his European tour and too impatient to put them in practice. Gandhiji realised this and moaned, "Differences between you and me appear to be so vast and so radical that there seems to be no meeting ground between us. I cannot conceal from you my grief that I will lose a comrade so valiant, so faithful, so able and so honest that you always have been; but in serving a cause comradeships have got to be sacrificed." But despite these differences- there was no break between the two; as usual, adjustments were made and the master brought the erring disciple round.

After the Congress session Nehru made a country-wide tour addressing hundreds of meetings and presiding over several provincial conferences. Because of his emphasis on socialism he also came nearer to labour and was elected, almost without his knowledge, President of the All-India Trade Union Congress. So far he had aligned himself with the peasants; now the workers also looked to him for a lead. He was able to give a new content to the national struggle, which was both radical and socialistic. He emphasised that the fight against the British was not only political but economic. From the youth, whose unchallenged leader he became, he demanded action. He sought for "the dynamic element" in Indian revolution, and made no secret of the fact that it was "the function of the youth to supply it".

Nehru could not have found a better time to propagate his new ideas. India was in ferment; labour was restless; and the peasantry was discontented. Specially in Bardoli, a district in Gujarat, the situation due to enhancement of land tax had become tense. The people were angry and to give their wrath a forceful direction there appeared on the scene — Vallabhbhai Patel, who later became the "Sardar" of the Congress and a co-architect with Nehru of India's freedom. Patel organised with Gandhiji's blessing satyagraha against the Government in Bardoli; the Government, on its part, retaliated with mass arrests and wholesale confiscation of lands. Patel did not budge. He asked his supporters not to worry, reminding them that the British could not take their land with them to Britain. The heroic struggle in Bardoli had its repercussions on other parts and even in the U. P., where the Congress was anxious to avoid a clash between peasants and zamindars, the tillers showed a new awakening.

In the field of labour also the position was no better; there were strikes and lockouts in many industrial centres. Trouble was in the air everywhere and it reached its climax at the time of the historic Meerut trials. Nehru raised funds and personally arranged for the defence of the accused, most of whom were members of the Communist Party and at the helm of the new movement among the workers. There was violence; British officers were murdered; trains carrying British dignitaries were derailed. Terrorism was used for gaining freedom and Bhagat Singh became a hero. All in all, India was on the verge of a revolution, essentially a non-violent mass upsurge besmirched by sporadic violence.

Such was the atmosphere when the Simon Commission arrived to study India's political conditions and to suggest constitutional remedies. It was an all-British commission; wherever it went it was greeted with black flags and boycotted. Processions and hartals became the order of the day. There was total non-cooperation and it gave a new fillip to the national movement. Further, it was while leading one such procession that the Punjab Congress leader, Lala Lajpat Rai was severely beaten by the police; within a week he succumbed to his injuries and died in a hospital. Nehru was horrified. If this could happen to one of India's foremost leaders, he asked, what security was there for others. He himself led a procession in Lucknow and received", as he admitted, "a tremendous hammering" at the hands of the police. "I felt half blind with the blows," he explained.

Meanwhile, efforts were being made for a *rapprochement* between the Hindus and the Muslims, which finally led to an All-Parties Conference in August that year, attended by both the delegates of the Muslim League and the Congress, already gathered in Lucknow for their respective annual sessions. After long deliberations the "Nehru Report" was signed, named after Motilal, the motive force behind it. Jawaharlal did not bother much about it, nor did he show any enthusiasm for it. He was particularly peeved at its adherence to the goal of "dominion status". To Gandhiji, Jawaharlal's deflection began to cause concern. He was conscious of the latter's growing hold on the people, specially the younger generation.

He was also anxious to allow Jawaharlal to play his natural role; nevertheless the Mahatma wanted him to be tempered and, therefore, suggested his name for the next Congress presidentship in supersession of his own and Patel's nomination. Furthermore, the one-year deadline given to the British for declaring India a dominion was also to end by then, and there could be no better person to herald the call of *Puma Swaraj* or "complete independence". The British did not remain quiet. The new Viceroy, Lord Irwin (later Halifax) was too alarmed about people's upsurge to ignore it. He pressed London to re-affirm India's goal as that of "dominion status" and to take steps to sponsor a Round Table Conference of British and Indian leaders, to draft a Constitution. This was a clever move and it succeeded to some extent in diverting the current of popular reaction.

At first, Nehru under pressure from his elders welcomed the move; later he realised the full implication of the Viceregal statement and retraced his step. He even resigned along with Subhash Bose "from the Congress Working Committee. At that time Sapru and Jayakar, two Liberal leaders, who were to play a prominent mediatory role between the Congress and the Government, came on the scene and tried to heal the breach. It took several months but their efforts culminated in the famous Gandhi-Irwin Pact, under which the Congress agreed to participate in the Round Table Conference, and the British, in return, made several concessions to the Congress including the release of political prisoners and the restoration of confiscated land.

Nehru did not like the Pact; he thought it almost humiliating but as Congress President he reluctantly accepted it. He did not have the heart to break away from Gandhiji and his elders but neither did he make any secret of his dislike of their approach and methods. He was torn between the two forces, tossed in a sea-saw struggle between them. In such a mood of hesitancy and uncertainty he accepted the leadership from his father and embarked on his presidential task, determined to give a more revolutionary and radical turn to the affairs of the Congress.

Congress Presidentship

At Lahore in 1929 Nehru as well as the Congress came of age. The historic session ushered in a new era — an era which gave out a declaration of an all-out war against the British. A new zeal was generated among the people by Nehru and the whole country was charged. The struggle could, no longer, be delayed; the Congress authorised it under the leadership of Gandhiji. There was no doubt much excitement, but the final programme of civil disobedience was yet to be chalked out.

Though thrilled at the awakening, as Nehru admitted, he was anxious to canalise it properly. As the first step in this direction, the Congress legislators at the Centre and in the provinces were called on to resign; more than 178 of them immediately responded. As a symbolic expression the 26th day of January was christened as "Independence Day". Thousands of meetings were held all over India that day in 1930 and in a solemn tone the people pledged: "It is the inalienable right of the Indian people, as of any other people, to have freedom and to enjoy the fruits of their toil." They also resolved that "if any government deprives a people of these rights and oppresses them they have a further right to alter it or abolish it". Exactly twenty years were to elapse before this pledge could be redeemed and a free India could give to her people a Constitution of her own making.

Soon after, Gandhiji met the Viceroy several times and carried on negotiations. Irwin was himself anxious for a settlement. He had gauged the intensity of popular feeling and was eager to arrest the widening of the rift between the Congress and the Government. Finally he succeeded in persuading Whitehall to associate the Indian leaders in the task of framing a Constitution for India. The response from the other political parties was enthusiastic; but the Congress paid little heed to the move.

Irwin was keen on Congress participation, but there were difficulties on either side. All the goodwill between Irwin and Gandhi, therefore, proved to be of no avail; both were adamant on fundamentals, and these were irreconcilable. And so in the early hours of March 12, 1930 Gandhiji, with a small band of followers, left his Sabarmati Ashram and began his famous 200-mile march to Dandi on the shores of the Arabian sea with a solemn vow to break the salt law. This was a novel move, symbolic of a new mood of defiance, and it electrified the entire country.

For his part, Nehru was most jubilant and gave vent to his feeling in these words: "Today the pilgrim marches onwards on his long trek.... The fire of a great resolve is in him and surpassing love of his miserable countrymen. And love of truth that scorches and love of freedom that inspires. And none that pass him can escape the spell, and men of common clay feel the spark of life." His people, especially the youth, he asked: "Will you be mere lookers-on in this glorious struggle?" reminding them that, "the field of battle lies before you, the flag of India beckons to you and freedom herself awaits your coming". And with deep emotion he cried out, "Who lives if India dies? Who dies if India lives?"

As President of the Congress, Nehru busied himself with the details of the new movement and issued like a Commander-in-Chief directions to soldiers of freedom in different parts of the land. Within a fortnight, however, he was arrested in Allahabad and sentenced to six months' imprisonment. This time his destination was the Naini Central Prison. Soon after Gandhiji himself was whisked away in a car and taken to Yeravda Prison, near Poona.

These arrests released a wave of resentment among the people; there were strikes in textiles mills, hartals all over India. A most extraordinary situation developed. Irwin could not rule India with ordinary laws; he had to issue one ordinance after another. He assumed almost dictatorial powers but still the upsurge could not be crushed. He, therefore, prevailed upon his Government to make a gesture of a substantial constitutional advance; the result was the Round Table Conference, hurriedly called in London.

To Nehru such a gesture meant little; he was more excited about civil disobedience and particularly the role of women in it. He felt proud of the part that his wife Kamala took; and was greatly moved by the heroic manner in which his aged mother participated. On the whole, the movement was non-violent, but here and there some lapses were inevitable, as for instance, in

Chittagong, where the police and the army fired on an unarmed crowd; in Sholapur, where people took over the administration and then clashed with the military; in Peshawar, where under the leadership of Khan Abdul Ghaffar Khan, popularly known as "Frontier Gandhi", the Red Shkts faced police bullets, which killed more than thirty and wounded an equal number. However, what upset the authorities considerably was the refusal by two army platoons to fire on their own unarmed countrymen in Peshawar. It showed not only a new alliance between the Congress and the Muslims but a new spirit of defiance in those officers and men upon whom the Raj relied for its existence.

All this time, Nehru languished in a small cell in the Naini Central Prison with no contact beyond. It was an exasperating experience and wrecked his nerves. He organised his life to a schedule — rising early, spinning a few hours, doing yoga and reading. He conformed to strict discipline and kept himself occupied most of the time. A month later, he was joined in prison by his ailing father and Syed Mahmud. Despite his age — he was seventy then and in poor health — Motilal plunged into the struggle and was sentenced to six months imprisonment. He was taken to Naini and his one consolation was his reunion with his son in the jail. Motilal became worse steadily and by September, 1930, he had to be released. His father's condition shocked and saddened Jawaharlal who was soon joined by his brother-in-law, Ranjit Pandit.

Outside, the two Liberal leaders, Sapru and Jayakar, were trying to bring about peace between the Congress and the Government. They contacted the Nehrus in jail, but both the father and son refused to commit themselves, one way or the other, unless they had met Gandhiji and held consultations with the other members of the Congress Working Committee. They were, therefore, taken along with Syed Mahmud to Yeravda, where Gandhiji was detained. The talks lasted several days. Jawaharlal was released soon after but before taking any further part in political discussions, he rushed to his father's bedside. Finding him a little better he moved out for keeping the agitation alive. Hardly had he enjoyed a week of freedom when he was again arrested and sentenced to twenty-eight months' rigorous imprisonment. He returned to his old cell in Naini — isolated and cut off. Though dying, both the son's arrest and the severity of his sentence angered Motilal who called on the people to observe Jawaharlal Day, on November 14, the day he was born. The response was enthusiastic. More than 5,000 persons courted arrest and hundreds of thousands showed their sympathy with their beloved prisoner. In jail Nehru read avidly and wrote a series of letters to his daughter which he later published as *Glimpses of World History,*

Outside the jail, there was a lull in the storm. In London the Round Table Conference had just been inaugurated and the first session adjourned after discussing only the preliminaries. The socialist Ramsay MacDonald was then the Prime Minister and in order to win over the Congress, he promised that the British would make the executive responsible to the legislature subject to certain safeguards. His statement created a more congenial atmosphere and Irwin improved it by releasing as an earnest all the Congress leaders. Meanwhile, on February 6, 1931, Motilal passed away, plunging not only Jawaharlal but millions of his countrymen in mourning. In his last days, Gandhiji remained with Motilal; Jawaharlal found a haven of solace and peace in the Mahatma.

Politically there was less of tension especially because of the frantic efforts that were being made by Sapru and Jayakar. These paved the way for the Gandhi-Irwin negotiations on February 7, which culminated in the famous Delhi Pact on March 5. At the Karachi Congress the Pact was approved and Gandhiji left soon thereafter for London, accompanied by Sarojini Naidu. He participated in the Second Round Table Conference in the autumn of 1931; but returned by the end of the year empty-handed, disillusioned and disheartened. For Nehru neither the Pact nor the London Conference gave any comfort. He did not expect anything out of them. He even expressed a sneaking admiration for the terrorists. As he told the Karachi session of the Congress, "The corpse of Bhagat Singh shall stand between us and England." He was all for a fight but he found that neither Gandhiji nor the country was ready for it. At the session, therefore, he busied himself with drafting a resolution on "fundamental rights". Earlier, he had met M. N. Roy and under his influence and guidance, prepared "a minimum programme for the Congress, which guaranteed such freedoms as those of expression, religion, thought and assembly; equality before the law, irrespective of sex, creed or caste; protection to regional languages and cultures; for the industrial workers, living wages, limited hours of work, old-age insurance; safeguards against unemployment; abolition of untouchability; universal adult franchise; free primary education; prohibition; state control and management of key industries, services and public undertakings; and the establishment of a secular state. The resolution, despite some opposition from the right wing, was passed, and most of it has since then found an honoured place in the new Constitution. For Nehru, it was a personal triumph; it laid the foundation of the welfare state that he was to try and build in free India.

Differences with Gandhi

Frustrated, tired and exhausted, Nehru left for Ceylon on a holiday with his wife. In India the political situation threatened to become worse, with tension mounting in Gujarat, Bengal, Bombay and the Frontier Province. Irwin had retired and in his place Lord Wellington took over as the new Viceroy. In London also the Round Table Conference headed towards a communal deadlock. Finally, the Mahatma lost hope of a constitutional settlement and returned home by Christmas of 1931.

On his arrival he found his followers disorganised and dissipated. There were ordinances in force in Bengal, the U.P. and the Frontier. Many Congress leaders were behind bar. The truce had not only been broken, but the new Viceroy had declared war against the Congress. Gandhiji sought an interview with him, but in vain. Soon he himself was taken into custody. To quote Sir Samuel Hoare, who was then the Secretary of State for India, *"I admit that the ordinances that we have approved are very drastic and severe. They cover almost every activity of Indian life."* Furthermore, the Congress was banned; its records destroyed; its properties seized; its funds confiscated. Even affiliated or sympathetic organisations were not spared the onslaught. Political meetings were prohibited. Processions were not allowed. The press was gagged. Thousands were put in prison. Huge fines and penalties were imposed. Wellington struck pitilessly with all the force that his administration could generate. He struck so suddenly and severely that even a stoic Congress was taken aback.

Nehru continued to languish in prison. In his helplessness his anger rose. He learned of the savage attack of the police on his aged mother in Allahabad. She was leading a procession when she was battered and left on the road, alone and uncared for. He was so hurt that he began to doubt the very efficacy of non-violence; on such brutes would human goodness have any effect, he wondered. In February, 1932 the Government transferred him from Naini to the Bareilly District Jail and thereafter to Dehra Dun Jail, where he spent the last 14 months of his imprisonment until August, 1933. This time Nehru did not keep his health. He often fell ill and suffered from exhaustion. Soon he realised that he must reconcile himself to a futile existence in jail. He, therefore, occupied himself with odd jobs.

Abroad, Hitler had risen to power and the great economic depression had hit the Western world. He feared that there would be another world war. He saw darkness all around in Europe, perceiving a ray of hope in Soviet Russia. As he said, "I do believe that fundamentally the choice before the world today is between some form of communism and some form of fascism and I am all for the former." He did not then see any "middle road" as he put it.

At home, the Communal Award of the British Prime Minister Ramsay Macdonald had created a new situation; and as a protest against it Gandhiji decided to go on a fast unto death unless the award, which provided for separate electorates for the untouchables, was revoked. Nehru did not like the fast or the manner in which it was undertaken. One thought alone troubled him: What would happen to India if Gandhiji died? As a result of the efforts of several people, a settlement was, however, brought about between the Mahatma and the leader of the untouchables, B. R. Ambedkar, who later became a minister in Nehru's Cabinet and forged free India's Constitution. Separate electorates were given up. The Government accepted the Poona Pact, as it was called, and Gandhiji ended his fast, only to begin, some time later, another 21-day fast. It was strictly for self-purification. A perplexed Nehru then told Gandhiji that he felt lost "in a strange country" where "he groped his way in the dark but stumbled". As the fast was non-political, the Government released Gandhiji. He suspended the civil disobedience movement. Soon after, he sought an interview with the Viceroy, but it was denied again. To Nehru all this came as "one of the biggest shocks I ever had." He almost lost faith in Gandhiji's leadership. To quote his words, "I had a sudden and intense feeling that something broke inside me, a bond that I had valued very greatly snapped." As if groping for some light, Gandhiji offered individual satyagraha. The Government arrested him. True to his own technique, he began yet another fast. The Government released him. This time he decided to abjure all agitation for one year.

Meanwhile, Jawaharlal's mother took seriously ill. He was released and rushed to her bedside in Lucknow; then he came to Poona to see the Mahatma. They talked at length but instead of understanding each other they found the gulf between them yawning both politically and ideologically. Their affection for each other remained, but there was no common ground for action. To Nehru, Gandhiji's new-fangled emphasis on constructive work seemed meaningless, his moral fads irritable. To him, the uppermost task before India was the attainment of freedom. Still he lacked the courage to break away from the Mahatma. As Subhash Bose, who was Nehru's chief lieutenant then, pointed out, "With a popularity only second to that of the Mahatma, with unbounded prestige among his countrymen, with a clear brain possessing the finest ideas, with an up-to-date knowledge of modern world movement" he lacked "the essential quality of leadership, viz. the capacity to make decisions and face unpopularity if need be".

Agitated, Nehru became more conscious of his role in the national struggle and began to strengthen the leftist forces. For this purpose he openly condemned the reactionary part played by capitalists, communalists, zamindars and princes. In an address to Banaras Hindu University he attacked the Hindu Mahasabha; and later entered into correspondence with the famous poet of Islam, Iqbal, on the destructive role of Muslim communalism. To Nehru there was only one solution to India's problem: a free Constitution framed by a fully representative Constituent

Assembly and a plan for the economic uplift of all sections of the people. At the Bombay session of the Congress in 1934 held under the presidentship of Rajendra Prasad, now President of the Republic of India, Nehru moved the resolution for convening a Constituent Assembly to frame a suitable Constitution for free India.

About this time an earthquake shattered the landscape of Bihar, rocking some 20,000 people to their doom and destroying a million homes. Nehru with Prasad rushed to the shambles to give immediate succour to the victims and floated a fund. Gandhiji called the earthquake a punishment for the sin of untouchability. Nehru reacted angrily and said that there was only one sin and that was the continuance of British rule in India. Until it was ended he was not prepared to relax or relent. He carried 'on with his fiery orations both in Bengal and the U.P. and was again arrested on February 11, 1934. He was first kept in the Presidency Jail, Calcutta, and then taken to the Alipore Central Jail. By now Nehru had become so used to jail routine that he found no difficulty in adjusting himself. Most of his time he spent reading books and contemplating the next step. He was puzzled by Gandhiji's methods, especially the manner in which he terminated all forms of civil disobedience on the slim ground, that some valued comrade of his had not performed his prison task fully. Nehru could not restrain himself and called the decision "a monstrous proposition and an immoral one". In Alipore Jail he began to lose weight. He was transferred to Dehra Dun Jail.

Outside, the political situation grew none the better; nor was there any improvement in Kamala's health. Nehru rushed to Allahabad and was released temporarily. The parole lasted only eleven days and he was back in prison. This time he was taken to Naini in order to be nearer his wife, in case of any emergency.

Politically also he was becoming more and more disillusioned. He found it difficult to comprehend Gandhiji's tactics. The Mahatma found him rash and impetuous. But such was their affection for each other that neither was prepared for a break. Nehru was young and therefore he could be erratic. Gandhiji was older and more understanding. He could not react in the same manner as Nehru did. As he told Patel, "No amount of political differences will ever separate him from me." To Gandhiji, Nehru was "the rightful helmsman of the Congress". Perceiving that he was becoming out of tune with Nehru, and out of court with the radical trend, Gandhiji decided to retire from Congress politics. He gave up his Congress membership. He declared, "I am a dead weight in the Congress now." At the Bombay session of the Congress, his retirement was announced. Gandhiji, none the less, exercised his leadership but now more from outside than inside the Congress; it became more moral than political and hence less controversial and more effective.

As Kamala's condition grew worse Nehru was moved to Almora District Jail so that he could visit her in the sanatorium. He added a few pages, now and then, to his *Autobiography* or visited Kamala. In May, 1935 her health became critical and she had to be taken to Europe for special treatment. Jawaharlal saw her off, but was not allowed to accompany her. A few months later as life was ebbing out of Kamala the Government released him. Nehru flew to Europe to face a great personal misfortune. On February 20, 1936 Kamala passed away. His *Autobiography,* which, as Mahadeo Desai commented, "carried many honest Englishmen off their feet", was about to be published; he dedicated it "To Kamala who is no more."

Electoral Success

Forlorn and heart-broken, Nehru returned to India in March, 1936; in his absence he was elected President of the Lucknow session of the Congress. He was touched by the gesture. As he said, "I am weary and I have come back like a tired child yearning for solace in the bosom of our common mother, India." Apart from his colleagues that solace came from his people in abundance. He was moved and exclaimed, "How can I thank you, men and women of India? How can I express in words feelings that are too deep for utterance?"

Gloom continued to envelop the national scene. Gandhiji had withdrawn into his ashram. All round, there was frustration and despondency. In the Congress, the orthodox group, which had never sympathised with Nehru's views, was in control of the organisation, while his socialist friends were bitter and frustrated. They organised themselves into a separate group within the

Congress and asked Nehru to join them. At first he vacillated but finally said no. Nehru was not prepared for an open fight with his colleagues; he felt that it would put Gandhiji in an awkward position and that, at any rate, he wanted to avoid. His love for his leader was deep-rooted; and, despite differences, he did not want to weaken that leadership in which somehow he had faith. Nehru also knew that but for Gandhiji he could never have been elected President. Leaders like Patel, Prasad and Bajaj did not like his ideas nor were they willing to play his tune. They gave him latitude because of Gandhiji.

For his part, Nehru was anxious to use his influence with Gandhiji and his personal popularity in taking the Congress along a more radical course of action. That is why, though reluctant at first, he accepted the presidentship so that he could act as "a link between various groups within the Congress". The Mahatma also believed that Nehru alone would be able to bridge the gulf between different groups in the Congress and give to the movement that unity of purpose and action which it badly needed.

The immediate task before the Congress was the preparation for a fight against the Government of India Act, 1935, which Nehru described as "a new charter of slavery to strengthen the bonds of imperialist domination and to intensify the exploitation of our masses". It bestowed a kind of provincial autonomy on the provinces in British India and provided for a federal legislature with restricted responsible government at the Centre. To Nehru the Act was a challenge, which if not met earnestly would bolster anti-national forces. He was, therefore, determined to tear it to bits, to burn it.

In Europe the crisis was deepening and Nehru was anxious that the Congress should give — both nationally and internationally — a correct lead to India. He believed in a socialistic approach to Indian and world problems and towards that end wanted to play his full part. He became less and less inclined to put up with the rightist leadership in the Congress and demanded a radical approach to the main issues. But while the rightists were not bothered about the outside world and gave Nehru all the latitude in the international sphere, approving resolutions bristling with socialistic interpretations, in internal matters they refused to budge and stuck to their views. There Nehru gave in. He was caught in an atmosphere of give and take and lacked the courage to be firm with the result that the Congress decided to contest the elections under the new Act which Nehru had threatened to wreck. Even on the question of office acceptance his opposition was resisted and finally rejected. He was, no doubt, .distressed. Three times he decided to resign but, as usual, he was afraid to weaken the forces of unity, especially in view of the international crisis. True, in his new Working Committee he dropped four rightists and nominated others with pronounced socialist leanings; but soon there was trouble. In July, 1936 six rightist leaders, including Prasad, Patel and Rajagopalachari, tendered their resignations. They wrote, "We feel that the preaching and emphasising of socialism particularly at this stage by the President and other." As he told Bose, "That struggle without Gandhiji's active participation and leadership was not likely to be an effective one." He admitted that though Bose had always shown great affection and regard for him, the two were temperamentally different and "our approach to life and its problems is not the same".

He did not like Bose's softness towards Nazi Germany and Fascist Italy; or his political methods at home. Nehru was, no doubt, aware that many of his own followers did not understand or even like the stand he had taken in this controversy. As he put it, "I have succeeded in becoming very unpopular with them, quite a remarkable feat — to displease almost everybody concerned." But until the last he tried to bridge the rift between Gandhiji and Bose. He did not succeed. Ultimately, perhaps inevitably also, Bose had to resign the presidentship. In his place the AICC elected Prasad. To prove his impartiality Nehru kept out of the new Working Committee but the gesture did not bring Bose any the nearer. In fact, he left the Congress soon thereafter and formed his Forward Bloc. Amidst the internal confusion, Nehru took advantage of an invitation from China and spent four weeks there as the guest of Marshal and Madame Chiang Kai-shek, then in power in that land.

World War

As a result of the deepening of the international crisis, which soon engulfed the world in a catastrophic war, Nehru had to cut short his Chinese visit and rush back to India. Stung by the victories of the Nazis he cried out in anguish, "The world is tragic to those who are sensitive, heart-breaking to those who feel". And as Europe sat on the edge of the sword, he sought new thoughts on the situation at home. The country was declared belligerent by Lord Linlithgow, who had taken over the Viceroyalty from Wellington. For Nehru this was not a patriotic war but a struggle between fascism on the one side and imperialism as represented by Britain and France on the other. In such a conflict, India could have no place and hence the Viceregal ukase was criticised, condemned and totally opposed by him. His heart was, no doubt, with the Allies, but he made it clear that if India were to participate in the war, it would have to be on equal terms. Freedom was a pre-requisite for India joining the Allies.

Nehru's reaction was later endorsed by the Congress Working Committee in a resolution, which stated: "If the war is to defend the *status quo,* imperialist possessions, colonies, vested interests and privilege, then India can have nothing to do with it. If, however, the issue is democracy and a world order based on democracy, then India is intensely interested in it." The British must first declare "in unequivocal terms what their war aims are" and in particular how these were going "to apply to India and to be given effect to in the present". Gandhiji hailed the resolution, described its author as an artist who had the friendliest feeling towards the English. He spoke of Nehru's "nationalism" being "enriched by his fine internationalism" and emphasised that his disciple stood not only for India, but "for all the exploited nations".

However, as the war situation worsened and there was serious talk of active cooperation with the British, differences in approach between the master and the disciple again came to the fore. Linlithgow made an offer to include representative Indians in his Executive Council, but rejected the Congress demand for an immediate transfer of power as impracticable. In the circumstances, the Congress declared that it could not possibly give any support to the British. The Viceroy became rigid in his approach. Nehru was disappointed and fell in line with Gandhiji, whose attitude was hardening. But at the same time another development took place which was equally tragic: the growing rift between the Congress and the League. In a desperate effort to bridge the gulf,

Nehru met Jinnah several times, but to no avail. The League leader liked Nehru, spoke of his personal regard for him and even admired "his character and integrity"; but he disapproved of his politics and compared him to "Peter Pan who never grows up". Meanwhile, as the cleavage between the Congress and the Government widened, Congress Ministries resigned. Jinnah, as a shrewd politician, exploited the situation and proclaimed a "Day of Deliverance" for the Muslims. Nehru was hurt. He believed that Jinnah had become in-possible. He disliked his politics as much as he detested his tactics.

As the war situation worsened further, there was renewed talk of wresting freedom for India; there was a feeling that despite Jinnah and his League it could be achieved. At the Ramgarh session of the Congress, held under Azad's presidentship there was a move for a struggle against the British, but no concrete plan was formulated. In Europe, Hitler's armies were on the march, overrunning one country after another; even France collapsed. Nehru was aghast and did not want the Congress to exploit Britain's perilous position. His heart went out to the Allies and he yearned to help them. Gandhiji agreed with his logic but was not prepared to offer armed assistance. At the AICC meeting in Poona, Rajagopalachari, ignoring Gandhiji's stand, made an offer to the British of armed cooperation if there was a political settlement. Nehru supported him in spite of the misgivings that his attitude caused among his socialist supporters who wanted to struck "with this imperialist war". The Viceroy, however, showed no enthusiasm and Nehru reconciled himself to a struggle which Gandhiji was planning. As in the past Gandhiji first held talks with Linlithgow and these having failed, as they were bound to, he embarked upon an individual civil disobedience movement in 1941.

His first satyagrahi was Vinoba Bhave — now world famous as the Bhoodan leader — and the second Nehru/The British reacted strongly and arrested the satyagrahis. At his trial Nehru was sentenced to four years' rigorous imprisonment; it shocked even Churchill. India was stunned; hundreds of meetings were organised to protest against it. For Nehru neither the punishment nor the sentence was of any consequence because, as he told the judge, "It is a small matter to me what happens to me in this trial or subsequently. Individuals count for little; they come and go as I shall go when my time is up. ... But it is no small matter what happens to India and her millions of sons and daughters. That is the issue before me, and that ultimately is the issue before you, sir." He lamented the parting of the ways but declared that it was inevitable. To use his own words, "Let those who seek the favour and the protection of this imperialism go their way, we go ours."

Not long after, the Japanese attack on Pearl Harbour took place and it brought the United States into the war. In consequence, Nehru along with other Congress leaders was released. The external situation became critical enough for the British. It was too risky and unwise to keep any longer the Indian leaders in jail. Nehru still showed no bitterness and continued to believe that the progressive forces were with the Allies; but he could not cooperate with them, unless his cooperation could be effective. Under his pressure, therefore, the Congress made another bid for a settlement with the British, but failed. On his part, Gandhiji was still averse to the idea of armed cooperation but in deference to Nehru's wishes remained quiet. He had faith in his leadership; on international issues especially he preferred to rely on Nehru's judgement. He believed that the future lay in his hands. To quote the Mahatma, "Jawaharlal will be my successor. He says that he does not understand my language and that he speaks a language foreign to me. This may or may not be true but language is no bar to a union of hearts. I know this that when I am gone he will speak my language." The declaration was unambiguous and unequivocal. From then on, Nehru became the acknowledged heir of Gandhiji.

In South-East Asia, the Japanese forces overran Hongkong, the Philippines, Malaya, Singapore, Thailand; they conquered Burma and came to the doors of India. For Nehru, Japan's "co-prosperity sphere" theory held no attraction. Despite the intransigence of the British his heart was still with the Allies. He, therefore, welcomed the visit of Marshal and Madame Chiang Kai-shek to India. They prevailed upon President Roosevelt to use his good offices with Churchill and arrange for an immediate transfer of power to Indian leaders to ensure the successful prosecution of the war. Churchill sent Sir Stafford Cripps to Delhi for a political settlement with the Congress and the League, but his mission failed.

Jinnah and his League had propounded by now their two-nation theory and refused to compromise on their demand for Pakistan. But the failure of the Cripps Mission generated a new bitterness in the Congress and there was once again talk of a fight to the finish. The issue was debated with much heat and passion at the AICC meeting in Allahabad, where the Congress decided on a programme of parallel resistance to the Japanese by resorting to a "scorched earth" policy. The British would no doubt be hindered in their war efforts but the Congress could not help it; it had to organise people's resistance to Japanese invaders.

At the next meeting of the AICC in Bombay on August 8, 1942 Gandhiji gave the dramatic slogan of "Quit India" and with those two simple, clear words, he asked the British to pack up and go, so that India could mobilise her full strength against a Japanese invasion. Nehru was not happy with Gandhiji's unbending attitude for he believed that it might jeopardise the chances of an Allied victory. But he was also aware that the Congress could not remain idle; inaction on its part would be suicidal.

Until the last, therefore, Nehru tried for a settlement and, as Gandhiji later revealed, he almost "forgot his old quarrel with the imperialists". But the British did not respond; on the contrary, within a few hours of the passing of the "Quit India" resolution, which had left the door open for negotiation, the authorities swooped on Gandhiji, Nehru and other Congress leaders and whisked them away in a special train. Gandhiji was taken to the Agha Khan's Palace in Poona; the rest, including Nehru, to the Ahmednagar Fort, where they remained detained until June 15, 1945. These arrests sparked a new rebellion in the whole country and, for a few months, India was caught in a fire of agitation and revolt unparalleled in her annals.

The people took Gandhiji's *mantra* of "Do or Die" literally to heart; in consequence, they set out either to free India or to die in the attempt. For months chaos prevailed. A sense of insecurity overwhelmed the Government. Gandhiji later regretted these happenings; but to Nehru they were inevitable and showed people's impatience. As he observed, "If we did not pacify them, I think we would have lost all strength." For the three years that Nehru remained in the Ahmednagar Fort with his colleagues like

Azad, Patel, Kripalani and Narendra Deva, he read a lot as usual and took an active part in the community life within the jail. His special interest was gardening and he devoted a great deal of time to it. He also did much writing and completed his last book, entitled the *Discovery of India,* which gives his interpretation, of the currents and cross-currents in Indian life through the ages,

Transfer of Power

As the world war neared its end in 1945, with the Allies emerging victorious on all fronts, there was renewed talk of a political settlement between India and Britain. But the unprecedented stress of a bloody holocaust into which India had been unwillingly drawn, the phenomenal shortage of food for her civilian population, and the insensitivity of an unimaginative bureaucratic machine — all these had culminated in mass starvation and widespread famine, the situation being particularly serious in Malabar, Bijapur and Orissa. But the worst happened in Bengal, where thousands died of hunger and millions lay starving. More than the political deadlock it was the economic challenge that perturbed the authorities. As months passed, tension mounted. It shook up even the steel-frame of the Raj.

Churchill had sent Wavell, a general with a magnificent war record, to India as the Viceroy; but before he could embark on his unenviable task, the Tories were unseated at home and a Labour Government, headed by Clement Attlee, captured power. Nevertheless, Wavell plunged into his work with energy and earnestness. He offered to reconstitute his Executive Council so as to make it representative of the people and towards that end called a conference in Shimla on June 25, 1945.

Invitations were sent to many leaders but the focus was on the participation of the Congress, whose leaders were released for the purpose, and the League. Although Nehru took part in the conference, he neither showed excessive enthusiasm nor pinned great hopes on it. He knew Jinnah and the obstacles that he would create in the way of a settlement. About the attitude of the Government also he was not very sanguine. As the conference dragged on, Nehru escaped for a fortnight's holiday in the "loveliness of the land" of Kashmir to enjoy "its beauty of river and valley, lake and graceful creeks". Meanwhile, the new Labour Government, determined to break the political deadlock, summoned Wavell to London, where he held talks for about a month. He returned to India with a fresh constitutional offer, much more radical than before. As an earnest of British intentions general elections were ordered and the decision to convene a Constituent Assembly was announced. Efforts were simultaneously made to reconstitute the Viceroy's Executive Council. At first the Congress entertained several misgivings, but later it appeared convinced of the change in the British attitude.

The elections, however, did not improve the situation; they confirmed the hold of the Congress among the non-Muslims and of the League among the Muslims. The latter won all Muslim seats in the Central Assembly and about 75 per cent of the Muslim seats in the provincial legislatures. Only in the North-West Frontier Province it lost to the Red Shirts of the Khan Brothers who obtained a clear majority. Consequently, the Congress formed Ministries in eight of the eleven provinces, the League in Bengal and Sindh, and the Unionist Party, with Congress support, in the Punjab.

The next stage was the reconstitution of the Viceroy's Executive Council and the convening of a Constituent Assembly. As further proof of their earnestness, the British Government sent to India a three-member high-power Cabinet Mission consisting of Lord Pethick Lawrence, the new Secretary of State for India, Sir Stafford Cripps and A. V. Alexander. At the same time, two other developments took place. One was the trial of the members of the Indian National Army (INA) which had been organised in South-East Asia by its Netaji, Subhash Bose, from among the Indian prisoners-of-war in South-East Asia, and the second was the naval mutiny in Bombay. To Nehru both were symbols of a new resurgence in India. Some officers of the INA were picked and brought for trial as deserters; to Nehru and his followers they were a "fine body of young men" whose "dominant motive was love for India's freedom". "They deserve to be treated", he said, "as prisoners-of-war" because they "functioned as regular, organised, disciplined and uniformed combatant forces." Their alliance with Japan was only to facilitate India's freedom. Nor could Nehru doubt, as he pointed out, Bose's "passion for independence". An INA Defence Committee was, therefore, set up by the Congress to assist the accused at their trial, Nehru himself put on the robes he had discarded years earlier and in the company of Bhulabhai Desai, Sapru, Katju, and Asaf Ali, appeared for the defence. The trial took place in the Red Fort. Though the officers were convicted, such was the popular adoration of their valour and the public resentment against their conviction that the authorities had to commute their sentences.

On February 18, 1945 in the wake of an RAF disturbance at Dum Dum airport, Calcutta, ratings of the Royal Indian Navy in Bombay rose in revolt. There was tremendous excitement among the people and even talk of an armed usurpation of power. Nehru disapproved of violent methods, especially when a peaceful transfer was in the offing. The ratings eventually surrendered both in Bombay as well as in Karachi, where a similar revolt had been organised.

As the negotiations with the Cabinet Mission progressed, Nehru became convinced that the British meant to quit and, hence, he went about his task seriously. For several months the Mission endeavoured to bring about an agreed settlement between the Congress and the League. Having failed in that, its members produced on May 16, 1946 a scheme of its own under which there was to be a Union at the Centre with three subjects: Foreign Affairs, Defence and Communications; three groups of provinces, one predominantly Hindu and the other two predominantly Muslim, dealing with the other subjects, and below them the provinces themselves. This three-tiered plan, as it came to be called, was not drafted in precise terms and, therefore, a battle of interpretations raged between the Congress and the League, especially on the question whether grouping was optional or compulsory. The Mission also outlined a scheme for the formation of an Interim Government at the Centre. Nehru did not care much for the Mission's long-term or short-term plan but as the former provided for a Constituent Assembly, he saw no harm in accepting it. On the other hand, he saw too many catches in the Interim Government arrangement. The Mission, therefore, left India without achieving any results; both the Congress and the League stuck to their viewpoints.

Meanwhile, Nehru was elected President of the Congress in succession to Azad. Tired of the deadlock, the Congress accepted the long-term plan with its own interpretations. So did the League with its interpretations. But a storm broke out as a result of a speech made by Nehru at the AICC meeting in Bombay on July 10, 1946, when he declared that the Congress was not bound by any conditions and that the Constituent Assembly would function as a completely sovereign body. On that pretext Jinnah at once pulled the League out of its earlier commitment and rejected the plan. Further, he called for direct action to achieve Pakistan. Suddenly the atmosphere became so charged that widespread communal riots took place and broke the peace in many parts of India, particularly Calcutta. In a desperate attempt, Nehru met Jinnah but their talks were fruitless. In their failure crashed all hopes of a settlement between the Congress and the League.

From London the Labour Government demanded swift action by Wavell. He was perplexed, unable to bring the Congress and the League together. Finally he called on Nehru on September 2, 1946 to form an Interim Government. In a broadcast, five days later, Nehru outlined the broad policies, both domestic and foreign, of the new Government and sought the cooperation of all people in this historic undertaking. He emphasised the urgency of raising the living standard, appealed for communal harmony and promised to ameliorate the condition of the untouchables and the backward tribes. In foreign affairs, he declared non-alignment with power blocs as the kernel of his policy and called for the liberation of the colonial people.

He urged the League to join the Interim Government in a spirit of harmony and cooperation and said that the door would be kept open for its representatives. A month elapsed before Wavell was able to bring the League into the new Government; but, instead of improving the situation, its coming in created new problems. Squabbling became the order of the day and the Government a house divided, with the result that there were two Governments instead of one, each functioning against the other. Nehru was fed up and at the next session of the Congress declared, "Our patience is reaching the limit and if these things continue a struggle on a large scale is inevitable." He could not say how "long we will remain in the Interim Government". Jinnah was not impressed. He ridiculed Nehru's efforts to turn the Viceroy's Council into a Dominion Government. As the League leader put it, "Little things please little minds; you cannot turn a donkey into an elephant by calling it an elephant." As allegations and counter-allegations worsened the situation, Attlee invited two representatives of the Congress, two of the League and one Sikh leader to London in a final effort to bridge the gulf. Both Nehru and Jinnah were among those who went to London; for four days the talks lasted but to no avail. Distrust had gone too far and any understanding between the Congress and the League was found impossible.

Immediately on Nehru's return from London, the Constituent Assembly met in Delhi on December 9, 1946. The League boycotted it. In moving the Objectives Resolution, Nehru, in a memorable speech, declared, "It is a resolution and yet it is something much more than a resolution. It is a declaration. It is a firm resolve. It is a pledge and an undertaking and it is for all of us, I hope, a dedication."

He pleaded with the League to abandon its boycott, called upon the princes to play their proper role, but made no secret of his determination to go ahead, with them if possible, without them if necessary. He declared, "India, as she is constituted today, wants no one's advice and no one's imposition upon her." She would be proclaimed a sovereign, democratic republic and whatever Constitution her representatives in the Constituent Assembly framed would become the Constitution of free India — whether Britain accepted it or not.

At this time Nehru faced another difficulty: the growing rift between himself and his principal deputy, Patel. At times it was ideological; often temperamental. Gandhiji intervened and brought them together; but there was no real unison. From outside Jinnah gave trouble and obstructed the finalisation of a constitutional settlement. The Congress tried to woo him by compromising on the grouping issue; but the League leader was no longer interested in a united India. The challenge of Pakistan had become real; and even Nehru with all his antipathy to the two-nation theory began to have second thoughts. Patel had already reconciled himself to partition. Wavell continued to waver and was eventually replaced by Lord Mountbatten to bring a fresh mind to the problem.

In his desire to put an end to the stalemate, Attlee was agreeable to any solution. Hence, without waiting for an agreement between the Congress and the League, the British Prime Minister announced on February 20, 1947 in the House of Commons that the British would quit India "by a date not later than June, 1948", transferring power "as a whole to some form of Central Government for British India, or in some areas to the existing Provincial Governments, or in such other way as may seem most reasonable and in the best interests of the Indian people". At last, the die was cast. Nehru hailed it as a "clear and definite declaration" which was "a challenge to all of us". Though not very happy, Jinnah also welcomed it. Only Gandhiji was sad; he saw in the declaration the germs of Pakistan. As he told Nehru, "It may lead to Pakistan for those provinces or portions which may want it." Strangely enough Churchill also raised his voice against it; he foresaw that it might lead to "partition" and even "fragmentation" of India but the British leader was more concerned about his country's "shameful flight, by a premature, hurried scuttle", which only added "the taint and smear of shame" to Britain's glorious heritage.

The Fulfilment

At last, there was fulfilment. But the dawn of freedom brought in its wake partition and its terrible aftermath. Nehru's joy was, therefore, warped by a tragic touch in an unexpected manner. In hastening the coming of independence, Mountbatten's dynamism, no doubt, played a helpful part; but it also added to the tension. Clear in his mind about the objective, he imparted to his mission all the military speed and efficiency of which he was capable. He knew that the British had to quit and, hence, ensured that they withdrew in good time and good grace. Of its internal consequences he was not so careful. Power was transferred to Nehru on the one side and Jinnah on the other hurriedly, much earlier than scheduled; in fact within less than six months of his arrival, Mountbatten had completed the operation, irrespective of the blood that it spilled. One reason for this extraordinary haste was, no doubt, the rapid deterioration in Hindu-Muslim relations, which in its train, had sapped the morale and vitality of the administration. Mountbatten foresaw the outbreak of a sanguinary conflict. The atmosphere, especially in North India, was tense. Blood flowed in Lahore, Amritsar, Multan, Rawalpindi, Sialkot and Jalandhar in the northwest, and in several places in Bengal.

To these terrible events, Nehru himself was witness. He visited many areas reduced to a shambles by rioters. He was appalled by such behaviour of human beings as "would have disgraced brutes". There was growing insecurity and fear among the Hindus and the Sikhs of West Punjab and the Hindus of East Bengal. There was transparent nervousness among the Muslims living on the proposed frontiers of Pakistan. Slowly but steadily, massacre and looting became the order of the day and hooligans made no distinction between children and women, or between the aged and the young. Millions, in search of safety, left their hearth and home on both sides of the border. They recorded the biggest migration in history.

But, while India was in the grip of such unprecedented violence, Nehru organised in Purana Qila on March 27, 1947, the first Asian Relations Conference. Present at the conference were representatives of many countries of Asia, including the Arabs from West Asia and comrades from Soviet Central Asia.

To Nehru, this was indeed a great occasion. He declared in his inaugural address, "Asia after a long period of quiescence has suddenly become important again in world affairs." Though it was only the beginning of that awakening and the period ahead would still have to be a period of transition, Asia was determined to take, as Nehru put it, "her rightful place with other continents".

He was proud that India was playing "her part in this new phase of Asian development". But to others engaged in the task of finalising the transfer of power, the conference did not mean much. Neither Nehru's colleagues in the Congress nor the League leaders bothered about it. To them, the task nearer home demanded all attention; nor were they, temperamentally or politically, much enamoured of such assemblies. To Nehru, India ever remained a part of Asia and the world and, hence, even in the midst of her tragedy, the internationalist in him could not forget her obligation to the rest of the exploited people.

True to his task, Mountbatten busied himself with giving the finishing touches to the last act. He met Gandhiji, Jinnah, Nehru, Azad and other leaders, of both the Congress and the League, several times. Having satisfied himself that there was no basis for a united India, he made them accept the inevitable — Partition. Time and circumstance had already brought Nehru and Patel round. Jinnah first ridiculed the idea of a "moth-eaten" Pakistan, as he called the Mountbatten plan, and then reconciled himself to whatever he could get.

Even the British initially were not happy over partition but Mountbatten brought home to them that there was no other choice; it was the only plan which could produce the minimum agreement among the parties for the withdrawal of the British. He paid a hurried visit to London and secured the imprimatur of the British Government on his scheme. Returning to India, he called a conference of prominent leaders on June 2, 1947, and after receiving their endorsement, announced the details of his partition plan the next day. Nehru, sad at heart, declared, "It is with no joy in my heart that I commend these proposals, though I have no doubt in my mind that this is the right course. The distinction between the "heart and the "mind was significant. At a historic AICC meeting held two weeks later, Gandhiji was the unhappiest person present; he could not approve of the plan but was too unnerved to say anything. Apparently, he did not have either the heart *ox* the courage to oppose his own proteges and plunge the country into another struggle. Nehru tersely commended the plan and it was approved by 153 votes to 29 with 36 abstentions.

For two months, thereafter, until the zero hour on August 15, 1947, the communal situation steadily deteriorated despite the agreement between the Congress and the League. In the law of the jungle, loosed by the brutes, where was the place for security of life or property?

In London, the constitutional formalities were rushed through and by the end of July, the Indian Independence Bill had been passed by both Houses of Parliament. The Act brought into existence the Dominion of India and the Dominion of Pakistan consisting of the Provinces of Sindh, the North-West Frontier and West Punjab in the west, and East Bengal in the east. Nehru and the Congress decided to let Mountbatten continue as the first Governor-General of the Dominion of India, but Jinnah appointed himself as the head of Pakistan.

Thourfi criticised at that time, Nehru's gesture in retaining Mountbatten proved beneficial to India. He not only helped Nehru and his colleagues to settle many thorny problems of partition but exercised a moderating influence on Indian princes who, on a characteristic interpretation of the lapse of paramountcy, seemed to aspire to freedom. Mountbatten was clear in his mind about the role the princes would have to play in the new set-up and, consequently, advised them, in private and in public, to take a realistic view of the constitutional position and to accede to one Dominion or the other, mindful of their geographical position and the religious character of their subjects.

At the stroke of midnight on the appointed day, Nehru rose to the occasion and to the full stature of his leadership. In the Constituent Assembly, he declared, "Long ago, we made a tryst with destiny and now the time comes when we shall redeem our pledge, not wholly or in full measure but very substantially. At the stroke of the midnight hour, when the world sleeps, India will awake to life and freedom." He concluded with the exhortation, "This is no time for petty and destructive criticism, no time for ill-will or blaming others. We have to build the noble mansion of free India where all her children may dwell." Most of India celebrated the birth of free India with great rejoicing and enthusiasm but there was one who, though the architect of it all, kept himself aloof. He sensed no happiness in his heart or fulfilment of his dream. He continued his one-man mercy mission in far-off villages in East Bengal, bringing help to the needy, comfort to the distressed and balm to the lacerated — all victims of independence in the country's very hour of glory.

Blood and Sacrifice

True, independence brought joy to millions but it plunged Bengal and the Punjab into an agony unknown in India's history.

As months passed both Hindus and Muslims, on either side of the border, realised that partition might have solved the constitutional tangle, but at a price immeasurable in terms of human misery. The uprooted did not know where to go. To many of them it was a journey to doom. Protection was guaranteed to the minorities by the infant Dominions; but neither was able to implement it. In the wake of the holocaust came the Radcliff Award, demarcating the boundaries between the two States, but instead of settling the dispute it only fanned the flames of communal frenzy, especially in the border areas. More than half a million people died in search of rehabilitation; those who survived came to a new soil free but not their own.

As trainloads of refugees from West Pakistan poured into India, the atmosphere in Delhi and East Punjab became charged with hatred. There was indiscriminate looting, and even murder and rape. Gandhiji was a disillusioned soul. His faith in the intrinsic goodness of humanity was shaken. As he saw those orgies he was appalled by the cruelty of man to man. Every day, at his prayer meeting, he enlarged the theme of peace and communal harmony with a messianic fervour. People heard him but he did not find in them the proper response.

Nehru, as he confessed in a broadcast, was also "full of horror with the things I saw and that I heard". To the Prime Minister, it was a challenge, a challenge to his leadership and to the secular character of India. He was distressed to find even some of his own colleagues in the Congress and the Cabinet wavering in their faith in secularism. But in no circumstance could he be untrue to himself; in that flood of hostility he stood firm as a rock. Alone he gave battle to the communalists, without truth or fear. He braved the wrath of fanatics who, with dagger in hand, sought to stab at the back of his secular state. He declared, unmindful of his popularity, that whatever Pakistan might have done, he would not let India shape as a Hindu State. He said, "India is not a communal state but a democratic state in which every citizen has equal rights." To this pledge, he received the unequivocal support of Gandhiji. In retrospect it emerges as a miracle how the master and the disciple held back the dark forces of communalism that had gripped the people from one end of the country to another. Was freedom worth the price of partition?

Nehru ruefully admitted, "We consented to partition because we thought that, thereby, we were purchasing peace and security." He was not sure, if he had the same choice again, what he would do. The period of trial and anguish brought Nehru much closer to Gandhiji, perhaps closer than at any time. He rushed to him every day for advice and guidance, even on trifles. He looked to him for moral support in his differences with Patel, which were ever widening on account of a fundamental divergence in outlook. Nor were his other colleagues, particularly J. B. Kripalani, who was then the Congress President, very happy with him or with the relations that subsisted between the Government and the Congress. His socialist friends like Narendra Deva and Jayaprakash Narayan considered Nehru weak-kneed and wanted him to break away from Patel. In the midst of growing disaffection all round, he found reassurance and renewed faith in Gandhiji.

In October, 1947 Path in tribesmen from Pakistan invaded Kashmir, Maharaja Hari Singh acceded to India and Nehru had to rush his troops in order to defend the frontier State from the advancing raiders. The tribal invasion hardly helped to restore faith in the *bona fides* of Pakistan; or in her declaration of protection to the Hindu minority. Hence, there was a sudden communal flare-up, especially in Delhi. Pained by these developments Gandhiji embarked on a fast unto death so that he could persuade all Indians, irrespective of caste or creed, to "live like brothers'". Nehru believed that "the loss of Gandhiji's life would mean the loss of India's soul". He told the people so.

The Mahatma's fast had its moral effect. Within five days, not only did the communal situation in Delhi improve but, as a corollary to it, even the gulf between Nehru and Patel was bridged. But that was not enough. There was no genuine meeting of hearts. Little did the nation then know that a supreme sacrifice would have to be made in the next few weeks. During those anxious days, Nehru vindicated, as a British observer said, "one's faith in the humanist and civilized intellect". In the "turmoil of communalism, with all its variations from individual intrigue to mass madness, he not only spoke "almost alone" but acted so. In the eyes of Hindu communalists, the secularism of Gandhiji and Nehru was a serious challenge to their creed. Nehru could be tackled on a material plane but Gandhiji's sway over the people was too spiritual to be negatived. They vowed to destroy him in order to eliminate that moral force.

There was hushed talk of a despicable conspiracy and on January 20, 1948, a young man dropped a crude bomb at a prayer meeting. Ten evenings later, a Hindu fanatic, Nathuram Godse, snuffed out the life of the Mahatma with three shots from his revolver as Gandhiji was coming to his prayer meeting. The apostle of non-violence had at last found by a violent act company in his "incomparable friend". Stunned and overwhelmed by grief, Nehru rushed to Birla House, where Gandhiji lay in state.

A nation was orphaned; so was Nehru. He wept like a child and told his people, "The light has gone out of our lives and there is darkness everywhere.' An inconsolable Nehru moaned in the Constituent Assembly, "I have a sense of utter shame, both as an individual and as the head of the Government, that we should have failed to keep the greatest treasure that we possessed." With tears in his eyes, he declared, "A glory has departed and the sun that warmed and brightened our hearts has set and we shiver in the cold and dark".

Slowly as the days passed the wound began to heal. Nehru recovered and told the nation in his own inimitable way, "We mourn him; we shall always mourn him, because we are human, and cannot forget our valued master; but I know that he would not like us to mourn him. No tears came to his eyes when his dearest and closest went away; there was only the firm resolve to persevere, to serve the great cause that he had chosen.

So, he would chide us if we merely mourn. That is a poor way of doing homage to him. The only way is to express our determination, to pledge ourselves anew, to conduct ourselves so, and to dedicate ourselves to the great task which he undertook and which he accomplished to such a large extent."

And so Nehru returned to his post to redeem that pledge, to carry on that task, with unswerving faith in the nation, with unreserved loyalty to the master, with the unbending response of a *karmayogi* to the call of duty.

Administrative Problems

One immediate good that the Mahatma's martyrdom did was to bring home to the people the degeneration into which Indian society had fallen. There was a welcome spirit of repentance among them and a rededication to the ideal of communal harmony. The tidal wave had been checked for the most part. Nehru and his colleagues were anxious to put to constructive purpose the new spirit of amity at home. But while the atmosphere in India was improving there was a fresh outburst of communal hatred in East Bengal which promptly had its impact on West Bengal. Thousands of Hindu refugees crossed the border into West Bengal; and the intensity of their distress evoked sympathy with them as also resentment against Pakistanis and those Indian Muslims who had supported the conception of Pakistan.

Again, Hindu-Muslim relations became strained. Several responsible people demanded a war against Pakistan, unmindful of its repercussions. Their cry was a big challenge to Nehru's leadership; but it was a benevolent circumstance that at that crucial moment Patel stood firmly by the Prime Minister, even though he showed no particular concern for the fate of Indian Muslims. He was anxious that Nehru, without being bellicose, should be tough towards Pakistan. This policy bore fruit, and the Pakistani Premier, Liaqat Ali Khan, rushed to New Delhi from Karachi and held a series of talks with Nehru. An agreement was eventually signed on April 8, 1950 under which refugees were guaranteed the right to return to their original homes, protection in transit and the right to transfer movable property and to dispose of immovable property. Safeguards were also provided for the recovery of looted property and abducted women.

The two Premiers promised to provide equal rights for minorities in both countries. Nevertheless, West Bengal leaders considered the Nehru-Liaqat Pact an act of appeasement and the two Bengali members of Nehru's Cabinet, S. P. Mukherjee and K. C. Niyogi, resigned. Had it not been for the unequivocal support that Patel gave to the Pact, the situation might have worsened.

The Sardar, however, was not too happy at Nehru's unqualified secularism; nor did he like his radical attitude towards social reforms, in particular the codification of Hindu law and his insistence on socialistic measures in the economic field. He was indifferent to the Planning Commission, which Nehru so eagerly set up; nor did he approve of Nehru's hostility towards the landed and moneyed interests. In selecting Purushottamdas Tandon for the Congress Presidentship in 1950, he threw a challenge to Nehru because Tandon stood for orthodox values in social affairs and for economic development on private lines. He also favoured a strong policy towards Pakistan.

Against Tandon, the Nehruites put up Kripalani, who is now one of the chief opponents of Nehru, but Tandon won, proving the superior hold of Patel on the party machine. Nehru himself kept aloof from the contest, but later refused to cooperate with Tandon or join the latter's Working Committee. At the Nasik session of the Congress, over which Tandon presided, Patel saw that for the masses, Congress meant Nehru. He, therefore, relented and persuaded him to accept the membership. Nehru agreed, unwillingly, for the sake of party unity. A few months later, Patel died and with him the only serious challenge to Nehru's leadership in the Congress ended. Nothing could thereafter happen in the Congress without Nehru's approval; he was the lord and master of the party.

That was why Tandon, with his peculiar ideas, could not continue as President and by September, 1951 he had to resign. Nehru took over the presidentship and the dual role of controlling the executive as Prime Minister and managing the party as President continued until 1954, when one of his nominees, U. N. Dhebar, took charge of the Congress organisation. Dhebar guided the organisation for five years until Nehru's own daughter, Indira Gandhi, succeeded him.

Meanwhile, the Constituent Assembly concluded its labours at the end of four years and adopted a Constitution on November 26, 1949. It came into force on January 26, 1950 making India a sovereign, democratic Republic.

While Nehru was busy giving a new dynamism to people's aspirations and occasionally a necessary lead to the rest of Asia — as he did by calling a 19-Nation Asian Conference in January, 1949 in New Delhi to protest against the Dutch "police action" in

Indonesia — Deputy Prime Minister Patel was engaged in integrating 650 odd princely States into the Indian Union. By August 15, 1947, he had managed to bring about the accession of all but Junagadh, Hyderabad and Kashmir. These taxed the patience and resourcefulness of India's new administrators. Of them, Junagadh proved to be a storm in a tea cup. Hyderabad with the Nizam at its head and fanatical Razakars running amuck among its people, was a tough affair. Its size and historical background could not be ignored. Nehru and Patel gave a long rope to His Exalted Highness, who dreamt of an independent kingdom and whose advisers even flirted with Pakistan. Ultimately, on September 13, 1948, Indian troops marched into Hyderabad, launched police action and took over the State.

Broadcasting on the occasion, Nehru declared, "We are men of peace, hating war, and the last thing we desire is to come into armed conflict with anyone. Nevertheless, circumstances, which you know well, compelled us to take this action in Hyderabad. Fortunately, it was brief and we return with relief to paths of peace again." He was pleased with the "restraint and discipline" shown by both Muslims and non-Muslims. He was happy that, despite the communal danger inherent in the situation, "not a single communal incident occurred in the length and breadth of this great country."

In Kashmir, the situation was different because of the aggression committed by Pakistan and the consequential complaint of India to the Security Council. In a speech to the Constituent Assembly in March, 1948, Nehru explained the position thus: "...Kashmir is not a case of communal conflict; it may be a case of political conflict, if you like; it may be a case of any other conflict, but it is essentially not a case of communal conflict.

Therefore, this struggle in Kashmir, although it has brought great suffering in its train to the people of Kashmir and placed a burden on the Government and the people of India, nevertheless, stands out as a sign of hope that we see a certain kind of cooperation, combination and coordination among certain elements, Hindu, Muslim, Sikh and other, on an equal level, and for a political fight for their own freedom. I wish to stress this because it is continually being said by our opponents and critics on the other side that this is a communal affair and that we are there to support the Hindu or the Sikh minorities as against the Muslim masses of Kashmir. Nothing can be more fantastically untrue. We could not for instance send our armies and we would not be there if we were not supported by very large sections of the population, which means the Muslims of Kashmir. We would not have gone there in spite of the invitation of the Maharaja of Kashmir if that invitation had not been backed by the representatives of the people of Kashmir and may I say to the House that in spite of our armies having functioned with great gallantry, even our armies could not have succeeded except with the help and cooperation of the people of Kashmir."

Nearer home, two major problems — rehabilitation of refugees and economic planning — engaged Nehru's attention. In less than a year more than five million Hindus had crossed over from West Pakistan, and three million from East Pakistan. Their absorption was a gigantic task. But, by November, 1950, Nehru could report to Parliament that "compared with the way in which the refugee problem has been dealt with in other countries, our results have been creditable".

In regard to planning, the Planning Commission constituted by him in March, 1950, with himself as Chairman, prepared after labouring for fifteen months the blue print of the First Five-Year Plan, which primarily aimed at self-sufficiency in food. Nehru created two sectors, the public and the private, for undertaking the work of national development, with the former exercising, as the Prime Minister emphasised, "strategic control" over the latter. Under the Plan, multi-purpose irrigation and power projects were given priority. Of such, the gigantic Bhakra-Nangal project in the Punjab, the massive Hirakud dam in Orissa, the sprawling Damodar Valley project in West Bengal, the Kosi project in Bihar, the Tungabhadra project in Andhra, the Mayurakshi project in West Bengal, the Koyna project in Bombay and the Kundah Valley project in Madras are all monuments to Nehru's planning. He often refers to them as places of pilgrimage in modern India.

Speaking about the targets of the First Five-Year Plan in 1952, Nehru declared, "Our ideals are high and our objectives are great. Compared with them, the Five-Year Plan appears to be a modest beginning. But let us remember that this is the first great effort of its kind and that it is based on the realities of today and not on our wishes. It must, therefore, be related to our present resources or else it will remain unreal. ..."

The first general election under the new Constitution in 1951-52 was a triumph of Nehru's leadership; it was a historic experiment carried out magnificently. The electorate was colossal and consisted of 173 million voters — the biggest in the world — more than eighty per cent, of whom were too illiterate to understand the technique of voting. They had to elect 4,000 representatives, 489 to the Lok Sabha and 3,375 to the various State Assemblies. They were required to vote at one of 196,000 polling booths. True, Nehru was anxious to canvass their votes for the Congress candidates; but he was more particular about building a sound and solid democratic structure. As he reported to the AICC, "The coming elections are important, but it is far more important to know exactly what we stand for and how we want to function in the future. It is better to keep our soul and to lose an election than to win that election in the wrong way and with wrong methods."

Electioneering was not new for Nehru; he had done it in 1937 and 1945. But the present election was different; it was based on adult franchise. The 170 odd million voters were spread over thousands of villages and hundreds of towns; to reach them all was an impossible task. But Nehru toured extensively, covering about 30,000 miles and addressing no fewer than 30 million people. The result was that the Congress swept the polls. In Parliament it won 362 of 489 seats and secured a majority in most of the States. Nehru had good reason to be satisfied with the outcome, even proud of it. He was victorious both in his experiment of democracy as well as in bringing his party back to power.

Foreign Affairs

Under her new Constitution, India ceased to be a Dominion and became a Sovereign Democratic Republic; nevertheless, she did not leave the Commonwealth. For years Nehru had advocated a complete severance of the British connection, but the manner in which the British left and the new forces, "full of strife", looming on the world horizon compelled him to take *a*, more realistic view.

Hence, at the conclusion of the conference of the Commonwealth Prime Ministers in London on April 27, 1949 he agreed to a declaration endorsed by all other members that India, though a Republic, would remain within the British Commonwealth of Nations. Under the new formula, the British Sovereign became the symbolic Head of the Commonwealth.

On his return home, Nehru defended his decision in a broadcast to his people. As he put it, "I have naturally looked to the interests of India, for that is my first duty. I have always conceived that duty in terms of the larger good of the world. That is the lesson that our master taught us and he told us also to pursue the ways of peace and of friendship with others, always maintaining the freedom and dignity of India." He saw hatred in men's hearts and fear and suspicion clouding their vision. He was, therefore, anxious to welcome every step that would lead to a lessening of the tension in the world. In that light, it could not but be a good augury for the future that the old conflict between India and England should have been resolved in a friendly way, honourable to both countries.

There were too many disruptive forces in the world and the Prime Minister was averse to throwing "our weight in favour of further disruption, and any opportunity that offers itself to heal old wounds and to further the cause of cooperation should be welcomed". He, however, made it clear that "the evil part" of the Empire would have to be broken; as also anything that came in the way of any member-nation's growth. He added ". . . it is better to keep a cooperative association going which may do good in this world rather than break it."

In less than a week after his arrival, Nehru took steps for the ratification of the London decision in the Constituent Assembly and, despite opposition from socialists and communists, was able to obtain overwhelming support of the members; thus was put India's seal on the new relationship with Britain. Later, the Congress also approved the decision at its Jaipur session. In Britain and other Commonwealth countries, it created a further reservoir of goodwill for India. To the rest of the world, it was a fine lesson in co-existence; it enhanced the prestige of India.

Before returning from his historic visit to London, Nehru stopped at Paris, where the General Assembly of the United Nations was in session. He was invited to address it. In an eloquent appeal for a revaluation of Asia's role in world affairs, Nehru declared in a passage which has assumed historic importance: "May I say, as a representative from Asia, that we honour Europe for its culture and for the great advance in human civilization which it represents? May I say that we are equally interested in the solution of European problems; but may I also say that the world is something bigger than Europe, and you will not solve your problems by thinking that the problems of the world are mainly European problems. There are vast tracts of the world which may not in the past, for a few generations, have taken much part in world affairs. But they are awake; their people are moving and they have no intention whatever of being ignored or of being passed by. It is a simple fact that I think we have to remember because, unless you have the full picture of the world before you, you will not even understand the problem, and if you isolate any single problem in the world from the rest, you do not understand the problem. Today, I do venture to submit that Asia counts in world affairs. Tomorrow, it will count much more than today."

To convey the same message, Nehru undertook a year later at the invitation of President Truman a trip to the United States. It was his first visit to America. He was impressed by the gigantic strides in technological and material fields made by Americans, but he did not find depth in their approach to life. He was amazed by the reaction to his policy of non-alignment. He took pains to explain it but he found little response among responsible Americans. He assured the House of Representatives, "We have to achieve freedom and defend it. We have to meet aggression and to resist it, and the force employed must be adequate for the purpose. But even when preparing to resist aggression, the ultimate objective, the objective of peace and reconciliation, must never be lost sight of, and heart and mind must be attuned to this supreme aim, and not swayed or clouded by hatred or fear. This is the basis and the goal of our foreign policy. We are neither blind to reality nor do we propose to acquiesce in any challenge to man's freedom, from whatever quarter it may come. Where freedom is menaced, or justice threatened; or where aggression takes place, we cannot be and shall not be neutral. What we plead for, and endeavour to practice in our own important way, is a binding faith in peace, and an unfailing endeavour of thought and action to ensure it." He hoped that the great democracy of the United States would understand and appreciate India's approach to life's problems because Nehru was anxious to develop friendship and cooperation between the two republics. In a tone ringing with sincerity he told America, "I stand here to offer both in the pursuit of justice, liberty and peace."

Nehru's first visit to America was, however, not very fruitful; it only hardened his attitude to the West. He believed that it had not yet got over the colonial complex and continued to take Asia and Africa for granted. That was not so in the East; from there he received both admiration and sympathy, even public support to his international stand.

In the latter half of October, 1954, Nehru visited China and in a triumphant tour was able to see the many changes that the communists had brought about in a short time. He saw, as he himself said, "This ancient country in new garb, and it is the face of youth here that I shall especially remember, the vital, active joyful faces of young men and young women, boys and girls and children, that is the memory especially that I shall carry with me."

He was convinced that China was anxious to be friends with India and emphasised that both could learn something from each other. To use his own words: "Both can cooperate in many ways even though their problems may differ to some extent and their methods might not be the same. The essential thing between two nations and two peoples is tolerance and friendly feelings. If these are present, then, other things follow. I am convinced that these are present in China and India." Earlier, during the visit to India of the Chinese Prime Minister, Chou En-lai, concrete shape to this understanding had been given by a re-affirmation of the five principles incorporated in the preamble to the Sino-Indian agreement on trade with Tibet. In a joint declaration the two Prime Ministers declared in June, 1954 that they would abide by those principles which came to be known as the Panchsheela; these are: (1) mutual respect for each other's territorial integrity and sovereignty; (2) non-aggression; (3) non-interference in each other's internal affairs; (4) equality and mutual advantage; and (5) peaceful co-existence and economic cooperation.

In their opinion, if these principles were applied not only between various countries but in international relationship generally, they would surely lay a sound foundation for peace and security, and the fears and apprehensions that exist today would give place to a feeling of confidence. In their subsequent meetings, which took place periodically, the two Prime Ministers tried to apply them in practice in their relation with each other but on the question of Tibet and the undemarcated Sino-Indian frontiers, the Chinese were always stiff and became "aggressive" towards India after the revolt of the Dalai Lama and his followers in 1959.

However, at the Afro-Asian Conference held in Bandung in 1955, where both Nehru and Chou played a prominent part, these principles held sway and were elaborated into Ten Principles for world peace. They were approved by 29 participating Governments of Asia and Africa. Since then, "Bandung" has become a symbol of the new awakening of the Afro-Asian world and of its determination to take its rightful place among the nations.

Soon after Bandung, Nehru made his historic journey to the Soviet Union; two years later he went again to the United States but this time at the invitation of a friend, President Eisenhower. Both the visits were of tremendous significance. The one because it brought India and the Soviet Union closer together than ever before; subsequently the return visit to India of Bulganin and Khrushchev strengthened that friendship still more. The other, because of the clearing of several misunderstandings between the two great republics.

Despite the risk of Western reaction Nehru showed courage in undertaking the visit to the Soviet Union and still more in inviting the Soviet leaders to India but he was amply rewarded by the firm attitude taken by the Soviet Union in favour of India on the questions of Kashmir and Goa — a part of India still in Portuguese possession — and the large-scale economic aid that came from Russia. In fact, these visits reinforced Nehru's position, both nationally and internationally. Though the West was not happy at first and did not make any secret of its misgivings about these developments it soon realised that India could not be taken for granted and hence there was a keener desire on its part to come to terms with India.

On his second visit to the United States in 1956 the treatment given to Nehru was different. He was listened to more respectfully and even his non-alignment policy was not devalued. In this, Eisenhower, no doubt, played a great part; but Nehru also assured the Congressmen and Senators of America that though India might be neutral in her international dealings, she would not be neutral where freedom was in peril or democracy was threatened.

In his meetings with Western leaders in Europe on several occasions, especially during the Commonwealth Prime Ministers' Conferences, Nehru sought to clarify his foreign policy. It goes to his credit that despite the adverse and sometimes hostile press in the West he was able to convince those who came into personal contact with him about the sincerity of his approach and his *bona fides*. In consequence, there was better understanding even in the West of the role of India in world affairs. In the newly-freed countries of Asia and Africa Nehru had already won a reservoir of goodwill and affection. To most of them he was the inspirer and guide of their own liberation. That was why Kings and Prime Ministers came to India, paid glowing tribute to Nehru's leadership and in return invited him to their countries and publicly idolised him. This was so specially in Burma and Indonesia in South-East Asia and Egypt, Syria and Saudi Arabia in West Asia. Leaders from Africa also came to him, including the Prime Ministers of the Sudan and Ghana. In particular, Nkrumah impressed him greatly. Nehru hailed him as a "shining star in the new firmament of Africa". Africa is one of the few continents which Nehru has not yet visited. He has been invited and even pressed by the African leaders but he has as yet not been able to fulfil his promise. He has declared that nothing would make him happier than to do so as soon as time permitted because he has always had a great fascination for the African people and their culture.

Planning for the Future

In India Nehru's leadership, though criticised sometimes by the left, sometimes by the right, continued unchallenged. In 1957, it was put to another democratic test in the second general election. The ruling Congress Party relied more on his personality than on its programme for its electoral success.

A vote for the Congress was openly solicited as a vote for Nehru. But the leader himself spoke more about the achievements of the party in power — of the Five-Year Plans, the community development projects, the objective of a socialistic pattern of society and finally, India's growing status in the world. It was, however, accepted on all hands that with most voters, it was the magic of the Nehru name which weighed. As a result, the Congress won 75 per cent, of the seats in the Lok Sabha and 65 per cent, of the seats in the State Legislatures. For Nehru it was a magnificent achievement; it confirmed his immense hold on his people and added to his international stature. Except in Kerala, the Congress was able to form ministries in all other reorganised States. At the Centre its sway was overwhelming.

Soon after the formation of a new Government, Nehru faced a crisis in India's economy, caused by an acute shortage of foreign exchange and food. The Prime Minister exhorted the nation to produce more food and warned his Party that unless the economic situation was retrieved, freedom would be jeopardised. He also called for the speedy introduction of land reforms and eventually made the Nagpur session of the Congress approve such radical measures as State trading in food grains, cooperative farming and service cooperatives. Nevertheless, the economy was giving way at many points and there was strong criticism of his policies from different quarters; the left attacked him as being weak-kneed and the right thought he was going too fast. There were also attacks on his policy of non-alignment, which had resulted in a diminution of Western aid to India. Nehru replied, "I say with a challenge that even if Jawaharlal Nehru were to go mad, the Congress and the country will not depart from the policy of non-alignment and socialism." He was conscious of the difficulties the country faced; he was worried about the set-back to some of his cherished programmes. Still, he said, "We will never change our policy. If somebody does not want to give us aid, well, let him keep his money with him. We will go on without aid."

However, there was a time especially after the Gauhati Congress, when he felt "stale and flat". He wanted to give up office. As he told the Congress Parliamentary Party in April 1959, "I feel now that I must have a period when I can free myself from this daily burden ...". He did not want to escape from responsibility but was anxious to operate for at least six months as a private citizen untrammelled by office. The announcement came as a bombshell to the Congress, to the country. Neither his colleagues in the Cabinet nor the rank and file of the Congress Party were prepared to allow him to retire. From everywhere, pressure was put on him to continue; eventually he relented, rather grudgingly. "The atmosphere is getting heavier, murkier, more difficult for a sensitive person to breathe easily. What is one to do, I do not know," he said.

The episode over, Nehru returned to the saddle with renewed dedication to planning for the future. He was in a hurry to build the India of his dreams. Under his inspiration the framers of the Second Five-Year Plan had set specific tasks: *(i)* a sizable increase in national income so as to raise the level of living in the country; *(ii)* rapid industrialisation with particular emphasis on the development of basic and heavy industries; *(iii)* large expansion in employment opportunities; and *(iv)* the reduction of inequalities in income and wealth, and a more" even distribution of economic power.

Looking to the backward conditions and poverty of the people, these were not ambitious undertakings. By the end of the Plan in 1961, the national income would increase by 25 per cent.; there would be 10 million new jobs; production of food grains would go up by 25 per cent., cotton by 31 per cent, and jute by 25 per cent.; 21 million more acres of land would be brought under irrigation; industrial production would rise by 64 per cent., steel recording 231 per cent., partly because of the Soviet-aided Bhilai, the West-German-aided Rourkela, and the British-aided Durgapur — all fruits of Nehru's policy of non-alignment.

Moreover, railways would be modernised and extended; transport — both sea and land — would be enlarged; education would be widely spread; medical facilities would be greatly increased; and finally, the shape of rural India would be changed by the extension of the community development programme. At the inauguration of this last programme, which assured a new existence to 325 million people, Nehru exclaimed, "The work which has been started here today spells the revolution about which some people have been shouting for so long. This is not a revolution based on chaos and the breaking of heads, but on a sustained effort to eradicate poverty.' Essentially a scheme of self-help, it has brought to thousands of villages new roads, buildings, schools, hospitals and helped them in reclaiming virgin and waste lands, and given them more food, more clothing, better health and a modicum of education. Rightly Nehru boasted, "Nothing has happened in any country in the world during the last few years so big, in content and so revolutionary in design as the community development projects in India." His statement was supported by an acknowledged American authority on rural development — M. L. Wilson, who, after an extensive survey of these projects, recorded, "My admiration and enthusiasm for the programme as a whole, its vastness, its organisation and its objectives is such that I can hardly express my judgement and opinions except in superlatives. In many aspects, there has been nothing approaching its scope and objectives in the history of rural improvement and adult education throughout the entire world."

But the emphasis in the Second Plan has been on rapid industrialisation; according to Nehru it could be achieved, especially in the field of heavy industries by enlarging the public sector. By the resolution on Industrial Policy issued by his Government on April 30, 1956 the scope of State enterprise was considerably expanded and included "all industries of basic and strategic importance, or in the nature of public utility services," as also "other industries which are essential and require investment on a scale which only the State, in the present circumstances, could provide". In pursuance of this policy, Nehru went ahead with the installation of heavy plant and machinery for iron and steel production; with machine-tool manufacture; with mining and heavy electrical plants.

In other industries the State's interference in larger public interest was clearly stated; and though industrialists were assured that there would be no nationalisation of their private concerns, they would have to function within the new framework of a socialist economy. Naturally there was panic in the private sector. Nehru, however, assured it, "I do not want State socialism of that extreme in which the State is all-powerful and governs practically all activities ... I should, therefore, like decentralisation of economic power. We cannot, of course, decentralise iron and steel and locomotives and such other big industries but you can have small units of industries as far as possible on a cooperative basis with State control in a general way. I am not at all dogmatic about it." His economic adviser, P. C. Mahalanobis, had a solution: large machine-building industry as the basis for secondary industries; and cottage industries as the basis for large-scale employment. The private sector was alarmed at this approach; under its pressure considerable modifications were made, with the result that there is much greater harmony now between the public and private sectors than previously.

Nevertheless, as an earnest of Nehru's socialism, his Finance Minister, T. T. Krishnamachari, who later resigned under unhappy circumstances, presented a novel budget for increasing taxation and raising more revenue for financing the new schemes. It was such a radical departure from all budgetary precedents that it shook the whole economic structure. Krishnamachari, however, remained firm. He declared, "We could not have taken a different course; in democracy it is very difficult to get credit from people unless you do something substantial."

In 1958, the Second Plan faced serious trouble due to a large foreign exchange gap; it had to be pruned and one of the victims of pruning was the community development programme, which had to be slowed down. Nehru was, naturally, sad and distressed. Similarly, in the field of land reforms, despite his own convictions and personal enthusiasm, he had to mark time.

The subject falls in the State list and the State Ministries do not share to that extent his ideological concern for giving land to the tiller; some drastic measures have, no doubt, been taken by them but the situation has not improved. In his anxiety to hasten the process Nehru even amended the Constitution making compensation for acquired land non-justiciable and leaving the executive free to determine its quantum — a measure which provoked considerable opposition in various quarters. Equally slow and haphazard has been the progress of education, 80 per cent, of the population still remaining illiterate. Again on the question of over-population he is neither clear nor firm; in fact he seems to believe, much to the surprise of his own experts, that "India can support a larger population given economic growth".

In scientific and technological development, Nehru has always taken great interest; that is why he has set up twelve national laboratories in various parts of the country to do research in subjects as diverse as agriculture, industrial technology, nutrition, malaria, cancer, fuel, drugs, tropical medicine, leather, glass and ceramics. For nuclear research he has almost a passion; ever since its formation he has kept the Department of Atomic Energy under his own charge and established two nuclear-research institutes, one in Bombay and the other in Calcutta. One atomic reactor — Apsara — has already been commissioned; another is under way, with Canadian help.

Stresses and Strains

One of Nehru's outstanding contributions to the building up of free India is the sense of unity and stability that he has given to the administration; his personality itself has been the strongest cementing factor. In fact, people sometimes become alarmed and wonder what will happen to the whole fabric when he is gone. That is why the persistent question: After Nehru, what? Even in his life-time, disruptive tendencies have sought to raise their ugly heads; one of these was the linguistic agitation. Though based on "sound, scientific and cultural principles of administrative organisation, the language issue was exploited by interested parties and became a challenge to Indian unity. The first to wage a campaign were the Telugu-speaking people of Madras, who demanded a separate State of Andhra. A Congress worker, Potti Sriramulu, fasted to death. At last, Nehru gave in and formally inaugurated the new State in October 1953.

Once Andhra was conceded, the other demands for linguistic reorganisation could not be resisted. Although Nehru denounced them as "foolish and tribal attitudes", he was conscious of the intensity of the people's feelings and appointed a States Reorganisation Commission to go into the whole question and to suggest appropriate measures, bearing in mind the need to preserve and strengthen Indian unity. After two years of survey and investigation, the Commission reported, recommending the redivision of the country into sixteen States and three Territories. Not all were satisfied; in some parts like Bombay and the Punjab, discontent took a most violent form. Nehru vacillated, suggesting one modification after another. Finally, solutions were announced by him and even approved by Parliament but these did not resolve the conflict. In fact, in Bombay, the Congress suffered heavy electoral reverses and the Opposition parties forged a united front, took full advantage of popular discontent and strengthened their party positions.

Equally disturbing has been the opposition in the South to the introduction of Hindi as the official language of India; the appointment of an Official Language Commission to suggest the time and methods for the change-over from English to Hindi intensified it. In 1957, the report was published, recommending the replacement of English by Hindi by 1965; it made the situation worse, and some forty Congress MPs from the South petitioned for a delay until 1990. In Madras, particularly, popular agitation rose to fever pitch; Rajagopalachari publicly spoke of Hindi imperialism. Nehru favoured gradualness, rebuked Hindi fanatics and assured South Indians that he was himself "partial to English". But he was not prepared to give English an equal status with Hindi — recognised as the official language by the Constitution — but guaranteed the former's continued use for all official purposes as an "associate language". He declared, "I don't want people in the non-Hindi areas to feel that certain doors are closed to them."

From the left, Nehru had been facing organised opposition since independence; but recently the right also, alarmed by the speed of his socialism, took courage and came out openly against him. His life-long colleague and friend, Rajagopalachari, gave the lead and in a short time was able to organise a new party — the Swatantra (Freedom) Party — to halt what he described as the Congress march to communism. At first, Nehru scoffed at it, saying that it was a reactionary group having no roots among the people, but later he showed some concern at its growing influence, especially among the capitalist, middle-class and educated circles, and warned the Congress to be prepared to face its challenge.

From Kerala, where the Communists had obtained a majority in the State Legislature and formed the Government, came disquieting news of a mass upsurge; there was discontent all round and it threatened to paralyse the administrative machinery. Reluctantly Nehru intervened, dismissing the Communist Government and imposing President's rule in the State. He justified the action on grounds of internal security and peace, and said, "Everyone concerned, whether he said it or not, wanted this done in the totality of circumstances." The communists were furious and damned his action as a "betrayal of democracy"; in certain other quarters also, doubts were expressed about its legality and constitutionality.

From across the frontiers, Nehru's foreign policy was subjected to unexpected stresses. First came the danger from the rise of a military dictatorship, headed by General Ayyub Khan in Pakistan; it made the relations between the two countries more tense. There was talk of a possibility of war, but the Pakistani General showed commendable restraint. The clouds disappeared. On September 1, 1959, Nehru and Ayyub Khan met at Palam Airport, New Delhi, for about an hour and pledged the determination of the two Governments to formulate relations between them on "a rational and planned" basis, abandoning the old system of tackling issues in an *ad hoc* manner. The Pakistani leader spoke appreciatively of Nehru and said that he was inspired by "his personality and by his thoughts and feelings of goodwill".

From Communist China, whose case for admission into the United Nations he had been fighting valiantly, trouble came in a distressing and acute form. First was the internal revolt in Tibet, regarding whose autonomy Chou En-lai had personally given a guarantee to Nehru in 1954; but despite it the Tibetans were subjected to brutal communist repression, with the result that the Dalai Lama and his followers had to flee and take refuge in India. Because of cultural and historical affinities between India and Tibet, Nehru was pained at the Chinese behaviour. He told the Lok Sabha on April 27, 1959, "We have no desire whatever to interfere in Tibet; we have every desire to maintain the friendship between India and China; but at the same time we have every sympathy for the people of Tibet, and we are greatly distressed at their hapless plight." A week later, he declared in the Rajya Sabha that he was "grieved beyond measure" at the developments over Tibet and reminded the Chinese leaders who accused India of interfering in China's affairs and harbouring imperialist plans that all that India had done was to give shelter to the Dalai Lama and the Tibetan refugees. Though Nehru remained unshaken in his belief in the Panchsheela, he admitted that it was losing some of its glitter.

A few weeks later, he received a still bigger shock; the Chinese started indulging in "continued aggression" against India's northern borders. Reporting the "incidents" to the Lok Sabha in the middle of August 1959, he declared, "There is no alternative to us but to defend our borders and our integrity." Near those borders lay the tiny states of Bhutan and Sikkim, becoming nervous about their independence as they came to know about Chinese troop movements. Nehru re-assured them: "Our position is quite clear. Any aggression against Bhutan and Sikkim will be considered as aggression against India." Even in Ladakh district of Kashmir, the Chinese had been misbehaving; they had repeatedly ambushed and captured isolated Indian patrols. The Prime Minister also disclosed that in July 1959, an Indian detachment had been taken prisoner by Chinese troops "well within Indian territory". In a White Paper issued by his Government the full story about Chinese intentions was revealed. The Prime Minister was a disillusioned man. Despite his affection for the Chinese, he admitted, "What is happening in China today — I do not want to use strong words — is the pride and arrogance of power that is showing itself in their language and in their behaviour to us and in so many other things they have done."

In the midst of these disturbing developments the people were shocked to learn of the "temperamental differences" between the Defence Minister and the Chief of the Army Staff, who tendered his resignation. On the advice of Nehru, the resignation was withdrawn but the whole episode left a bad taste and did considerable damage to the morale of the armed forces and of the people in general.

Earlier, the Food Minister, A. P. Jain, resigned reporting to Parliament his inability to improve the food position. In his place,

Nehru appointed S. K. Patil, a dynamic figure in Congress politics, who promised to retrieve the situation. The overall economic position was not too bright, though the new Finance Minister, Morarji Desai, often spoken of as Nehru's likely successor, brought about a certain financial stability and by his visits to Europe and America procured sizable loans to tide over an exchange crisis.

Meanwhile, blue prints for the Third Five-Year Plan (1961-66) were under active consideration. Under Nehru's inspiration, the Dhebar Committee appointed by the Congress has recommended a further tightening up of the tax structure, increased production by an expansion of the public sector as a means of providing resources for additional development and wider employment, substantial steps to bridge social and economic inequalities, and finally the reorganisation of agriculture on cooperative lines on a voluntary basis. But all this is not expected to increase the national income by more than six per cent. It is a far cry from socialism, Nehru himself describing it as only "a leap forward to a socialist society".

Summary

As Nehru crosses the biblical span of threescore and ten, he is harassed on many fronts, both internal and external. He starts his day, as he himself revealed recently, in "not too pleasant a mood". First he has to open a "pretty big baggage of telegrams" received from either Peking, Lhasa, Gyantse or Yatung, giving the latest information about the border happenings. "I try to overcome that," he said, "and I am getting accustomed, to some extent, to do that." Then there are disputes and minor crises within his Congress Party; as also the temperamental differences among his own Cabinet colleagues and senior officials, leading sometimes to a Mundra scandal and sometimes to a Mathai episode. Also there is a flood in Kashmir or draught in Raj as than; a food riot in Calcutta or a linguistic upsurge in Bombay. On every issue he keeps an open mind. He tries to see every point of view. And in the process he often loses his own point of view, with the result that people feel he is not sufficiently firm or decisive.

Politically also, there is dissatisfaction with his policies — the left is annoyed with his compromising approach; the centre is unhappy with his radicalism; the right is openly accusing him of bringing in communism. To the vast majority of people, however, he remains by and large the hero he has always been. They may be irritated with him a little, even angry with him at times, but their faith in the man is unshaken — in his sincerity of purpose, honesty of action and above all in the intensity of his desire to do good to the poor and the downtrodden. But withal he is human. He is susceptible to praise, listens often to wrong people and gives in to friends, due more to past loyalties than to merit. He is, no doubt, brave and daring; he is also impulsive and impetuous, which often creates more problems for himself than he can solve. But he is as conscious of his failures as he is proud of his achievements. He is anxious always to do right but what is right eludes him now and again.

He becomes confused and loses clarity of vision. The ideals before him are still the same and still beckon to him but they seem to have lost some of their beauty and lustre. He sees the triumph of evil in unsuspected quarters and becomes a helpless spectator of the coarsening and distortion by his own colleagues of the values and objectives which he holds dear.

Today, Nehru himself has become a subject of debate; but against the few who have lost confidence in his leadership, there are still the many who do not hesitate to give him unquestioned loyalty. Therein lies the secret of Nehru's role in modern India. He has, as he himself pointed out in an anonymous article years ago, "all the makings of a dictator in him — vast popularity, a strong will directed to a well-defined purpose, energy, pride, organisational capacity, ability, hardness, and with all his love of the crowd, an intolerance of others and a certain contempt for the weak and the inefficient". Then there is "his overmastering desire to get things done and sweep away what he dislikes and build anew...". In that process "he may keep the husk" but he sees to it "that it bends to his will".

Is democracy safe in the hands of such a man? To quote Nehru again, "He calls himself a democrat and a socialist, and, no doubt, he does so in all earnestness, but every psychologist knows that the mind is ultimately a slave to the heart and that logic can always be made to fit in with the desires and irrepressible urges of man. A little twist and Jawaharlal might turn a dictator sweeping aside the paraphernalia of a slow-moving democracy." But the man who can give such a penetrating analysis of himself can never be a dictator; Nehru has always guarded himself, more so since his assumption of power, against that "little twist".

India's democracy lives because of him; the danger to its survival may arise when he is no more. But in the emergence of that danger his own part will have been far from negligible. The tragedy of his leadership is that, unlike Gandhiji, he has not produced the leaders — young, active and dynamic — who can carry on his mantle. And, worse still, he seems least concerned about it. Nevertheless, India prays that after him there will not be the deluge.

3

An Eventful Career

Jawaharlal Nehru, the man who made a tryst with destiny, was a leader who kept his promise and led India to freedom. The first Prime Minister of India, he came to the forefront of the Indian freedom struggle after Jalianwala Bagh massacre. Devoted to the cause of freedom, he was a representative of a whole new generation of India. World Peace and all round development of India were the main concerns of this great statesman. 'Chacha Nehru', as he was fondly called by children, was amongst the prominent names behind the establishment of the Non-aligned Movement (NAM).

Pt. Jawaharlal Nehru was not just a man or a Prime Minister, he was a phenomenon who gave shape to the dreams of independent India and permeated the lives of Indians.

Education

Jawaharlal Nehru was the first Prime Minister of India. He was also a major persona in the Indian Independence movement. The early education of Jawaharlal Nehru played a major role in his political views and economic policies.

Jawaharlal Nehru was the son of Motilal Nehru. Motilal Nehru was a wealthy barrister by profession. He practiced English law in the colonial Indian courts. The family belonged to the educated genteel class. It was also to a large extent anglicised. Jawaharlal Nehru received primary education under the guidance of an English governess. Young Jawaharlal was taught to converse in English from an early age. He also learnt the appropriate customs of the British Raj.

Motilal Nehru wanted his son to get a proper English education. He wished his son to qualify for and serve the Indian Civil Services or I.C.S. He sent his son Jawaharlal to Harrow, the elite Public school in England. Jawaharlal Nehru was to spend the next six years of his life by studying at the hallowed portals of Harrow and Cambridge.

The young Jawaharlal did not enjoy his schooling at Harrow. He found the school syllabus stifling and the standard of residency conditions unbearable. All students of the school were forced to condition themselves to the daily specter of bathing and washing themselves in cold water. After completing school, Nehru took the University of Cambridge entrance examinations in 1907. The same year, he got admission into the University.

Jawaharlal Nehru studied natural sciences at Cambridge University. His chosen subjects were physics, chemistry and geology. Jawaharlal Nehru was weak in mathematics. For this reason, Physics was later substituted by botany.

The tripos subjects taken up at Cambridge University were not voluntarily chosen by Nehru. He studied the three natural science subjects with only one aim, to pass the Indian Civil Services examination. Nevertheless, Jawaharlal Nehru enjoyed his stay at Cambridge. The liberal atmosphere of the University encouraged him to do a host of non-academic activities. Jawaharlal Nehru passed the final Cambridge degree examinations successfully, where he stood second.

Jawaharlal Nehru joined the Inner Temple for his legal studies in October 1910. This decision, again, was not taken due to Nehru's fascination with the law. The event merely marked a career move as charted by his barrister father Motilal Nehru. Jawaharlal Nehru passed the Bar final examination in 1912. After clearing the examination, he was called to the bar later that year.

Nehru's education years at England fostered in him the Indian nationalist movement. He believed that the colonial English administration wilfully discriminated against Indians. This thinking was further fuelled by the abrasive attitude of the British Imperial order against Indians. Jawaharlal was attracted by the socialism of the British Fabians. The forte of equality in socialism acted as a magnet for the impressionable Jawaharlal Nehru.

Jawaharlal Nehru was very much influenced by the socialist and liberal political atmosphere prevalent in Europe in those days. The 1900s heralded the culmination of the Western Age of Enlightenment. The atmosphere of liberalism prevalent in that era emphasised the importance of the rights of the individual. It also emphasised on the rights of the equality of opportunity. This liberal viewpoint came to prominence during Nehru's later years. His British sojourn also instilled in him a secular ethos that was far ahead of his time. This moral uprightness would help him to dream of a new India that would accommodate citizens of all religions.

London was a hotbed of political movements in the early part of the 20th century. The student Jawaharlal Nehru liked to visit the cultural attractions of the capital city of the British Empire. He frequented the museums, opera houses and the theatres of London. Nehru was influenced by the deep social cauldron of pre-World War I London. Socialism was one of the prominent influences affecting the English political class at that time.

The early education of Jawaharlal Nehru influenced him in his later life. The influence was clearly visible on the economic policies adopted by the Indian state after its independence in 1947. Nehru clearly favoured a more socialist approach when compared to other South Asian economies. The first Prime Minister was clearly thinking about his heady educational period in London when he promulgated the socialist ideology that influenced Indian government of the 1950s. The economy was treated with a mixed control. The Indian government was in control of the primary industries like electricity, mining and heavy engineering workshops.

The socialist leaning of Jawaharlal Nehru was apparent in the land redistribution programme announced by the Indian government in the middle of the 20th century. The rural sector was given importance. Nehru correctly thought that since the majority of the Indian population lived in its villages, the rural sector should also get a lion's share of the country's economic resources. Dams were built. Canals were dug. The British education of Nehru is starkly visible in the promotion of fertilizers to increase the crop yield of the land.

The British education of Jawaharlal Nehru is also displayed in the Prime Minister's quest for independent energy sufficiency. Nehru actively promoted the acquiring and development of Nuclear Energy. Hydroelectric power projects were also enthusiastically taken. The License Raj was also his creation.

The License Raj was a unique by-product of Nehru's combined Social-Liberal philosophy. The License Raj was started with the view to help the Indian industrial sector. The intention led to limited success. Indian industries soon became unprofitable and became globally uncompetitive. The failure of the License Raj led to its gradual scrapping by successive Indian governments from the 1980s.

Jawaharlal Nehru was the epitome of a resurgent India in the middle of the 20th century. He had the best of worlds, a privileged British education and an Indian upbringing. His study at the Harrow School helped him to get a firm grounding of the British cultural ethos. This was further cemented by his attendance at the Trinity College in the University of Cambridge. His stint as a Barrister at the Inner Temple in London helped to hone his already sharp negotiation skills at the bar. This legal training would help him to negotiate the treacherous minefield of pre-independence British politics from 1910 to 1947.

Joining Indian National Congress

Jawaharlal Nehru and the Indian National Congress maintained a close relationship that lasted for more than four long and eventful decades of Indian history. Nehru's relationship with the Indian National Congress officially started in 1919, two years after the birth of his daughter, Indira Priyadarshini, and seven years after his return from England. However, his close association with the Indian political scenario started much before his official initiation. Motilal Nehru, Jawaharlal's father, was a veteran

Congressman of the moderate school and closely associated with the cause of India's freedom. Soon after his return from England in 1912, Jawaharlal found himself at the very midst of the Indian political scenario.

However, Jawaharlal was not very sure of the ideological position that would be effective for a rapid attainment of Indian Independence. On one side, there was his attachment to the extremist mode of protest, and then there was his loyalty towards his father.

His initial dissociation from the ground realities of India also worked as a hindrance for him taking any definitive position. He was overall disturbed at the state of the inane Indian response to the British rule, with Anglophile Indian elite at the helm. The emergence of Gandhi worked as a great impetus to the Indian freedom struggle, and provided Nehru with the much needed direction that he was in search of. Gandhi's success at Champaran and Ahmedabad introduced the power of Satyagraha to the Indian masses. Civic resistance seemed to be a new political weapon that was powerful enough to put even the greatest imperialist power on the back-foot on issues of rightful governance and public rights.

Apprentice Congressman

Jawaharlal Nehru as a Congress apprentice started his political career soon after he returned from England. Although he worked in the legal firm of his father, yet it was India's predicament that concerned him more than his legal career. He was highly impressed by the Gandhian philosophy and way of life, and soon found in Gandhi the direction that he long yearned for. The entire Nehru family adopted Gandhian ways, however, but it was Nehru more than others who heartily accepted the Gandhian way of life, much to his father's dismay.

Nehru travelled the country extensively to preach Gandhi's ways and participate in the nationalist movements. The way he was received by the masses filled him with new confidence in his abilities and popular appeal. Gandhi himself was not slow to realise the great popular support that Nehru could harness with his background, charm and liberal education. These sojourns also provided Nehru with an opportunity to see the widespread exploitation that plagued every sphere of Indian civil life. The perils of the Indian populace that he witnessed first hand in these formative years shaped his policies during his tenure as a Prime Minister later on.

Jawaharlal Nehru participated whole-heartedly in the Non-cooperation Movement. However, he did not join his father to part ways with Gandhi when Motilal Nehru formed the Swaraj Party with C. R. Das after the movement was called off by Gandhi following the Chauri Chaura incident. Jawaharlal Nehru was caught between divided loyalties between his father and Gandhi. However, his strong faith in Gandhian methodologies made him close ranks with Gandhi in this crucial period of his life. This tension between father and son would be a regular feature in Jawaharlal's life, and it was only after the death of his father that Nehru despite his grief, felt fully free to pursue his own political course. The ascendancy of Nehru in the fullest sense happened only after the death of Motilal Nehru.

As Congress President

Jawaharlal Nehru's rise within the Indian National Congress (INC) was meteoric in the years following the Non-cooperation Movement. He, along with Subhash Chandra Bose, became two dynamic young leaders of the Congress to whom the Indians were glad to look up to for guidance.

The Calcutta Congress of 1928 saw the Congress divided on the Nehru report prepared by Motilal Nehru on India's being awarded dominion status by the British government. Jawaharlal himself took exception to the steps laid down by the Nehru report. Mahatma Gandhi worked towards a compromise, and also single handedly worked for Jawaharlal's election as the Congress President in the historic Lahore Congress in 1929. Despite the universally accepted organisational prowess of Vallabhbhai Patel, Jawaharlal Nehru was elected as the Congress president at a young age of forty, prior to the extremely significant Lahore Congress of 1929. Nehru was prompt to use the platform in order to declare his dream of Purna Swaraj or Complete Independence.

Prison Days

The monumental Lahore Congress introduced the Civil Disobedience Movement. Nehru plunged himself into the movement and courted arrest. It was not the first time Nehru went to prison, and it would not be the last time either. Over the period of the next decade, Nehru would spend most of the time of his life in prison as a political prisoner. However, he was determined to make his solitude count. During the days of imprisonment, Nehru wrote extensively on a number of topics, particularly history and other social issues. He read a lot and often lectured fellow prisoners. However, with Motilal, Gandhi and Nehru imprisoned, the Indian freedom movement suddenly found itself without a clear direction. A number of factions both within Congress and outside were trying to undermine Satyagraha and offer alternate ways to India's freedom.

Early Years in Freedom Movement

Jawaharlal Nehru was born into politics. His father Motilal Nehru was a veteran Congressman and committed to the cause of India's freedom for a very long time. Nehru spent much of his educational years in England studying first at Harrow and then at Trinity College, Cambridge. However, the freedom of India was always on his mind. It was therefore no surprise that after his return from the British shores in 1912, the job of a lawyer was the last of Nehru's priorities. As a student he already felt himself closely attached to the cause India's freedom, and had his sympathies with the Extremist leaders of Congress. After his return, he involved himself directly into the political scenario of the country.

However, Nehru was still comparatively without a firm direction in these early years, not sure which path was the right path that would lead towards India's freedom. His father's moderate ideologies and elitist way of life disturbed him, as he thought him, like many other Congressmen of his generation, to be much dissociated from the ground realities of the land and the lives of the common people of India. He also realised that the direct application of Socialist measures would not suit India's socio-economic profile. It was at that time that he found a direction in the mode of civil resistance as preached by Gandhi. Gandhi's success in Champaran and Ahmedabad renewed and established his belief in Satyagraha. He was not slow to adopt the cultural aspects of Satyagraha as well. He read the Indian scriptures of India, and dressed in home-spun clothes becoming a staunch Gandhian in all senses.

Motilal and his entire family adopted the Gandhian way of life. Nehru travelled across India, and was warmly received by the masses. This filled him with a renewed sense of self-confidence. It was time he decided to whole-heartedly commit himself to the cause of Indian freedom.

Great Leader of Freedom Movement

Nehru's Nationalism and his role in the Freedom Movement are closely inter-related, since it was the nature of Nehru's Nationalist ideas that dictated his course of action in the freedom movement of India.

Nehru's Nationalism

Nehru's nationalism was not one of mindless jingoism. He was able to reach a common ground between an erudite internationalism and a very keen understanding of the Indian condition. Nehru's nationalism was marked by a fiery pride in the heritage of the country. But he was willing to temper this pride with his readings and his rationalist views that he received from his Western education in the West.

Jawaharlal Nehru's role in the freedom movement of India has probably not received as much historical attention as it deserves. That is, of course no surprise, as Jawaharlal Nehru's astounding success as a statesman who ushered in a new era of international relations through the formation of the NAM, and his stature as the first Prime Minister of independent India often adumbrate his position as a significant figure in the freedom movement of India.

With his charm, highly impressive educational background, and selfless service to the nation, Nehru presented the face of a new and active India to thousands of Indians who looked up to him as a role model and a guide.

Leading Congress before Freedom

Nehru spent most of the 1930s in prison, far from the Indian freedom struggle and the Indian National Congress. However, he kept a close watch on the course the movement was taking. On his return from prison to mainstream politics, Nehru had to employ all his reconciliatory skills to bring the warring factions within his party to a common platform. Although his Socialist ideals differed significantly from Gandhi's spiritual bent of civil resistance and the cultural aspects that came along with it. His differences with Gandhian modes came into the open in the Lucknow Conference of 1936.

Throughout the early-40s, Nehru visited other Nationalist states as the Congress representative. He returned from China just before the World War II. The World War II brought in new problems for the Indian National Congress. Bose and his followers were willing to cooperate with the Axis forces in order to create pressure on the British officials, a move that Nehru summarily disapproved of. In the mean time, the Second Round Table Conference failed, and the Quit India movement was launched. Nehru was imprisoned once more. He was released in 1945 after the end of the War. Soon he started to work relentlessly towards forming the INA and preparing India for the hour of Independence. The end of the war brought the new Labour government in Britain, and the long held dream of Indian independence did not seem very far from then on.

Non-cooperation Movement

The first big involvement of Jawaharlal Nehru came at the onset of the Non-cooperation Movement in 1920. Nehru joined in whole-heartedly in this Satyagraha based movement that stormed India. Nehru was arrested on charges of anti-governmental activities and was released a few months later. In the rift formed within the Congress following the sudden closure of the Non-cooperation Movement after the Chauri Chaura incident, Nehru remained loyal to Gandhi's camp and denied to join the Swaraj Party formed by Motilal Nehru and CR Das. After his release, Nehru's fame as a dynamic Congress leader was well-established. He soon became the President of the Allahabad Congress

Committee in 1923. However, towards the end of the decade, Nehru grew increasingly impatient with the pacifist nature of the senior Congressman. Along with Subhash Chandra Bose, Nehru was intent on complete freedom and believed in giving an ultimatum to the British Government to grant India dominion status. The senior leaders were bent on a slower and more patient approach. The Calcutta Congress of 1928 brought the rift into the open. Jawaharlal openly decried the Nehru Commission framed by Motilal Nehru, and it needed the intervention of Mahatma Gandhi to persuade Nehru to abandon his fiery stance of more direct action.

Civil Disobedience Movement

The Lahore Congress of 1929 was monumental in the political career of Nehru as well as the history of India's freedom struggle. Nehru was elected the president of Congress for the first time at a young age of forty. He used the platform of the Lahore conference to declare the goal of complete freedom or Purna Swaraj. The Civil Disobedience movement was formally launched after the Lahore Congress, and Nehru whole heartedly plunged himself in the non-violent protests and picketing that took the nation by storm. Nehru was arrested again in 1930, beginning the second and the longest phase of his prison stays. On his release, he formed the Socialist party within the Congress and insisted on more stern and immediate measures to realise the goal of India's freedom.

Last Days of Indian Freedom Struggle

The Government of India Act of 1935 called for nation-wide elections. Nehru campaigned vigorously for Congress, although he himself did not contest directly in the elections. With Gandhi concentrating on the spiritual development of his followers and gradually dissociating himself from direct political action, the stature of Nehru within the Congress ranks was now more than ever. He became the Congress President in the consecutive years of 1936 and 1937. By 1938, the rift in Congress was clear. With Bose and Gandhi forming the two feuding camps, Nehru was once more faced with a political dilemma. However, he decided to side with Gandhi and his methods. Bose resigned as the Congress president, and Nehru's status in the Congress reached a height previously unattained. This year started a new phase in Nehru's career, especially after his denial to come to a compromise with the Muslim League.

With the clouds of World War II looming large in the horizon, Nehru's skill in international relations would be tested once more. Nehru did not support Bose's policy of siding with the Axis forces, and intended to extend support to the Allies. In the mean time, the Second Round Table conference failed and Gandhi launched the Quit India movement in 1942. Nehru was arrested and was released only in 1945. By the time the World War II was over and the new Labour Government of Britain seemed willing to grant India its long deserved freedom. However, the British Government wanted to adopt a policy of waiting and watching the result of the general elections of 1945.

Nehru was once again at the centre of activities. He was arrested. His refusal to comply with Jinnah's claims made partition inevitable, as Jinnah called for direct action. Although his fight for Indian freedom stood on the verge of success, Nehru knew his work was far from over. He had to build a new India and had to guide the nascent economy towards success.

Leading to Independence

The new government was willing to provide self dominion to India. With Nehru as the Congress president, negotiations were being worked out between the British government and the Congress Party, which was by then elected to be the single most popular party in India. However, the British were willing to play the waiting game and see the outcome of the elections. Moreover, a common ground between the Indian National Congress and the Muslim League was yet to be reached. Nehru tried his best to work out a solution through talks with Jinnah. The talks, expectedly failed. There was an absolute deadlock between the parties, and Partition seemed to be the only way for India to finally attain freedom.

The Indian Independence finally came in the year 1947; although the conditions of the much awaited freedom were far from what was expected. For Nehru as the President of the Indian national Congress, it was a bitter-sweet moment of truth. As the President of Congress, Nehru was the automatic choice as the first Prime Minister of Independent India. On 15th August, 1947 Nehru gave his famous 'Tryst with Destiny' speech from the Red Fort. However, it was hardly the end of his troubles. Mahatma Gandhi was murdered soon after and Patel died in 1950. Nehru was vested with the duty of steadying the rocking boat of the tottering economy of a newly emergent nation. This started the second phase of Nehru's work within the folds of the Indian National Congress, the post Independence phase.

Leading the Nation after Independence

Indian National Congress was committed to the primary idea of freeing India from British rule. Nehru thought otherwise, and he realised that the widespread popularity of the Congress could be used as a platform to address and solve much of the nation's problems. However, a sudden loss in a sense of direction was imminent in Congress. The Congress party itself had its due share of problems too. The Leftist forces provided a constant threat to the Party, as was the right wing within the Party who opposed Nehru's socialist ideals. At such a time, it was much because of Nehru's personal charisma that the integrity of the Congress could be successfully maintained.

Nehru's imposing internationalism somehow helped to soothe the problems back home. In fact, problems as mounting as the division of the provinces on linguistic lines and the Kashmir debate were also taken care of by Nehru's formidable success in foreign policies. It was with his stature, that Nehru managed to forge together the various warring forces within the Congress. However, Nehru himself was well aware of the decadence that has infested the party ranks and is known to have warned his party members after the Congress victory of 1957.

Nehru's commitment to the Congress party was life-long, and he is still considered to be one of the greatest Congressmen. However, the greatness of Nehru remains in the fact, that he successfully transcended his Congress identity to become a major international political figure.

A Great Social Reformer

Jawaharlal Nehru was the first Prime Minister of independent India. He was a key figure in the Indian independence movement. Nehru also initiated the process of social reform in the independent Indian Republic. The importance of Jawaharlal Nehru as a social reformer in Indian history cannot be denied.

India gained independence on 15 August, 1947. The India that existed in the 1940s was a cauldron of social unrest. The age-old problem of caste had reared its ugly head and was threatening to tear the social fabric apart. Religious tensions were also a reigning problem in India during those days. The partition of pre-independent India had divided the Indian subcontinent into two countries, India and Pakistan. Pakistan became an Islamic Republic as envisaged by its creator Muhammad Ali Jinnah. India became a secular republic by choice.

Jawaharlal Nehru inherited from the British a country that was bereft of social and economic stability. He inherited a mish-mash of people speaking as many as 16 different languages with different cultural moorings.

The genius of Jawaharlal Nehru as a social reformer shone through in this post-independence period. He took decisive steps to eradicate the evils of the all pervasive caste system. Nehru undertook corrective measures by changing existing Indian legal laws. Legal procedures were enacted to make caste discrimination illegal and punishable by law. The enacted laws were strictly enforced.

Jawaharlal Nehru was one of the few Indian statesmen at that time who understood the need of proper intellectual development of the Indian populace. He had exposure to European educational ideals during his stay at England, where he received education. Nehru also knew that British stress on proper education to run their colonial Empire. He understood the importance of proper and healthy intellectual development to run the nascent Indian state. Jawaharlal Nehru wished to combine the best of both worlds, the winning combination of western scientific prowess and Indian civilization wisdom.

Nehru realised that the only way the Indian Republic can re-establish its presence in the world stage is through the intellectual power of its citizens. Jawaharlal stressed on the teaching of science and its practical application fields. He took cognizance of the need of learning vocational science. The teaching of vocational science attracted him. Special focus was put on the development of technology. The famed Indian Institutes of Technology or IIT's were conceived and established during his Prime Ministership.

The Indian Institutes of Technology are now regarded as one of the premier scientific institutes of higher technological learning throughout the world. IIT graduates are much in demand among the corporate sector. The establishment of such learning centres also indirectly contributed to the emergence of the Indian Republic as a pharmaceutical major in the late-1980s. The cheapest medicines in the world are produced and sold in India. The capabilities of the Indian software industry have also amazed the world.

Jawaharlal Nehru was born in an era when the principal mode of communication was the postal service. Telephones were affordable only by the minuscule economically empowered Indian populace. There were few government hospitals. The rural Indian population lived in pitiable conditions amidst abject poverty.

Nehru was acutely aware of the rural situation of India. He had contested and won democratic elections in Pratapgarh district of Uttar Pradesh. Jawaharlal Nehru knew the many problems faced by the rural populace. The rural environment was feudal at that time. Literacy was low and social tensions were simmering below the societal surface. Nehru initiated the construction and functioning of a number of schools. The schools provided primary and secondary education to the rural population. The schools are spread throughout India. Primary education was provided free of cost.

The government schools also provided free meals to its students. This scheme was the trump card of Jawaharlal Nehru. The great statesmen understood the importance of food to attract students to schools. The purchasing power of the rural Indian population at that time was very low. A majority of the rural population subsisted on one meal a day. All members of the family were required to work to keep the home-fires burning. The children were also roped in to earn for the family. Jawaharlal Nehru knew the importance of food in the educational scheme. The food acts as a magnet for the impoverished hungry child. The family of the prospective student was also happy with the subsequent tangible cost savings.

The food given in the primary education programmes included milk in addition to pulses for a healthy meal. The specter of malnutrition in the 1950s and 1960s India were fought in this way. Jawaharlal Nehru also established vocational schools for adults. Adult education centres were created both in rural and urban areas. Higher technical schools were also established.

The Indian Republic has a substantial population. Almost half of the population is women. Jawaharlal Nehru enacted laws to guarantee practical universal suffrage to the women population of the country. The laws aimed to secure the social freedoms of Indian women. Female legal rights were also increased under Nehru's able Prime Ministership.

Jawaharlal Nehru was a highly educated man. His western education catalysed his aspirations for equality of the Indian populace. Nehru actively promoted and brought about the system of reservations in the Indian job sector. A certain percentage of government jobs were reserved for persons born into scheduled castes and scheduled tribes. This was done to ensure the participation of the less privileged Indian population to the mainstream.

Jawaharlal Nehru had many social successes to his credit. He was responsible for promoting the rights of religious minorities. His swift judgement along with his mentor Mahatma Gandhi at the time of independence ensured that the Indian Republic became a secular state. He understood the basic social nature of the Indian population. The Indian population is largely secular, plural and civil and has a number of practicing religions. Nehru fostered the need for tolerance of all religions and respect for people unlike own.

The success of Jawaharlal Nehru's reforms is apparent throughout the modern Indian Republic. The booming economy of contemporary India underscores this fact.

Economic Policies

The economic policies of Jawaharlal Nehru have been subject to much controversy in the past few decades. However, it is important to place Nehru's economic policies in context for a proper appreciation of his policies. Nehru's commitment to the cause of India's development remains unquestioned, and it is no doubt that much of his plans and speculations were jeopardised by the unexpected partition that came along with the independence of India, which brought about an unprecedented fissure in the economic resources of the Indian mainland. Nehru himself confessed that the partition brought about a large share of problems, including a great rift in the agricultural and the industrial sectors. A large portion of the most productive agricultural lands fell in Pakistan whereas the corresponding industries remained in Indian dominion. The problem faced by the Jute industry soon after Independence can be stated as a case in the point. The jute producing areas were in Pakistan whereas the Jute processing factories remained in India, thereby affecting jute productions on both sides of the border.

Early Economic Reforms

Nehru started his career as the Prime Minister of independent India in 1947, and immediately launched a number of economic reforms. Nehru was a firm believer in state control over the economic sectors. His socialist ideals revealed themselves in the way he introduced laws for land redistribution, in order to curtail the economic disparity in India among the landed and the landless classes. One of Nehru's key economic reforms was the introduction of the Five Years Plan in 1951. It was introduce to determine the mode of government expenditure and grants in important development sectors like agriculture, industries and education.

The Ideology Guiding Economic Policies

Nehru's economic policies have often been considered to be Socialist in nature. It is no doubt that Socialism did play a very important role in Nehru's ideological make-up. But at the same time, it is also important to consider that Nehru himself denied any kind of overt Socialist tendencies in the economic policies adopted by him. Nehru advocated a kind of mixed economy. Any kind of unquestioned ideological adherence to any form of economic tenet, or 'ism', he realised, would be detrimental to India's growth. He wanted a practical approach in framing the Indian economy, which would suit best the country's needs. On the one hand, as a devoted Gandhian, he had strong belief in the betterment of rural economy. On the other hand, he had a strong belief that heavy industrial development would be the best way to serve India's economic interests.

Industrial Policies

Nehru wanted to create a balance between the rural and the urban sectors in his economic policies. He stated there was no contradiction between the two and that both could go hand in hand. He denied to carry forward the age old city versus village controversy and hoped that in India, both could go hand in hand. Nehru was intent to harness and fully exploit the natural resources of India for the benefit of his countrymen. The main sector he identified was hydroelectricity, and he constructed a number of dams to achieve that end. The dams would not only harness energy, but would also support irrigation to a great degree. Nehru considered dams to be the very symbol of India's collective growth, as they were the platforms where industrial engineering and agriculture met on a common platform. Nehru also considered the possibility of nuclear growth during his tenure as the Prime Minister of India.

Foreign Investment

Nehru inspired the industrialists to provide a fillip to India's economy. However, he had strict reservations on the question of foreign investment. Nehru was wary of foreign investment. Nehru's nationalist ideals confirmed in him the belief that India was self-sufficient to bolster her own growth. Although he did not officially decry the possibility of foreign investment in direct terms, he did stress that the sectors of foreign investment would be regularised, and the terms and conditions of investment and employment would be strictly controlled by government rules in case there were possibilities of a foreign investment. Nehru, moreover, emphasised that the key sectors will always be in government hand. This step of Nehru is much criticised now. Yet, it cannot be denied that Nehru aptly looked forward to long term investments for which he banked more on Indian industries. It is also often suggested that his endeavour to harness international support to develop India's infra-structural profile between 1947 and 1955 did not meet with much success. It, however, remains a fact that Nehru's regime was not one of great economic growth for India. Although his economic policies are blamed for the failure of India to turn into a major economic force in the aftermath of independence, yet Nehru was probably thinking on a more long term basis. It is often inferred that the economic liberation of the later years was possible only because of Nehru's policies in the initial stages.

State Control on Economy

The most distinctive, and often debated feature of Nehru's economic policies, was the high level of state and central control that was exercised on the industrial and business sectors of the country. Nehru emphasised that the state would control almost all key areas of the country's economy, either centrally or on a state-wise basis. His Socialist emphasis on state control somehow seemed to undermine his stress on industrial policies. The rigorous state laws and License rules put a great degree of restrain on the free execution of industrial policies. Even the farmers, along with the business personnel, found themselves to be at the receiving end of rigorous state control policies and high taxation. Poverty and unemployment were widespread throughout Nehru's governance.

Rural Economy

Nehru's policy towards the rural economy of India was also significant. Nehru felt for the rural self-development of India very strongly. He tried to boost India's cottage industries. Much on the lines of Gandhi, Nehru believed that the rural and cottage industries of India played a major role in the economic fabric of the country. But most of his cottage industry development programmes were meant as a part of community development.

He was also of the belief that small scale industries and cottage industries were effective solutions to the massive employment problems that remained a perpetual issue of concern throughout his tenure.

The economic policies of Nehru are often blamed for the poor economy of India in the subsequent years. However, it cannot be denied that his decisions were necessitated by the needs of the times. India needed to effectively harness its domestic means as well as strengthen its governmental control to lay the base for future privatisation. It is often speculated that Nehru would have embraced the economic reforms and economic liberalisation of the late-20th century if he was alive.

First Prime Minister of India

Jawaharlal Nehru was the first Prime Minister of India. His Prime Ministership was marked by social and economic reforms of the Indian state. A number of foreign policy landmarks like the founding of the Non-aligned Movement also marked the tenure of Jawaharlal Nehru as Prime Minister.

Jawaharlal Nehru became Prime Minister on the 15th of August 1947. His ascension was plagued by controversy and a bitter power struggle within the Congress Party. The internal struggle of the party was symptomatic of the larger struggle within the Indian Republic itself. The initial period of Jawaharlal Nehru as Prime Minister was marked by communal violence.

Jawaharlal Nehru was forced to concede the creation of Pakistan as per the wishes of the Muslim League leader the leadership of Muhammad Ali Jinnah. Communal violence enveloped the entire country during this period. Maximum bloodshed was witnessed in the national capital Delhi. The Indian states of Punjab and Bengal also witnessed fierce bloodshed.

The first Prime Minister tried to defuse the explosive situation by visiting the violence affected areas. He toured the riot stricken areas with Pakistani leaders to reassure those affected by the violence. Nehru promoted peace in Punjab during that momentous period in Indian history. The secular nature of Jawaharlal Nehru was best exemplified during those times. He took active steps to safeguard the status of Indian Muslims.

The enduring legacy of Nehru rule is the effect of Nehru's economic poiicies. His economic policies were far reaching and its effects are felt to this day. Jawaharlal Nehru is best known for his enduring brand of 'Nehruvian Socialism' or the Indian version of Socialism. The original socialist policies were watered down by Nehru to gel with the Indian economic context. Jawaharlal Nehru was responsible for the special economic reform policy vehicle, Planning Commission of India.

The Planning Commission of India is Jawaharlal Nehru's brainchild. The Commission is responsible for formulating the 'Five-Year Plans' of the Indian economy. The Planning Commission also conducts a host of other economic functions. The first Five-Year Plan was presented by Prime Minister Jawaharlal Nehru on the 8th of December, 1951.

Prime Minister Jawaharlal Nehru concentrated his economic policies on the rural sector. The Indian rural economy was allotted a lion's share of the first Five-Year Plan fund money. More than 27 per cent of the total funding went to irrigation and energy production. The agricultural sector got more than 17 per cent of the budget resource. About 4 per cent of the fund money was earmarked for land rehabilitation.

The first Five-Year Plan also provided the seed money for setting up the five Indian Institutes of Technology or IIT's. The University Grants Commission or UGC was also set up during this period. The tenth Five-Year Plan is currently in vogue.

Land redistribution plans were undertaken during Jawaharlal Nehru's tenure as a Prime Minister. The redistribution of land ensured a more socially just Indian society. This move helped the Indian economy in many ways. The wealth disparity between sections of the populace lessened. This resulted in a more thriving and healthy societal landscape.

The first Prime Minister Jawaharlal Nehru was one of the first Indian policy-makers to understand the importance of cottage industries in the Indian economy. The development of such small scale industries infused much needed production efficiency into the rural Indian economy. The Cottage Industries also helped the agricultural workers to have a better quality of life. This is due to the additional profits generated by the farming community.

A number of educational and social reforms were undertaken when Jawaharlal Nehru was Prime Minister. He was instrumental in starting new Indian institutes of higher learning like the Indian Institutes of Technology, the All India Institute of Medical Sciences or AIIMS and the various branches of the Indian Institutes of Management among others. Primary education was made compulsory. It was also made free of cost. Adult educational units were also established.

Jawaharlal Nehru was also responsible for setting the direction of India's foreign policy. The policy is valid till now. The world in the 1950s was sharply divided into two opposite factions: one side was the west-comprising of the United States and western European countries and the other side was the East-dominated by the erstwhile USSR. India wisely joined neither faction during that period. The Republic of India was one of the founding members of the Non-aligned Movement or NAM.

The negotiating skills of Jawaharlal Nehru came into focus during his dealings with the Pakistani ruling establishment. His consummate skill was on display during the talks with Pakistan on the Kashmir issue. The first Indian Prime Minister cemented India's administrative hold on the northern Indian state. He also arrested the influential politician- Sheikh Abdullah on suspicion of anti-national activities. This led to a smoother administrative transition from the former Kashmiri ruler to civilian Indian rule.

The Indian Prime Minister Jawaharlal Nehru was feted around the world for his efforts to ease global political tensions. The middle of the 1950s saw India criticising the invasion of the Suez Canal by a combined military force comprising French, British and Israeli troops. Jawaharlal Nehru formally signed the Indus Water Treaty with Pakistan in 1960. This was done with a view to mitigate the long standing dispute between India and Pakistan in sharing the water resources of the major rivers in the shared geographical region of Punjab.

The invasion of India's northeastern territorial region by China in the 1960s dashed Jawaharlal Nehru's hopes for a peaceful South-East Asia. His decision to grant refuge to the Tibetan Buddhist leader Dalai Lama also came in for severe criticism. The Chinese invasion also forced him to re-examine India's security requirements and act accordingly.

Jawaharlal Nehru's last days as India's Prime Minister were marred by political problems. The Congress Party suffered from corruption within itself. He promoted his daughter Indira Gandhi to the Indian political landscape in that period. Indira Gandhi later became India's first woman Prime Minister. The last period of his Prime Ministership also included the Indian invasion of Portugal in 1961. Jawaharlal Nehru died in office on the 27th of May 1964.

Foreign Policy

Jawaharlal Nehru is considered to be the architect of modern India. Apart from his careful handling of India's tumultuous domestic situation in the years immediately after the Independence, Nehru's major contribution lies in the field of foreign policies. In fact, Nehru determined India's international profile to a great degree in the post-independence years, in his capacity as the foreign minister of India.

Jawaharlal Nehru's foreign policy has been made subject to much controversy and debate, like his economic policies. However, taken in the context of India's newly found status as a democratic republic, Nehru's foreign affairs policies seem to be extremely apt.

Socialism can be said to be one of the greatest international influences on Nehru, but Gandhi's ideals of Satyagraha also influenced him to a great degree. But he committed himself to neither point of view in framing his foreign policy. Nehru's foreign policies were characterised by two major ideological aspects.

First, he wanted India to have an identity that would be independent of any form of overt commitment to either power bloc, the USA or the Soviet. Secondly, he had an unshaken faith in goodwill and honesty in matters of international affairs. The first policy led ultimately to the founding of the Non-alignment Movement (NAM). His second faith was terribly shaken by the Chinese attack of 1962, openly disobeying all the clauses of the Panchsheel or five-point agreement of 1954 between New Delhi and Peking. This breach of faith was a major psychological shock for Nehru, and was partially the reason for his death.

Founding Principles of Foreign Policy

Nehru saw war and violent insurgency from very close quarters as a freedom fighter, and he believed in neither. In his foreign policies, Nehru tried to guide India in such a way, so as to steer clear from any form of violence and militarism. He rightly believed that a newly decolonised nation must invest all its economic and logistic resources towards development and not defence and armament. Just like his economic policies, which were non-committal towards any ideological position, Nehru wanted to bring in a healthy level of pragmatism in his dealings of India's foreign affairs as well. He understood that overt commitment to any of the two major power blocs to emerge in the aftermath of World War II, would not serve India's path. He therefore wanted to tread a third path, which was not necessarily the middle path.

It should be remembered that this dogged non-commitment of Nehru was not seen sympathetically by any of the super powers of either East or West at its initial stage. It was frequently termed as a kind of international opportunism and was accused of 'neutralism' - a stance reckoned to be not only dangerous but also equally immoral in the world of International politics. However, the increasing popularity of NAM among various Asian and African countries and Nehru's growing stature as a statesman situation changed their views.

India too benefited from this position, as it managed to secure rebuilding grants from member countries of either bloc. After Nehru's successful mediation in the Korean War and the Congo problem, putting an end to a long and violent struggle, his status as a commendable and efficient statesman reached new heights. Jawaharlal Nehru's theory of ideological non-commitment in a world that was rendered dangerous by the Cold War was appreciated by one and all.

Role in Non-alignment Movement

The greatest success of Jawaharlal Nehru's non-committal international politics was the formation of the Non-alignment Movement (NAM). Nehru found allies in Tito, Nasser, Soekarno, U Nu and Nkrumah at a later stage in his formation of this new alliance. An alliance of newly independent and long colonised nations was not taken seriously in the beginning, either by the Eastern or the Western bloc. However, the importance of the alliance was soon felt, and initially led to a great degree of international pressure from both parts of the globe. However, Nehru proceeded with his mission undaunted. It was great test for his courage and it was soon found out that the NAM was not merely a passive platform of neutral and inactive nations. It had clear objectives that included the gradual decolonisation of the world, and a strong statement that the member countries were not party to the ever escalating tension of the Cold War.

The favoured process of decolonisation as adopted by the NAM member countries was one of discussion and peaceful agreement. On many occasions, NAM met with success, often under the leadership of Nehru. Whoever supported its cause was an ally and a friend. Nehru preached a policy of issue based alliance and not one based on political and economic dogmas. He was proud of being an Asian, and wanted Asian nations to be the primary determinants of their political fate, not always guided by Western forces.

Nehru's unshaken belief in the force of international brotherhood was attested with his decision to continue with India's Commonwealth status. He was made subject to much criticism back home because of the support he extended towards the Commonwealth, particularly after the complication of the independence issue by the British government in the post World War II years, leading to the unwanted partition. However Nehru, always the believer in peaceful alliances and solution of international affairs based on discussions, went on with his ideals.

The Kashmir Problem

Nehru's Foreign policies did not augur well when it came to deal with the neighbours. Kashmir was a perpetual problem, and he failed to reach any successful negotiation regarding Kashmir with the neighbour Pakistan. Nehru had an innate belief in honest fellow-feeling and political generosity. He tried to force a negotiation with the Pakistani government through the United Nations. But the Pakistani military rulers denied any peaceful agreement. The offer of a possible plebiscite was also taken off in 1950. After India's dogged denial of the two-nation theory, a result in favour of Kashmir in the Muslim dominated Kashmir would be a strategic disaster for India. The Kashmir problem remained unresolved, and not even Nehru's diplomatic expertise could give any positive direction to the problem. It still continues to be the one of the key international problems in South Asia.

Indo-Pak War of 1947

The Indo-Pak War of 1947, sometimes known as the First Kashmir War, was fought between India and Pakistan over the region of Kashmir from 1947 to 1948. It was the first of four wars fought between the two newly independent nations. The result of the war still affects the geopolitics of both the countries.

The Backdrop

Prior to 1815 the area now known as "Kashmir" was referred to as the "Punjab Hill States" and comprised 22 small independent states carved out of Afghanistan Amir (King) controlled territories combined with local small rulers, from 900 AD, in Sultan Mehmood Ghaznavi time, to Afghan Amir Ahmed Shah Abdali time, born in southern Punjab Multan. Since 1757 it was ruled by the Muslim Mughal Empire, until 1857, when the British East India Company arrived to India.

These small states were ruled by Rajput Kings who had sworn allegiance to the Mughal Empire. In fact the Rajput of the Punjab Hill States were a major strength of the Mughal Empire and had fought many battles in support of the Mughals especially against the Sikhs. Following the rise of the British East India Company and the subsequent decline of the Mughal Empire, the power of the Punjab Hill States also began to decline. They therefore became easy targets for the Sikh leader Ranjit Singh who proceeded to conquer these small states one by one. Eventually all the Punjab Hill States were conquered by Ranjit Singh and merged into one state to be called the State of Jammu.

History of Punjab castes by J. Hutchinson and J. P. Vogel lists a total of 22 states 16 Hindu and 6 Muhammadan that formed the State of Jammu following the conquest of Raja Ranjit

Singh in 1820. Of these 6 Muhammadan States two (Kotli and Punch) were ruled by Mangrals, two (Bhimber and Khari-Khariyala) by Chibs, one (Rajouri) by the Jarrals and one (Khashtwar) by the Khashtwaria.

The First Anglo-Sikh War was fought between the Sikh Empire, which asserted sovereignty over Kashmir, and the East India Company between 1845 and 1846. In the Treaty of Lahore in 1846, the Sikhs were made to surrender the valuable region (the Jallandhar Doab) between the Beas River and Sutlej River and required to pay an indemnity of 1.2 million rupees.

Because they could not readily raise this sum, the East India Company allowed the Dogra ruler Gulab Singh to acquire Kashmir from the Sikh Kingdom in exchange for making a payment of 750,000 rupees to the East India Company. Gulab Singh became the first Maharaja of the newly formed princely state of Jammu and Kashmir, founding a dynasty, The Royal House of Jammu and Kashmir, that was to rule the state, the second-largest principality during the British Raj, until India gained its independence in 1947.

Partition of India

Before and after the withdrawal of the British from India in 1947, the princely state of Kashmir and Jammu came under pressure from both India and Pakistan to agree to become part of one of the newly independent countries. According to the instruments of accession relating to the Partition of India, the rulers of princely states were to be given the choice of either acceding to India or Pakistan, or remaining independent. The Maharaja of Kashmir, Hari Singh chose the latter and tried to avoid accession to either country. When British forces withdrew there was a Muslim revolution in western Kashmir and the region was invaded by Pashtun tribals from the North West Frontier Province (NWFP).

Fearing that his forces would be unable to withstand the assault, the Maharaja asked for Indian military assistance. India set a condition that Kashmir must accede to India for it to receive assistance. Whereupon the Government of India recognised the accession of the erstwhile princely state to India, and was considered the new Indian state of Jammu and Kashmir, Indian troops were sent to the state to defend it against the Pakistani forces. The legitimacy of this accession is still disputed. Due to a lack of demographic data concerning religious affiliations, it is difficult to determine whether public opinion was a factor in Hari Singh's decision.

Pakistan was of the view that the Maharaja of Kashmir had no right to call in the Indian Army, because it held that the Maharaja of Kashmir was not a heredity ruler, that he was merely a British appointee. There had been no such position as the "Maharaja of Kashmir" prior to British rule. Hence, Pakistan decided to take action, but the Army Chief of Pakistan General Douglas Gracey did not send troops to the Kashmir front and refused to obey the order to do so given by Muhammad Ali Jinnah, Governor-General of Pakistan. Gracey's justified his insubordination by arguing that Indian forces occupying Kashmir represented the British Crown and hence he could not engage in a military encounter with Indian forces. Pakistan finally did manage to send troops to Kashmir but by then the Indian forces had taken control of approximately two thirds of the former principality. The Gilgit and Baltistan terretories were secured for Pakistan by the Gilgit scouts and the forces of the state of Chitral, another princely state that had acceeded to Pakistan.

Summary of War

The war was fought within the borders of the former princely state of Kashmir and Jammu by Indian Army, paramilitary and the erstwhile princely state forces opposed by Pakistan Army, paramilitary and local militias from the NWFP (the Pakistani forces referred to themselves as the Azad Kashmir forces (Azad in Urdu means liberated or free). The princely state forces were unprepared for the initial assault of AZK forces, having been deployed thinly on the borders of the princely state for purposes of maintaining border security and deterring militant activity. The princely state defences quickly collapsed in the face of the assault, some individuals and units joining the AZK forces.

The initial successes by AZK forces were not vigorously pressed, giving an opportunity for India to airlift its forces into Kashmir after the state had acceded to India. With Indian reinforcements opposing AZK forces, the offensive ran out of steam towards the end of 1947, except in the High Himalayas sector where AZK forces made substantial progress until they were turned back at the outskirts of Leh in late-June 1948. Throughout 1948 many small-scale battles were fought, but none gave a strategic advantage to either side and the fronts gradually solidified along what would became known as the Line of Control. A formal cease-fire was declared on 31 December 1948.

Stages of the War

This war has been split into ten stages by time. The individual stages are detailed below.

Initial Invasion (Operation Gulmarg)

The objective of the initial invasion was to capture control of the Kashmir valley including its principal city, Srinagar, the summer capital of the state (Jammu being the winter capital). The state forces stationed in the border regions around Muzaffarabad and Domel were quickly defeated by AZK forces (some state forces mutinied and joined the AZK) and the way to the capital was open.

Rather than advancing towards Srinagar before state forces could regroup or be reinforced, the invading forces remained in the captured cities in the border region engaging in looting and other crimes against their inhabitants. In the Punch valley, the state forces retreated into towns where they were besieged.

Indian Operation in Kashmir Valley

After the accession, India airlifted troops and equipment to Srinagar, where they reinforced the princely state forces, established a defence perimeter and defeated the AZK forces on the outskirts of the city. The successful defence included an outflanking manoeuvre by Indian armoured cars. The defeated AZK forces were pursued as far as Baramula and Uri and these towns were recaptured.

In the Punch valley, AZK forces continued to besiege state forces.

In Gilgit, the state paramilitary forces (the Gilgit Scouts) joined the invading AZK forces, who thereby obtained control of this northern region of the state. The AZK forces were also joined by troops from Chitral, whose ruler, the Mehtar of Chitral, had acceded to Pakistan.

Attempted Link-up at Punch and Fall of Mirpur

Indian forces ceased pursuit of AZK forces after recapturing Uri and Baramula, and sent a relief column southwards, in an attempt to relieve Punch. Although the relief column eventually reached Punch, the siege could not be lifted. A second relief column reached Kotli, but was forced to evacuate its garrison.

Meanwhile, Mirpur was captured by AZK forces on the 25th of November 1947. Then there was a massacre of Hindus and Sikhs and loot, and more later in Alibeg camp. Around 20 thousand people reported killed, also atrocities on women were reported.

Fall of Jhanger and Attacks on Naoshera and Uri

The Pakistani/AZK forces attacked and captured Jhanger. They then attacked Naoshera unsuccessfully. Other Pakistani/AZK forces made a series of unsuccessful attacks on Uri. In the south a minor Indian attack secured Chamb. By this stage of the war the front line began to stabilise as more Indian troops became available.

Operation Vijay: Counterattack to Jhanger

The Indian forces launched a counterattack in the south recapturing Jhanger and Rajauri. In the Kashmir Valley the Pakistani/AZK forces continued attacking the Uri garrison. In the north Skardu was brought under siege by Pakistani/AZK forces.

Indian Spring Offensive

The Indians held onto Jhanger against numerous counterattacks from the AZK, who were increasingly supported by regular Pakistani Forces. In the Kashmir Valley the Indians attacked, recapturing Tithwail. The AZK made good progress in the High Himalayas sector, infiltrating troops to bring Leh under siege, capturing Kargil and defeating a relief column heading for Skardu.

Operations Gulab and Erase

The Indians continued to attack in the Kashmir Valley sector driving north to capture Keran and Gurais. They also repelled a counterattack aimed at Tithwail. In the Punch Valley the forces besieged in Punch broke out and temporarily linked up with the outside world again. The Kashmir State army was able to defend Skardu from the Gilgit Scouts and thus they were not able to proceed down the Indus valley towards Leh. In August the Chitral Forces under Mata-ul-Mulk besieged Skardu and with the help of artillery were able to take Skardu. This freed the Gilgit Scouts to push further into Ladakh.

Operation Duck

During this time the front began to settle down with less activity by either side, the only major event was an unsuccessful attack by the Indians towards Dras (Operation Duck). The siege of Punch continued.

Operation Easy; Punch Link-up

The Indians now started to get the upper hand in all sectors. Punch was finally relieved after a siege of over a year. The Gilgit forces in the High Himalayas, who had previously made good progress, were finally defeated. The Indians pursued as far as Kargil before being forced to halt due to supply problems. The Zoji-La pass was forced by using tanks (which had not been thought possible at that altitude) and Dras was recaptured. The use of tanks was based on experience gained in Burma in 1945.

Moves up to Cease-fire

At this stage Indian Prime Minister Jawahar Lal Nehru decided to ask UN to intervene. A UN cease-fire was arranged for the 31 December 1948. A few days before the cease-fire the Pakistanis launched a counter attack, which cut the road between Uri and Punch. After protracted negotiations a cease-fire was agreed to by both countries, which came into effect. The terms of the cease-fire as laid out in the UNCIP resolution of August 13, 1948 were adopted by the UN on January 5, 1949. This required Pakistan to withdraw its forces, both regular and irregular, while allowing India to maintain minimum strength of its forces in the state to preserve law and order. On compliance of these conditions a plebiscite was to be held to determine the future of the territory. In all, 1,500 soldiers died on each side during the war and Pakistan was able to acquire roughly two-fifths of Kashmir, including five of the fourteen eight thousanders plus peaks of the world, while India maintained the remaining three fifths of Kashmir, including the most populous and fertile regions.

Military Insights Gained from the War

Usage of Armour: The use of light tanks and armoured cars was important at two stages of the war. Both of these Indian victories involved very small numbers of AFVs. These were:

- The defeat of the initial thrust at Srinagar, which was aided by the arrival of 2 armoured cars in the rear of the irregular forces.
- The forcing of the Zoji-La pass with 11 Stuart M5 light tanks.

This may show that armour can have a significant psychological impact if it turns up at places thought of as impossible. It is also likely that the invaders did not deploy anti-tank weapons to counter these threats. Even the lightest weapons will significantly encumber leg infantry units, so they may well have been perceived as not worth the effort of carrying about, and left in rear areas.

This will greatly enhance the psychological impact of the armour when it does appear. The successful use of armour in this campaign strongly influenced Indian tactics in the 1962 war where great efforts were made to deploy armour to inhospitable regions (although with much less success in that case).

Progression of front lines:

- It is interesting to chart the progress of the front lines. After a certain troop density is reached progress was very slow with victories being counted in the capture of individual villages or peaks. Where troop density was lower (as it was in the High Himalayas sector and at the start of the war) rates of advance can be very high.

Deployment of forces:

- The Jammu and Kashmir state forces were spread out in small packets along the frontier to deal with militant incidents. This made them very vulnerable to a conventional attack. India used this tactic successfully against the Pakistan Army in East Pakistan (present day Bangladesh) in the 1971 war.

The China Crisis

Nehru's foreign policies concerning China have been made subject to much criticism. However, even in this case, it was Nehru's faith in transparency in the handling of International relations that is seen to be the root of all problems. Nehru was intent on a very warm and mutually beneficial relationship between India and China. The five-point agreement or the Panchsheel between New Delhi and Peking initiated in 1954 was a result of these negotiations. However, China started patrolling certain parts of the Indian border from 1955 onwards. Delhi started negotiations to solve the problem in a peaceful way. India, under the leadership of Nehru wanted to take one issue at a time and begin the discussions. The Chinese government, under Chou En-lai wanted to treat the border issue in its entirety at one go. It was gross violation of the five-point agreement. The Chinese denial for the arbitration from the International Court of Justice complicated the problem.

Amidst such tensions, the Chinese suddenly started a full-scale invasion in 1962. It was a rude shock, not only to Nehru, but to the entire international society. The Indian military was unprepared and also unequipped. Both USA and the Soviet extended token help. Soviet was quite busy with the Cuban crisis, however soon after the problem subsided, President Kruschev did extend some help. American help was minimum, compared to the massive military help that was extended to Pakistan in 1954.

On top of that, the Sandys-Rusk team visited India to hold talks in order to make India concede certain areas of Kashmir to Pakistan, a claim that was squarely denied. Nehru stood firm with this faith in the five-point principle. The international community stood by him, as China withdrew under growing international pressure, fearing isolation and global antagonism. Nehru played his last masterstroke in international policy, as he turned the military defeat in a moral victory for India.

The Chinese invasion had far reaching effects on India's foreign policy. It forced Nehru to change his stance on international affairs. He realised that unmitigated goodwill was not necessary the way the business of foreign affairs was conducted. Nehru's dreams were more or less shattered. It was also a great eye-opener. It made India to see that it is important to strengthen one's military strength and not overtly depend on peaceful negotiations in matters of international affairs. The Chinese invasion was a shock to Nehru, almost shaking his idealistic foundation to the very base. Domestic problems also kept escalating, putting a great degree of mental and physical stress on Nehru.

Nehru and Gandhi

Mahatma Gandhi and Jawaharlal Nehru were both stalwarts in Indian national struggle for independence. Motilal Nehru, Jawaharlal Nehru's father, was an eminent personality in the Indian National Congress and that fascinated young Jawaharlal Nehru to join politics too. He was greatly influenced by his father's charismatic personality and his elegance and style. Motilal Nehru and Mahatma Gandhi knew each other very well and it became easier for Jawaharlal Nehru to be closely acquainted to 'Bapu' — as the nation called him. Mahatma Gandhi first met Jawaharlal Nehru at the annual meeting of the Indian National Congress in the year 1916 at Lucknow. The first meeting was enough to impress Nehru regarding Gandhi and the charm of this relationship increased and flourished with passing time.

In Mahatma Gandhi, Jawaharlal Nehru had found the absolute leader who was capable of handling the entire nation. This quality he found missing in almost all the Indian political leaders of the time that included his father, Motilal Nehru. Even Motilal Nehru was highly impressed and influenced by Mahatma Gandhi's inner strength and self-confidence. The greatest quality that went in favour of Mahatma Gandhi was his image. General masses could identify themselves through Gandhiji. In the initial stages of his political career, Jawaharlal Nehru found everything regarding Gandhiji amazing and great. Gandhiji's plan of action in any field attracted Nehru to a great deal. The Satyagraha movement against the Rowlatt Act fascinated Jawaharlal Nehru greatly and he was keen to join the movement with great deal of enthusiasm. But he was dissuaded by his father to join the movement then and there and asked him to follow the proceedings of the mass-movement. With satyagrahas becoming the common form of revolt against the various forms of British atrocities, Mahatma Gandhi gained an important place in the Indian freedom struggle. There was also immense mass following that helped Gandhiji to attain that grand stature.

The heinous crime that the British committed in Jalianwala Bagh evoked Jawaharlal Nehru into action. He could no longer restrain himself from joining active politics and participate in the Indian independence struggle. Gandhiji also advocated the terms 'ahimsa', meaning non-violence and 'Swaraj', meaning self-rule. These were mainly aimed at improving and changing the economic scenario in the country. Jawaharlal Nehru joined the campaign with full fervour and enthusiasm. The Congress party was totally reformed and remodelled to reach to the people at the grass root level. This called for involvement of the masses in all the action that was planned for attaining freedom from the shackles of the British rule. Nehru completely supported the idea as he knew that without this support, attaining independence would be a next to impossible job.

In the year 1921, Jawaharlal Nehru was first arrested and sent to prison. After this, he was sent to the prison several times and passed nine years of his life in prison for the freedom struggle. Mahatma Gandhi in the mean time became the supremo of the Indian National Congress. The civil-disobedience movement was also called off by Gandhiji. There was also some political strife that was going on in the Indian National Congress at this time. In 1923, Jawaharlal Nehru was appointed the General Secretary of the Congress just for a period of two years. He again gained back the position in 1927 for two years. Along with this, he was deeply involved in the freedom struggle movement and under Gandhiji's leadership and care he was blooming as an efficient leader.

In 1929, under the patronage of Mahatma Gandhi, Jawaharlal was made the President of the Indian National Congress. This was declared at the annual Congress Session at Lahore. After that

Jawaharlal Nehru was made the President of the Indian National Congress six more times. He enjoyed the position and the glory that is attached to the post. But he was frequently arrested and put behind bars during the various movements that were launched to remove the British from India. Even during the Civil Disobedience Movement that was initiated by Mahatma Gandhi against the salt laws that were imposed by the British, Nehru was arrested.

Gandhiji even went to London to attend the Round Table Conference to figure out a peaceful way to attain freedom for the nation. But after coming back from there, he found the situation even worse. In 1932, both Gandhiji and Jawaharlal Nehru were arrested. Once, Motilal Nehru was also arrested and all three of them were behind bars. In 1942, with the beginning of the Quit India Movement, Jawaharlal Nehru was arrested and remained in prison for almost three years, one of the longest periods he had spent in jail. He was finally released in 1945.

In 1946, Jawaharlal Nehru with the influence of Gandhiji was summoned by the British with an idea of forming an interim government. This was done to organise the governmental structure during the transitional pre-independence period. Gandhiji was also against the partition that took place with the independence of the country. He tried his level best to avoid it and even advised the Congressmen to reject the proposals that were put forward by the Cabinet Mission. But the Congress leaders, including Jawaharlal Nehru tried to pacify Gandhiji by explaining that partition was the only way by, which a civil war between the Hindus and Muslims could be avoided. But in spite of this Gandhiji vehemently opposed this approach to freedom. Unfortunately, under great pressure from various sectors of the Congress Party and also from all parts of India, Gandhiji had to give his assent. But from his heart Gandhiji could not accept this and that troubled him till the last day of his life.

After Gandhiji's retirement from active politics, Jawaharlal Nehru became the leader of the Indian National Congress and took charge of the proceedings of the party completely. However, with passage of time and with Nehru's experience in the political field, there were certain difference of opinions and ideologies that cropped up between the two great Indian leaders. There were grave ideological differences between the two leaders. The formation of the Socialist Party within the Congress party by Jawaharlal Nehru was the first point of difference between the leaders. Though Nehru followed several rules of Satyagraha and many other principles of Gandhiji, he also opposed some of them vehemently. Nehru's ideologies matched completely with Subhash Chandra Bose and both of them also came together for the freedom struggle. But their extremist approach was strictly opposed by Gandhiji. The differences between Gandhiji and Jawaharlal Nehru also came to the forefront during the Quit India Movement. Gandhiji insisted that freedom had to be granted in 1942 and he would wait no longer, but Jawaharlal Nehru did not support this.

However, irrespective of the differences, Jawaharlal Nehru respected Mahatma Gandhi. He had influenced Nehru's personal, social as well as political life to a great deal. On his death, Jawaharlal Nehru addressed the nation and expressed his grief on the loss of the great leader. He felt that India had lost the greatest leader. With both good and bad times, the relationship that Jawaharlal Nehru and Mahatma Gandhi shared was a matter of envy for many leaders. It has become an interesting subject of study for many people, even in modern times.

Later Years

Jawaharlal Nehru was one of the pioneering leaders of India, who played an active role in the independence struggle of the country. He was also the first Prime Minister of Independent India. From childhood, Jawaharlal Nehru led a luxurious and glorious life. His father, Motilal Nehru was an eminent personality in the society, both in the social as well as in the political sphere. Jawaharlal Nehru also had a glorious political career and basked in name as well as fame for long time.

Though he had a good career record, his last eight-years as the Prime Minister of the country were not very successful. The country was facing both internal and external crisis during these eight years. Some of the economic policies that were set by Pandit Jawaharlal Nehru were not accepted in the country as well as in the foreign countries. It was also believed that he could not control the ongoing procedures in the country and there was anarchy all around. During the tenure of Nehru as the Prime Minister, Five-Year plans were initiated for the development and progress of the nation. The second Five Year Plan was initiated in the year 1956 and it mainly concentrated on the industrial development of the country. The establishment of several heavy engineering industries was emphasised in this Five Year Plan.

However, there was a problem that hampered the growth of these industries completely. Huge finances were required to set up these establishments, but the Government could fund only about one-third part of the total budget. The rest had to be funded by the several international institutions, World Bank and many more financing companies. This clearly depicted that India was greatly dependent on international financial aids and showed a clear picture of the economic conditions in the country. This pushed Jawaharlal Nehru into back gear. Within a year of the inception of the Second Five Year Plan, the whole plan failed to meet most of the targets that were set. Weather conditions were also unfavourable during this time and this hampered the growth of the nation to a great deal.

Though Jawaharlal Nehru was a great politician, but at some places he was a weak administrator and took some decisions as a Prime Minister, which went against him in various ways. Nehru was himself a devoted and clean man, away from any sort of corruption. But there were some people working in administrative bodies under him, who were corrupt. This was the only failure of Jawaharlal Nehru as a Prime Minister. At this very time, there were problems within the Congress Party. This became evident in the General Elections that were held in 1957. Every year the party framed radical policies that made them more unacceptable with the general masses.

There were also some linguistics problems that were faced by the nation during the period of Jawaharlal Nehru as Prime Minister. Hindi was prescribed as the national language of the country and that was accepted by all. But since, Jawaharlal Nehru had seen the world to a great extent; he knew the importance of the English language. He was a man with great foresight and could sense that

English would be the most important and commonly used language in the near future. He stressed on the fact that English should be used as an additional official language. There were also problems with the Urdu language. Jawaharlal Nehru wanted the language to be part of the pluralistic society in India. Urdu was spoken and followed by several people in the country and it was also recognised by the Constitution. These problems affected Nehru to a great deal and he sank deeper and deeper into this.

Jawaharlal Nehru had also established several foreign links that had helped him in enhancing his personal horizon and outlook. He used these experiences for the upliftment and progress of India. However, strains were also seen in the various foreign policies and foreign relations that he had established. During this time, India had managed to include Goa in the Indian Union by making it independent from the Portuguese rule. This was the only positive thing that had happened in the political and social sphere of India in those days. This boosted the morale of Jawaharlal Nehru to a great deal. Congress also won the elections in 1962 that provided some relief to the man, who had dreamt of making a new India.

The Indo-China Relationship was a major issue that had troubled Jawaharlal Nehru in his last days. He was the man, who had tried his best to cultivate harmonious and cordial relations with China. There are also several instances, where India did not react to certain hostilities that were shown by China. Jawaharlal Nehru even went to the extent of visiting the country for improving and enhancing the relation between the two countries. But Sino-Indian relations had reached nadir in the year 1959 with the advent of Dalai Lama in the social and political field.

Jawaharlal Nehru's health was also deteriorating with passing time. He was suffering from a kidney disorder, namely pyelonephritis. It was said that he suffered from this disorder due to excessive workload. He was diagnosed in London and doctors said that if he took rest for a long period of time, he would be absolutely fine. He was a man in his early-40s by then. During the last two years of his life, Jawaharlal Nehru had to endure several harsh conditions, both politically and socially. Several dissatisfactions and disapprovals in the country had made Nehru very upset and that added to the health deterioration.

On 8th January, 1964, he suffered a major stroke that paralysed him. Many people advised Jawaharlal Nehru to resign at this time, but he refused to do so. He still went to the Parliament on 10th February, but it clearly showed that he was not completely fit, though he denied that he was unwell. In the few months after this, he had recovered a bit and Congressmen were happy that they would get their leader back in power. But on 27th May, he fell severely ill and was in great pain. He was in great discomfort and doctors were called at once. Doctors confirmed that his aorta had ruptured and death was inevitable. He also asked for sedatives and was provided with it, but that did not bring him much relief. Doctors informed all his relatives that nothing more could be done to save him. On the same day at about 1.44 p.m. Jawaharlal Nehru breathed his last. This marked the end to a grand and glorious personality, who had excelled in political, social as well as in professional life. India lost a great leader on this day and his presence is still felt in times of crisis.

4

Great Leader of the Nation

Tactically speaking, Nehru was extremely successful given the fact that by the mid-1950s his leadership was virtually uncontested. In this chapter it will be demonstrated how Nehru tailored his 'Vision' in order to minimise the risk of being sidelined within the Congress party whilst at the same time carving out a distinct persona and agenda. To do this, the chapter examines each of Nehru's speeches as Congress President (1929, 1936, 1936/37, 1951, 1953, 1954) and conducts a content analysis to explore the influence of Socialism in Nehru's understanding of world events and as a platform upon which to launch his political agenda. The position of Congress president was of particular importance during the years prior to independence. Elected on an annual basis, the role of Congress President provided the individual with an opportunity to define his political persona and to make his beliefs known to a wide audience. At the same time, and in particular during the 1930s, the president-elect had to have Gandhi's backing and hence represented a position of power and prestige. Functioning like a 'government-in-waiting', the Congress body issued resolutions pertaining to organisational matters, responses to current developments as well as setting out general principles conveying the Congress position on policy matters even though the party lacked policy-making capability.

The chapter begins with a description of the key bodies within the Congress structure as it was in the early-1930s. This structure remained in place following independence in 1947 albeit with the addition of the Congress Parliamentary Board. Turning to Nehru's speeches as Congress President, an assessment is made of the extent to which socialism adopted a central place within his rhetoric as the representative of the Congress party. Following this a comparison is drawn with the speeches of three other contemporary presidents: Rajendra Prasad, Vallabhbhai Patel and Subhash Chandra Bose. Such an exercise, it is argued will help contextualise Nehru in terms of contrasting him with other political figures, each of whom was a representative Congress figure in his own right. The chapter begins with the 1930s and ends in the mid-1950s when, it is posited, Nehru was at the peak of his power. For the period following independence two decision-making bodies emerged as important instruments of influence: the Congress Working Committee and the Prime Minister's Cabinet. Both are examined and used as barometers for Nehru's rising power. The conclusion summarises the shifting 'structure of opportunities' and explains the importance of this changing context for the following analyses of individual policies.

Organisation of the Indian National Congress

In the pre-independence days the Congress organisation consisted of a pyramidal national decision-making structure. At the base were the 21 Provincial Congress Committee (PCC) which were obliged to send a list to the Working Committee of the members qualifies to vote for the delegates who would then represent the PCC at the All-India Congress Committee (AICC). The numbers of delegates each province was entitled to was set according to whether the province was designated a 'rural' or 'urban' area and the density of population. The elected delegates of each province were obliged to meet on a specific date and to propose the candidate or candidates for the Presidentship of the Congress for the ensuing year and to elect from among themselves one-twelfth of their number as representatives of the province to the AICC. The AICC was treated as an unofficial Parliament, responsible for carrying out the work programme laid down by the Congress from session to session.

At the apex was the Working Committee, a small executive subcommittee of the AICC which acted as the Cabinet of the movement. The President was allowed to select fourteen members from among the members of the AICC to constitute his Working Committee. Under the 1934 Constitution, the Working Committee was to 'be the executive authority and as such shall have the power to carry into effect the policy and programme laid down by the AICC and the Congress.' It had the power to (a) frame rules and issue instructions for the proper working of the Constitution; (b) to superintend, direct and control all Congress Committees subject to review by the AICC; (c) to take such disciplinary action as it may deem fit against a committee or individual for misconduct, wilful neglect or default.

After tallying the number of votes recorded in favour of all the PCC-recommended candidates, the Working Committee announced the new President-elect. Initially, the President had been chosen annually by an ad hoc committee appointed at the yearly Congress session. After 1934 however, he was elected directly by the delegates, a change introduced by Gandhi who thought a popularly elected President would help centralise leadership and galvanise the movement. In preparation of the Annual Session of the Congress, which all delegates from each province attended, the new AICC met as a Subjects Committee a few days before. The out-going Working Committee submitted a draft programme of the work for the upcoming annual session along with the resolutions carried out by the different PCCs. to the President-elect.

Following the formation of the Interim Government in 1946, the setting up of Congress ministries in the states and finally, complete independence in August 1947, the role of the Indian National Congress underwent a dramatic change. This had to be matched with appropriate changes to the organisational set-up so that a new relationship between party and government could be formed.

To decentralise the structure, new tiers had been introduced including the District Congress Committee in cities with a population of more than 200,000 and the Mandal Congress Committee. Each Provincial Committee was to return delegates to the Congress in the proportion of one to every 100,000 population from which one eight would act as representatives to the AICC. The rules for electing the Congress President changed from PCCs proposing candidates to any ten delegates jointly suggesting the name of any delegate for election as President of the Congress. Each delegate was then entitled to vote. The Working Committee was to consist of the President and twenty members, including a Treasurer and one or more General Secretaries.

As the highest executive authority of the Congress, the Working Committee had the responsibility of setting up a Parliamentary Board consisting of the Congress President and five other members for the purpose of regulating and coordinating parliamentary activities of the Congress Legislature Parties.

A Central Election Committee consisting of Parliamentary Board members and five other members elected by the AICC was responsible for conducting election campaigns and making the final selection of candidates for the State and Central legislatures.

As Kochanek describes in his book, *The Congress Party of India. The Dynamics of One-Party Democracy*, there were three phases in the evolution of party-government relations: 'The first, a period of transition which lasted from 1946 to 1951, was marked by conflict between party and government and by disorder and confusion at the executive level of the party organisation as the Congress sought to adapt a nationalist movement to a political party.' This was followed by a 'period of convergence' where under Nehru's guidance, the Working Committee 'came to perform the functions of party-government coordination, centre-state coordination and conflict resolution'.

A third phase, 'a period of divergence saw the development of a certain equilibrium of power between party and government, centre and states.' For the purpose of the thesis the focus here is on the first two phases of transformation when the relationship between the Prime Minister and the Congress President was in the process of being redefined and the Working Committee took on a new function. First, the chapter examines Nehru in his capacity as Congress President.

As Congress President

No systematic analysis of Nehru's presidential addresses is available in the vast Nehru-related literature. Given that he was elected president three times before and three times after independence, his speeches provide a useful medium through which to examine any notable shifts in his position. Nehru's worldview and political beliefs drew heavily from the school of Fabien socialism that was popular at the time.

Hence, this section seeks to investigate the presence of Nehru's socialist beliefs in his speeches, to explore the way in which he packaged them so as to enhance their appeal to the Congress party while minimising the risk of earning the reputation of being a radical and isolating himself. Throughout the 1930s Nehru was aware of his tenuous position within the Congress establishment given that he had not worked his way up though grassroots activism as had Patel and Prasad nor did he represent a solid regional basis of power, as did Bose. Thus, it is interesting to examine how Nehru tailored his 'image' and rhetoric given the compulsions.

The first observation that strikes one is the radicalism of the young Congress President. His speeches from 1929 and the two in 1936 were impassioned and daring, openly expressing an admiration for the Soviet Union and the merits of socialism. Aware of the lack of support for him in 1929 Nehru was nevertheless willing to cast himself as the radical reformer who was ready to take on the 'old guard' including his father, Pandit Motilal Nehru who had been the Congress President in 1928 and who supported gradual transformation through cooperation with the British and constitutional change.

Nehru's subsequent speeches, in contrast are far more reserved and cautious reflecting a wiser, more guarded politician at work. It is however, interesting to note that by 1954 Nehru felt comfortable again about referring directly to socialism. This propensity grew more marked in the following years as the Congress party was brought securely under his wing. By 1955 Nehru felt secure enough to relinquish the post of Congress president and to hand it over to a loyalist, U. N. Dhebar, who remained Congress president for the next four years.

In 1928 Jawaharlal Nehru's father, Pandit Motilal Nehru, had been Congress president. Named after him, the Nehru Report issued in the same year, proposed Dominion status for India as an alternative to 'Complete Independence'. Representing an older generation of leaders who had favoured gradual constitutional change to a revolutionary overthrowing of the system, Motilal Nehru's presidential speech had been mostly about questions of strategy and how to engage with the British and whether, in settling for Dominion status, this might be a small step in the direction of ultimate independence.

One year later, the period of grace granted by the Nehrū report, having met with no response from the British, Jawaharlal Nehru's election as Congress President was intended to inject a breath of fresh air. In accordance, his presidential speech asserted, 'The brief day of European domination is already approaching its end...The future lies with America and Asia....India today is a part of the world movement we march forward unfettered to our goal....for this Congress is to declare in favour of independence and devise sanctions to achieve it.' The first resolution passed at this session announced 'Complete Independence' (*purna swaraj*) as the new goal of Congress and India and, directed all current Congress members of any government legislatures or committees to 'resign their seats'. To establish his credentials as a radical reformer, Jawaharlal declared himself in this speech to be a socialist and a republican. Three major problems were identified by Jawaharlal as issues of the day: the minorities, the Indian States, and labour and peasantry, of which the last was in his opinion, the greatest concern of all. Reflecting a turn towards socio-economic concerns the All India Congress Committee adopted a resolution calling for 'revolutionary changes in the present economic and social structures of society and to remove the gross inequalities.'

The following year at the 1931 Karachi session it is interesting to draw a comparison with Sardar Vallabhbhai Patel's presidential speech which was altogether more down-to-earth than Nehru's. Much shorter in length, it addressed the practical considerations arising from the *Purna Swaraj* or *Complete Independence* resolution of 1930. 'This independence', Patel explained, 'does not mean, was not intended to mean, a churlish refusal to associate with

Britain or any other power. Independence therefore does not preclude the possibility of equal partnership for mutual benefit and dissolvable at the will of either party....I am aware there is a strong body of opinion in the country to the effect that before a partnership could possibly be conceived, there must be a period of complete dissociation. I do not belong to that school. It is, as I think, a sign of weakness and of disbelief in human nature.' Mentioned by Patel only in passing, the Resolution on Fundamental Rights, was a result of Nehru's efforts and would later be described as the first commitment of the Congress to an economic programme. However, the relatively moderate tone and wording reflected the careful balancing act that was at play with Gandhi trying to keep Nehru within the fold of the Congress, whilst tempering his radicalism.

Over the next two years the Congress party annual sessions were hampered by the widespread arrest of many of its leaders and the threat by the Government to break up gatherings. It was only in 1934 that the Congress was able to return to its normal functions and under Rajendra Prasad an attempt was made to revive the campaign. In the aftermath of the 1935 Government of India Act, Jawaharlal returned to India following the death of his wife in Switzerland to preside over the 1936 Lucknow Congress. As in the past, Nehru's speech was longer than other presidential addresses, had a grandstanding style about it and was as much about himself as it was about issues. The 1936 session however, reflected a leaning towards the left wing of the Congress for, in his Working Committee Nehru had managed to install two fellow socialists, Narendra Dev and Achyut Patwardhan. Also in his speech, Nehru made no concessions and stated clearly his preferences and ideological inclination. Hence, having cast the challenges facing him, India and the Congress within the context of global developments, Nehru pronounced, 'I am convinced that the only key to the solution of the world's problems and of India's problems lies in socialism'.

Going on to explain the 'scientific, economic sense' in which he meant the term socialism, Nehru stated, 'That means the ending of private property, except in a restricted sense, and the replacement of the present profit system by a higher ideal of cooperative service.' Furthermore, 'I have cooperated whole-heartedly in the past with the *khadi* programme and I hope to do so in the future because I believe that *khadi* and village industries have a definite place in our present economy....... But I look upon them more as temporary expedients of a transition stage rather than as solutions of our vital problems.'

Another issue upon which different factions of the Congress were to come to loggerheads on was the question of whether provincial elections, as promised in the 1935 India Act, ought to be contested. Nehru's suggestion was to contest the elections in order to 'carry the message of the Congress to the millions of voters and to the scores of millions of disfranchised' but 'to accept office and ministry, under the conditions of the Act, is to negative our rejection to it and to stand self-condemned. National honour and self-respect cannot accept this position, for it would inevitably mean our cooperation in some measure with the repressive apparatus of imperialism, and we would become partners in this repression and in the exploitation of our people'. A further controversial proposal was that the Congress party amend its Constitution to provide for affiliations with separate, functional, peasant and worker organisations so that 'the Congress could have an individual as well as a corporate membership'. The question of functional representation, as a result, became a central issue upon which the conflict between the Congress Socialists and the rightist Gandhians came to be centred.

Despite Nehru's public pronouncements on socialism and, his views on how to change the organisation and priorities of the Congress movement, there were limits to the extent of his influence and power. No major resolutions were adopted that year giving effect to Nehru's propositions. Although the election manifesto carried a strong imprint of Nehru in terms of its emphasis on poverty and unemployment amongst the agrarian and working classes as well as a reference to the Karachi Fundamental Rights resolution it did not mention the word socialism anywhere.

Re-elected as Congress President at the Faizpur Congress of 1936/37, Nehru spoke of a 'revolutionary remedy: the socialist structure of society' to combat the problems of imperialism and to understand the 'real content of the swaraj to come'. Although

Nehru made a reference to a 'Backward Russia (which) with one mighty jump established a Soviet Socialist State and an economic order which has resulted in tremendous progress in all directions', there was no further clarification in his presidential address about what he meant by socialism, how it would come about and, with what implications. All in all there seems to have been a considerable toning down of Nehru's radical rhetoric. Nor were any major resolutions on foreign policy or economic concerns passed in 1936/37 which could have reflected Nehru's influence and engagement. This was a contrast compared with the previous Lucknow Congress where Nehru's presence had been much more evident. It is also noteworthy that during the controversy over the Presidency in 1939 when Subhash Chandra Bose was nominated for re-election, Nehru was careful not to publicly take sides. Whilst Sardar Patel, Rajendra Prasad made public statements expressing their disapproval of Bose's candidature, Nehru was visibly silent.

The 1951 New Delhi session is interesting for the moderate tone adopted by Nehru on all the core issues raised in the Presidential address. With the country's first general elections approaching it seems logical that he felt the need to cast as broad an appeal as possible within the party and across the country. In fact a rather non-committal approach and lack of substantive pledges was evident in the Congress Election Manifesto adopted by the All India Congress Committee in July 1951. Nehru's speech to the Congress session reflected this. On foreign policy, there was no mention of non-alignment, simply that 'we have a definite and positive approach to world problems'.

Similarly, the issue of the Hindu Code Bill was referred to but carefully sidestepped: 'the Hindu Code Bill, which has given rise to so many arguments, became a symbol of this conflict between progress and reaction in the social domain. I do not refer to any particular clause of that Bill, which might or might not be changed, but rather to the spirit underlying that Bill.' With regards to Planning, it is significant that no mention was made of Socialism. Instead the Five Year Plan was simply portrayed as, 'a realistic survey of what it is possible to do with the resources likely to be available within the limitations of our Constitution and without a marked break from our existing social and economic framework'.

Following its electoral success, the Congress party found itself in government at the centre and in most of the states. However, as is reflected in the two following Congress sessions, it was as if the party was being made to take a clear back seat in the formulation of policy. Elected yet again as President to both the 1953 and 1954 sessions, Nehru's Presidential speeches are cautious and aimed at maintaining a consensus. No landmark resolutions were adopted and little was revealed about the party's concrete plan for action. As will be demonstrated further on in this chapter, this reflected a struggle that was going on at the time between the Congress in its organisational capacity and Congress as the party in government.

Only in 1955 was Nehru sufficiently in command to relinquish the position and to allow someone else to become Congress President. It was also at the 1955 Avadi session that most of Nehru's policies were explicitly articulated and adopted by the Congress. A survey of the resolutions adopted by the 1955 Indian National Congress proves this point nicely. The resolution on a 'Socialistic Pattern of Society' declared the official goal of planning to be, 'where the principal means of production are under social ownership or control, production is progressively speeded up and there is equitable distribution of the national wealth'.

On international affairs, the principles which ought to govern relations with the countries of the world were officially proclaimed to be those 'set out in the joint statements issued by India, China and Burma, and more recently by India and Yugoslavia.' Furthermore, 'the Congress warmly welcom(ed) these five principles of Panchsheela. They represent the approach and policy of India in international affairs, and put forward the alternatives of collective peace to the preparation for collective war'. Finally, on the front of social reform the Hindu Code Bills were hailed as significant steps towards improving 'the welfare of women and children'.

In each of the three areas Nehru's 'pet projects', as they had evolved over the first eight years of independence, were finally officially endorsed by the Congress party. This came about as a result of unforeseeable events (such as the death of Sardar Patel in 1950) but was also due to the strategic and careful consolidation of power by Nehru within the party.

His Contemporaries

Three central figures are chosen as representative of views that could be described as having been to the left and right of Nehru. Rajendra Prasad, a veteran freedom fighter went on to become the first President of the independent Republic of India and whose position on particular issues such as partition, Hindu-Muslim relations, consolidation of the nation, economic policy, relations with the industrialists, were popular amongst the more conservative wing of the Congress party which included other key political figures such as Vallabhbhai Patel. To represent the other end of the spectrum is Subhash Chandra Bose. The parallel drawn between Bose and Nehru is interesting given that they shared a tendency towards radical thinking particularly in the realm of economic policy but Nehru proved to be the cannier tactician, willing to temper his radicalism in order to consolidate his position within the Congress party first.

To highlight the span of differences between the three contemporaries and Nehru the table below juxtaposes the positions of each in the three main policy fields of economic development, social reform and foreign policy. Each of the above served as Congress President during the 1930s and hence their presidential addresses were used to extract the broad contours of their positions. The 1930s was a period when Gandhi more or less reigned supreme as the maker and breaker of political destinies within the Congress party and the position of Congress president was a highly prestigious one as it carried with it the support and favour of the Mahatma. Hence, although the four figures were not in direct competition against one other they each nevertheless came to occupy a distinct place within the space of political agenda-making.

The four leaders varied greatly in terms of methods espoused, general outlook and the particular objectives voiced. Sardar Vallabhbhai Patel, known for his good relations with the business community and pragmatic attitude, already in 1931 was calling for moves to stimulate and support local enterprise. Unlike Nehru, who in 1936, foretold the end of private property, Patel saw the need to make use of what was available before inflicting unnecessary destruction simply to make way for something new and bigger. On issues relating to social reform Patel's presidential speech had little to say except for the statement relating the abolition of untouchability to an act of self-purification. Much more strongly imbued with the language and practices of Gandhi than Nehru was, Patel also adhered more to the idea that the individual can, through his actions cleanse society of certain evils. This differed from Nehru's rather top-down approach where state-driven programmes changing the economy or issuing sweeping legislation would secularise society. Both Prasad and Patel saw India's use of non-violence as a contribution to humanity and possibly to the conduct of international politics.

Prasad comes across as more 'traditionalist', firmly embedded in the ideals and methods advocated by Gandhi, committed to the notion of truth and non-violence as essential guiding principles. Patel, on the other hand, while similarly well-versed in Gandhian thought, envisioned the need for arrangements that would provide material benefits to various parties at the same time, such as the federal system. While Nehru and Bose occupied the left end of the political spectrum, clear differences are also evident between the two. Both had a focus on economic problems and solutions, reflecting a shared belief in the benefits of a planned economy and rapid industrialisation.

However, on the issue of social reform and India's international profile it is interesting to note a crucial divergence. Nehru, especially in the 1930s, tended to cast his worldview, his analysis of India's problems as well as his agenda for reform all in terms of socialism. Bose, on the other hand, comes across as more multi-faceted given that his view on cultural, identity-related issues proposed they be left out of the ambit of state-induced reform. With regards India's reputation and interests in the international arena, Bose anticipated non-alignment as a strategy with his advice that India ought to judge according to her interests rather than primarily following principles.

This, in conjunction with the proposal that India should not simply rely upon a bestowed image but ought instead to carefully manufacture one, imply an unexpected closeness between Patel and Bose in their pragmatic, matter-of-fact diagnoses. Nehru and Prasad on the other hand seem closer in their more strictly doctrinaire approaches. Having briefly surveyed the scope for differences in the ideas and prognoses that were 'on offer' in the 1930s the following section looks more closely at the individuals.

Rajendra Prasad

Born in 1884 in Bihar, Rajendra Prasad was trained as a lawyer when in 1911 he joined the Congress party and was elected to the All India Congress Committee. Having set up a legal practice in Calcutta, Prasad became a known figure in the Eastern provinces of Bengal, Bihar and Orissa. Unlike Jawaharlal Nehru, Prasad entered the freedom struggle through his experience of grassroots activism in the form of the *Champaran* movement. One of the first movements initiated by Gandhi, the Champaran agitation of 1918-19 highlighted the dire conditions of the indigo workers in Bihar. Prasad's book on *Satyagraha in Champaran* provides an insight into these early experiences and together with a book on partition, *India Divided*, there are contrasts with Nehru which can be drawn.

Written shortly after his experience of the Champaran *satygarha* Prasad described the long history of peasant struggles in the area, stating that the first recorded outbreak against the cultivation of indigo occurred in 1867. Prasad's experiences and study of the peasant movement contrast starkly with Nehru's amazement and shock when he first encountered the plight and resilience of the *kisans* (farmers) in 1920 in the province of Uttar Pradesh. In his *Autobiography* for instance Nehru described how he was 'thrown almost without any will of my own, into contact, with the peasantry. I realised more than ever how cut off we were from our people and how we lived and worked and agitated in a little world apart from them. This realisation came to me during these Partabargh visits and ever since then my mental picture of India always contains this naked, hungry mass'.

With regards to basic political, philosophical outlook, Rajendra Prasad seems to have been primarily concerned with the *means* of political action and in the second place, with the *goals*. This reflects a position that was closer to Mahatma Gandhi's thinking and approach which emphasised that the nature of action ultimately affected the aims too. Writing in 1919 when Gandhi had assumed national leadership in the movement against the Rowlatt Bills, *Satyagraha*, was defined as, 'insistence on truth, and force derivable from such insistence' was a crucial mechanism of the movement which was as important as the goal of liberation itself. Hence, the need for regular self-purification and the conscious implementation of the 'truth force' which was to act as the 'binding force between province and province and the millions of Hindustan.' As a result, in 1922 Gandhi was willing to suspend non-cooperation and to risk jeopardising the movement due to the violence that had taken place at Chauri Chaura which was a demonstration for him that the movement was not yet ready.

Prasad, who from the beginning had claimed an affinity with Gandhi's ideas and methods unlike Nehru, who was more sceptical to begin with, echoes this prioritisation. For example in his presidential address to the 1934 session of the INC he said, 'To my mind Truth, Non-Violence and Khadi represent a triple force whereby we can achieve the whole of the Karachi programme and more...... Whilst I would have no objection to amplifying the Karachi programme and elucidating it... I would say emphatically that we should do nothing that compromises by one iota the creed of non-violence.' Whereas Nehru, who had been one of the key figures behind the Karachi Resolution, invested in the ideals and long-run goals of the movement, Prasad remained firmly committed to Gandhi's focus on the means and methods of the struggle.

A further difference compared with Jawaharlal Nehru's politics can be seen in Prasad's critique of the kind of radicalism for which Nehru stood: 'My friends the socialists, are keen on a more inspiring ideology and would hasten the elimination of all that stands for exploitation. I should like to tell them in all humility that there is no greater ideology than is expressed by the creed of truth and non-violence and the determination of the country not to eliminate the men that stand for exploitation but the forces that do so. Our quarrel is with the sin and not the sinner which we all are to a greater or lesser degree.'

Another interesting difference in approach is evident in Prasad's world view. Commenting on Nehru's presidency of the Congress party in 1935 Prasad wrote that: 'An atmosphere of war was fast developing in Europe. Italy had invaded Ethiopia. England did not approve of Italy's action but avoided a direct clash with Italy on the issue. All that the League of Nations did was to express lip sympathy for Ethiopia...... Our socialist colleagues wanted the Congress to adopt a resolution sympathising with Ethiopia and refusing India's help to Britain in any future war because of her attitude to the victim of aggression...although nothing was father from my mind than that we should help Britain in case of war, I thought it premature for the Congress to express an opinion on international affairs'. Unlike Nehru, Prasad did not believe in the need to be internationalist for the sake of being internationalist. Without having the means to actually implement the action and standards one preached, there was a danger of turning such statements into empty words and, in the process, losing credibility and influence in the future.

On economic policy there is a revealing difference in the way both Nehru and Prasad argued about the cow and its dual importance as a symbol of Hindu sentiments and as an economic unit of value. Brought to the fore in 1955 when The Indian Cattle Preservation Bill was placed before the Indian Parliament seeking a ban on cow slaughter, Nehru's position was to depict the cow only in terms of an economic unit and as part of the wider debate on agriculture and economic development. Nehru rejected the Bill on procedural grounds, arguing that as agricultural subject it fell under the jurisdiction of state legislatures.

Rajendra Prasad on the other hand examined the issue of cow slaughter from a perspective that *combined* the two dimensions of identity and economic value. Hence, in his opinion legislation was not needed. Instead what was required was an improvement in the conditions of keeping and breeding of cows: 'If goshalas (sheds and facilities which could be provided by the government) are managed properly, cows will become a paying proposition and their slaughter will cease automatically'.

Unlike Nehru who chose to skirt the debate and to turn it into a discussion about the secular state, Prasad's proposition rested upon providing an economic solution to a socio-cultural problem by pinpointing its economic, and hence negotiable, roots. While Nehru, invested hope and faith in the ability of the state to mould its citizens, Prasad's approach drew upon the inherent basic instincts of the individual to secure the best possible conditions given his constraints. Hence, instead of proposing policies that entailed the State imposing its interpretation of modernity, top-down, Prasad's approach favoured the creation of incentives for people to behave in a way that was considered by them to be the more efficient and rational choice.

Accompanying this divergence in premises is the very different style adopted in his writing. Each of Nehru's main books examined here, *An Autobiography, Glimpses of World History* and *Discovery of India* are written in a very narrative and pedagogical manner whilst Prasad's texts read more like an analytical treatise. For example in a book outlining the grounds for partition, Prasad lays out his argument in a scientific manner.

Beginning with the problem of how to identify the overlapping contours between State and Nationality, he concluded that 'a State need not be coterminous with a nationality, that in fact the experience of national States has ended in failure and created new problems', Prasad goes on to prove that the Muslims do not constitute a nation and do not need a separate State given that there is much that is shared, such as customs, rites, dress codes and sources of inspiration, which have created syncretic blends of language and art and which, most importantly, have a given rise to a shared history.

Moving on to analyse the role of the British in fanning communal consciousness, Prasad ends with a clever image from geometry: 'In this race between Muslim League demands and British Government concessions, the League is always ahead of the British Government by a few lengths and the Hindu majority and all other minorities cannot have even an entry. No wonder the base of the Communal triangle lengthens and the angle of communal difference widens.'

Prasad's analysis leads from one fact and inference to another and he even details various alternate schemes providing for complete independence versus the reorganisation of the provinces along cultural principles. His final conclusion is insightful and remains prescient today: 'It will be a stupendous task to carry out a division of all this..... It may well be that when the actual division has been accomplished, the result may turn out to be a veritable Dead Sea Apple or a *Delhi ka Laddu*, which the man who gets it regrets as much as the man who does not.'

Subhash Chandra Bose

As one of Jawaharlal Nehru's closest contemporaries Subhash Chandra Bose is invaluable as a basis for comparison particularly with regards Nehru's socialism and radicalism. Bose was a popular student leader and active in the trade union movement. A few key publications and various published documents provide an insight into Bose's world view and belief system such as his unfinished autobiography, *An Indian Pilgrim* and historical work, *The Indian Struggle, 1920-42* which provide an interesting contrast to Nehru's *Autobiography* and *Discovery of India* in terms of how Bose purviews his life within the larger context of India's colonial history.

For example, on the matter of religion Bose's writing implies that he was much more comfortable with the particular mix of spirituality and politics that India's historical experience had generated than Nehru ever was. Surveying the Bengal Renaissance and the figures it produced, Bose described a continuing trend where spirituality became wedded to politics through Ram Mohan Roy, Sasadhar Tarkachuramani, Pandit Iswar Chandra Vidyasagar, Ramakrishna Paramahansa, Swami Vivekananda, Aurobindo and affected other leaders across the country like B. G. Tilak and Mahatma Gandhi.

Experimenting personally with yoga and immersing himself in Indian philosophy, Bose's adolescent and young adult experiences and inclinations are a marked contrast to the preferences for Western sources of thought and action that Nehru pursued from an early stage. Though spending eighteen months at Cambridge, Subhash Bose retained a strong nationalist streak and tendency towards extremist politics, ultimately resigning from his Indian Civil Service position to join the freedom struggle. By their late-20s both Jawaharlal and Bose were 'the heroes of India's youth and the *bêtes noires* of the British authorities.

Interestingly while the two shared an affinity for radical politics what ultimately divided them was their response and strategy towards Gandhi's personality and politics. While Jawaharlal was to move closer and closer to Gandhi, Bose remained loyal to C. R. Das, his mentor, a major Bengali leader in the independence movement who, in the 1920s, had been one of the sharpest critics of Gandhi's methods of non-cooperation. Bose therefore, as a protege of C. R. Das, was more willing to openly express his scepticism about Gandhi's political wisdom and style while Nehru, who had decided quite early on to cast his lot with Gandhi, opted not to confront him publicly on issues of disagreement and more often than not, to do as he was bid. An early indication of this parting of their ways came in 1928. In response to pressure from within the Congress Party (led by Motilal Nehru) to accept Dominion Status as the party's objective, Bose and Nehru formed the 'Independence for India League' to propagate the goal of *complete* independence.

On the eve of the Calcutta Congress, Gandhi negotiated a via media, proposing that Congress formally adopt the proposition of Dominion Status but that if this were not accepted by the British government within one year, the Congress would opt for complete independence and engage in civil disobedience. Bose who opposed the resolution, saw it as 'shirking the duty of launching a struggle against the British imperialists' while Nehru, chose to support the resolution, probably in the realisation that it heralded the return of Gandhi as central power broker and in the knowledge that the one year ultimatum to the British was unlikely to yield anything.

Jawaharlal's election as INC president the following year at the Lahore Congress added to the gulf that had been created by the above incident. This was seen by Bose as a stratagem by Gandhi to draw Nehru away from the left wing of the Congress. Discovering that he was not included in the newly formed Working Committee, Bose decided to walk out, accusing Jawaharlal of having sold out to the 'Dominion Status school'. Once again, at the 1931 Karachi Congress, Bose was critical of Gandhi regarding the Gandhi-Irwin Pact and the Round Table Conference.

In 1935, Bose's *The Indian Struggle*, was published in which he acknowledged that Gandhi had transformed the INC from 'a talking body into a live and fighting organisation' but he was also highly critical: "The asceticism of Gandhiji, his simple life, his vegetarian diet, his adherence to truth and his consequent fearlessness – all combined to give him a halo of saintliness.... Consciously or unconsciously, the Mahatma fully exploited the mass psychology of the people, just as Lenin did the same thing in Russia, Mussolini in Italy and Hitler in Germany." Bose deplored the religious and moral undertones of satyagraha and the campaign against untouchability which he felt distracted from the main political objectives. These were opinions which were very close to Jawaharlal's impressions at the time. However, although the two may have shared the desire to turn Congress towards a more progressive direction, Jawaharlal had realised at the 1936 Congress over which he presided, that Socialism threatened to divide the party more than unite it. Socialist slogans of class struggle, it was argued by the more conservative wing, did not help the Congress-led movement which was aimed at freedom first and then socio-economic reform but in fact hindered it by helping the government gain the support of landlords and feudal elements.

Arrested upon his return to India, Bose was in prison for almost one year and in a gesture both to Bose and to Bengal, Gandhi supported Bose's candidature for INC president in 1938. At the 1938 Haripura Session of the INC, Bose's presidential address provides an insight into his outlook and approach to politics. One of Nehru's specialities was an internationalism which manifested itself in the emphasis he gave to international problems and the need for India to be an active participant in the international arena, albeit more in terms of rhetoric than concrete action.

Bose, seems to be as, if not more, internationalist than Nehru in terms of the broad historical contexts he was able to give his speeches and the radical commitments made to internationalist agendas. For example the struggle for political freedom of India was portrayed as incidentally also the fight 'for the economic emancipation of the British people as well.' Analysing the ebb and flow of past Empires, Bose's speech had a clear historical and structural argument in which he analysed the inherent weaknesses and contradictions of the British Empire and the challenges of attaining and preserving India's unity.

Referring directly to future policy, Bose took a clear stand on the problems of accommodating differences within a framework of equal rights and obligations. Hence, on the issue of religion he emphasised that 'the Congress policy is one of live and let live – a policy of complete non-interference in matters of conscience, religion and culture, as well as of cultural autonomy for the different linguistic areas.'

Unlike Nehru's speeches as Congress party president, Bose dwelt upon a number of looming practical challenges such as how to ensure the continued vitality of the Congress party when, after winning freedom, it would also became the party to put into effect the entire programme of post-war reconstruction. Other problems he considered included generating national unity through mechanisms like a *lingua franca* and a common script; reforming and modernising agricultural production as well as industrial development; changing the outlook of the permanent services like the bureaucracy to instil a national outlook and mentality. On the matter of foreign policy Bose also had a distinctive brand of pragmatism: 'we should take a leaf out of Soviet diplomacy. Though Soviet Russia is a Communist State her diplomats have not hesitated to make alliances with non-socialist States and have not declined sympathy or support coming from any quarter. We should therefore aim at developing a nucleus of men and women in every country who would feel sympathetic towards India.'

The case of Subhash Chandra Bose is also interesting in terms of the difference in strategy pursued by him. Unlike Nehru who was careful to restrain and temper his beliefs and actions in order to maintain a consensus and avoid crises, Bose was willing to openly challenge even the Mahatma himself. Standing for re-election as Congress president in 1939, against the express wishes of Gandhi and, on top of that, winning the elections, Bose brought the rift within the Congress movement between right and left to the fore. Most of the members of the Congress Working Committee resigned and Nehru, despite sharing the ideological underpinnings of economic policy with Bose, chose not to publicly support him.

As Bose himself described it, Nehru typically opted for an ambiguous stance: 'The election was followed by sensational developments, culminating in the resignation of twelve out of the fifteen members of the Working Committee, headed by Sardar Patel, Maulana Azad and Mr. Rajendra Prasad. Another distinguished and eminent member of the Working Committee, Pandit Jawaharlal Nehru, though he did not formally resign, issued a statement which led everybody to believe that he had also resigned.' After failed attempts to form a consensus cabinet, none of which Gandhi agreed to endorse, Bose finally decided to quit in May 1939.

Although remaining a member of the INC, Bose attempted to rally leftist forces under the umbrella of a Forward Bloc within the Congress party which basically advocated two key positions: issuing an ultimatum for self-government to the British and, establishing Socialism as the political creed for independent India. In addition, at the following Congress session in March 1940, Bose convened an alternative 'Anti-Compromise Conference' close to the official site. Lambasting an All India Congress Committee resolution to curb the power of the provincial Congress committees, Bose refused to hold elections to the Bengal Provincial Congress Committee, of which he was president and in response, the Congress Working Committee decided to disqualify him from holding any elective office for a period of three years. In July 1940 Bose was arrested and detained by the Government under the Defence of India Act but released in early-December on medical grounds. He successfully escaped from house arrest in January 1941 and set off to Germany and Japan to seek help from the Axis powers in liberating India from British rule.

A deeper insight into Bose's political thinking is provided by a lengthy document titled 'Forward Bloc: Its Justification' dated 22 March, 1941 which came to be known as the Kabul Thesis since it was written in Kabul, where Bose was secretly in transit, having escaped house arrest in Calcutta and ultimately reaching Berlin via Moscow. In this document he used Hegelian dialectics to demonstrate the emergence of a 'Leftist Antithesis' in response to a 'Rightist Thesis' and to argue how his initiative of the Forward Bloc would act as a rejuvenating force.

Hence, the Forward Bloc had 'saved the Congress from stagnation and death at the hands of the Rightists...It has served to stem the drift towards Constitutionalism, to create a new revolutionary mentality among the people and to bring the Congress back to the path of struggle....(it) has clarified the issues which separate the Left from the Right and has stimulated the intellectual and ideological progress of the Congress'. To Bose, Leftism meant in the first place anti-imperialism and only after the attainment of independence, would it be equated with Socialism. Unlike Nehru who already in his pre-independence days spoke of the need for a socialist outlook and socialist policies,

Bose was in some ways more pragmatic when asserting that 'Socialism or Socialist reconstruction before achieving our political emancipation is altogether premature'.

Ultimately sidelined within the Congress party, Bose's strategy was not an effective one as he ended up isolating himself amongst the High Command which, apart from Mahatma Gandhi, included others like Sardar Vallabhbhai Patel, Rajendra Prasad, J. B. Kripalani, Bhulabhai Desai, Sarojini Naidu. Nevertheless, Bose played a central role in terms of articulating the Leftist position and in paving some of the ground so that Nehru's visions could later take root. The most obvious evidence of this lies in the formation of the Planning Commission which was installed under the leadership of Bose.

During the early-1930s Bose's relations with Nehru were good enough for him to ask Nehru to become the first chairman of the newly initiated Planning Commission. However, after the 1939 re-election fiasco, Bose's comments on Nehru are deeply bitter. His sense of betrayal and disappointment is palpable in a letter to Nehru dated March 28, 1939 in which he outlined various grievances and highlighted the differences between them: 'You are in the habit of proclaiming that you stand by yourself and represent nobody else and that you are not attached to any party...

By bearing a non-party label one can be popular with all parties, but what is the value of it?' Another difference in approach is revealed in Bose's criticism of Nehru's statements on international affairs: 'I feel that we should take international politics seriously and utilise the international situation for our benefit — nor not talk about it at all. It is no use making a show, if we do not mean business.'

By 1941 Subhash Chandra Bose was out of the country and increasingly out of the picture in terms of Congress politics. It is alleged that he died in a plane accident on 18 August, 1945 although his body was never recovered. His death in removed a potential rival to Nehru from the political scene and in effect, Bose's vision of India's economic development strategy was absorbed into Nehru's programme.

Sardar Vallabhbhai Patel

Born, it is estimated in 1875, into a formerly important clan in the princely state of Gujarat, Vallabhbhai Patel was brought up adhering to religious beliefs as a way of life and in a family with limited resources. Unlike both Nehru and Bose, Patel's education began through a village school from which he worked his way up to complete his studies in law. Setting up his own practice in Godra in 1900 Patel self-financed his training as a barrister in London in 1910 and returned to India in 1913.

Patel's youth seems to have been spent mostly on acquiring an education and setting up his legal practice in order to support his own and his brothers' families. Brought into close contact with Gandhi in 1917 when Patel was elected as Secretary to the Gujarat Sabha and Gandhi was invited to be its President, his career in politics was launched. Together with Gandhi, Patel fought for the rights of farmers to be exempted from payment of land tax when the yield was less than 25 per cent of the normal, organising a campaign of non-violent resistance by the peasants which was ultimately successful. An older man when he came into contact with Gandhi and joined forces with him, Patel was a solid supporter and unquestioning follower; a different generation compared to the spirited, idealistic young men that Nehru and Bose were when they joined the nationalist movement.

With Gandhi sentenced to six years imprisonment in 1922, Patel was looked upon as the leader of the Congress movement in Gujarat and in 1928 with the campaign in Bardoli, Patel acquired the status of a hero. Challenging once again the British policy of land taxation, in 1928 a tax increase of 22 per cent was announced, Patel launched a non-violent, civil disobedience movement protesting the fact that peasants had to pay periodically increasing taxes regardless of the size of their land-holdings and the yield produced. Appealing to all sections of society, Vallabhbhai managed to put together a united front of Muslims and Hindus to fight the Government. After a long campaign an independent enquiry was launched into whether the land revenue increase had been justified. Concluding that an increase of 5.7 per cent was reasonable as against the 22 per cent sanctioned by the Government, the Bardoli settlement was hailed a triumph for satyagraha.

Catapulted into the limelight of Congress politics as a result of the peasant campaign, Patel was elected Congress President in 1931, but only after Jawaharlal Nehru had served in 1929 when, at the behest of his father, Motilal Nehru to Gandhi, Jawaharlal's name was proposed.

The differences in style and substance between Jawaharlal and Patel were evident from early on. Unlike Nehru, who went through a long period of questioning the effectiveness of Gandhi's techniques and had trouble with the religiosity that Gandhi represented, Patel, despite his lawyer's conviction for negotiated agreements and the rule of law, was more easily able to engage with and implement Gandhi's principles and methods of action. Perhaps this was a result of his upbringing which was closer to Gandhi's than Jawaharlal's had been or perhaps Patel's solid rootedness of being connected to the land and peasantry in Gujarat gave him a confidence and stability which the young Jawaharlal lacked and which compelled him to seek structural solutions and explanations in doctrines and ideologies.

In the mid-1930s although Jawaharlal propounded socialist ideas and had the support of the Congress socialists it was Rajendra Prasad and Sardar Patel who held the upper hand in determining the content of Congress resolutions and the membership of the Working Committee. Excerpts of Patel's statement in response to Jawaharlal's presidential speech of 1936 are worth reproducing to note the difference in tone and worldview: 'While I detest imperialism and admit the inequality between capitalist class and the famishing poor, I do believe that it is possible to purge capitalism of its hideousness. There is no difficulty in my subscribing to the doctrine that all land and wealth belonged to all. When we have attained (freedom) it will be time to enforce our theories and plans.'

In 1947, at independence Jawaharlal Nehru was sworn in as Prime Minister on account of his election to President of Congress in 1946 although Patel had been the favoured candidate and only in acquiescence to Gandhi had withdrawn his candidature. Sharing power with Nehru as his Deputy Prime Minister, their divergent views on economic matters and others came to the fore. Additionally Home Minister and Minister for States and

Information and Broadcasting and together with his control over the Congress Party machine, Patel maintained a formidable concentration of power in his hands. Decrying Prime Minister Nehru's tendency towards appeasement and idealism, Patel had the tendency to give voice to the concerns of the Hindu majority, calling for Muslims who had opted to stay on in India to demonstrate their loyalty by not demanding special treatment as minorities or by denouncing the acts of aggression committed by Pakistan in Kashmir.

Differences between the two were also evident in the Constituent Assembly Debates where on the issue of property rights Patel was firmly in favour of securing their protection, allowing the State acquisition only for the sake of a public purpose and on payment of fair compensation. Nehru, who was concerned about implementing a socialistic programme and introducing a reform of the land tenure system pressed that the legislatures should have full powers, in the larger national interest, to decide the scale of compensation to be paid. Finally, in a victory for Patel over Nehru, the Constituent Assembly accepted that the right to property be protected by the Constitution and that the rate of compensation should be subject to review by the courts.

Combining a toughness and sense of pragmatism, Patel achieved other miracles of negotiation such as persuading minorities, including the Muslims, to give up the tradition of separate electorates introduced by the British, and the integration of the 554 princely states, which was achieved peacefully with the exception of Hyderabad and Kashmir (the latter being handled personally by Nehru). It is interesting to note that working closely with Patel were figures who in their own right were great public personalities such as Rajendra Prasad, who served as President of the Constituent Assembly and later as President of the nation, and V. P. Menon who acted as secretary to Patel in the States Department.

As has been pointed out by Patel's biographer, Patel was an adept party man, capable of managing the party machine so that important members of all different hues continued to support the Congress-led movement. Not so often at the forefront like Nehru and lacking his international exposure and persona, Patel had worked closely with Gandhi during the 1930s to manage the party organisation to the extent that he was one of the few leading figures to have widespread support and respect from across the country. As treasurer of the Congress he raised money, courting powerful industrialists and feudal landlords. Later, as President of the Parliamentary Sub-Committee Patel experienced firsthand the running of election campaigns and the enforcement of discipline in the Congress Ministries.

Consolidation of Power

Having examined the structure of the Congress Party and the various contending figures and viewpoints, the chapter explores the processes through which Nehru consolidated his power within the party.

Position within Congress: 1947-55

Invited by the Viceroy of India, Lord Wavell, to form an interim government, Jawaharlal Nehru took the helm on 2 September 1946. It is interesting to note that this occurred manifestly because Nehru happened, at the time, to be the President of the Indian National Congress, a position he held largely thanks to Gandhi's powerful intervention in his favour for it appears that Congressmen in general favoured Sardar Patel for this office. As a result, when independence came less than one year later, Nehru had precedence and it seemed automatic that he should become the first Prime Minister of sovereign, independent India. The leadership rivalry between Nehru and Patel, though not apparent on the outside, soon revealed itself in terms of their fundamentally opposing positions on various issues.

A description of the two by a contemporary, C. D. Deshmukh, who was to become Finance Minister in 1950, aptly captures the differences between the two, 'Temperamentally, Patel was a realist, with the common sense characteristic of the sturdy peasantry from Kaira District, Gujarat, from which stock he had sprung. Nehru on the other hand, was an intellectual with a theoretical commitment to socialism dating back to the days of his early manhood and traceable to his sojourns in Europe in the early-1930s. At the core of Vallabhbhai's realism was the recognition of the foibles of human nature and an awareness of its limitations, which stamped him as a conservative. Nehru, unsure as a judge of men, was inclined to overestimate the achievement potential of his fellow-beings; he was in consequence only too ready to respond to the appeal of socialism. The Nehru-Patel balance in the Cabinet was therefore a case of unstable equilibrium, maintained only by a common effort on either side not to encroach on each other's assigned territory'.

The Congress presidential elections of 1950 proved to be one such point of contestation. Two candidates, J. B. Kripalani and Purushottamdas Tandon had the support of Nehru and Patel respectively and their contest was watched as a trial of strength between the Prime Minister and his Deputy in the Cabinet. Furthermore, with the First General Elections impending, it was recognised that the party office bearers would play a decisive role in the selection of candidates for the elections. It is revealing that despite having experienced an acrimonious relationship with Kripalani in 1946-47 when Kripalani was Congress President and Nehru, the interim Prime Minister, eventually leading to Kripalani's resignation in 1947, Nehru opted to support Kripalani over Tandon in the 1950 contest.

Nehru made it known that apart from supporting Kripalani, if Tandon were to be elected he would treat it as a vote of no-confidence against himself by the Congress party and would resign as Prime Minister. The election took place on 29 August 1950 and the result was announced on 1 September. Tandon secured a majority, with 1,306 votes, Kripalani having won 1,052 and Shankar Rao Deo, 202. In response to Tandon's election, Nehru decided to place before the 1950 Nasik session a series of resolutions to test whether the party was willing to endorse his policies and positions.

These resolutions referred to foreign policy, particularly towards Pakistan, condemned communalism, reaffirmed the secular state concept, and approved the government's economic policy. All of them were passed by huge majorities. However, the unity which Nehru had hoped to test through these resolutions quickly revealed cracks when it came to discussing the composition of the party executive, the Working Committee. Despite an invitation from Tandon, Nehru refused at first to join the new

Working Committee. Discussions over the members were brought to a temporary halt with only thirteen of twenty members selected. When the rest were announced on October 16, 1950 it was evident that Nehru had been unable to exert his preferences, for Tandon had dropped all those who had opposed him and created a committee containing eight Provincial Congress Presidents. This represented a break with the past when the Working Committee had been dominated by individuals who had a broad, all-India appeal as opposed to being provincial, party bosses.

On December 15, 1950 Sardar Vallabhbhai Patel's death removed a formidable challenge to Nehru's leadership and the central bastion of the conservative wing of the Congress party. However, the next road block emerged in the form of a confrontation between Tandon and his Working Committee on the one hand against Kripalani and the Democratic Front, which he had formed following his failure to win the presidency.

The objective of the Front was to 'purify' the Congress and, to carry out the central economic, social and foreign policies that had been articulated in the Nasik resolutions. With matters gradually coming to a head, Nehru eventually took action by writing to Tandon on August 6, 1951 stating his decision to resign from the Working Committee and the Congress Election Committee. In the following week, Nehru addressed the Congress Parliamentary Party, explaining his reasons for his resignation. A motion of confidence in Nehru's leadership was introduced and passed, implying that the conflict was about individuals, leadership and policy rather than a clash of roles and procedure.

Eventually Tandon stepped down and on September 8, 1951 Nehru was elected to the Congress presidency by a vote of 295 to 4. Appointing Tandon to his Working Committee Nehru invited all those who had seceded from the Congress to rejoin the party. Meeting in October, the Congress passed a series of resolutions embodying Nehru's policies on the economy, communalism and foreign policy. Although in late-1951 it already looked as though Nehru was the undisputed leader within the party, concrete actions had to be taken to sustain this position. As Congress President for the next three years, Nehru worked to consolidate and secure his power. Handing over the Presidentship in 1954 to U. N. Dhebar, formerly Chief Minister of the State of Saurashtra and at forty-nine, a 'new generation' compared with earlier leaders, Nehru could be sure of his protege's loyalty In one of his first public speeches Dhebar acknowledged the pre-eminence of Nehru in particular: 'There is only one leader in India today and that is Jawaharlal Nehru. Whether he carries the mantle of Congress Presidentship on his shoulders or not, ultimately, the whole country looks to him for support and guidance'.

As a Political Entrepreneur

Using the resources available to him, Nehru managed to secure his position. Two institutions provided the means through which to exert his influence and establish a power base: the Congress Working Committee (CWC) and the parliamentary Cabinet. The struggle to control the Congress Working Committee was an old one since, as a subcommittee of the AICC it was the highest authority of the Congress and the chief policy-maker of the organisation. It framed the rules for the working of the organisation, controlled the Pradesh Congress Committees and took disciplinary action against committees or individuals within the Congress.

Post-independence, the CWC was charged with coordinating party-government relations through the Parliamentary Board and through a second committee, the Central Election Committee it exerted great influence in the selection of election candidates. However, with independence the relationship between the Congress party and the central government became a central concern, raising questions about the extent to which the CWC ought to continue issuing all-India policies under a federal system, whether a membership criteria ought to be developed and the need to introduce fair organisational elections.

In the transformation from a mass movement into a political party in government, the composition of the CWC took on a greater importance. On the one hand, it was argued that close cooperation and overlapping membership of the CWC and government positions was necessary to preserve unity, but at the same time a majority seemed to believe that this represented too much of a concentration of power. As mentioned above, Purshottamdas Tandon's CWC was composed largely of party bosses from the major states, many of whom opposed the social and economic policies of the Nehru government. Under Nehru the composition of the CWC underwent a significant alteration. At the 1951 AICC session, in preparation for the General Elections, the Congress President was given full freedom to select his Working Committee, enabling Nehru to drawn upon Central Ministers and Chief Ministers. In this way, the Working Committee became a means of coordinating all-India Congress policy informally, ensuring that there was little divergence between party resolutions and government action. Nehru had also instituted a practice of writing regularly to his Chief Ministers and the letters demonstrate how closely he sought to guide and monitor their actions.

By 1951 therefore Nehru was in a position to give institutional form to his vision and priorities for a modern, independent India. By strategically compromising on some issues, such as the degree of socialist rhetoric in order to secure a consensus on economic policy or, by encouraging a polemic debate on other fronts, as in the case of the Hindu Code bills, Nehru had managed to favourably alter the 'structure of opportunities' in his favour. By 1951 he combined the post of Prime Minister with that of Congress president and was able to exert his influence through both the working committee and, as we shall see below, the Cabinet. However, the extent to which Nehru was able in fact to shape the political arena and the limits to his power. As suggested, the instrumentalisation of a policy issue, (an indicator of this being when the actor refers to a particular policy more in terms of its symbolism rather than its substantive content), is unlikely to generate uncontested policy outcomes. On the contrary, such a style of politics and policy-making is inherently more likely to run into strong opposition and stringent bargaining positions.

The changing composition of the Cabinet is yet another prism through which to follow the growing predominance of Nehru. According to the Constitution it was stated that 'there shall be a Council of Ministers, with the Prime Minister at the head, to aid and advise the President in the exercise of his functions....The Prime Minister shall be appointed by the President and the other Ministers shall be appointed by the President on the advice of the Prime Minister'. Thus, the Westminster British model of parliamentary Cabinet government was instituted and some of the unwritten conventions of the British system were written into the Indian Constitution.

The first Cabinet in fact predated the Indian Constitution. Following the acceptance by the Indian National Congress of the British Cabinet Mission Plan, the then Viceroy, Lord Wavell, invited Jawaharlal Nehru (in the latter's capacity as the then head of the Congress), to form an Interim Government. Nehru was to the Vice-President of the Viceroy's Executive Council under the proposed arrangement and all the Departments (including the previously reserved or British-controlled Departments of External Affairs, Defence, and Communications) were to be under the charge of Indian Members.

Technically, the Viceroy remained the President of the Council but before forming the government, Nehru obtained the assurance from Lord Wavell that the Interim Government would, in practice, function like a Dominion Cabinet. In other words, the Interim Government was to act like a Cabinet and Nehru was the *de facto* Prime Minister. In reality, Nehru was not quite as free as the Prime Minister under a Cabinet system. The task of forming the Government was entrusted by the Congress to a special parliamentary committee comprising Jawaharlal Nehru, Sardar Patel, Maulana Azad and Rajendra Prasad, demonstrating who the helm-leaders were at the time. The Cabinet was also not characterised by political homogeneity with some of its Members (out of an initial team of nine) also non-Congressmen, namely C. H. Bhabha, John Matthai, Baldev Singh, and S. P. Mukherjee.

Jawaharlal Nehru's first Cabinet after independence was sworn in on 15 August 1947 and consisted of a Deputy Prime Minister (Patel) and twelve other Ministers. Patel it is said was virtually self-appointed for, having withdrawn in favour of Nehru at Gandhi's insistence in the leadership contest of 1946, he expected his due. Also in the Cabinet, Rajendra Prasad was one of the party stalwarts, leaning more towards the right. Three other members, N. V. Gadgil, Rajkumari Amrit Kaur and Jairamdas Daulatram were not Nehru's own choices. Gadgil himself attributed his first appointment in 1947 and, retention in the first Cabinet of 1950, to Sardar Patel. Both Amrit Kaur and Daulatram had not been in the forefront of all-India Congress leadership, but had been closely associated with Gandhi. Subsequent appointments of K. M. Munshi, R. R. Diwarkar and K. Santhanam were seen as falling under Patel's special area of influence, at the time, mainly Bombay and the South. Significantly, all of them were dropped after the general election of 1952, Patel having passed away in the meantime and Nehru being in a position of strength within the party. In addition to these, two other members of the Cabinet – Jagjivan Ram and C. H. Bhabha – owed their positions to factors other than the Prime Minister's personal choice. Jagjivan Ram was included to provide representation to the numerous *harijans* or Scheduled Castes and C. H. Bhabha was included following a decision by the Congress High Command to give representation in the government to the affluent and influential Parsee community.

The limits to Nehru's power during the early years of independence are evident from various aspects. Firstly, there was his inability to remove Patel despite Nehru's own threats to resign. N. V. Gadgil, a 'Patelite' also proved to be an obstacle to Nehru. In the early years after independence Nehru also had to cope with some very vocal critics who were also Cabinet members. S. P. Mukherjee for instance served as cabinet minister for Industry and Supply for two and a half years after which he resigned from the Cabinet on 19th April, 1950.

He held strong views on the path to economic development given India's conditions. According to his biographer, Mukherjee was convinced that in an industrially backward country, the primary task was to mobilise all resources, private and governmental to make the country self-sufficient, especially in terms of defence requirements. Total nationalisation was unwise given the lack of trained personnel and expertise to run industries efficiently. Hence, collaboration with private industry was essential. This view in addition to the strong stance he adopted with regards treating Pakistan as India's number one enemy brought him into conflict with Nehru on issues like how to handle the integration of Kashmir and Hyderabad into the Indian Union.

Following the death of Patel in December 1950 and the weakening of the 'Patelites' in the Cabinet, Mukherjee was approached to lead a new organisation, the All India Bharatiya

Jana Sangh which was launched in late-1951. Explaining the need for the new party he said, "one of the chief reasons for the manifestation of dictatorship in Congress rule is the absence of well-organised opposition parties which alone can act as a healthy check on the majority party and can hold out before the country the prospect of an alternative government".

It can be argued that Nehru as an uncontested leader really came into his own after the success of the 1952 elections. The election manifestos for the country's first general elections offer a useful insight into the political terrain of the time. Whilst the Indian National Congress held the clear advantage in terms of resources, a pan-India network and the undisputed association with the Freedom Struggle, a few other parties stood for clear alternatives to the Congress programme.

The Hindu Mahasabha for example, apart from projecting itself as the party, that 'stands for establishment of a Hindu Raj in Bharat with a form of Government in accordance with Hindu conception of policy and economy', and a key player in the Civil Resistance movement, differentiated itself from the Congress on specific policy matters as well. Thus, in foreign policy the Hindu Mahasabha criticised 'the unrealistic and theoretical approach in the sphere of foreign policy (that) has left Bharat friendless in the whole world', on the economy, 'the vacillating and indecisive policy of the Congress Government in dealing with industry has alienated successfully both capital and labour. It has created a sense of insecurity in the minds of investors and has retarded the growth of industry.'

On the subject of social reform, the Hindu Mahasabha protested the 'attempt by the Congress Government to pass the Hindu Code Bill in spite of general protest against the disruption of Hindu society.' The policy alternatives promised included, a 'foreign policy guided by the principle of enlightened self-interest and reciprocity', recognition of 'the sanctity of private property and guarantee(ing) its possession and inheritance to its owners', and a clear position 'against legislative interference in religious matters, measures like the Hindu Code Bill would be opposed'. In all the three policy arenas therefore the Hindu Mahasabha took a clear stand.

The Jana Sangh, formed on the eve of the elections, decided to contest for seats in both the State and Central legislatures. Challenging the government on a number of issues, the Jana Sangh expressed alternative views on topics including the economy, foreign policy and communalism. On the whole however, the election results were a debacle for the Jana Sangh which succeeded in getting only three of its candidates through out of the 93 who had contested on its ticket. In the State legislatures it fared not much better where out of the 742 candidates that had contested, only 33 were elected. In some provinces like East Punjab, where the Jana Sangh appeared to be the strongest, it could not secure a single vote. The most significant gain for the party however, was the recognition of the Jana Sangh as one of the four All India Parties by the Election Commission of India, on the basis of the number of votes polled by it.

The Communist Party of India (CPI) fared well, emerging only second to the ruling Congress Party in Parliament and as the second largest party in a number of State Assemblies. However, even with 26 seats, the CPI did not get more than 4.45 per cent of the total polled votes while the Socialist Party which got only twelve seats, and the Kisan Mazdoor Praja Party (KMPP) obtained nine seats, polled respectively 10.50 per cent and 5.81 per cent. Its election manifesto criticised the Congress Party on a number of points, most importantly the slowness of its land reforms. Lambasting the Nehru Government as 'a Government of Landlords and Monopolists' the CPI manifesto declared 'We have before us the glorious example of China which under a government of People's Democracy has registered an advance that has amazed the whole world. It has freed the peasants from feudal shackles and increased food production by ten million tons. It is fast building its industries and roads....... it should not be forgotten that China was more backward than India, had to support a far bigger population and its economy was shattered by decades of war and devastation'.

On the whole the opposition fared rather poorly. Collectively, the opposition parties secured more than 55 per cent of the total vote polled as compared with the 44.63 per cent garnered by the Congress. Yet in terms of seats this translated into an absolute victory for the Congress which acquired 364 seats as against 125 won by the opposition put together. Furthermore, the opposition front of 125 was badly divided. The Communists and their allies, who had 26 members in the new Parliament, constituted the largest organised group in the opposition. The Socialists had 12 members and the Kisan Mazdoor Praja Party of Acharya Kripalani had 10. Their merger to form the Praja Socialist Party, combined to produce 22 seats. The Bharatiya Jana Sangh, the fourth All-India Party, secured only 3 members and the rest were represented by smaller regional parties or independents. Despite not being able to muster together the requisite number of seats to constitute a formal opposition group (50 seats were required), MP Shyma Prasad Mukherjee emerged as the unofficial spokesman of the opposition. Criticising the Government's kid-glove approach towards Kashmir for example, Mukherjee raised an important question, "I would like to know are Kashmiris Indian first and Kashmiri next or they are Kashmiris first and Indian next, or they are Kashmiris first, second and third and not Indian at all?"

Following the resounding victory in the 1952 elections, Nehru's Cabinets began to reflect the new arrangement of power. His new Cabinet dropped all the 'Patelites', including Gadgil, Munshi, Diwarkar and Santhanam. It consisted of fourteen cabinet ministers (excluding Nehru) and four Ministers of State. Among the fourteen ministers were Kailas Nath Katju (Home Minister) and Lal Bahadur Shastri (Railways) – both from Allahabad, Nehru's hometown in Uttar Pradesh. Rafi Ahmed Kidwai (Food and Agriculture), who had been close to the Nehrus since the days of Motilal Nehru, was retained. In addition to these confidantes, several other Cabinet Ministers like Gopalaswamy Ayyangar, C. D. Deshmukh, T. T. Krishnamachari, Amrit Kaur and C. C. Biswas were otherwise political non-entities and owed their positions to the Prime Minister.

The Summary

This chapter sought to contextualise Nehru at first, in terms of the ideological and intellectual parameters of the time, by comparing him with three contemporaries, Sardar Vallabhbhai Patel, Dr. Rajendra Prasad and Subhash Chandra Bose. An attempt was made to summarise the differences in positions on key issues as revealed in their presidential speeches in the mid to late-1930s. The analysis of these speeches served to highlight how each responded to the challenges of the freedom struggle and the differences in the emphasis given to issues. Secondly, the chapter demonstrated the institutional constraints of the Congress party organisation over which Nehru managed to gradually assert control. By examining the various resolutions adopted by the Congress party and the speeches of different Congress presidents, the aim was to track Nehru's emergence as a central figure within the Congress party organisation.

The chapter has revealed how Nehru's position on various policy issues seemed to harden in some cases and in others, to soften and furthermore, how the organisational and institutional mechanisms of the Congress party, as a party in power came to serve as instruments of influence and power consolidation. By 1955 it is posited that Nehru was at the peak of his power. For the next five sessions the President of the Congress party, U. N. Dhebar served as a reliable stooge, allowing Nehru to focus on flaunting his international persona and skills of diplomacy, on hammering out the second five year plan and fine-tuning his idea of a 'socialist pattern of society'.

The information presented in this chapter was meant to convey the 'structure of opportunities' which Nehru sought to mould in his favour, especially after he was chosen to be Prime Minister of newly independent India in 1947. Faced with important rivals such as Vallabhbhai Patel, Rajendra Prasad and their respective constituencies, Nehru sought to position himself strategically on a number of central themes, namely economic policy, social reform and foreign policy.

Opting for a different spatial standpoint on the spectrum of positions depending on the issue, Nehru had, by the mid-1950s managed to turn himself into the pivotal actor whose choices were to set the parameters for future policy-making. Observing this tendency towards dominance, authors such as Rajni Kothari developed the idea of a one-dominant party system under the Congress party which, after independence continued as a broad-based movement, 'involving within itself both dominant and dissident groups, and functioning alongside government as an agency of political penetration.' However, Kothari's analysis really focuses on the period after 1962 and how the 'Congress System' survived the shocks of the 1967 state assembly elections and, not so much on the 1950s. This period, like in so many other books about India's modern political development, is neglected.

Arguing that time and sequence are important components of the analytic narrative, the thesis emphasises the need for 'pre-history' and a more in-depth investigation into the origins of institutional arrangements rather than focusing on their replication. Hence, the transition to independence and the early years just after independence are considered to be crucial in understanding how Nehru consolidated his power.

5

Nehru and Non-aligned Movement

The Brainchild of Pt. Nehru

The Non-aligned Movement (NAM) is an intergovernmental organisation of states considering themselves not formally aligned with or against any major power bloc. The movement is largely the brainchild of India's first Prime Minister Jawaharlal Nehru, President of Egypt Gamal Abdul Nasser and Yugoslav President Josip Broz Tito. It was founded in Belgrade (1961); as of 2009, it has 118 members and 17 observer countries. The purpose of the organisation as stated in the Havana Declaration of 1979 is to ensure "the national independence, sovereignty, territorial integrity and security of non-aligned countries" in their "struggle against imperialism, colonialism, neo-colonialism, racism, and all forms of foreign aggression, occupation, domination, interference or hegemony as well as against great power and bloc politics." They represent nearly two-thirds of the United Nations's members and comprise 55 per cent of the world population, particularly countries considered to be developing or part of the third world.

Members have, at various times, included: Yugoslavia, Argentina, SWAPO, Cyprus and Malta. Brazil has never been a formal member of the movement, but shares many of the aims of NAM and frequently sends observers to the Non-aligned Movement's summits. While the organisation was intended to be as close an alliance as NATO (1949) or the Warsaw Pact (1955), it has little cohesion and many of its members were actually quite closely aligned with one or another of the great powers. Additionally, some members were involved in serious conflicts with other members (e.g. India and Pakistan, Iran and Iraq).

The movement fractured from its own internal contradictions when the Soviet Union invaded Afghanistan in 1979. While the Soviet allies supported the invasion, other members (particularly Islamic nations) of the movement did not.

Because the Non-aligned Movement was formed as an attempt to thwart the Cold War, it has struggled to find relevance since the Cold War ended. After the break-up of Yugoslavia, a founding member, its membership was suspended in 1992 at the regular Ministerial Meeting of the Movement, held in New York during the regular yearly session of the General Assembly of the United Nations. At the Summit of the Movement in Jakarta, Indonesia (September 1, 1992 - September 6, 1992) Yugoslavia was suspended or expelled from the Movement.

The successor states of the SFR Yugoslavia have expressed little interest in membership, though some have observer status. In 2004, Malta and Cyprus ceased to be members and joined the European Union. Belarus remains the sole member of the Movement in Europe. Turkmenistan, Belarus and Dominican Republic are the most recent entrants. The application of Bosnia-Herzegovina and Costa Rica were rejected in 1995 and 1998.

The Origin

Independent countries, who chose not to join any of the Cold War blocs, were also known as non-aligned nations.

The term "non-alignment" itself was coined by Indian Prime Minister Nehru during his speech in 1954 in Colombo, Sri Lanka. In this speech, Nehru described the five pillars to be used as a guide for Sino-Indian relations, which were first put forth by Chinese Premier Zhou Enlai. Called Panchsheel (five restraints), these principles would later serve as the basis of the Non-aligned Movement. The five principles were:

- Mutual respect for each other's territorial integrity and sovereignty.
- Mutual non-aggression.
- Mutual non-interference in domestic affairs.
- Equality and mutual benefit.
- Peaceful co-existence.

A significant milestone in the development of the Non-aligned Movement was the 1955 Bandung Conference, a conference of Asian and African states hosted by Indonesian President Sukarno. Sukarno has given a significant contribution to promote this movement. The attending nations declared their desire not to become involved in the Cold War and adopted a "declaration on promotion of world peace and cooperation", which included Nehru's five principles. Six years after Bandung, an initiative of Yugoslav President Tito led to the first official Non-aligned Movement Summit, which was held in September 1961 in Belgrade.

At the Lusaka Conference in September 1970, the member nations added as aims of the movement the peaceful resolution of disputes and the abstention from the big power military alliances and pacts. Another added aim was opposition to stationing of military bases in foreign countries.

The founding fathers of the Non-aligned Movement were: Sukarno of Indonesia, Nehru of India, and Josip Broz Tito of Yugoslavia, Gamal Abdul Nasser of Egypt and Kwame Nkrumah of Ghana. Their actions were known as 'The Initiative of Five'.

Organisational Structure and Membership

Requirements of the NAM with the key beliefs of the United Nations. The latest requirements are now that the candidate country has displayed practices in accordance with:

- Respect for fundamental human rights and for the purposes and principles of the Charter of the United Nations.

- Respect for the sovereignty and territorial integrity of all nations.
- Recognition of the equality of all races and of the equality of all nations, large and small.
- Abstention from intervention or interference in the internal affairs of another country.
- Respect for the right of each nation to defend itself singly or collectively, in conformity with the Charter of the United Nations.
- Refraining from acts or threats of aggression or the use of force against the territorial integrity or political independence of any country.
- Settlement of all international disputes by peaceful means, in conformity with the Charter of the United Nations.
- Promotion of mutual interests and cooperation.
- Respect for justice and international obligations.

Policies and Ideology

Secretaries General of the NAM had included such diversified figures as Suharto, an authoritarian anti-communist, and Nelson Mandela, a democratic socialist and famous anti-apartheid activist. Consisting of many governments with vastly different ideologies, the NAM is unified by its commitment in world peace and security. At the seventh summit held in New Delhi in March 1983, the movement described itself as the "history's biggest peace movement". The movement places equal emphasis on disarmament. NAM's commitment to peace pre-dates its formal institutionalisation in 1961. The Brioni meeting between heads of governments of India, Egypt and Yugoslavia in 1956 recognised that there exists a vital link between struggle for peace and endeavours for disarmament.

The Non-aligned Movement believes in policies and practices of cooperation, especially those that are multilateral and provide mutual benefit to all those involved. Many of the members of the NAM are also members of the United Nations and both organisations have a stated policy of peaceful cooperation, yet successes that the NAM has had in multilateral agreements tends to be ignored by the larger, western and developed nation dominated UN. African concerns about apartheid were linked with Arab-Asian concerns about Palestine and success of multilateral cooperation in these areas has been a stamp of moderate success for the NAM.

The NAM has played a major role in various ideological conflicts throughout its existence, including extreme opposition to apartheid regimes and support of liberation movements in various locations including Zimbabwe and South Africa. The support of these sorts of movements stems from a belief that every state has the right to base policies and practices with national interests in mind and not as a result of relations to a particular power bloc. The Non-aligned Movement has become a voice of support for issues facing developing nations and is still contains ideals that are legitimate within this context.

Contemporary Relevance

Since the end of the Cold War and the formal end of colonialism, the Non-aligned Movement has been forced to redefine itself and reinvent its purpose in the current world system. A major question has been whether many of its foundational ideologies, principally national independence, territorial integrity, and the struggle against colonialism and imperialism, can be applied to contemporary issues.

The movement has emphasised its principles of multilateralism, equality, and mutual non-aggression in attempting to become a stronger voice for the global South, and an instrument that can be utilised to promote the needs of member nations at the international level and strengthen their political leverage when negotiating with developed nations.

In its efforts to advance Southern interests, the movement has stressed the importance of cooperation and unity amongst member states, but as in the past, cohesion remains a problem since the size of the organisation and the divergence of agendas and allegiances present the ongoing potential for fragmentation. While agreement on basic principles has been smooth, taking definitive action vis-a-vis particular international issues has been rare, with the movement preferring to assert its criticism or support rather than pass hard-line resolutions.

The movement continues to see a role for itself, as in its view, the world's poorest nations remain exploited and marginalised, no longer by opposing superpowers, but rather in a unipolar world, and it is Western hegemony and neo-colonialism that the movement has really realigned itself against.

It opposes foreign occupation, interference in internal affairs, and aggressive unilateral measures, but it has also shifted to focus on the socio-economic challenges facing member states, especially the inequalities manifested by globalisation and the implications of neo-liberal policies.

The Non-aligned Movement has identified economic underdevelopment, poverty, and social injustices as growing threats to peace and security.

Later Activities and Positions

Criticism of US Policy: In recent years the US has become a target of the organisation. The US invasion of Iraq and the War on Terrorism, its attempts to stifle Iran and North Korea's nuclear plans, and its other actions have been denounced as human rights violations and attempts to run roughshod over the sovereignty of smaller nations.

The movement's leaders have also criticised the American control over the United Nations and other international structures. While the organisation has rejected terrorism, it condemns the association of terrorism with a particular religion, nationality, or ethnicity, and recognises the rights of those struggling against colonialism and foreign occupation.

Self-determination of Puerto Rico

Since 1961, the group have supported the discussion of the case of Puerto Rico's self-determination before the United Nations. A resolution on the matter will be proposed on the XV Summit by the Hostosian National Independence Movement.

Anti-Zionism

NAM's Havana Declaration of 1979 adopted anti-Zionism as part of the movement's agenda. The movement has denounced Israel's occupation of the West Bank and Gaza Strip. It has called upon Israel to halt its settlement activities, open up border crossings, and cease the use of force and violence against civilians. The UN has also been asked to pressure Israel and to do more to prevent human rights abuses.

Sustainable Development

The movement is publicly committed to the tenets of sustainable development and the attainment of the Millennium Development Goals, but it believes that the international community has not created conditions conducive to development and has infringed upon the right to sovereign development by each member state.

Issues such as globalisation, the debt burden, unfair trade practices, the decline in foreign aid, donor conditionalities, and the lack of democracy in international financial decision-making are cited as factors inhibiting development.

Reform of the UN

The Non-aligned Movement has been quite outspoken in its criticism of current UN structures and power dynamics, mostly in how the organisation has been utilised by powerful states in ways that violate the movement's principles. It has made a number of recommendations that would strengthen the representation and power of 'non-aligned' states. The proposed reforms are also aimed at improving the transparency and democracy of UN decision-making. The UN Security Council is the element considered the most distorted, undemocratic, and in need of reshaping.

South-South Cooperation

Lately the Non-aligned Movement has collaborated with other organisations of the developing world, primarily the Group of 77, forming a number of joint committees and releasing statements and document representing the shared interests of both groups. This dialogue and cooperation can be taken as an effort to increase the global awareness about the organisation and bolster its political clout.

Cultural Diversity and Human Rights

The movement accepts the universality of human rights and social justice, but fiercely resists cultural homogenisation. In line with its views on sovereignty, the organisation appeals for the protection of cultural diversity, and the tolerance of the religious, socio-cultural, and historical particularities that define human rights in a specific region.

Working Groups, Task Forces, Committees

- High-Level Working Group for the Restructuring of the United Nations.
- Working Group on Human Rights.
- Working Group on Peace-keeping Operations.
- Working Group on Disarmament.
- Committee on Palestine.
- Task Force on Somalia.
- Non-aligned Security Caucus.
- Standing Ministerial Committee for Economic Cooperation.
- Joint Coordinating Committee (chaired by Chairman of G-77 and Chairman of NAM).

Summits

- Belgrade, September 1-6, 1961.
- Cairo, October 5-10, 1964.
- Lusaka, September 8-10, 1970.
- Algiers, September 5-9, 1973.
- Colombo, August 16-19, 1976.
- Havana, September 3-9, 1979.

- New Delhi (originally planned for Baghdad), March 7-12, 1983.
- Harare, September 1-6, 1986.
- Belgrade, September 4-7, 1989.
- Jakarta, September 1-6, 1992.
- Cartagena de Indias, October 18-20, 1995.
- Durban, September 2-3, 1998.
- Kuala Lumpur, February 20-25, 2003.
- Havana, September 15-16, 2006.
- Sharm El Sheikh, July 11-16, 2009.
- Kish Island, 2012.

6

Great Policy Maker

This text examines a second case of policy-making under Nehru: the signing of the Panchsheela Agreement. It explores the sequence of strategies employed and analyses the variation in tactics and manoeuvres compared with those used to institute planning as the stratagem for India's economic development. Signed on 29th April 1954, the Panchsheela Agreement was at the time hailed as a major foreign policy achievement for India. In Nehru's words:

> "India does not propose to join any camp or alliance. But we wish to cooperate with all in the quest for peace and security and human brotherhood..... Peaceful coexistence is not a new idea for us in India. It has been our way of life and is as old as our thought and culture.....From this it has naturally followed that we should keep ourselves free from military and like alliances and have not joined any of the great power groups that dominate the world today. It is in no spirit of pride or arrogance that we pursue our independent policy. We should not do otherwise unless we were false to everything India has stood for in the past and stands for today. We welcome

association and friendship with all and the flow of thought and ideas of all kinds, but we reserve the right to choose our own path. That is the essence of *Panchsheela"*.

During the years leading up to independence Jawaharlal Nehru is usually portrayed as one of the few leaders with an interest in foreign affairs and international politics. His travels abroad and engagement with international causes like the Sino-Japanese war, the Spanish civil war and the anti-colonial movement (Brussels conference) established him as the expert in foreign policy. It is certainly the case that Nehru wrote extensively on international issues in the form of articles and books in which he often revealed a concern for global problems.

The perception of India abroad and the country's potential to be a major player in the international arena were also repeated themes in Nehru's analyses although the envisioned instruments of India's foreign policy remained vague. Contrary to common thinking however, Nehru was not the sole source of thinking on foreign affairs and the only formulator of options that were open to India. Both during the freedom struggle as well as after independence, alternative views were being voiced but these have been ignored in the literature since, by and large, these failed to be incorporated into the early phase of independent India's foreign policy.

The policy towards China in particular generated heated discussions, both in terms of India's bilateral relations with its unpredictable and relatively unknown neighbour, the newly established communist People's Republic of China, as well as raising questions about the general principles underlying India's foreign policy. As a result, the Panchsheela Agreement serves to concentrate the debate on India's China policy and India's international strategy of non-alignment, providing a useful prism through which to explore the rationale behind India's foreign policy choices in the early-1950s.

The Panchsheela Agreement is a crucial point in recent Indian history because it officially endorsed India's recognition of Tibet being a part of China and as a result, what had been Tibet-India borders became China-India borders for the first time. What is curious about the agreement is why Nehru went ahead with it despite there being a substantial amount of scepticism and objection voiced in Parliament and secondly, why Nehru felt it necessary to be conciliatory towards China when India was under no immediate pressure to do so.

These questions have not been answered in the existing literature. In fact the existing material on Nehru's foreign policy is surprisingly thin given that he was hailed and continues to be seen as the progenitor of modern Indian foreign policy. Various publications are available which simply describe the international context at the time and the various foreign policy challenges India faced. Furthermore, while Nehru's contribution to the policy of Non-Alignment is a popular topic it has not generated analytical works. This is particularly the case with regards Panchsheela, about which for a long time there was only one book in English that examined the Agreement and its repercussions: *Born in Sin: The Panchsheela Agreement, the Sacrifice of Tibet* by the French scholar, Claude Arpi. However, like Neville Maxwell's infamous *India's China War*, Arpi's book is highly polemical and considered to have been heavily biased. In Arpi's case the book is seen as leaning heavily against the Chinese whilst in Maxwell's case, he was regarded as having been far too critical of India.

In 2004, to commemorate the fifty years anniversary of the agreement, a retrospective volume of collected articles edited by former ambassador, C. V. Ranganathan was published under the title, *Panchsheela and the Future. Perspectives on India-China Relations.* Whilst interesting as material through which to assess the ongoing relevance and symbolic value of Panchsheela the contributions to these volumes are uniformly uncritical, providing little insight into the motivations and politics behind the agreement of 1954. Another example is that of the respected India scholar, Rothermund who points out the inherent problems with Nehru's China policy in a succinct paragraph:

> 'Nehru relied on the anti-imperialism of the Chinese revolutionaries. When they occupied Tibet in 1950, he did not object and immediately ceded the extra-territorial rights in Tibet. In 1954 India and China

> concluded a border treaty which unfortunately did not specify the border but only mentioned some passes open for trade between India and Tibet. The treaty also included the five principles (Panchsheela) of peaceful coexistence which Nehru repeatedly emphasised in subsequent years but which did not mean anything to the Chinese'.

However, his analysis does not go on to explore the reasons behind Nehru's fallacies, leaving the reader instead to speculate about Nehru's intentions and capabilities. This text begins with a pre-history to India's foreign policy options and priorities as moulded by the experience of being a British colony. The subject of India's borders is intimately linked to the colonial period, given that Britain maintained a strict control over defence policy and was, in fact, responsible for the treaties to which India refers to in claiming its modern-day frontiers. This is followed by a quick summary of Nehru's insights on India's foreign policy, the instruments and goals and the priorities that would set India apart from other nations and the prevailing norms of realpolitik.

His position as revealed in the Constituent Assembly Debates is examined to identify whether there was any change from his pre-independence writings.

Given that Nehru chose to associate himself so closely and intimately with the making and implementation of Indian foreign policy, the controversy surrounding his China policy-makes for an ideal window into the discussions of the time. Using an analytic narrative, the various stages of policy-formulation, articulation, debate and implementation are examined, with the 1954 agreement acting as the culminating policy outcome. By following the sequence of events, exploring the alternatives that were voiced and rejected whilst keeping in mind the particular domestic political context, a case is made that Panchsheela took shape as a politically expedient choice aimed at disarming critics at home and sceptics abroad. Like with the Planning Commission, the *political* origins of Panchsheela are explored and the argument is made that while the 'visionary' element was certainly present, this was overshadowed by the political gain Nehru hoped to achieve as a result of his foreign policy 'coup'.

A concluding section argues that Nehru misjudged the Chinese. This was both a result of misinformation and bad advice at home from close advisors that Nehru chose to surround himself with as well as a deliberate effort by the Chinese to mislead. Leaving Chinese motivations aside the point still holds that Nehru *chose* to ignore warnings, objections and cautionary advice from across the political spectrum in order to sign a document which entailed no material gains for India.

In the case of Panchsheela Nehru's strategy consisted of steamrolling his way forward in the face of opposition and calls for prudence and a concerted attempt to turn Panchsheela and India's relations with China at large, into a *non-issue* within parliamentary discussions. *Ex post facto* he justified his decision as part of India's new way of diplomacy. Unlike the Planning Commission, which took shape as part of a process of consensus-driven politics, Panchsheela emerged as a highly personal choice on Nehru's part, serving to boost his international persona and to prove his unchallenged position on international affairs at home. The proposition is considered that, having set such a precedent, subsequent foreign policy-making suffered from a highly under-institutionalised framework.

British India's Foreign Policy

Today India claims the McMahon Line to be its international border with China. This is a line that dates back to the 1914 Shimla agreement brokered by the British which calls for a brief historical background since the legacy India inherited with regards the India-Tibet/China border was a particularly complicated one. The rise of Britain and Russia as colonial powers at the beginning of the nineteenth century coincided with the decline of China and as a result Tibet took on strategic relevance in the Anglo-Russian rivalry, known then as 'The Great Game' seeking to contain Russian influence in the region and establish a British presence, army officer Francis Younghusband led a British expedition in 1903-04 to Tibet. Finding the Chinese unwilling to negotiate, since for them the Anglo-Chinese Convention of 1890 was still valid in which the British Government had implicitly recognised China's right to speak for, and on behalf of Tibet, and when no resistance was met, Younghusband marched on to Lhasa. The Anglo-Tibetan Agreement of 1904 was eventually extracted but, it was a treaty to which neither the Chinese nor the actual Dalai Lama at the time was party to and was signed instead by the acting regent. The treaty allowed the British to trade in Yadong, Gyantse and Gartok, called for Tibet to pay a large indemnity, formally recognised the Sikkim-Tibet border and declared Tibet to be a British protectorate.

By 1906 the terms of the treaty had been re-negotiated and more ambiguity was injected into the status of Tibet with the privileged position accrued to Britain under the 1904 agreement appearing to be surrendered and China recognised as having supremacy over the Tibetan Government.

The October 1911 Revolution which led to the downfall of the imperial Qing Dynasty and to the establishment of the Republic of China in 1912 exposed the country's weakness, leading to a gradual erosion of Peking's authority over large parts of western China including Mongolia, Sichuan and eventually Tibet. Taking advantage of the turmoil and Tibet's attempt to reassert its independence from China, the British restarted direct negotiations with the Tibetan Government which resulted in the Shimla Conference of 1913 where Tibet, China and British interests were to be represented. For the British, Sir Arthur Henry McMahon was the representative.

He was then Foreign Secretary of the Indian Government and brought to the negotiating table a long experience in boundary-making. It was at this conference that the crucial play on words was introduced, the agreement referring to Tibet's status as being 'under the *suzerainty* but not the *sovereignty*' (italics added) of China. As Mehra explains in his excellent book, *The McMahon Line and After*, this sought to impose a legalistic rigidity onto what had essentially been an elastic, flexible relationship between the Chinese Emperor and the Dalai Lama. The other area of long-lasting controversy pertained to the delimitation of the India-Tibet boundary which ultimately gave rise to the famed McMahon line and which remained shrouded in legal uncertainty throughout the 1920s and 30s given that it was a part of the Shimla Convention to which the Chinese ultimately had *not* been a party.

The issue of borders took on urgent relevance in 1935 when, under India's new Constitution, it became necessary to define the tribal areas in the North-East in order to place them under the control of the government of Assam. The impending separation of Burma from the rest of British India made the definition of borders all the more imperative. A clash of interests however, was emerging at the time between the India Office and Whitehall which appeared less than enthusiastic to publish any maps for fear of antagonising the Chinese and losing their trading privileges.

World War II was an additional complication given that China was an important bulwark against the Japanese onslaught that threatened British India and British interests in South East Asia. By the time of India's independence the exact status of Tibet and the Indo-Tibetan border remained beset by ambiguity. This point was driven home at the 1947 Asian Relations Conference in New Delhi, convened by Jawaharlal Nehru, to which the Tibetans made a point of attending as a distinct group separate from the Chinese with their own independent flag.

In addition to the preoccupations at home and the overwhelming logistics and trauma of the partition which divided British India into the two separate nations of Pakistan and India, New Delhi at the time of independence had to cope with Tibetan as well as Chinese encroachments along its eastern frontier. In Tawang for instance, south of the McMahon line and the seat of an important lamaist monastery, a struggle was underway between Tibet and the Assam government to establish authority for example in the form of tax collection.

However, both Whitehall and later New Delhi seem to have had their hands tied, unwilling to negotiate directly with the Tibetans for fear of upsetting Peking.

On October 1st, 1949 the new People's Republic of China was proclaimed, bringing an end to more than two decades of civil war and driving out the Kuomintang regime under Chiang Kai Shek from the mainland to Taiwan whilst the Communists took charge in Beijing. Not long after taking control, the Communists proclaimed as a central objective, the 'liberation' of Tibet from the alleged intrigues and interferences of western imperialists and on October 7th, 1950 the People's Liberation Army marched into Tibet.

Nehru on Foreign Affairs: the Constituent Assembly Debates

The linkage between foreign policy and nation-building was strongly advocated by Nehru and is a theme that became increasingly prevalent in his speeches on foreign policy in the run-up to and after independence. In a speech to the Constituent Assembly in December 1947, Nehru clearly stated that 'Ultimately foreign policy is the outcome of economic policy, and till that time, when India has properly evolved her economic policy, her foreign policy will be rather vague, rather inchoate, and will grope about.' This link drawn between the economy and foreign policy was to persist and explains to some extent India's policy of non-alignment which also consisted of receiving economic aid from both blocs, sometimes at the same time.

What is noteworthy is how little the topic of non-alignment came up for discussion in the Constituent Assembly for there are comparatively speaking, few debates specifically on the subject. In some of the rare occasions when the topic was raised, Nehru spoke of the need to navigate the emerging tensions and faultiness of the Cold War where "India, in so far as it has a foreign policy, has declared that it wants to remain independent and free of all these blocks and that it wants to cooperate on equal terms with all countries".

However, it was acknowledged that India was going to have to use, what has been called, weapons of the weak, or, as Nehru himself put it, "to function as peace-makers and peace-bringers because today we are not strong enough to be able to have our way". Following the logic underlying the implementation of 'weapons of the weak', Nehru opted for an international stance which frequently castigated the great powers on their actions and their motives. His reprimands and scolding style was perfected by his representative to the United Nations, Krishna Menon.

By March 1948, Nehru's statements had become grander with him arguing that 'India even today counts in world affairs and the trouble you see in the United Nations or in the Security Council is because she counts, not because she does not count..... It is not a question of our viewpoint or of attaching ourselves to this or that bloc; it is merely the fact that we are potentially a great nation and big power.....' The trouble Nehru referred to pertained to the quagmire that was developing over the issue of Kashmir and the often unwelcome interventions that India was making on the question of Palestine among other issues. It is this tone and belief in the manifest destiny of India to play a major role in world politics which progressively intensified in the following years and during the decade of the 1950s.

The Discourse on Foreign Policy: Alternatives to and Critics of Nehru

Right from the early days, Nehru's speeches are laden with references to world problems. In Nehru's outlook, India's interests often seemed to be global rather than national.

The 1950 war in Korea was one of the first international missions for Nehru and India, and China already featured prominently in this for it was India's special access to China which Nehru often referred to. For example, in a speech to the interim Parliament in 1950 Nehru announced, 'we were in intimate touch with our Ambassador in Peking and we asked him, as we asked our representatives in other countries, to tell us how the various Governments were viewing the scene. We had perhaps a rather special responsibility in regard to China, because we were one of the very few countries represented there, and we were the only country, apart from the countries of the Soviet group, which could find out through the Ambassador what the reactions of the Chinese Government were to the developing events'.

In the same speech Nehru talked about the Chinese 'liberation' of Tibet and acknowledged that the government was taken by surprise when China sent military troops into Tibet, especially since China had agreed to settling the matter through peaceful negotiations. Nevertheless Nehru saw no indication in this of China's duplicity nor did he doubt the reliability and credibility of his ambassador, K. M. Panikkar in Beijing.

In fact it was either rather naive of Nehru or highly presumptuous to imagine that the information which the Chinese were passing on to Ambassador Pannikkar could be taken at face value. To either assume that India had special access or that China was not politically savvy enough to be playing its own international game of diplomacy, smacks of arrogance. A further slap in the face came on 30 October 1950 when China made it clear in a Government note, that Tibet was part of China and therefore entirely a domestic problem and no foreign interference would be tolerated. The Chinese army had been dispatched to 'liberate the Tibetan people and defend the frontiers of China'. It also denounced India's attempt to link the Tibet issue with that of China's United Nations membership and alleged that India had been 'affected by foreign influences hostile to China in Tibet'.

It is interesting to note that India's reply was strongly worded. The note described India's amazement at being referred to as an instrument of the foreign hand and assured China that 'it had no desire to interfere or gain any advantage' and that it had sought a peaceful settlement to the Tibet issue, 'adjusting the legitimate Tibetan claim to autonomy within the framework of Chinese suzerainty'. India had no territorial ambitions in Tibet but 'certain rights have grown out of usage and agreements which are natural among neighbours with close cultural and commercial relations'. These had emerged in the form of trade agencies in Gyantse and Yatung and the maintenance of post and telegraph services on the route as well as a small military escort to protect the trade route. India, the note stated, was 'anxious that these establishments, which are to the mutual interest of India and Tibet, and do not detract in any way from Chinese suzerainty in Tibet', should continue. The position taken in this document is revealing since it makes clear that while India recognised Tibet as part of China, it was keen to maintain its extra-territorial rights. China's reply of 16 November ignored the reference to these rights.

Criticising Nehru's stance, N. G. Ranga's interpretation provides a *realist* alternative to the Nehru vision of foreign policy, drawing attention to the fact that the Chinese people may be favourable towards India but the important factor was to gauge the leaders of the Chinese people: 'Who is in charge of the Chinese Government today? Could we be indifferent to the fact that only the other day it was none else than the Chinese Government which had hinted that India was the foreign power in Tibet which was supposed to be queering the pitch?'

Dr. S. P. Mukherjee, another vocal member of Parliament and critic of Nehru's foreign policy made the point that instead of the laurels Nehru bestowed upon himself and India for its role in the Korean crisis, the country ought to learn from the incident, and in particular be aware to the fact that China had acquired enormous strength to the extent of being able to meet on the battle-ground the finest forces of the United States and other allied powers. Following in the wake of China's intervention in Tibet, the Korean crisis ought to have been treated with greater gravity by the Indian government. As he pointed out, 'We have got to look at these problems undoubtedly from the point of view of world peace but principally also from the manner in which our own position may be affected'.

Yet another valid critique was given by Acharya Kripalani, whose speeches in Parliament presented a logical dissection of Indian foreign policy, beginning with the underlying premises guiding policy to the final intended and unintended outcomes that such a policy was likely to produce. As he rightly pointed out in 1950, despite India and Nehru's vocal stance on international issues, at the end of 1950 India could claim no friends in the international arena amongst the major powers like China, Russia, and United States. An explanation for this was offered by Kripalani, 'I suppose all these things have happened because our basic philosophy is wrong, that is we want to judge every action on its own merits. Another reason for this is that we think we will fight for just causes, or is it lost causes? Neutrality cannot be combined with the urge to reform the world'. Minoo Masani, who later went on to co-found the conservative Swatantra party, endorsed India's commitment to world peace but cautioned about the need to develop a system of collective security. As he rightly asked, had India tried to develop a regional system of collective security? Apart from the moralistic rhetoric, Masani argued that India needed to take a more proactive stance which would demonstrate that the country was not willing to appease or condone aggression of any kind. As he pointed out, 'if we do not do these things....... we shall be strengthening those forces of isolationism in the West which will be prepared to write off Asia, because Asia is not prepared under its present leadership to defend its own freedom and its own collective security'.

On the subject of China, Masani like the other critics, cautioned that in light of China's actions in Korea, Tibet and Indo-China, together with China's rhetoric accusing India of instigating resistance in Tibet and of Nehru being the running dog of Anglo-American imperialism, 'there can be no longer any illusions about friendship in Asia. By the one act of attacking Tibet and deceiving the Indian Government after their assurances given repeatedly, they have shown their utter contempt for the idea that we embraced, namely of a free and united Asia'.

Of course there were defenders of Nehru's position but it is noteworthy that in 1950 the critics far outnumbered the supporters. Among the arguments promoting Nehru's vision in its early days included the point that 'with so small a military force at our disposal he has succeeded in making India respected out of all proportion to our military strength and today the world recognises that we are really independent and that we follow an independent foreign policy'. The discussions in Parliament are also valuable for providing an insight into the dilemmas facing the newly founded Indian state in formulating a foreign policy that could be billed as both radically new as well as encapsulating an ancient Indian genius.

Hence, there were those who advocated Communism as the only way to bring about far-reaching changes to India's economic and social situation and which in turn implied a more favourable attitude towards other fellow communist countries. Others, recognising the merits in the goals of Communism rejected its methods, as manifested in domestic politics as well as international behaviour. Whilst some proposed that Communism would be more appropriate for the Indian condition where discipline, direction and regimentation would bring about more results than democracy which reinforced the existing tendency towards a lack of cohesion and discipline, others pointed out that in a country where religion played such a vital role, Communism would require a spiritual dissolution.

In responding to his critics, Nehru was adamant that 'the real development and strength of an army and a country lies in developing the industrial resources and the economy of the country out of which armies and defence forces and everything come'. On the whole Nehru's tendency in reacting to criticism seems to have been to call into question the expertise and proficiency of his critics. For example, closing the December 6-7th parliamentary consideration of the International Situation and India's foreign policy, Nehru's speech challenges each of his detractors. Thus, he accuses members of being 'full of light – they have no need to grope ....in the darkness that surrounds us..... They know exactly what should be done at any moment. I envy them for this feeling of brightness and lightness'.

On the point that India's foreign policy lacked realism, Nehru countered, 'It seemed to me that those people who pride themselves of being practical politicians normally know nothing about realism or about the state of affairs'. On the subject of whether India ought to lean towards any one of the two blocs, or whether if at all there were two blocs, Nehru sharply retorted, 'these questions and these arguments are completely out-of-date. They do not count today... And today if a person thinks in this manner it merely means he is yesterday's man...... and not keeping pace with the changing world and changing events'.

To dismiss the alternatives and questions proposed and raised by members on India's approach to China, Nehru's words were often mocking, 'Do you meant to tell me that I should issue an ultimatum to China not to do this or that..... and tell them that it is foolish to have a doctrine of Communism'. To those who worried about India's foreign policy as being one of sitting on the fence, Nehru again demonstrated an inclination towards denigrating those who opposed him: 'I say we have taken a more active part in the past two or three years in foreign policy than many other countries, barring the Big Powers. I do not understand this business, except that these people who talk like that know nothing about what they are talking of and do not study or read or understand what is happening around them.'

The extensive debates in Parliament on international affairs reveal that in the very early-1950s there was a great interest in the subject and most importantly, there were a number of dissenting voices. In particular with regards to India's strategy towards China much caution and circumspection was advocated. The parameters of discourse were wide open and it is surprising to read the various standpoints being articulated in opposition to or in criticism of Nehru's policies. Judging from the various stances taken during the parliamentary discussions in the early-1950s, it appears that there was a healthy framework for debate in place, representing a variety of positions ranging from the extremely hawkish, to the pacifist, from those advocating world peace to the more realist-driven interpretations of international politics, the primacy of the national interest and the vital importance of defence.

This is surprising because the literature on India's foreign relations of the 1950s tends to cast Nehru as the sole articulator, formulator and executor of Indian foreign policy, unchallenged and unmatched in his expertise and reading of the international situation. The narrative above has demonstrated that this was clearly not the case and there were harbingers of the problems India was to encounter with China following the 'liberation' of Tibet. Hence, as one speaker warned, 'This uncertain boundary line between Tibet and India will be another excuse for intervention'.

Sardar Vallabhbhai Patel, then the Home Minister, was among the most prescient, writing a long letter to Jawaharlal on November 7, 1950 in which he drew Nehru's attention to the danger from China and also recommended certain actions. It is necessary to quote Patel at length to get a taste of his perceptive analysis at a time when he himself was very ill and soon to die: "I have carefully gone through the correspondence between the External Affairs Ministry and our Ambassador in Peking and through him the Chinese Government. There can be no doubt that during the period covered by this correspondence the Chinese must have been concentrating for an onslaught on Tibet.

The final action of the Chinese, in my judgement, is little short of perfidy...... Even though we regard ourselves as friends of China, the Chinese do not regard us as their friends. During the last several months, outside the Russian camp, we have practically been alone in championing the cause of Chinese entry into the UNO and in securing from the Americans assurances on the question of Formosa...... I doubt if we can go any further than we have done already to convince China of our good intentions, friendliness and goodwill.... Their last telegram to us is an act of gross discourtesy not only in the summary way it disposes of our protest against the entry of Chinese forces into Tibet but also in the wild insinuation that our attitude is determined by foreign influences. It looks as though it is not a friend speaking in that language but a *potential enemy*.". Sardar Patel continued, "In the background of this, we have to consider the situation that now faces us as a result of the disappearance of Tibet...... The Chinese interpretation of suzerainty seems to be different. We can, therefore, safely assume that very soon they will disown all the stipulations which Tibet has entered into with us in the past".

In addition to this, Patel provided a list of actions India ought to take with regards to improving intelligence-gathering, consolidating military guards at important routes or areas likely to be under dispute, updating communications with frontier outposts, developing a policy on the issue of the MacMahon line. Of critical importance, Patel strongly advised the need to improve relations with the population on the North-East frontier who needed to be fully assimilated into the Union of India which was both a political and administrative task.

In contrast with Nehru, who spoke always in terms of the international consequences of foreign policy or how India's reputation was at stake, Patel possessed a hardnosed practical realism with a primary concern for domestic politics. A note sent by Jawaharlal Nehru guiding the foreign department and instructions to be sent to B. N. Rao, India's representative at the UNO on the position to be taken should Tibet come up for discussion in the Security Council, provides an apt contrast.

In one place the note states, "I think that it is exceedingly unlikely that we may have to face any real military invasion from the Chinese side... in the foreseeable future. I base this conclusion on a consideration of various world factors." Going on, Nehru provided his assessment of China's strategic situation: "China, though internally big, is in a way amorphous and easily capable of being attacked on its sea coasts and by air. ...It is inconceivable that it should divert its forces and its strength across the inhospitable terrain of Tibet and undertake a wild adventure across the Himalayas. Any such attempt will greatly weaken its capacity to meet its real enemies on other fronts." That this precisely might have been the right time for India to take a forceful position before China got any stronger did not fit Nehru's self-perception of being the magnanimous statesman.

Nevertheless events proved Patel to be the more accurate reader of relations between the two countries, and this was despite the fact that he was not the external affairs minister nor did he profess to have an understanding of 'world factors'.

The Panchsheela Agreement: An Analytic Narrative of Intentions, Functions and Constraints

The Agreement on Tibet (otherwise known as the Panchsheela Agreement) was signed in Beijing on 29 April, 1954. Its practical provisions pertained to the:

- Establishment of three trade agencies by each side;
- Recognition of a number of trade marts; and
- Facilities for traditional pilgrimages in both countries by persons of Hindu and Buddhist faiths.

Apart from Gartok, to the east of Shimla in Himachal Pradesh, the trade agencies granted to India were in locations where India already possessed rights and was choosing to relinquish these as an act of good faith. These included military escorts stationed at Yatung and Gyantse in Tibet and postal, telegraph and public-telephone services along with twelve rest-houses and other buildings owned by the Government of India in Tibet. In contrast China was not only given completely new rights to set up trade agencies in India but in addition, these were to be located in such important cities as the capital, New Delhi and in the state of West Bengal Calcutta and Kalimpong which could have been strategically important trade portals.

It is also noteworthy that throughout the document Tibet was referred to as the 'Tibet Region of China', clearly endorsing China's legitimate control over Tibet.

The preamble contains the famed 'Five Principles of Peaceful Coexistence' or *Panchsheela*. Literally meaning, the 'five principles of rules of conduct' in Sanskrit, Panchsheela was drawn from the original Buddhist conception of ten negative prohibitions and 18 positive injunctions that must be followed in the pursuit of enlightenment. The five principles refer to the basic concepts of moral behaviour which all must follow, known in Buddhism as *Pansil*. This was first applied to politics in Indonesia by President Sukarno who in 1945 formulated the five basic principles of his state policy: belief in God, humanitarianism, nationalism, democracy and social justice. Given the close relationship between Nehru and Sukarno and India's support of Indonesia's freedom struggle against the Dutch it is quite possible that Nehru borrowed the idea, going one step further to apply the guiding principles to inter-state relations.

Signed by India's Ambassador to China, N. R. Raghavan and China's Vice-Minister for Foreign Affairs, Change Han-Fu, the document's preamble contained the five principles of:

- Mutual respect for each other's territorial integrity and sovereignty;
- Mutual non-aggression;
- Mutual non-interference in each other's internal affairs;
- Equality and mutual benefit; and
- Peaceful coexistence.

Describing the agreement in Parliament on 15 May, 1954 (after it had been signed), Nehru proclaimed, 'These principles not only indicate the policy that we pursue in regard to these matters not only with China but with any neighbouring country, or, for that matter, any other country, but it is also a statement of wholesome principles'. The way Nehru projected the Panchsheela Agreement, it is clear that he considered it to be something which could teach the international community something about diplomacy.

Arguing that 'Collective Security' initiatives are equivalent to 'preparations for collective war', he portrayed Panchsheela as an exercise in 'collective peace, with no element of aggression against any country'. Further on in the speech after having covered, what he saw to be, India's unofficial but morally correct stance on the Indo-China problem and the highly independent position taken by India advocating clemency for Japanese war criminals, Nehru reiterated the importance of India's approach which 'is that of trying to work for collective peace.... The other collective security that, – all the time, by threats and fear of mounting armaments — is not even bringing a climate of peace'.

Significantly, Nehru attached the most meaning to the Preamble. The individual articles which contained the substance of the agreement and basically signed away India's privileges in exchange for next to nothing were, it seems, not the crux of the matter. The emphasis and attention was directed at the preamble containing the five principles of peaceful coexistence, which in fact the Chinese were initially reluctant to include! It is also telling that the document was signed as the dryly titled, 'Agreement between the Government of the Republic of India and the Government of the People's Republic of China on Trade and Inter-Course between Tibet Region of China and India' and did not technically go by the name *Panchsheela,* the 'Five Principles of Peaceful Coexistence'. The large number of issues dealt with in the document, did not include any reference to border concerns, but addressed trade, pilgrim traffic, communications. All these, Nehru explained are small points in comparison to 'the major thing about this agreement...the preamble'.

On the issue of Tibet and the fact that the 1954 agreement gave *de facto* recognition to China's recently acquired position in Tibet, Nehru's defence interestingly, consisted of trying to further blur the already thin lines of distinction between the concepts of 'sovereignty' and 'suzerainty'. Granted that the difference between the two is subtle it is important to note that in his speech, Nehru used them interchangeably which must have been a deliberate choice for he could have alternatively chosen to emphasise the differences in meaning and to dissect the implications for India. Instead, he stated, 'I am not aware of any time during the last few hundred years when Chinese sovereignty or if you like suzerainty was challenged by any outside country'.

Although, by May 1954 the open criticism of Nehru in parliamentary debates on foreign affairs was considerably less compared with the discussions in 1950, a few voices persisted in raising questions about Nehru's choice of action. It is interesting to note that among the last to oppose or question Nehru's arguments and policy choices, was Acharya Kripalani, leader in the Socialist Party. In 1953 Kripalani sharply criticised what he referred to as India's 'posturing on the international stage'. Describing India's involvement in the aftermath of the Korean crisis, Kripalani provided a synopsis of how India's dabbling in international affairs ended up annoying all the parties involved to the point where India's volunteered custodian troops, provided to man the ceasefire line, could not even touch the soil of South Korea and had to be airdropped into the neutral zone.

In a criticism aimed at Nehru's high profile style of diplomacy, Kripalani advocated that especially in times 'when nations are suffering from a kind of hysteria, it will be best for us to cultivate our garden and confine ourselves largely to the four corners of the home front'. In the 1954 discussion Kripalani was a lone voice in condemning China's actions in Tibet and questioning the trustworthiness of China.

In the May 15, 1954 debate Acharya Kripalani was clear in his denunciation of China's actions in Tibet. If India was going to stand up to Western acts of colonial aggression, he argued, then India should also be able to condemn China's act of colonial aggression. Describing Tibet as culturally more akin to India than Communist China, China's act of deliberate aggression constituted a case where, 'one nation by force of arms, or fraud occupies the territory of another nation'. Going on to puncture the grandiose portrayal of the Asian Prime Ministers Conference held in Ceylon which Nehru had depicted as unique and historical, Kripalani pointed out that 'An Asian Prime Minister's Conference without the Near East, without Japan, without even China, does not become an Asian conference'.

Cautioning that neutrality lasted only as long as it served a nation's purpose, Kripalani was one of the few to openly state that the conference did not contribute anything concrete other than simply adding to the prestige of India and Ceylon.

This is interesting because by 1954, communist voices, like H. N. Mukherjee had considerably toned down their opposition to Nehru, especially following the 1954 Panchsheela Agreement which had bestowed so many advantages on Communist China.

Since the early-1950s, Mukherjee had been advocating an even more positive and pro-China stance to be taken up by India for instance on the question of China's membership of the United Nations. Even in September 1953 Mukherjee's response to Nehru's opening speech was full of censuring remarks and observations. On the issue of Kashmir (treated as a foreign policy subject in the Lok Sabha debates) Mukherjee demanded stronger action and on the subject of relations with Nepal he was highly critical of India's attempt to meddle in Nepalese politics.

Most crucially perhaps was Mukherjee's stance regarding India's membership of the Commonwealth. Given Nehru's support for India's membership and continued close association with Britain this must have threatened to turn into a politically explosive issue with sufficient emotive value to be able to rally popular opposition. In his contribution to the debates of 17 September, 1953 Mukherjee's speech was largely devoted to criticising Nehru's relations with Britain and the image that was being created of India and Pakistan acting as 'the brokers doing the dirty job for these imperialists'. Here he was referring to the emerging Suez Crisis and the suggestions that were being made at the time in the international press that India and Pakistan, fresh from the Coronation and the Commonwealth Conference in London, could carry Britain's message and press for Britain's case.

In this speech Mukherjee accused Nehru's policies of being pusillanimous, daring him to act 'really and truly in consistency with the spirit of our national movement'. Such spirited criticism was almost non-existent in the foreign policy debates from the mid-1950s on.

Defending the agreement in the Lok Sabha on 30 September 1954, Nehru lambasted his critics who had referred to the 'melancholy chapter of Tibet'. Advising members of the House to read the history of British India, China and Tibet, Nehru asked 'What did any honourable member of this House expect us to do in regard to Tibet any time?... Where do we come into the picture unless we want to assume the aggressive role of interfering with other countries?' Answering his own question Nehru added, 'We do not go like Don Quixote with lance in hand against everything we dislike; we put up with these things because we would be, without making any difference, only getting into trouble'.

With the 1954 Panchsheela Agreement, it is possible to note a crucial change in the political arena, both in terms of the parameters of debate and in the actual style of foreign policy-making. Criticism, dissenting views and a consideration of alternatives to the Prime Minister's views on India's foreign policy had become markedly reduced whilst those supporting the government dominated the debate. Sycophancy towards Nehru had become commonplace by the mid-1950s. Take for example the words of parliamentary member, Mr. Joachim Alva: 'It should not be merely enough that we have a foreign policy. We have a Prime Minister who has perhaps given us the best foreign policy. He will perhaps be known in history as the greatest Foreign Minister our country ever had. Perhaps he is the greatest Foreign Minister in the world today'.

Furthermore, the explicitly pro-Chinese tilt which the Agreement symbolised and endorsed through its provisions, resulted in the implantation of a bias towards China in the foreign policy-making establishment, a constraint which continues to influence India's policy towards China. While the communists were appeased to a large extent by the pro-China nature of the agreement, the Socialists remained on the fringes. Kripalani's views for instance were usually dismissed as unworkable, illogical or even fantastical. As a result, the 'socialist' position, despite Nehru's professed socialist inclinations, was not incorporated into the general corpus of foreign policy goals and priorities. One possible explanation, for this is the undue influence that Krishna Menon and K. N. Panikkar wielded over Nehru and the fact that they were themselves more inclined towards communism rather than a more moderate form of socialism.

This was probably compounded by the long-running rivalry between Nehru and Kripalani dating back to pre-independence days, even continuing into 1962 when Kripalani contested a seat in the general elections from North Bombay, in opposition to Krishna Menon who was being openly backed by Nehru and the Congress party machinery. Furthermore, in the mid-1950s it was only the communists who posed any real challenge to Nehru as a political force, the rest of the opposition being far too fragmented to constitute a real front against Nehru. Hence, policies which also won the approval of the Communists meant that Nehru faced no real threat to his position in power.

The Implications of Panchsheela

Taking the 1954 agreement to be an affirmation of the good relations between India and China, Nehru projected Panchsheela as an internationally-applicable code of conduct. A joint statement issued by Prime Ministers Zhou En-Lai and Jawaharlal Nehru on June 28, 1954 proclaimed, "If these principles are applied not only between various countries but also in international relations generally, they would form a solid foundation for peace and security and the fears and apprehensions, that exist today would give place to a feeling of confidence". At the Bandung Afro-Asian summit of April 1955 the five principles were fully embodied in a ten point declaration which set out the framework governing relations amongst member countries and on Independence day, August 15, 1955, Nehru hailed Panchsheela as the guarantee of international peace and amity and as a code of conduct for application to international problems.

While Bandung represented a convergence of Indian and Chinese policies on the Panchsheela principles, it was China that emerged as the star of the conference. Chou En-Lai's speech of 19 April, affirmed China's allegiance to the Five Principles and underlined his endeavour to 'seek common ground and not create divergence' but a deadlock quickly ensured between countries that were aligned and those that professed a commitment to non-alignment.

The draft resolution on colonialism reached a stalemate when some participants insisted that communism should be denounced as a new form of colonialism. An impassioned speech by Nehru deprecated the approach of the pro-Western participants whilst Ceylon's Sir John Kotewala demanded that in pursuit of co-existence, China should ask all local communist parties in Asia and Africa to disband and use its influence with the Soviet Union to dissolve the Cominform. Nehru, trying to bring about a consensus, recognised that both communism and anti-communism (equated with the Cominform and SEATO respectively) were dangerous and, that if co-existence was to be real, such organisations would have to wind up. The show however, was stolen by Chou En-Lai who made an unexpected and sensational statement, announcing China's willingness to negotiate with the United States and to discuss the relaxation of tensions in the Far East and especially in the Formosa area. This was regarded as a major breakthrough and a highly praiseworthy gesture on China's part. As a result it was China, and particularly in the form of the individual, Chou En-Lai, who was seen to have been the central player at the Bandung Conference. Nehru himself recognised this, writing to his Chief Ministers afterwards that, 'The Prime Minister of China, Chou Enlai, attracted the most attention both in public and in the Conference. This was natural as he was not only playing a great part in the crisis of the Far East (Indo-China) but was rather a mysterious figure whom people had not seen.'

As a result, China at Bandung clearly outdid India, making critical diplomatic gains whilst India came away with little that was concrete in terms of policy achievements, apart from providing Nehru with the opportunity to play the role of chairperson. Providing China with a platform through which to demonstrate its independence from the Soviet Union, the Bandung Conference enabled China to make contacts with Indonesia, Egypt and Pakistan, countries which were later to become important allies. To demonstrate, China's diplomatic offensive it is noteworthy that between November 1955 and February 1956, Chou En-Lai visited eight Asian countries (North Vietnam, Cambodia, India, Burma, Pakistan, Afghanistan, Nepal and Ceylon).

By the end of 1955, Panchsheela had been internationally launched, heralded in speeches at home and abroad, enshrined in agreements and used to cement bi-lateral relations. Nehru had made a concerted effort to embed Panchsheela within a legacy of Indian tradition and ethos, portraying it as the natural choice for a country with India's ancient history and experience of peaceful resistance during the freedom struggle.

Furthermore 'Peaceful Coexistence' was often described as the 'perfect approach between two countries to rule out aggression or interference.' During these years, leading up to the 1954 agreement and into 1955, Panchsheela was also promoted as a cornerstone for the country's non-alignment policy. For example in his report to the AICC on 10 January 1955, Nehru proclaimed that 'At a moment when the countries of the world become increasingly intolerant towards each other, we have to remember that tolerance is not only a virtue but the only practical approach to the problems of today..... In the international field this may be called coexistence and the application of the *Panchsheela*, the Five Principles.... This coexistence is not merely an absence of war and conflict but a recognition that each country should live its own life and not interfere with others and should have friendly approach to other countries, even though they differ from it in many ways.'

Vision and Strategy in the Panchsheela Agreement

Tibet plays a critical role in India's national security given that it shares a 2000 mile border with India. Despite the fact that India and China went to war in 1962 over the border and that the Panchsheela Agreement effectively came to an end after its eight year validity lapsed, the issue of Tibet and the symbolism behind the agreement continue to be of relevance in terms of the constraints they impose on India's China policy. What emerges from a close analysis of the sequence of events is that Nehru did not possess a well thought-out strategy towards China. His early writings reveal that he spent little time considering this subject which mostly consisted of visualising Asian unity based on Indian leadership and Sino-Indian friendship. Once in power, his policy-making style indicated a tendency to respond in an *ad hoc* fashion to events. This was on occasion justified by Nehru who claimed India's approach to international politics was to think of a response on the basis of assessing events as they occurred and on their own terms, rather than part of an overall string of causally related moves. However, in 1950 Nehru's policy on China faced a major crisis.

China's 'liberation' of Tibet through the use of military force called into question India's ability to influence China let alone world peace. At the time Nehru was proclaiming that India had a special role to play in international affairs and was strenuously projecting the country's role as mediator in the Korean crisis. This was to be a way of launching India on the international podium. China's military intervention in Tibet was however, a flagrant rejection of Nehru's advice to use peaceful methods and furthermore, it exposed the weaknesses in Nehru's defence policy which had not planned for a scenario where India would share a direct border with China.

The confusion and errors surrounding the use of sovereignty versus suzerainty in official notes did not add to Nehru's credentials as an effective statesman and the debates in Parliament in 1950 and 1951 contained a number of disapproving voices. Furthermore it has to be remembered that Nehru's position within the Congress party was far from secure during this period. As a result, a foreign policy breakthrough was imperative and Panchsheela developed into a timely opportunity to showcase India's, or rather, Nehru's diplomatic skills and, to confirm the wisdom of non-alignment. With the agreement India waived its rights in Tibet as a gesture of good will to China, in consonance with India's stand on inherited colonial privileges, and at the same time, the preamble's 'Five Principles of Peaceful Coexistence', acted as India's voice to the world, through which Nehru hoped to be heard and lauded. For a document of such significance, Panchsheela evolved within a relatively short space of time, in response to the changed circumstances of the border region. There is no evidence in Nehru's writings of his having pondered or conceived of the idea early on.

Hence, the move by India to relinquish its rights in Tibet has to be seen as a calculated move given that the McMahon line, despite being a colonial legacy, was not put up for negotiation.

The technicalities of the agreement were worked out in a relatively short period of time (talks were initiated in December 1953 and four months later, the agreement was signed) which also implies that there was an urgency underlying the initiative which could only have been political in nature since there were no economic gains or interests to be made or satisfied.

India's security was also not directly at risk since China was concerned with other threats at the time from within and in the Korean Peninsula. As a result, the agreement on Tibet need not have taken place at all or, alternatively, it could have restricted itself to its functional purpose of clarifying India's status with regards Tibet, minus the preamble which was essentially superfluous.

Instead, by turning the document into an enunciation of visionary principles the treaty was given an unrealistic and unsustainable significance. To claim that Panchsheela was going to act as a code of conduct was foolhardy given that (a) India did not have the defence system in place to ensure its territorial integrity nor (b) an internationally recognised border with China. In essence the agreement relied on goodwill on the part of the Chinese as the superior military force, and India's interpretations of the border, as the 'superior' moral force.

Since India's security in the early-1950s was not threatened by China to the point that last measures had to be resorted to, and since India's security was not enhanced by the 1954 agreement, as quickly became apparent, it is possible to conclude that the agreement was primarily a means through which to boost Nehru's prestige as a statesman.

It appears therefore, that Panchsheela, despite its visionary content and the visionary proclamations used to promote it, had a clearly instrumental role to play and, was aimed at both audiences at home and abroad. Unfortunately, this instrumental value was directly related to Nehru's kudos and not to serving the security interests of the country.

The example of Panchsheela demonstrates how Nehru successfully used the structure of opportunities to his advantage. Unlike in the case of Planning, there did not exist as wide a spectrum of well-formed and well-represented alternatives to Nehru's worldview and prognoses.

Hence there was no need, nor was it in his interest to encourage any institutional framework for the formulation and conduct of foreign policy, to the extent that foreign policy was turned into a non-issue in parliamentary debates and press conferences. Only with the outbreak of crises such as the 1950 PRC 'liberation' of Tibet or in the build-up to the 1962 war was Nehru's decision-making and foreign policy choices brought under scrutiny.

The Panchsheela agreement, emerged not so much as a basis for foreign policy-making (it was far too vague in its pronouncements for that) but rather to symbolise the success of Nehru's diplomacy. Serving to silence sceptics and critics both on the Left and the Right, the agreement was a coup for Nehru in the short run but failed to set guidelines for Indian foreign policy in the longer run. What is noteworthy is that despite the highly favourable conditions to mould India's foreign policy according to his preferences, Nehru's legacy in foreign policy unravelled quite early on after his death.

Father of Planning

Planning Commission (India)

The Planning Commission is an institution in the Government of India, which formulates India's Five-Year Plans, among other functions.

History

Rudimentary economic planning, deriving the sovereign authority of the state, first began in India in 1930s under the British Raj, and the colonial government of India formally established a planning board that functioned from 1944 to 1946. Private industrialists and economist formulated at least three development plans in 1944.

After India gained independence, a formal model of planning was adopted, and the planning commission, reporting directly to the Prime Minister of India was established. Accordingly, the Planning Commission was set up on 15 March 1950, with Prime Minister Jawaharlal Nehru as the chairman. Planing Commission though is a non-statutory as well extra constitutional body, i.e. has been brought by an executive order.

The first Five-year Plan was launched in 1951 and two subsequent five-year plans were formulated till 1965, when there was a break because of the Indo-Pakistan Conflict. Two successive years of drought, devaluation of the currency, a general rise in prices and erosion of resources disrupted the planning process and after three Annual Plans between 1966 and 1969, the fourth Five-year plan was started in 1969.

The Eighth Plan could not take off in 1990 due to the fast changing political situation at the Centre and the years 1990-91 and 1991-92 were treated as Annual Plans. The Eighth Plan was finally launched in 1992 after the initiation of structural adjustment policies.

For the first eight Plans the emphasis was on a growing public sector with massive investments in basic and heavy industries, but since the launch of the Ninth Plan in 1997, the emphasis on the public sector has become less pronounced and the current thinking on planning in the country, in general, is that it should increasingly be of an indicative nature.

Organisation

The composition of the Commission has undergone a lot of change since its inception. With the Prime Minister as the ex-officio Chairman, the committee has a nominated Deputy Chairman, who is given the rank of a full Cabinet Minister. Mr. Montek Singh Ahluwalia is presently the Deputy Chairman of the Commission.

Cabinet Ministers with certain important portfolios act as part-time members of the Commission, while the full-time members are experts of various fields like Economics, Industry, Science and General Administration.

The Commission works through its various divisions, of which there are three kind:

- General Planning Divisions.
- Programme Administration Divisions.

The majority of experts in the Commission are economists, making the Commission the biggest employer of the Indian Economic Services.

Functions:

- Assessment of resources of the country.
- Formulation of Five-Year Plans for effective use of these resources.
- Determination of priorities, and allocation of resources for the Plans.
- Determination of requisite machinery for successful implementation of the Plans.
- Periodical appraisal of the progress of the Plan.

- To formulate plans for the most effective and balanced utilisation of country's resources.
- To indicate the factors which are hampering economic development.

The Background

Jawaharlal Nehru, as the First Chairman of the Planning Commission: The Planning Commission was set up by a Resolution of the Government of India in March 1950 in pursuance of declared objectives of the Government to promote a rapid rise in the standard of living of the people by efficient exploitation of the resources of the country, increasing production and offering opportunities to all for employment in the service of the community. The Planning Commission was charged with the responsibility of making assessment of all resources of the country, augmenting deficient resources, formulating plans for the most effective and balanced utilisation of resources and determining priorities. Jawaharlal Nehru was the first Chairman of the Planning Commission.

The first Five-year Plan was launched in 1951 and two subsequent five-year plans were formulated till 1965, when there was a break because of the Indo-Pakistan Conflict. Two successive years of drought, devaluation of the currency, a general rise in prices and erosion of resources disrupted the planning process and after three Annual Plans between 1966 and 1969, the fourth Five-year plan was started in 1969.

The Eighth Plan could not take off in 1990 due to the fast changing political situation at the Centre and the years 1990-91 and 1991-92 were treated as Annual Plans. The Eighth Plan was finally launched in 1992 after the initiation of structural adjustment policies.

For the first eight Plans the emphasis was on a growing public sector with massive investments in basic and heavy industries, but since the launch of the Ninth Plan in 1997, the emphasis on the public sector has become less pronounced and the current thinking on planning in the country, in general, is that it should increasingly be of an indicative nature.

7

Nehru's Global View

The aim of this chapter is to provide a systematic analysis of Nehru's worldview. This will be done in three different steps. At first, a chronological account of his rise to power within the Congress party will be presented. This section provides the basic biographical details that framed his political career prior to independence. The narrative stops in 1940 when Nehru began his longest period of prison sentences which lasted into 1945. Between the end of World War Two and India's independence, the transfer of power from British to Indian hands was worked out. The purpose that this biographical interlude serves is to observe Nehru's gradual ascendance within the party, to highlight his relationship with Mahatma Gandhi and, to take note of the events and issues that may have shaped him. Due to constraints of space this has been deliberately kept short.

The chapter then shifts its focus to the core ideas that were to form the pillars of his political programme as Prime Minister. The context is still the pre-independence years because this is when Nehru did most of his writing during frequent prison terms. The quality of this material is generally considered to be high, partly because as a 'Class A' political prisoner, Nehru had privileges which usually included the opportunity to order books and newspapers. Hence, the books written in the 1930s and early-40s are not only deeply self-reflective, wide-ranging and extensively referenced, but are also well-informed about current politics and, as a result, serve as a useful window into Nehru's concerns and thought processes. This requires a second step, which is to contextualise Nehru intellectually within the currents of political and economic thinking that were popular at the turn of the century in Britain and Europe. Corresponding with the three policy choices that have been selected as the thesis' focus (the Hindu Code Bills, the Planning Commission and the Panchasheel Agreement), are three broader conceptual fields. These are the extent of state involvement in developing the economy, the role of the state in reforming society and the nature of the state in international politics. In this section therefore, the Fabian and utilitarian discourse, popular at the time in Britain, will be presented in order to understand the origins of some of Nehru's beliefs and priorities.

Finally, the chapter seeks to explore the inner consistency of Nehru's thought process. To do this a selection of central statements by Nehru on the three policy themes is presented and analysed by means of a 'cognitive map'. By creating a 'cognitive map', the aim is to gain an insight into the inner logic and premises underpinning Nehru's thinking and the conclusions that he came to. Since *vision* is one of the central explanatory variables proposed by the thesis, an attempt is made to conduct a comparative analysis of Nehru's thinking across the three issue areas mentioned above. It is argued that such an exercise helps to understand the preferences of the actor, his internal logic and, as a result will add to an explanation of the choices made in his/her decision-making.

A conclusion summarises Nehru's position on the role, nature and goals of the state which acts as a basis for the contrast between him and his contemporaries, two of which will be studied in order to locate him within a spectrum of political thinking at the time. Subhash Chandra Bose and Rajendra Prasad were both important figures in the freedom struggle and each, in their own way, represented and set the bases for an alternative to Nehru's vision of modern Indian politics. While the literature on Subhash Chandra Bose is quite substantial and parallels and contrasts are often drawn between the two contemporaries, Bose and Nehru, Rajendra Prasad, despite being the first President of the Republic, tends to have been a neglected figure in modern India's politics. This could, in part, be due to the fact that Bose's home state, West Bengal has made a concerted effort to encourage scholarship about the leader and to preserve his 'hero-status' whilst Prasad's state of Bihar has invested little in the creation or preservation of an icon. Nevertheless Prasad's letters of correspondence and publications are available which, along with his statements in the constituent assembly debates, generate the contrast and comparison with Nehru.

His Formative Phase

Biographical material on Nehru is bountiful and the thesis does not claim to make any new discoveries about the *sources* of his ideas and preferences and the external influences on him. Rather, the aim here is to present a method by which to compare his thinking in the three issue areas of secularism, socialism and internationalism. The prime purpose therefore that this brief biographical interlude serves, is to contextualise Nehru in terms of key happenings in India and major developments in European politics.

The period prior to independence is referred to here as Jawaharlal Nehru's 'formative phase'. This was a time of great political activity in India and using Nehru as the reference point, this section seeks to highlight some of the major events and developments leading to independence in 1947.

Born in 1889 into a wealthy, Brahmin family settled in Allahabad, in the northern state of Uttar Pradesh but who originally hailed from Kashmir, Jawaharlal had a childhood that was exposed to both, great religiosity on his mother, Swarup Rani's part and the highly westernised habits and views of his father, Motilal Nehru. From 1901 to 1904 Jawaharlal was educated at home by a European tutor, then sent, at the age of sixteen, to Harrow and from there to Trinity College, Cambridge where he graduated with a Lower Second in the Natural Sciences Tripos in 1910. In accordance with the wishes of his father, Motilal Nehru, a highly successful barrister and political figure in his own right, Jawaharlal went on to read law at Gray's Inn, London, the same place where before him Mohandas Karamchand Gandhi and Muhammad Ali

Jinnah, among others, had studied. It is during this time that Jawaharlal encountered the movement of *Fabian Socialism*, popular at the time in Britain, through the lectures of Harold Laski at the London School of Economics and began to develop a more extreme political outlook, distancing himself from his father's preference for gradual constitutional reform. This reflected the growing schism within Indian politics back home.

In 1907 the Indian National Congress (INC) had split at the Surat session, divided between the *Moderates*, which included Motilal Nehru who favoured British-induced reforms and the *Extremists* who called for direct action like boycotts. Importantly, the Extremists at this time were largely those advocating a religious nationalism, as in the case of the All-India Hindu Sabha founded in 1911, an alternative which, as shall emerge, did not appeal to Jawaharlal. Not having attained much academic success, Jawaharlal returned to India in August 1912 and began to work for his father's law practice in Ahmedabad. Politics at this point in time in India was relatively quiet with leaders of the *Swadeshi* movement in jail. The outbreak of World War One in 1914 stirred the political environment and prompted anti-British movements to take shape.

The Defence of India Act, passed in March 1915 empowered the government to suppress civil liberties and imprison anyone deemed to be a threat to British interests. Rallying together, the Moderates and Extremists reunited in 1915 and initiated the Home Rule Movement which in addition to demanding self-government argued, that the British war effort was to be supported not opposed in exchange for concessions later on. The Muslim League also accepted the argument and in December 1916 the INC and Muslim League reached an agreement, known as the 'Lucknow Pact' in which the Congress accepted separate electorates and the League accepted under-representation for Muslims in Muslim-majority areas in return for over-representation in Muslim-minority areas.

Responding to the events around him, Jawaharlal's views began to take a clearer shape, in particular as he engaged directly in politics for example through Annie Besant's Home Rule League. Meeting Mohandas Karamchand Gandhi for the first time in the winter of 1916 at the Lucknow Congress of the INC, Jawaharlal was unable to relate to his style and rhetoric of politics which he found to be an unfamiliar blend of grass-root activism, asceticism, religion and philosophy. However, in 1919 when the Rowlatt Act was passed, extending wartime repressive legislation into peacetime, it was Gandhi who galvanised the Indian response through his first nation-wide campaign in an all-India *Satyagraha* to resist the Act through non-violent civil disobedience. This entailed courting arrest, returning of titles bestowed by the Raj, boycotts of schools and colleges, withdrawal of lawyers from courts, campaigns against the use of foreign cloth.

Marking the beginning of Jawaharlal's direct involvement in active politics, another major event of 1919, the Jalianwala Bagh massacre, soon came to eclipse the Rowlatt Act. On April 13, opening fire on a peaceful gathering of people, General Dyer's battalion killed hundreds of people, official estimates put the number of dead at 379 though it was widely agreed that the actual figure was much higher. The Congress began to organise relief work in the Punjab and set up its own enquiry committee in which Jawaharlal was involved. During the investigation Jawaharlal was in close contact with Gandhi and from then on seems to have found in him, his mentor.

The momentum generated in Punjab and the unity and solidarity which infused the Amritsar Congress session was carried forward into the *Non-cooperation Khilafat Movement* of the 1920s. Following the defeat of Turkey in World War One and the harsh Treaty of Sevres signed on May 14, 1920, Indian Muslims were growing increasingly agitated over the fate of the *Khalifa* in Turkey. Recognising the potency of the issue, Gandhi announced a Non-cooperation Movement which was accepted by the Khilafat Committee and the Congress party in 1920. Motilal Nehru also changed from his earlier position which had disapproved of anti-constitutional means, to support Gandhi. Boycotting November 1920 elections, the movement represented a dramatic new phase in Indian politics for it witnessed the emergence of a popular mass movement entailing radical pan-Islamic and Hindu believers, united by the method of non-violent, civil disobedience. The success of the movement carried over into the empty streets and *hartals* which greeted the Prince of Wales, future King Edward VIII on his visit to India in 1921.

This period seems to have marked a turning point in Nehru's political career for he also began to gain first-hand knowledge about working conditions in factories and the state of the peasantry. In 1920 Jawaharlal participated in the Congress' Allahabad district conference and was elected vice-president of the district committee, his first official position. This was also the year when Jawaharlal 'discovered' the peasants in his first rural, campaigns within the Kisan (farmers) movement. Carrying Gandhi's message of non-violence to the kisans in the Uttar Pradesh countryside, it was precisely these principles of satyagraha, entailing self-restraint which was to clash with Jawaharlal's own inclinations towards socialism and its ideals of radical and revolutionary change. However, for both the Nehrus, this seems to have been a period of transition and greater involvement in active resistance against the government and on December 6, 1921 both father and son were arrested and sentenced to six months in jail each.

Three months into their jail sentence, at what seemed to be the peak of the Non-cooperation Movement, Gandhi called off the movement in response to an outbreak of violence at a place called Chauri Chaura in UP. Shocked by Gandhi's unexpected move, Jawaharlal felt along with others as though the cause of the movement, as well as his own sacrifices, had been betrayed. His Autobiography noted, 'The sudden suspension of our movement after the Chauri Chaura incident was resented.... What troubled us even more were the reasons given for this suspension and the consequences that seemed to flow from them. Chauri Chaura may have been and was a deplorable occurrence and wholly opposed to the spirit of the non-violent movement; but were a remote village and a mob of excited peasants in an out-of-the-way place going to put an end, for some time at least, to our national struggle for freedom?' For Gandhi however, Chauri Chaura was a sign, a warning from God that 'that there is not as yet in India that truthful and non-violent atmosphere which alone can justify mass disobedience' and for which he had to atone. Both the language and methods that Gandhi employed stand in stark contrast to Nehru's reasoning.

Briefly released, Jawaharlal was re-arrested on a new charge and commenced his first long spell of imprisonment that lasted till January 31, 1923. Upon his release he agreed to become chairman of the Allahabad (UP) Municipal Board where Jawaharlal gained experience in administrative work. Disillusioned with the abrupt ending of non-cooperation and Gandhi having withdrawn himself to reflect and reconsider the methods of the struggle, Jawaharlal sought other sources of inspiration. The aftermath of the Russian Revolution was felt in India during the mid and late-1920s with the growth of left-wing parties, Workers' and Peasants' parties, an increase in trade unionism, worker's agitations and strikes. In this context, Jawaharlal's intellectual moorings began to lean more towards the left.

In March 1926 Jawaharlal, his wife and daughter left for Europe to treat his wife's condition of tuberculosis. During this stay, Jawaharlal travelled to major European cities and met with prominent intellectuals. For example at the International Conference against Colonial Oppression and Imperialism at Brussels, which he attended as the representative of the INC, Jawaharlal encountered Romain Rolland, Albert Einstein, Sun Yat Sen's widow, Song Qingling. Playing a large part in the proceedings, in the drafting of resolutions and making of public statements, Jawaharlal was beginning to carve out for himself an international persona.

Upon returning to India, Nehru was to participate in a new phase of Indian politics beginning with the arrival of the Simon Commission which was to review India's progress towards higher political development and to determine its fitness for self-government. Adding insult to injury, the Commission was composed of all-white members. A boycott was to be organised and an All-Parties Conference coordinated cooperation between the INC, the Muslim League and other groups. A committee was formed to draw up a rival constitutional framework to that of the Simon Commission, and was chaired by Motilal Nehru who, continued to favour constitutional reform and gradual progression from dominion status to eventual independence. In contrast, Jawaharlal had piloted a resolution at the Madras session of Congress in December 1927 declaring 'independence with full control over the defence forces of the country, the financial and economic policy and the relations with foreign countries' to be the goal of the Indian people. The resolution was criticised by contemporaries such as Rajendra Prasad who called it 'silly', and feared it would turn Congress into 'the laughing stock of the world'. The resolution was also criticised by Gandhi who wrote to Nehru to warm him 'You are going too fast....Most of the resolutions you framed and got carried could have been delayed.' Although the resolution was ultimately passed, a public confrontation was avoided.

The anti-Simon Commission black flag demonstrations brought large numbers of people out onto the streets and pursued the Commission across the country. The Nehru Report which emerged from Motilal's Committee recommended the abolition of separate electorates but, treading a fine balance between Muslim League and Hindu Mahasabha demands, the Nehru Report ultimately failed to produce a consensus on the issue of reserved seats. Carrying out an admirable attempt to foster Hindu-Muslim unity, the Nehru Report was an example of how the constitutional approach to self-government could fall hostage to internecine disputes and bickering over details, a result that, in Jawaharlal's view, only served to perpetuate British rule.

As a last resort, the Nehru Report accepted dominion status on the basis that it would be granted within a year, failing which the Congress would demand complete independence. One year later, with no clear moves from the government, the Congress passed the *Purna Swaraj* (Complete Independence) Resolution in Lahore on December 31, 1929. Elected as Congress president, this represented a high point in Jawaharlal's pre-independence career. On January 26, 1930, the flag of the INC was unfurled and hoisted as the national flag and 'Independence Day' was marked across India (a date that is still commemorated today).

In his presidential speech, Jawaharlal recognised that he had not been the favoured choice amongst Congress members. Jawaharlal Nehru was still a relatively unknown figure in politics and the masses, workers and peasants, along with the provincial Congress' elites had gathered to cast their votes for either Mahatma Gandhi or Vallabhbhai Patel. Correspondence between Gandhi and Jawaharlal's father, Motilal Nehru are revelatory. In mid- 1929 Motilal wrote to Gandhi, "The revolt of the youth has become an accomplished fact..... It would be sheer flattery to say that you have today the same influence as you had on the youth of the country some years ago All this would indicate that the need of the hour is the head of Gandhi and the voice of Jawahar...... There are strong reasons for either you or Jawahar to wear the 'crown'....". Nevertheless, once in the position, Jawaharlal attempted to set out his manifesto with a distinct socialist orientation and having been recently elected president of the All-India Trades Union Congress (AITUC), he advocated greater cooperation between the AITUC and the INC.

In February 1930 Gandhi declared the British salt tax to be the target of the next civil disobedience movement. The government had a monopoly on the manufacture of salt and the tax on salt was paid by Indians. Gandhi planned to launch the campaign with a 240-mile 'Salt March' on March 12 beginning at his Ashram near Ahmedabad and ending at Dandi on the west coast where Gandhi would break the law by collecting salt. With this act, civil disobedience across the country was ignited and, took the form of either illegal manufacturing of salt or the boycotting and burning of foreign textiles.

In response, a British crackdown put many into jail including Jawaharlal who was incarcerated from April 14 to October 11 and again from, October 19 to January 1931. The year 1931, must stand as a significant turning point in Jawaharlal's life for in February the death of his father, Motilal left him grief stricken. Furthermore, on March 5, 1931 a truce was signed by Gandhi and the Viceroy, Lord Irwin in which Gandhi had agreed to give up boycotts as a political weapon.

Nehru's reaction to this was 'tremendous shock', or as he put it in his *Autobiography*, 'The Civil Disobedience Movement was ended....Was it for this that our people had behaved so gallantly for a year? Were all our brave words and deeds to end in this.... This is the way the world ends, Not with a bang but with a whimper'. Despite the disappointment and sense of betrayal at Gandhi's unilateral decision to end the campaign, Jawaharlal was unwilling to publicly break with Gandhi. Recognising his vulnerability - the Working Committee (central decision-making body of the Congress party) had proposed a unanimous choice of Sardar Patel as Congress president — Nehru was aware of how little support he commanded within the party and hence, chose not to risk further alienation by openly opposing Gandhi. Asked by Gandhi to move the resolution ratifying the Gandhi-Irwin Pact, Nehru ultimately gave in to his survival instincts and as he recalls, "Almost at the last moment, a few minutes before the resolution was taken in the open Congress, I decided to sponsor it. In my speech I tried to lay before the great gathering quite frankly what my feelings were and why I had wholeheartedly accepted that resolution and pleaded with them to accept it." Perhaps as a gesture in return, Gandhi condoned the resolution on fundamental rights which Jawaharlal had drafted and introduced, committing the Congress to a comprehensive programme of social and economic reforms.

After a short period of release, Jawaharlal was back in jail on December 26, 1931 to begin his longest term that lasted until August 30, 1933. As has been noted by many of his biographers this was a time that Jawaharlal put well to use, reading and writing widely. A book of essays and letters to his daughter, Indira Gandhi written during this time was published as *Glimpses of World History* in 1934. To quell the growing vagueness surrounding his thoughts and political inclinations, Jawaharlal published *Whither India* in October 1933 in pamphlet form which sought to answer questions about what was to come after independence and the implementation of socialism into policies. Arrested again in February 1934 for having denounced imperialism and tried for sedition, Jawaharlal was sentenced to two years imprisonment during which he wrote his autobiography (published in 1936 with the same title).

In September 1935 with Kamala Nehru's condition deteriorating, Jawaharlal was granted early release on the condition that he would go with her to Europe and not return to India before his sentence expired in February 1936. In the meantime the Government of India Act of 1935 was finally passed setting out a scheme of provincial autonomy, in which British Indian provinces would be ruled by elected Indian ministries but the governor would retain reserve powers. Separate electorates were maintained and safeguards granted for British business and financial interests.

In all of this Jawaharlal's role appears to have been minimal, neither having played a major role in formulating nor in resisting the provisions.

Kamala Nehru died on February 28, 1936 and Jawaharlal returned to India in March 1936 to assume the mantle of Congress President for the second time. By then, rival factions within the INC were clearly emerging. Founded in 1934 as a group within the Congress, the Congress Socialist Party (CSP) called for the formation of a United Front of anti-imperialist forces including the Communist Party of India. One of its most influential spokesmen, Jayprakash Narayan advocated a Marxist-Leninist programme. Although Jawaharlal never joined the CSP he was regarded by many of its members as a sympathiser.

Furthermore, thanks to Jawaharlal's close relationship with Gandhi he was increasingly perceived as the bridge between two broad trends that were emerging within the Congress. This included, on the one hand the 'modernists' referring to industrialists and socialists, united in their faith in industrialisation and, on the other hand, the 'indigenists', which meant the Gandhians and Hindu sectarians who aspired towards a society based on indigenous traditions. Although Gandhi may have seen Jawaharlal as a unifier, others, such as his contemporary, Subhash Chandra Bose accused Jawaharlal of never having the courage to oppose the Mahatma and of drifting along, trying to please both the Right and the Left.

As President of the 1936 Congress Jawaharlal's statements implied a turn towards socialism, alarming businessmen and Congress members on the right of the ideological spectrum and adding to the strains caused by a central dilemma about the nature of Indian nationalism: was the Indian nationalist movement to be defined as a loose, broad, all-inclusive, secular movement but one that essentially lacked an ideological core? Right-wing tendencies within and without the Congress tended to be Hindu, upper-caste property owners, the dominance of whom was likely to alienate the 'Depressed Classes', minorities and particularly Muslims. On the other hand, the Muslim League at the time was also inclined more towards maintaining the *zamindar* (land owner)-based social order, pushing Muslims in favour of radical social change closer to the left wing of the Congress. Within the right wing, prominent businessman, such as G. D. Birla and political figures like Vallabhbhai Patel and Bhulabhai Desai also identified themselves as 'Gandhians'.

Confronted by the prospect of provincial elections (as a result of the Government of India Act, 1935), the Congress was split between those, especially the leftists, who wanted to boycott the elections, and those, especially business leaders and landlords, who wanted Congress to work with the Constitution. In the end Congress contested the elections held in early-1937 and emerged with massive victories. Contesting 1,161 out of a total of 1,585 seats, the Congress won 716 of them. From April 1937, the Congress was running nine out of eleven provincial governments, six on its own and three in coalitions. A crucial experience in governance and power-sharing, office acceptance also brought the Congress into conflict with itself. With ministries containing few representatives of the Left, the CSP and its affiliated organisations like the *Kisan sabhas* and the trade union movement, found themselves engaged in a struggle against the Congress which was in effect seen to be helping to run an imperialist system.

Till the mid-thirties the philosophy of the Congress-led movement had been to provide an institutional umbrella incorporating all hues of political outlook. The crisis over Subhash Chandra Bose's re-election as Congress president in 1939 brought tensions to the fore allowing Jawaharlal to emerge as a consensus candidate. By this time, Jawaharlal had begun to appear as the one of the few possible unifiers within the Congress movement. In November 1937, an anonymous article appeared in the Calcutta-based *Modern Review*, titled *The Rashtrapati* (President), warned that there was a tendency to see Nehru as a kind of saviour and that the man might be in danger of seeing himself as a latter day Napoleon or Caesar. It turned out that Jawaharlal himself was the author and while the intentions behind publishing such a piece are debated, the point is that he was increasingly in the limelight. From 1937, following the first provincial elections in which the Congress won easily in six of the eleven provinces and dominated two more, Jawaharlal took it upon himself to become the 'conscience of the ministries', reprimanding premiers of various provinces on their policies and statements as well as lecturing Congress on the need to keep an eye on the main goal of independence. Afraid of losing the collective momentum as the day-to-day running of provincial administrations distracted Congress members, and observing fractionalisation within Congress, the 'Mass Contact Programme' was launched in 1937 with Jawaharlal Nehru as one of its main leaders. Aimed at bringing Congress into close contact with those who were not yet Congress supporters, *Muslim* mass contact was deemed a priority.

Drawn into 'high' politics more directly, Jawaharlal views on the role of religion in politics and the potential for communal violence took on a harder line. For instance, writing to Stafford Cripps, at the time an upcoming figure in Labour politics to whom he had been introduced to by his friend, Krishna Menon in London, Jawaharlal was intent on conveying the influence of the Congress on the Muslims, claiming that "I come into greater touch with the Muslim masses than most of the members of the Muslim League. I know more about their hunger and poverty and misery than those who talk in terms of percentages and seats in the councils and places in the state services."

Issuing such an open challenge, released in the form of a statement to the press, Jawaharlal's actions had the effect of spurning the Muslim League to launch a far more successful 'mass contact' campaign of its own as well as setting the leader of the Muslim League, Muhammad Ali Jinnah on a war path. Other examples can be given of occasions when Jawaharlal's publicly advertised principles did not serve the cause of gaining support for the Congress and are an early indication of Jawaharlal's discomfort with, and inability to manage religion as a force in politics. Approaching the problem of communal politics in highly dichotomous terms, Nehru more often than not depicted the Congress as 'an advanced organisation' pitted against 'a politically reactionary organisation like the League', ruling out the possibility of Congress sharing power with any minorities in the provincial ministries, a move which may have helped to dispel accusation that Congress provincial rule, particularly in the heavily Muslim-populated state of Uttar Pradesh, was discriminatory and repressive against Muslims.

As an escape from the political infighting, Jawaharlal looked to international affairs and foreign travel. In 1937 he visited Burma and Malaya and in June 1938 left for Europe where he experienced the Spanish Civil War, made numerous public appearances in which he spoke on subjects such as the dangers of fascism, imperialist aggression and the world situation. Witnessing the Munich pact of 1938, Jawaharlal Nehru observed, first hand, the growing sense of crisis and approaching war that was building up in Europe. Reflecting the growing tendency of British policy-makers to regard Jawaharlal Nehru as a potential partner, in June 1938 he was invited to a weekend discussion on the possible terms for a treaty on the transfer of power with participants such as Sir Stafford Cripps, Harold Laski, Labour politicians as well as Krishna Menon of the Independence for India League.

By December 1939, when the Congress ministries had resigned in protest against Britain's declaration of war on India's behalf without consulting any of the 'representative' bodies of Indians, the Congress party organisational capabilities had been diminished, a right-left fault line had been exposed and communalist politics was on the rise. For most of the Second World War, Nehru was behind bars, jailed from November 1940 to December 1941 and again, from August 1942 to June 1945.

His Intellectual Context

Key developments in the political and intellectual climate of turn-of-the-century Britain were to play a crucial role in shaping the policies of both post-war Britain and independent India. Amongst these, the influence of the Fabian society is an important prism through which to observe the change and continuity in ideas and practices from the age of Victorian utilitarianism to the post-war social democracy and welfare politics of the Labour party. Founded in 1883, the Fabian society attracted a number of intellectuals including among others, George Bernard Shaw, H. G. Wells, Annie Besant, Harold Laski, Beatrice and Sidney Webb. What is interesting is how closely Nehru's thoughts on the state, modernisation and development reflected the twin sources of ideas popular at the time in Britain: utilitarianism and fabianism.

As Governor-General of India in the mid-nineteenth century, Lord Dalhousie upon reviewing his years of administration, is supposed to have described the railways, electric telegraph and uniform postage which he introduced to India as the 'three great engines of social improvement'. Such a reading of legacy reflected the philosophy of utilitarianism, as articulated by Jeremy Bentham and James Mill. In his *History of British India,* Mill had questioned the values of Indian society and proposed reforms along Benthamite ideals.

Despite being a Conservative, Dalhousie was therefore advocating that the key to progress in India was the introduction of Western science and knowledge. Crucial to note, is that the utilitarian idea of progress was not only progress brought about through scientific innovation but also reform of the existing social order. Hence, Dalhousie saw it as his duty to tackle the problems of infanticide, female education, the treatment of Hindu widows. Unity of authority, uniformity of management and legal practices were essential principles within this vision of governance. Codification was to emerge as one central instrument to put these principles into practice. References by Dalhousie to 'the good of the community', 'the interests of the public', 'the welfare of mankind' were echoes of the central utilitarian, 'Greatest-happiness precept'.

His farewell address on 5 March 1856 in Calcutta is a good example of this: 'While we have a right to congratulate ourselves on what has already been done, while we may regard with complacency the introduction into the East of those great instruments of public benefit which Science has long since created in the West; while we may rejoice that measures have been already taken for opening new sources of public wealth, for ministering to the convenience of increasing the happiness, and for raising the mental and social condition of the endless millions, whom providence for its own wise ends has committed to our charge; I trust we still shall feel that all we have yet done must be regarded as no more than the first beginning of greater things that are to come.'

Nehru, in some ways represented continuity with this line of thinking. His speeches and writings, often claimed the interests of mankind and of society as a whole, to be at stake. Even more striking was Nehru's propensity to believe in the wisdom and acumen of eminent individuals who could conceptualise and grasp the good of the community and take action from a neutral, benevolent position. His tendency to concentrate power and decision-making in the hands of a few individuals, his persistent monitoring and correspondence with chief ministers throughout his term as Prime Minister, attest to this.

Fabianism, as a current of political thought emerged in response, or rather in dialogue with the dominant ideas and in reaction to the experiences of industrialisation during the Victorian age. Believing in the possibility of gradual transition and reform, the Fabian Society rejected notions of class struggle and revolutionary change advocated by Marx's followers. Instead, it was argued that evolutionary and constitutional methods, the use of persuasion and permeation would bring about a gradual process of socialisation. Although Fabianism came to be embraced by the post-war Labour government it was never a doctrinal set of principles. The main goal of its adherents was to tackle the great injustices wrought by the capitalist system and to spread the theory of evolutionary socialism. As a result, democracy was to play a central part in the Fabian outlook as it provided the opportunity to bring about change peacefully and gradually.

The position of Fabianism on the State did not reject the utilitarian notions of the 'greatest happiness for the greatest number' and the need for society to be reorganised from above but instead, sought to extend them. Sidney Webb for instance is a good example of how utilitarianism was enhanced through his faith in positivism. Hence, science and experts were to be essential sources of neutral, rational advice. Much of the activity of government then could be left to 'the disinterested professional expert who invents, discovers, inspects, audits, costs, tests of measures' so as to pinpoint the facts about social life and its requirements. The knowledge, accumulated by the scientist, would enable them to administer effectively and to indicate priorities on policy matters. Elections, while not to be abolished, were to some extent in Webb's view a symbolic exercise through which popular consent for expertly designed policies could be raised. A belief in the inevitability of society to become ever more differentiated into functional units, held together through cooperation and coordination, meant the broad path of social development was set and, the job of politicians and experts was to develop proposals that would ease the way along this route.

A strong alternative to Webb's view was represented at the time by John Maynard Keynes who advocated fiscal and monetary measures to stimulate the economy essentially by expanding demand and employment. Furthermore, unlike Webb, Keynes focused on the individual as opposed to the common good. Reacting to the depression and unemployment of interwar years, Webb criticised Keynes for advocating short-term solutions within the framework of a capitalist economy when what was needed was a long-term industrial reorganisation within a collectivist economy. Turning therefore to the Soviet Union, which he visited in 1932 and 1934, solutions such as 'planned production for community consumption' appeared to have rationalised the economy for the social good in a way that had abolished 'mass unemployment, together with the devastating alteration of commercial booms and slumps.'

In spite of the control exerted by the Communist Part, Webb regarded the Soviet political system as a 'multiform democracy' in which the individual can participate as a citizen, producer, and consumer. Ignoring the ineluctable place of conflict in social life, Webb was committed to the ideal of there being an evolutionary movement towards a society where conflict would be largely absent since everyone would be working towards a common good upon which they agreed. Seeing the market as the epitome of immoral and irrational conflict, Webb did not want to recognise the extent to which the Soviet model too, embodied violence and conflict. As will be revealed in the rest of the chapter, Nehru's thoughts and ideas about the role of the market and state and, the nature of societal development carry a striking resemblance.

The Cognitive Maps of Political Elites

Written in 1976, Robert Axelrod's *Structure of Decision*, introduced cognitive mapping as a modelling technique in political science. Defining a cognitive map as a "specific way of representing a person's assertions about some limited domain, such as a policy problem" Axelrod explained that the aim was "to capture the structure of the person's causal assertions and to generate the consequences that follow from this structure." Underlying this statement is the argument that beliefs matter and can make a difference when it comes to policy choices and policy outcomes. Referring to another eminent political scientist whose work on cognitive psychology is widely known, Axelrod quoted Herbert Simon to justify the strategy of inference that he adopts where 'given the properties of the parts and the laws of their interaction, it is not a trivial matter to infer the properties of the whole'. Having established these two elements, only then is it possible, according to Axelrod to make predictions and assessments about the way an individual behaves or reacts to changes in his environment. The model, while positing that individuals do operate in accordance with the laws of cognitive maps does not assume unlimited rationality.

Rather, bounded rationality is revealed not so much 'as failures in (the decision-maker's) ability to draw correct inferences from the beliefs that he does state, but rather as limitations in the structure of the beliefs he presents as an image of the policy environment." As Axelrod points out it is precisely because of what may be unconscious but, which are essentially self-imposed, restrictions that serious distortions of the external policy environment are likely to occur. A year later, Jeffrey A. Hart in a critical journal article, applied the notion of 'cognitive maps' to a comparative study of three Latin American policy-makers.

Since this thesis is not aiming at an in-depth study of Nehru's belief system, its goals for developing a cognitive map are more modest. The prime concern is to explore whether Nehru's thoughts in the three policy areas of social reform, economic development and foreign policy, were equally well-conceptualised and internally consistent. Hence, the chapter has its own self-imposed limitation, in that it does not seek to develop a mathematical model for Nehru's overall belief system in order to *explain* his subsequent policy choices. This would be only half the explanation for the contextual constraints and exigencies of power politics, it is argued, play a central role in understanding why Nehru acted the way he did. However, a central proposition being made is that in the policy areas where Nehru's vision was more clearly articulated, he was more successful in getting results in terms of designing policies and institutions to put his ideas into action. In order to test this hypothesis it is necessary to conduct a *comparative* analysis of Nehru's cognitive map as applied to the three policy areas specified. As Axelrod himself admitted, a cognitive map cannot capture the nuances of individual causal beliefs and must leave out beliefs that are not causal by nature, hence the comparisons that are to be drawn in this chapter are based on a process that drastically simplifies reality.

A cognitive map, Axelrod specifies, has only two basic elements: concept and causal beliefs. 'The concepts are treated as variables, and the causal beliefs are treated as relationships between the variables'. To apply this to Nehru's belief system, the thesis refers to various arguments put forward by Jawaharlal Nehru in speeches and books on the three themes of secularism, economic development and foreign policy. An attempt is made to discuss the three areas comparatively and to examine whether there is a variation in the inner consistency and complexity of Nehru's thoughts on the subject.

A representative statement is chosen from three different sources each of which were important platforms from where Nehru could launch his position. Hence, in the first case of religion and secularism an ardent speech delivered when he was invited to preside over the Congress' Punjab Provincial Political Conference in 1928, was one of Nehru's early opportunities to make his views on critical issues known to a wider audience. On economic policy, a section from Nehru's Presidential address to Congress in 1936 is examined. This was an important occasion given that provincial elections were just around the corner and Nehru had been advocating a focus on economic issues and socialism.

Finally, on foreign policy Nehru's 1934 book, *Glimpses of World History*, a key text on his understanding of international diplomacy and world politics, is used for a representative extract. Although the timing and specific purposes of each source differs, the texts are considered insightful since each carried a particular focus related to the three policy areas of secularism, economic development and foreign policy. Hence, it was assumed that they could be used to reflect Nehru's concerns and considerations on the particular theme. While views and interpretations of the world certainly change over time it is posited that actors retain predispositions, especially on issues that have been singled out for attention from an early stage on. In Nehru's case, this chapter demonstrates that the issues of communalism and secularism, economic development and socialism, diplomacy and internationalism were matters of central concern to him.

Having extracted some initial observations based on a simple codification, the analysis made at the end of the chapter serves as a prism through which to examine Nehru's choices and decisions that feature on the Planning Commission, Panchasheel and the Hindu Code Bills respectively. The following steps are taken: (1) All 'conceptual variables' are pinpointed. These are terms that can take on different values such as 'security' which can be of a greater or smaller amount. Following Axelrod's methodology, cognitive maps frequently contain concepts variables for utility which refers to the unspecified best interests of the actor or what he considers to be in the best interests of the country or community. Other typologies include 'goal' variables which are variables that directly affect the utility variables and 'policy' variables which the individual seems to designate as being susceptible to control or manipulation. (2) Additional properties of the cognitive map concern the nature of the causal *paths*, or the chains of causation. There are basically two types of path: *positive* paths which contain an even number of negative assertions and *negative* paths with an odd number. (3) An important property of the cognitive map is *path balance* or the degree to which parallel paths between pairs of related variables have the same sign. This is held to indicate the *consistency* of the policy choice implied which is defined as 'the setting of a policy variable to a certain value so that all causal effects, direct or indirect, have a positive effect on utility.'

Nehru and Socialism

The relevance of Jawaharlal Nehru remains undiminished today. In fact, his ideas and approach to political, economic and social issues are more relevant now than even in his life-time.

It is necessary to state this basic truth and assess the continuing validity and vitality of his approach, because some who unabashedly use his name seek to project him as a pragmatist rather than as the firmly committed socialist that he was.

It is the fashion these days to say that socialism is a vague term, that it is a slogan, that there is no precise definition of what it means. This is essentially the argument of the believers in the *status quo*, of those who are afraid of radical change that will either hurt their own interests or destroy their pet theories.

It is no doubt true the despite his massive personal popularity and the power at his disposal in the government and in the party, Jawaharlal Nehru could not put into practice many of the ideas he spelt out regarding the radical changes, social and economic, that our society required. But this must be seen in the background of the dilemma he faced as an honest politician committed to socialism on the one hand and to democracy on the other. Rightly, he saw no contradiction between the two, for, who can deny that true democracy is the only viable basis for genuine socialism and that without advance towards the goal of socialism democracy will be bereft of meaning? Nehru would not discard the democratic processes or bypass the democratic institutions in order to put his ideas into pratice. In our context, with a long history of feudalism, caste hierarchy, religious divergence, multiplicity of languages and customs, in fact of stratification of society in a variety of ways, it has not been easy to correlate tradition and change, to work out a viable compromise between the best of cherished values and the urgency of eliminating social and economic inequalities. Jawaharlal Nehru realised that revolution in our situation had to be by consent and could not be by imposition. He admired the Soviet achievements and accepted the ultimate ideals of Marxism, but he did not make a secret of his reservations about applying the same methods in the case of our country.

In an underdeveloped nation with many layers of development within itself, both vertical and horizontal, and with a variety of vested interests wielding tremendous influence and extremely articulate, the difficulties involved in bringing about radical changes by consent were obvious enough. Yet the alternatives to the democratic system are so risky and unpredictable that he would not lightly discard his faith, even if this meant a visible, often frustating, slowing down of the process of change.

Nehru's acceptance of political democracy was not unqualified. "I am perfectly prepared to accept political democracy," he said, "only in the hope that this will lead to social democracy." He was clear in his mind that political democracy "is only the way to the goal and is not the final objective". He saw clearly that if profound economic changes did not take place fast enough, the political structure would be rendered unstable.

If political or social institutions stand in the way of such change, they have to be removed.

Socialism, whose essence is the removal of poverty and establishment of equal opportunities if not of equality in the strictest sense, has necessarily to suit the conditions of each country, and Nehru's constant effort was to bring about changes without destroying the fabric of Indian society, even if certain parts of that fabric were to be replaced.

Nehru saw the socialist society as some kind of a cooperative society, in which each individual would give of his best and would find full scope for his own development. The very first step had to be the ending of the profit motive of the acquisitive society to which we are accustomed. The dilemma he faced was the result of his desire to avoid a violent upheaval that could have disastrous consequences for future generations of our people and to take the maximum number of people along with him on the new path. This was no easy task, for the vested interests in the acquisitive society which he wanted to end were entrenched in the party and in the administrative apparatus which had necessarily to be his major instruments. Also, it was these interests which were active during the freedom struggle, and even more in the years of freedom, and they were able to create the illusion of democratic functioning without active participation by the masses of our population who were to gain by the changes Nehru envisaged.

Once Nehru said that two contradictory and conflicting processes could not go on side by side. That unfortunately is what has been happening. The Directive Principles contain a broad outline of the kind of socialist society envisaged, but the many amendments to other chapters of the Constitution that have been necessited have brought out the dichotomy in thinking that characterised the Constitution-making body. On another plane, the formulation of the concept of "mixed economy" representated on the one hand the "half-way house" Nehru thought of and on the other the ability of the vested interests to keep "two contradictory and conflicting processes" going on side by side, a situation Nehru did not desire. It is no coincidence that the "mixed economy" in operation has resulted in a strengthening of the monopoly and big business houses, and a consequent tightening of their hold on the administrative apparatus. If corruption has increased and the public sector has not been enlarged and strengthened to the extent it should have been, this is because of acceptance of the "mixed economy" as something of a "half-way house".

It must be said that Jawaharlal Nehru fully realised the difficulties inherent in seeking radical change through democratic processes.

I think it is possible to establish socialism by democratic means provided, of course, the full democratic process is avail able. (emphasis added)

There has been mass awakening as never before in our history, and despite massive illiteracy our people have demonstrated their capacity to reject what is against their interests. But the real problem is that the democratic process is not yet fully developed, and the people have only limited choice. The limitations imposed by our circumstances, both historical and man-made, have helped both the urban and rural vested interests to twist the democratic process to suit their own ends which are diametrically opposed to the interests of the masses.

In thinking of a form of socialism suited to our national needs and national genius, Nehru envisaged a limited place for the private sector, but he was quite clear about the framework.

In all that counts, in a material sense, nationalisation of the instruments of production and distribution seems to be inevitable. The question is whether there can be a step-by-step approach in this matter. Our experience with the takeover of the wholesale trade in foodgrains shows that partial measures in dealing with production and distribution of essential commodities can defeat the very objective. The fate of the land reform measures has shown that an administrative machinery that is not geared to the task can work havoc. The continuing importance and influence of the big business houses must be seem as the direct result of the failure to involve the people at the grassroots level more and more in the processes of planning, production and distribution.

It is possible to find fault with Jawaharlal Nehru for not having made the maximum use of his popularity to force the pace of change, but to do so is to overlook the historical forces that had shaped him and the historical circumstances in which he had to function, apart from his own commitment to the democratic processes as well as to the instruments at his disposal. It is debatable how much more he could have achieved in his life-time, but it is indisputable that he laid firm foundations for the kind of society we want to build in this country. It is for us and for future generations to build on these foundations.

Nehru was conscious that the Indian Revolution would be long and arduous, for he said: "Leaders and individuals may come and go; they may get tired and slacken off; they may compromise and betray; but the exploited and suffering masses must carry on the struggle, for their drill sergeant is hunger."

If the social and economic burdens of the masses "continue and are actually added to, the fight must not only continue but grow more intense". The masses would ultimately assert themselves, and of this he had not the least doubt. It was his hope that the political parties and the administrative apparatus would help the masses to assert themselves and secure their rights. He was quite clear in his mind that a leadership that failed to take the masses nearer the goal of socialism would be thrown aside, and the mass upsurge in 1969 following the elimination of the Syndicate from the Congress would appear to bear this out, even if only in a very limited sense.

Nehru Said: We have to plan at both ends. We have to stop the cumulative forces that make the rich richer and we have to start the cumulative forces which enable the poor to get over the barrier of poverty.

The planning process unfortunately has not gone on the way he had intended it to, and this is where the two main instruments on which he had to depend come in.

Nehru wanted the services to "cease to think of themselves as some select coterie apart from the rest of the people", and he rejected people with the "coat and necktie" mentality.

In other words, he wanted a new type of administrator to emerge, who could identify himself with the common people without effort and who would not become either a tool in the hands of vested interests or a self-seeker without a conscience. Unfortunately this kind of change has not come about; on the other hand, the expanded administrative structure has careerists and self-seekers in many key positions. This has to change.

As for the other instrument, the Congress, it may now be in better shape than in Nehru's time, but what he said about Congressmen remains relevant. Congressmen should make the organisation strong and effective. Use of money for boosting individuals in the organisations is extremely undesirable. Bogus members should be weeded out. Those in the organisation for whom the Congress is not an instrument for serving the country, who serve themselves and exploit it for their own ends...should be turned out.

He wanted the party to be a mass party, constantly in touch with the people and reflecting their aspirations, constantly struggling to end social and economic injustice. Some changes have taken place in the party in recent times, but it is still far from being the kind of instrument for change that Jawaharlal Nehru wanted it to be. It is to be hoped that the new forces at work within the Congress and the mass consciousness that has developed in the country will make it so.

Our aim and our problems were succinctly summed up when Jawaharlal Nehru said:

> Socialism is the inevitable outcome of democracy. Political democracy has no meaning if it does not embrace economic democracy. And economic democracy is nothing but socialism. Monopoly is the enemy of socialism. To that extent it has grown during the last few years, we have drifted away from the goal of socialism.

Summary

Through this exercise of examining Nehru's thinking in three different policy areas one is able to identify some of the core ideas that were likely to have influenced Nehru's later choices and preferences. Such an assumption draws upon the work of Axelrod, Shapiro and Alexander George all of whom held that individuals construct a specific rationale for a particular set of actions.

While earlier writers such as Alexander George and Nathan Leites used the concept of an 'operational code', the thesis uses the tool of a 'cognitive map' which allows for an analysis of causal beliefs or assertions held by the individual. The additional proposition being made here is that by looking at the three 'mini' cognitive maps it is possible to draw comparisons with regards to how far Nehru had conceptualised the three areas of economic development, social reform and foreign policy prior to India's independence.

Such an approach offers a marked contrast from the usual biographical accounts of Nehru that are so widely available which simply recount the narrative of his youth and entry into politics. What this chapter has sought to do is identify the actor's beliefs and premises and with the help of a cognitive map to create the prism through which the actor perceived and diagnosed the flow of political events. These beliefs are considered important given that they provide the norms, standards and guidelines that influence the actor's choice of strategy and tactics, his structuring and weighting of alternative courses of action.

With regards religion and secularism, Nehru's thought process indicated a tendency towards seeing things in black and white and of understanding problems in terms of stark contrasts. On the subject of economic development and socialism the vision conveyed by Nehru demonstrated a greater concern with policy, the applicability of socialist goals to India and the need to establish consensus-driven methods of attaining socialism.

Finally, on the subject of foreign policy there is surprisingly little in his writings and the tendency is towards sweeping statements and comments rather than concrete-policy related and India-specific observations. Having seen that Nehru's vision of a secular, socialist and internationalist, independent India varied greatly in terms of the challenges foreseen and the possible solutions envisioned, it will be easier to explain some of his later tactical choices. Using the Constituent Assembly debates, Nehru's 'vision' will be contextualised in terms of the alternatives that were being voiced and the extent to which his views faced criticism.

Before this however, it is necessary to briefly turn to the institutional and ideological setting within which Nehru emerged during the 1930s and 40s for it is recognised that the actor's belief system does not unilaterally determine decision-making but that it is an important variable affecting the range of options considered by the actor.

8

Nehru as a Writer

Freedom fighter, nationalist, politician, secularist, lawyer, world statesman, uncle (chacha), and patriot — these are commonly used nouns for Jawaharlal Nehru, the first Prime Minister of India. However, the noun "writer" is rarely used in his case, even though he has written several books. His books — The Autobiography of Jawaharlal Nehru Towards Freedom, Letters from a Father to His Daughter, Glimpses of World History, and The Discovery of India — are considered classic. These and his other books enrich the Indian literature, as do his essays, articles, speeches, and statements.

A Man of Letters

A master of the English language and a man of letters, Jawaharlal Nehru would not sign a document that had been prepared by anyone else. He was proud of his command of the language and wrote all of his works in English. He once told the court at his own trial, "I am a lover of words and try to use them appropriately." Indeed, he used words precisely, and it is easy to read his works. Once delving into them, it is difficult to set his any of books aside for long! Nehru is not merely chronicling events but enlivening them, telling readers how these events have affected his thoughts, moods, actions, hopes, and fears. Dull and dry historical details come alive in his books, which seem to tell stories without lecturing or teaching. The conversational style of his writings seems to come from two things: first, he wrote only after he experienced an action; and second, he frequently had conversations with the masses, who were largely uneducated and who needed to be spoken to in simple words.

Where did Jawaharlal Nehru write? He wrote most of his works in British gaols. British authorities imprisoned him numerous times during India's freedom movement; however, it is hard to ascertain the number of years he remained behind bars. On October 17, 1949, Time magazine reports that he spent 13 years in jail. The issue of July 30, 1956, however, reports 14 years. At any rate, any time behind bars for a wrongful reason is too long for anyone. In one book, he asks himself a question about his time in prison: "Was it worthwhile?" He then replies, "There is no hesitation about the answer." Why did Nehru write? "The primary object in writing...was to occupy myself with a definite task, so necessary in the long solitudes of jail life."

Nehru's book Towards the Freedom is his autobiography and was written entirely in prison from June of 1934 to February of 1935. However, the postscript and certain minor changes were added at a later time. In this book, he writes among other subjects about his life and the animals in prison, his roots and childhood, his education at Harrow and at Cambridge in Britain, his wedding, the arrival of Mahatma Gandhi in India, his time in and out of jails, the death of his father, the first Round Table Conference, and India old and new.

The book Letters from a Father to His Daughter contains letters from Jawaharlal Nehru to his only child, Indira Priyadarshini, when she was ten years old and in Mussoorie without him during the summer of 1928. Over the summer, he wrote to her about the making of the earth, the evolution of human and animal life, the formation of tribes and languages, the evolvement of civilizations and societies, the Aryans, and the epics of India.

The book Glimpses of World History is actually a series of lengthy letters (196) that Nehru began writing from Dehra Dun

Jail in 1930 to then his 13-year-old daughter. In this book, he introduces his daughter to the world from the early Indus Valley civilization to the beginning of World War II (1938). It contains Nehru's opinions about the events and his strong sentiments about British imperialism.

Nehru wrote The Discovery of India during his imprisonment from 1942 to 1945(1040 days) in the Ahmadnagar Fort. This book is also culled from letters to his daughter and was published in 1946. He wrote with pride about his motherland, his nation's ancient culture, history, and heritage, his people's strengths and weaknesses, his land's ancient books (such as the Vedas, Upanishads, Ramayana, and Mahabharata), and his mentor, Mahatma Gandhi. This book is known to fill a reader's eyes with tears, his heart with joy, and his chest with pride for being an Indian.

In Jawaharlal Nehru, John Alphonso-Karkala comes to the conclusion that, "Jawaharlal Nehru was not a professional author who devoted his lifetime to writing but a man of public affairs who became a writer by necessity. By training he was a scientist and a lawyer; by choice he was a politician; by attitude he was a humanist; and by sensibilities he was a poet. Yet what he wrote was historical prose, or prose that has become historical...Perhaps Jawaharlal Nehru may survive longer in the memory of mankind as an author than as a politician."

For whom did he write? Jawaharlal Nehru did not have a specific group in mind when he wrote: "But, if I thought of an audience, it was my own countrymen and countrywomen." November 14, marks the anniversary of Nehru's birth; we celebrate his birthday as Children's Day — Bal Din. What better way to remember him on his birthday than by having our countrymen and countrywomen read a few pages from his any of books? Furthermore, what better way to remember him every day than by teaching his books in our schools and colleges?

As a Writer of English Prose

"I am not a man of letters," wrote Jawaharlal Nehru in one of his missives from jail to his daughter Indira, but of course he was. All through his life Nehru lost no opportunity to write. His words took the form of drafts and resolutions for the Congress party, essays on the great issues of the day for newspapers and journals, and letters to friends, family, and colleagues in the independence movement. When he became Prime Minister of India, Nehru wrote a long letter addressed jointly to his chief ministers every fortnight, containing his deliberations on domestic and world affairs. It is clear that, despite the burdens of his worldly commitments, words set down on paper were for Nehru a way of making sense of the commotion of life, politics and ideas.

But Nehru was also a man of letters in a more abiding sense, as readers of any of his major works (his autobiography, *Glimpses of World History*, and *The Discovery of India*) know, and as *The Oxford India Nehru*, a selection of his most representative speeches and writings, again proves. That is to say that we can read Nehru not just for his ideas, or for insights into his personality, but also for the way in which expressed himself, for the grace and rhythm of his English. "At its best," wrote the editor Frank Moraes, one of Nehru's best biographers, "Nehru's style shows a vigour and clarity as pleasing and compelling to the ear as to the mind." Indeed, Nehru was among a handful of Indian writers, among which Gandhi and Tagore were also prominent, who found a way to domesticate what for most other Indians born in the nineteenth century was an often puzzling colonial tongue, a language the rules and moves of which could of course be learnt, as did many young people wanting to make a career under the Raj, but could never be used with the same vigour or pliability.

"English made the empire," observes the historian Sunil Khilnani in an essay called "Gandhi and Nehru: The Uses of English", "but (Gandhi and Nehru) showed how it could be used to unmake it — how the language could be a tool of insubordination and, ultimately, freedom." The two men, neither of them professional writers, shaped the place and form of English in India in three decisive ways. Gandhi was born in 1869; Nehru died in 1964: their lives encompassed a linguistic century that stretched from the English of legal petitions and imperial proclamations, of diwans, pleaders, and officers of the early Raj, to the official bureaucratese of the Five-Year Plans and the ministries of the independent Indian state. The sheer bulk of their spoken and written words (combined, the published work of Gandhi and Nehru exceed 150 volumes), as well as its historical span, ensured for the English language a countrywide currency. Second, though often ambivalent about the function of English in India, they kept a political commitment to English as a language of public communication. English may have been 'the language of the enemy', yet both wished to accommodate it alongside other Indian languages, recognising it as a vital link not just to the wider world but also between Indians themselves. Finally, the forms in which they wrote — autobiographies, public and private letters, journalistic essays and articles, and works of history — helped to define how these genres came to be understood and used in India, by their contemporaries and those who came after.

Although he sometimes chose a romantic and elevated tone that could grow monotonous, there is never in Nehru's work that tendency towards vagueness and bombast, the use of cliches and archaisms, that to this day disfigures so much Indian prose in English. Indeed, Nehru deserves to be seen, independently of the political man, as one of the best Indian prose writers of the twentieth century.

Uma Iyengar's selection of extracts for *The Oxford India Nehru* organises Nehru's work by theme rather than by chronology, grouping together Nehru's thoughts on Indian history and culture, on Gandhi, on India before and after independence, on the changing world situation, and so on. The great preoccupations and leanings of Nehru's work quickly emerge: his rationalism, his natural egalitarianism and his commitment to democratic institutions and practice, his impatience with, if not outright contempt for, religion, his espousal, after the fashion of his times, of socialism, his sometimes qualified admiration for and complicated relationship with Gandhi, his keen interest in world politics, and his sense of India as one indivisible composite culture and his desire to overlay upon it "the garb of modernity".

Many of these thoughts are still relevant; in fact, sometimes they seem never more relevant than today. Attacking the demands made by various communal organisations in 1934, Nehru writes that communalism is "another name for social and political reaction", and that "it has often sailed under false colours and taken in many an unwary person". Writing in 1953, Nehru remarks that although nationalism can be a rousing and unifying force, one of the problems with it is "the narrowness of mind that it develops within a country, when a majority thinks itself as the entire nation and in its attempt to absorb the minority actually separates them even more". Objecting to the very name of the Backward Classes Commission, he writes, "It is as if we are first branding them and then, from our superior position, we shall try and uplift them".

In more than four decades of writing to convince, persuade, engage, describe, attack, defend, reminisce, synthesise, and understand, Nehru wrote upon every possible subject on which opinions were divided, from cow slaughter to public health to the national flag and anthem to divorce ("Divorce," he opines with characteristic clarity, "must not be looked upon as something which makes the custom of marriage fragile"). Iyengar even includes a letter to his chief ministers on the subject of brooms, observing that the commonly found short-handled ones make for tiring and backbreaking work and encourage "a certain subservience in mind", and insisting that municipal sweepers be supplied with long-handled brooms.

Here, from *The Discovery of India*, is a classic example of Nehru's elevated style: a sentence multi-claused, expansive yet syntactically balanced and clear in sense, and proceeding steadily from specifics to generalities, generalities that exemplify his professed humanism and universalism:

The story of the Ganges, from her source to the sea, from old times to new, is the story of India's civilization and culture, of the rise and fall of empires, of great and proud cities, of the adventure of man and the quest of the mind which has so occupied India's thinkers, of the richness and fulfilment of life as well as its denial and renunciation, of ups and downs, of growth and decay, of life and death.

The only phrase that mars these sonorous cadences is "ups and downs", which is a favourite Nehru phrase. In a letter written in 1930 from jail to Gandhi, also in jail following the success of the Dandi march, Nehru exulted that Gandhi had made a new

India with his "magic touch", and remarked that "our prosaic existence has developed something of epic greatness in it." His writing about India, too, can often seem like a project to lift up an India of prosaic realities and trying to infuse in it, by harking back to the past and to the universal story of man, an epic greatness.

Nehru becomes a more interesting writer when irked or riled; the expression of annoyance or dissent adds muscle to his writing. Here, for example, is a paragraph from one of a series of letters he exchanged with the Englishman Lord Lothian in 1936 over the future direction of India. In it he attacks Lothian's argument that Indian people should stick to constitutional methods of protest:

> You refer also to the 'constitutional road' in India. What exactly is this constitutional road? I can understand constitutional activities where there is a democratic Constitution, but where there is no such thing, constitutional methods have no meaning. The word constitutional then simply means legal, and legal simply means in accordance with the wishes of an autocratic executive which can make laws and issue decrees and ordinances regardless of public opinion. What is the constitutional method in Germany or Italy today? [These countries had just come under Fascist rule] What was this method in the India of the nineteenth century or of the early-20th century or even now? ... The mere fact that it is impossible for the great majority of the people of India to make their will effective shows that they have no constitutional way open to them. They can either submit to something they dislike intensely or adopt other than so-called constitutional methods. Such methods may be wise or unwise, under the particular circumstances, but the question of their being constitutional or not does not arise.

Nehru's key rhetorical tactic is to ally "constitutional" to "democratic", and to insist that one is nothing without the other. Cutting and hacking away sentence by sentence, he leaves his adversary with no ground to stand on.

And in an essay in the *Tribune* early in 1934, he launches a broadside against organisations motivated by communal considerations:

> What are communal organisations? They are not religious, although they confine themselves to religious groups and exploit the name of religion. They are not cultural and have done nothing for culture, although they talk bravely of a past culture. They are not ethical or moral groups, for their teachings are singularly devoid of ethics and morality. They are certainly not economic groupings, for there is no economic link binding their members and they have no shadow of an economic programme. Some of them claim not to be political even. What then are they?

As a matter of fact they function politically and their demands are political, but calling themselves non-political, they avoid the real issues and only succeed in obstructing the path of others.

Nehru had a naturally metaphorical cast of mind. He is often found on these pages comparing history to a great river. Indeed, he thought a lot about history, and felt keenly the pressure of history. In a speech to the Constituent Assembly in 1947, he imagines himself "standing on the sword's edge of the present between the mighty past and the mightier future" — a particularly good metaphor, because it suggests how fraught with uncertainty the present is, possessing the power to cut sharply even as attempts are made to work with it. Elsewhere, he likens the taking of risks to the exhilaration of climbing the mountains, while those who hold back, desiring safety and security, are seen as living in the valley, "with their unhealthy mists and fogs". This metaphor shows among other things Nehru's love of mountains, for most Indians would hardly go along with his negative characterisation of valleys.

Although he read widely and well, Nehru was curiously not much given to quoting from the works of other writers, perhaps because he spent so much time on the move or else in prison, with limited access to books in either case. Despite frequent references to the defects and excesses of capitalism and the merits of socialism, for instance, he can only be found quoting Marx once on these pages. Also, Nehru's relationship to his reading was intensely practical, a means of learning something about the world past or present. He liked to read travellers' accounts — Huen Tsang, Marco Polo, Ibn Battutah — and surveys of history and society — Marx, Oswald Spengler, Reinold Neibuhr — but we know that he disliked reading novels, saying they left him "mentally slack". Gandhi appears to have been a more adventurous and open-minded reader, fond not only of the *Gita* and the works of Tolstoy, Ruskin and Plato but also of Walter Scott, Jules Verne and Goethe.

Perhaps it is to these tendencies we may attribute one fault of his writing, which is a fondness for generalities and groupings and a disregard for bracing and often necessary specificities. Consider that, although he travelled widely for decades on end, and was a captivating speaker who drew huge crowds, his references to the Indian peasantry almost always take the form of the generalised description — "the sunken eyes and hopeless looks of the people", "the starving peasant" for whom "hunger gnaws at his stomach". There is no account in his letters or essays of an actual conversation with a peasant whose name is provided or who is seen as more than a downtrodden man or a hungry stomach, and it does not seem to have occurred to him that his work would be all the more forceful by his doing so.

Yet the most stirring sentences of twentieth-century Indian writing in English were composed by Nehru. These are the opening lines of his speech to the constituent assembly on the hour of India's independence. It was a situation made for a man of his talents and predilections. "Long years ago we made a tryst with destiny, and now the time comes when we shall redeem our pledge, not wholly or in full measure, but very substantially. At the stroke of the midnight hour, when the world sleeps, India will awake to life and freedom," he begins, before moving onto a majestic seven-part sentence.

"A moment comes, which comes but rarely in history, when we step out from the old to the new, when an age ends, and when the soul of a nation, long suppressed, finds utterance." Nehru never wrote a better or more deeply felt line - it was what he had been waiting to say almost all his life.

His Writings

Nehru was a prolific writer in English language and wrote a number of books, namely *The Discovery of India, Glimpses of World History,* and his autobiography, *Towards Freedom.* Written in 1936, it ran nine editions in the first year alone. "Towards Freedom" is also popularly known as "An Autobiography."

The Discovery of India

The *Discovery of India* was written by India's first Prime Minister Jawaharlal Nehru during his imprisonment in 1942-46 at Ahmednagar in the Ahmednagar Fort.

Nehru was jailed for his participation in the Quit India movement along with other Indian leaders, and he used this time to write down his thoughts and knowledge about India's history. The book is widely regarded as a classic in India since its first publication in 1946, and provides a broad view of Indian history, philosophy and culture, as viewed from the eyes of a liberal Indian fighting for the independence of his country.

In The Discovery of India Nehru argued that India was an historic nation with a right to sovereignty.

In this book Pandit Jawaharlal Nehru tries to study the history of India starting from the Indus Valley Civilization, and then covers the country's history from the arrival of the Aryans to government under the British Empire. The effect of these various people on Indian culture and their incorporation into Indian society is examined.

This book also analyses in depth the philosophy of Indian life.

Glimpses of World History

Glimpses of World History, a book written by Jawaharlal Nehru in 1934, is a panoramic sweep of the history of humankind. It is a collection of 196 letters on world history written from various prisons in British India between 1930-33. The letters were written to his young daughter Indira, and was meant to introduce her to world history.

The letters start off with one he sends to his daughter on her birthday. He says he is sad about not being able to send her any "material" gift from prison, so he would try to give her something he can "afford", a series of letters from his heart.

Written from prison, where he had no recourse to reference books or a library but his personal notes, *Glimpses of World History* contains the history of humankind from 6000 BC to the time of writing of the book. It covers the rise and fall of great empires and civilizations from Greece and Rome to China and West Asia; great figures such as Ashoka and Genghis Khan, Gandhi and Lenin; wars and revolutions, democracies and dictatorships.

He wrote about many cultures throughout the globe in detail because, as he himself said, he didn't like the way history was taught in schools where it was confined to the history of a single country and that too narrow, and he wanted his daughter Priyadarshini to know why people did what they did. It was possible only through knowing the history of the whole world.

The letters are written in informal language, with the contemporary and personal events too are mentioned. They reflect the world view of Nehru, and his grasp of history. It could be considered as one of the first attempts at historiography from a non-Eurocentric angle.

The book is comparable to The Outline of History by H. G. Wells. The New York Times described it as... one of the most remarkable books ever written... Nehru makes even H. G. Wells seem singularly insular... One is awed by the breadth of Nehru's culture.

In particular, his chapter on Genghis Khan and the Mongol invasion runs counter to dominant European views of the time. Prefacing his introduction to the Mongol Empire, which was practically as large as the British Empire and lasted as long, he said:

> It would be foolish not to recognise the greatness of Europe. But it would be equally foolish to forget the greatness of Asia.

and he goes on to state:

> Genghis is, without doubt, the greatest military genius and leader in history.... Alexander and Caesar seem petty before him.

According to Jack Weatherford, his was possibly the first re-evaluation of the Mongol Empire since the 18th century.

An Autobiography

An Autobiography (1936) is an autobiographical book written by the first Prime Minister of India, Jawaharlal Nehru while he was in prison.

He was concerned that his father, Motilal Nehru, who was a prominent lawyer in India, disapproved of him going to prison, and he began to wonder how he had ended up there. To sort out this question for himself, he wrote this book.

Nehru starts his history with how his ancestors had to flee Kashmir, and then goes on to tell about his own life, with a particular emphasis on the parts of his life that had brought him to this point in time.

His entire life history, from even before his father was born, seems to have led him naturally to where he was.

As a child he seems quiet, observing, and thoughtful. As a (very tall) grownup he is still thoughtful. One sees his admiration for humble people, and his aversion to any form of violence very early in the book.

9

Significant Speeches

Jawaharlal Nehru, the first Prime Minister of independent India, was a man, who could influence the masses with his oration. He was an immensely learned man and could feel the pulse of the masses. Nehru's Message to the Nation on the Independence Day was delivered on the brink of midnight of the 14th of August, 1947. The speech focused on various topics related to India and the freedom that she had achieved from the shackles of British colonial rule. The speech also encourages and inspires the countrymen to wake from the long slumber and take steps for the upliftment and development of India.

Jawaharlal Nehru's independence speech aimed at motivating the general masses at building a new India. The speech aimed at boosting the people for working harder and with real zeal and enthusiasm to make India the numero uno nation in the world. There were certain social evils that were dominant in the Indian society in the form of illiteracy, poverty, ignorance, poor health conditions and many more in pre-independent India. The message propagated for the eradication of these social evils and to make India a prospering nation.

The message of the first Prime Minister of independent India, Jawaharlal Nehru, also requested the people of the country to actively participate in the process of nation-building. He also urged the people to have and show confidence in the national leaders of the country, who were bestowed with the duty of carrying the nation forward. The concept of equality was also emphasised in the independence speech made by Jawaharlal Nehru.

The Father of the Nation, Mahatma Gandhi, also finds reference in the speech made by Nehru. He also pays homage to the various freedom fighters, who had sacrificed their lives for the purpose of attaining freedom from the bond of British rule. He also makes a mention of the pains that several people had to endure due to the partition of the country. The speech also motivates the common masses to undergo the initial pains and troubles in the process of making a glorious India.

Last but not the least, Jawaharlal Nehru in his speeches pay homage to Mother India and takes vows to defend her in all troubles. He also summons all the countrymen to bind themselves to the services of the Motherland.

Pledge Taken on Independence Day

January, 1930

We believe that it is the inalienable right of the Indian people, as of any other people, to have freedom and to enjoy the fruits of their toil and have the necessities of life, so that they may have full opportunities of growth. We believe also that if any government deprives a people of these rights and oppresses them, the people have a further right to alter it or to abolish it. The British Government in India has not only deprived the Indian people of their freedom but has based itself on the exploitation of the masses, and has ruined India economically, politically, culturally, and spiritually. We believe, therefore, that India must sever the British connection and attain Puma Swaraj or complete independence.

India has been ruined economically. The revenue derived from our people is out of all proportion to our income. Our average income is seven pice (less than two pence) per day, and of the heavy taxes we pay, are raised from the land revenue derived from the peasantry and 3 per cent, from the salt tax, which falls most heavily on the poor.

Village industries, such as hand-spinning, have been destroyed, leaving the peasantry idle for at least four months in the year, and dulling their intellect for want of handicrafts, and nothing has been substituted, as in other countries, for the crafts thus destroyed.

Customs and currency have been so manipulated as to heap further burdens on the peasantry. British manufactured goods constitute the bulk of our imports. Customs duties betray clear partiality for British manufactures, and revenue from them is used not to lessen the burden on the masses but for sustaining a highly extravagant administration. Still more arbitrary has been the manipulation of the exchange ratio which has resulted in millions being drained away from the country.

Politically, India's status has never been so reduced as under the British regime. No reforms have given real political power to the people. The tallest of us have to bend before foreign authority. The rights of free expression of opinion and free association have been denied to us, and many of our countrymen are compelled to live in exile abroad and cannot return to their homes. All administrative talent is killed, and the masses have to be satisfied with petty village offices and clerkships.

Culturally, the system of education has torn us from our moorings, and our training has made us hug the very chains that bind us.

Spiritually, compulsory disarmament has made us unmanly and the presence of an alien army of occupation, employed with deadly effect to crush in us the spirit of resistance, has made us think that we cannot look after ourselves or put up a defence against foreign aggression, or even defend our homes and families from the attacks of thieves, robbers, and miscreants.

We hold it to be a crime against man and God to submit any longer to a rule that has caused this fourfold disaster to our country. We recognise, however, that the most effective way of gaining our freedom is not through violence. We will therefore prepare ourselves by withdrawing, so far as we can, all voluntary association from the British Government, and will prepare for civil disobedience, including non-payment of taxes. We are convinced that if we can but withdraw our voluntary help and stop payment of taxes without doing violence, even under provocation, the end of this inhuman rule is assured. We therefore hereby solemnly resolve to carry out the Congress instructions issued from time to time for the purpose of establishing Purna Swaraj.

Tryst with Destiny

[Tryst with Destiny was a speech made by Jawaharlal Nehru, the first Prime Minister of independent India. The speech was made to the Indian Constituent Assembly, on the eve of India's independence, towards midnight on 14 August 1947. It focuses on the aspects that transcend India's history. It is considered in modern India to be a landmark oration that captures the essence of the triumphant culmination of the hundred-year Indian freedom struggle against the British Empire in India].

Long years ago we made a tryst with destiny, and now the time comes when we shall redeem our pledge, not wholly or in full measure, but very substantially. At the stroke of the midnight hour, when the world sleeps, India will awake to life and freedom. A moment comes, which comes but rarely in history, when we step out from the old to the new, when an age ends, and when the soul of a nation, long suppressed, finds utterance. It is fitting that at this solemn moment we take the pledge of dedication to the service of India and her people and to the still larger cause of humanity.

At the dawn of history India started on her unending quest, and trackless centuries are filled with her striving and the grandeur of her success and her failures. Through good and ill fortune alike she has never lost sight of that quest or forgotten the ideals which gave her strength. We end today a period of ill fortune and India discovers herself again. The achievement we celebrate today is but a step, an opening of opportunity, to the greater triumphs and achievements that await us. Are we brave enough and wise enough to grasp this opportunity and accept the challenge of the future?

Freedom and power bring responsibility. The responsibility rests upon this Assembly, a sovereign body representing the sovereign people of India. Before the birth of freedom we have endured all the pains of labour and our hearts are heavy with the memory of this sorrow. Some of those pains continue even now. Nevertheless, the past is over and it is the future that beckons to us now.

That future is not one of ease or resting but of incessant striving so that we may fulfil the pledges we have so often taken and the one we shall take today. The service of India means the service of the millions who suffer. It means the ending of poverty and ignorance and disease and inequality of opportunity. The ambition of the greatest man of our generation has been to wipe every tear from every eye. That may be beyond us, but as long as there are tears and suffering, so long our work will not be over.

And so we have to labour and to work, and work hard, to give reality to our dreams. Those dreams are for India, but they are also for the world, for all the nations and peoples are too closely knit together today for any one of them to imagine that it can live apart Peace has been said to be indivisible; so is freedom, so is prosperity now, and so also is disaster in this One World that can no longer be split into isolated fragments.

To the people of India, whose representatives we are, we make an appeal to join us with faith and confidence in this great adventure. This is no time for petty and destructive criticism, no time for ill-will or blaming others. We have to build the noble mansion of free India where all her children may dwell.

The appointed day has come-the day appointed by destiny-and India stands forth again, after long slumber and struggle, awake, vital, free and independent. The past clings on to us still in some measure and we have to do much before we redeem the pledges we have so often taken. Yet the turning-point is past, and history begins anew for us, the history which we shall live and act and others will write about.

It is a fateful moment for us in India, for all Asia and for the world. A new star rises, the star of freedom in the East, a new hope comes into being, a vision long cherished materialises. May the star never set and that hope never be betrayed!

We rejoice in that freedom, even though clouds surround us, and many of our people are sorrowstricken and difficult problems encompass us. But freedom brings responsibilities and burdens and we have to face them in the spirit of a free and disciplined people.

On this day our first thoughts go to the architect of this freedom, the Father of our Nation [Gandhi], who, embodying the old spirit of India, held aloft the torch of freedom and lighted up the darkness that surrounded us. We have often been unworthy followers of his and have strayed from his message, but not only we but succeeding generations will remember this message and bear the imprint in their hearts of this great son of India, magnificent in his faith and strength and courage and humility. We shall never allow that torch of freedom to be blown out, however high the wind or stormy the tempest.

Our next thoughts must be of the unknown volunteers and soldiers of freedom who, without praise or reward, have served India even unto death.

We think also of our brothers and sisters who have been cut off from us by political boundaries and who unhappily cannot share at present in the freedom that has come. They are of us and will remain of us whatever may happen, and we shall be sharers in their good and ill fortune alike.

The future beckons to us. Whither do we go and what shall be our endeavour? To bring freedom and opportunity to the common man, to the peasants and workers of India; to fight and end poverty and ignorance and disease; to build up a prosperous, democratic and progressive nation, and to create social, economic and political institutions which will ensure justice and fullness of life to every man and woman.

We have hard work ahead. There is no resting for any one of us till we redeem our pledge in full, till we make all the people of India what destiny intended them to be. We are citizens of a great country on the verge of bold advance, and we have to live up to that high standard. All of us, to whatever religion we may belong, are equally the children of India with equal rights, privileges and obligations. We cannot encourage communalism or narrow-mindedness, for no nation can be great whose people are narrow in thought or in action.

To the nations and peoples of the world we send greetings and pledge ourselves to cooperate with them in furthering peace, freedom and democracy.

And to India, our much-loved motherland, the ancient, the eternal and the ever-new, we pay our reverent homage and we bind ourselves afresh to her service.

Jai Hind!

Resolution of Remembrance

January 26th, 1931

We, the citizens of .... record our proud and grateful appreciation of the sons and daughters of India who have taken part in the great struggle for independence and have suffered and sacrificed so that the motherland may be free; of our great and beloved leader, Mahatma Gandhi, who has been a constant inspiration for us, ever pointing to the path of high purpose and noble endeavour; of the hundreds of our brave youths who have laid down their lives at the altar of freedom; of the martyrs of Peshawar and the whole Frontier Province, Sholapur, Midnapur District, and Bombay; of the scores of thousands who have faced and suffered barbarous lathi attacks from the forces of the enemy; of the men of the Garhwali Regiment, and all other Indians in the military and the police ranks of the Government, who have refused, at the peril of their own lives, to fire or take other action against their own countrymen; of the indomitable peasantry of Gujrat, which has faced without flinching and turning back all manner of acts of terrorism, and the brave and long-suffering peasantry of the other parts of India, which has taken full pan in the struggle despite every effort to suppress it; of the merchants and the other members of the commercial community, who have helped, at great loss to themselves, in the national struggle and especially in the boycotts of foreign cloth and British goods; of the one hundred thousand men and women who have gone to the prisons and suffered all manner of privation and sometimes assaults and beatings even inside the goal walls; and especially of the ordinary volunteer who, like a true soldier of India, without care of fame or reward, thinking only of the great cause he served, has laboured unceasingly and peacefully through suffering and hardship.

And we record our homage and deep admiration for the womanhood of India, who, in the hour of peril for the motherland forsook the shelter of their homes and, with unfailing courage and endurance, stood shoulder to shoulder with their menfolk in the front line of India's national army, to share with them the sacrifices and triumphs of the struggle; and our pride at the youth of the country and the Vanar Sena, whom even their tender age could not prevent from participating in the struggle and offering martyrs for the cause.

And, further, we record our grateful appreciation of the fact that all the major and minor communities and classes in India have joined together in the great struggle and given of their best to the cause; of, particularly, the minority communities — the Muslims, Sikhs, Parsis, Christians and others who, by their valour and loyal devotion to the cause of the common mother land, have helped in building up a united and indissoluble nation, certain of victory, and resolved to achieve and maintain the independence of India, and to use this new freedom to raise the shackles from, and to remove the inequalities among, all classes of the people of India, and thus also to serve the larger cause of humanity. And with this splendid and inspiring example of sacrifice and suffering in India's cause before us, we repeat our Pledge of Independence, and resolve to carry on the fight till India is completely free.

Asian Relations Conference

24 March 1947

Friends and fellow Asians! What has brought you here, men and women of Asia? Why have you come from the various countries of this mother continent of ours and gathered together in the ancient city of Delhi? Some of us, greatly daring, sent you invitation for this Conference and you gave a warm welcome to that invitation. And yet it was not merely that call from us but some deeper urge that brought you here.

We stand at the end of an era and on the threshold of a new period of history. Standing on this watershed which divides two epochs of human history and endeavour, we can look back on our long past and look forward to the future that is taking shape before our eyes. Asia, after a long period of quiescence, has suddenly become important again in world affairs. If we view the millennia of history, this continent of Asia, with which Egypt has been so intimately connected in cultural fellowship, has played a mighty role in the evolution of humanity. It was there that civilization began and man started on his unending adventure of life. Here the mind of man searched unceasingly for truth and the spirit of man shone out like a beacon which lightened up the whole world.

This dynamic Asia from which great streams of culture flowed in all directions, gradually became static and unchanging. Other peoples and other continents came to the fore and with their dynamism spread out and took possession of great parts of the world. This mighty continent became just a field for the rival imperialisms of Europe, and Europe became the centre of history and progress in human affairs.

A change is coming over the scene now and Asia is again finding herself. We live in a tremendous age of transition and already the next stage takes shape when Asia takes her rightful place with the other continents.

It is at this great moment that we meet here and it is the pride and privilege of the people of India to welcome their fellow Asians from other countries, to confer with them about the present and the future, and lay the foundation of our mutual progress, well-being and friendship.

The idea of having an Asian Conference is not new and many people have thought of it. It is indeed surprising that it should not have been held many years earlier, yet perhaps the time was not ripe for it and any attempt to do so would have been superficial and not in tune with world events. It so happened that we in India convened this Conference, but the idea of such a Conference arose simultaneously in many minds and in many countries of Asia. There was a widespread urge and an awareness that the time had come for us, peoples of Asia, to meet together, to hold together and to advance together. It was not only a vague desire but a compulsion of events that forced all of us to think along these lines. Because of this, the invitation we in India sent out brought an answering echo and a magnificent response from every country of Asia.

We welcome you delegates and representatives from China, that great country to which Asia owes so much and from which so much is expected; from Egypt and the Arab countries of western Asia, inheritors of a proud culture which spread far and wide and influenced India greatly; from Iran whose contacts with India go back to the dawn of history; from Indonesia and Indo-China whose history in intertwined with India's culture, and where recently the battle of freedom has continued — a reminder to us that freedom must be won and cannot come as a gift; from Turkey that has been rejuvenated by the genious of a great leader; from Korea and Mongolia, Siam, Malaya and the Philippines; from the Soviet Republics of Asia which have advanced so rapidly in our generation and which have so many lessons to teach us; from our neighbours Afghanistan, Tibet, Nepal, Bhutan, Burma and Ceylon to whom we look especially for cooperation and close and friendly intercourse. Asia is very well represented at this Conference, and if one or two countries have been unable to send representatives, this was due to no lack of desire on their part or ours, but circumstances beyond our control came in the way. We welcome also observers from Australia and New Zealand because we have many problems in common, especially in the Pacific and in the Southeast region of Asia, and we have to cooperate together to find solutions.

As we meet here today, the long past of Asia rises up before us, the troubles of recent years fade away, and a thousand memories revive. But I shall not speak to you of these past ages with their glories and triumphs and failures, nor of more recent times which have oppressed us so much and which still pursue us in some measure.

During the past two hundred years we have seen the growth of Western imperialism and of the reduction of large parts of Asia to colonial or semi-colonial status. Much has happened during these years, but perhaps one of the notable consequences of the European domination of Asia has been the isolation of the countries of Asia from one another. India always had contacts and intercourse with her neighbour countries in the Northwest, the Northeast, the East and the Southeast. With the coming of British rule in India these contacts were broken off and India was almost completely isolated from the rest of Asia. The old land routes almost ceased to function and our chief window to the outer world looked out on the sea routes which led to England. A similar process affected the other countries of Asia also. Their entire economy was bound up with some European imperialism or other; even culturally they looked towards Europe and not to their own friends and neighbours from whom they had derived so much in the past.

Today this isolation is breaking down because of many reasons, political and other. The old imperialisms are fading away. The land routes have revived and air travel suddenly brings us very near to each other. This Conference itself is significant as an expression of that deeper urge to the mind and spirit of Asia which has persisted in spite of the isolationism which grew up during the years of European domination. As that domination goes, the walls that surrounded us fall down and we look at each other again and meet as old friends long parted.

In this Conference and in this work there are no leaders and no followers. All countries of Asia have to meet together on an equal basis in a common task and endeavour. It is fitting that India should play her part in this new phase of Asian development. Apart from the fact that India herself is emerging into freedom and independence, she is the compelling factor, and a geographically she is so situated as to be the meeting point of western and northern and eastern and South East Asia. Streams of culture have come to India from the west and the east and been absorbed in India, producing the rich and variegated culture which is India today. At the same time, streams of culture have flowed from India to distant parts of Asia. If you would know India you have to go to Afghanistan and Western Asia, to Central Asia, to China and Japan and to the countries of South East Asia. There you will find magnificent evidence of the vitality of India's culture which spread out and influenced vast numbers of people.

There came the great cultural stream from Iran to India in remote antiquity. And then the constant intercourse between India and the Far East, notably China. In later years South East Asia witnessed an amazing efflorescence of Indian art and culture. The mighty stream which started from Arabia and developed as a mixed Irano-Arabic culture poured into India. All these came to us and influenced us and yet so great was the powerful impress of India's own mind and culture that it could accept them without being itself swept away or overwhelmed. Nevertheless we all changed in the process and in India today all of us are mixed products of these various influences. An Indian, wherever he may go in Asia, feels a sense of kinship with the land he visits and the people he meets.

I do not wish to speak to you of the past but rather of the present. We meet here not to discuss our past history and contacts but to forge links for the future. And may I say here that this Conference, and the idea underlying it, is no way aggressive or against any other continent or country. Ever since news of this Conference went abroad some people in Europe and America have viewed it with doubt imagining that this was some kind of a Pan-Asian movement directed against Europe or America. We have no designs against anybody; ours is the great design of promoting peace and progress all over the world. For too long we Asia have been petitioners in Western courts and chancellories. That story must now belong to the past. We propose to stand on our own feet and to cooperate with all others who are prepared to cooperate with us. We do not intend to be the plaything of others.

In this crisis in world history Asia will necessarily play a vital role. The countries of Asia can no longer be used as pawns by others; they are bound to have their own policies in world affairs. Europe and America have contributed very greatly to human progress and for that we must yield them praise and honour, and learn from them the many lessons they hay to teach. But the West has also driven us into wars and conflicts without number and even now, the day after a terrible war, there is talk of further wars in the atomic age that is upon us. In this atomic age Asia will have to function effectively in the maintenance of peace. Indeed there can be no peace unless Asia plays her part. There is today conflict in many countries, and all of us in Asia are full of our own troubles. Nevertheless, the whole spirit and outlook of Asia are peaceful, and the emergence of Asia in world affairs will be powerful influence for world peace.

Peace can only come when nations are free and also when human beings everywhere have freedom and security and opportunity. Peace and freedom, therefore, have to be considered both in their political and economic aspects. The countries of Asia, we must remember, are very backward and the standards of life are appealingly low. These economic problems demand urgent solution or else crisis and disaster might overwhelm us. We have, therefore, to think in terms of the common man and fashion our political, social, and economic structure so that the burdens that have crushed him be removed, and he may have full opportunity for growth.

We have arrived at a stage in human affairs when the ideal of that 'One World' and some kind of a world federation seems to be essential though there are many dangers and obstacles in the way. We should work for that ideal and not any grouping which comes in the way of this larger world group. We therefore support the United Nations structure which is painfully emerging from its infancy but in order to have 'One World', we must also in Asia think of the countries of Asia cooperating together for that larger ideal.

This conference, in a small measure, represents this bringing together of the countries of Asia. Whatever it may achieve, the mere fact of its taking place is itself of historic significance. Indeed this occasion is unique in history for never before has such a gathering met together at any place. So even in meeting we have achieved much and I have no doubt that out of this meeting greater things will come. When the history of our present times is written, this event may well stand out as a landmark which divides the past of Asia from the future. And because we are participating in this making of history something of the greatness of historic events comes to us all.

This Conference will split up into committees and groups to discuss various problems which are common concerns to all of us. We shall not discuss the internal politics of any country because that is rather beyond the scope of our present meeting. Naturally we are interested in these internal politics because they act and react on each other, but we may not discuss them at this stage, for if we do so, we may lose ourselves in interminable arguments and complications. We may fail to achieve the purpose for which we have met. I hope that out of this Conference some permanent Asian Institute for the study of common problems and to bring about closer relations will emerge; also perhaps a School of Asian Studies. Further, we might be able to organise interchange of visits and exchanges of students and professors so that we might know each other better. There is much else we can do, but I shall not venture to enumerate all the subjects for it is for you to discuss them and arrive at some decisions.

We seek no narrow nationalism. Nationalism has a place in each country and should be fostered, but it must not be allowed to become aggressive and come in the way of international development. Asia stretches her hand out in friendship to Europe and America as well as to our suffering brethren in Africa. We must help them to take their rightful place in the human family. The freedom that we envisage is not to be confined to this nation or that or to a particular people, but must spread out over the whole human race. That universal human freedom cannot also be based in the supremacy of any particular class. It must be the freedom of the common man everywhere and full of opportunities for him to develop.

We think today of the great architects of Asian freedom — Sun Yat-sen, Zaghlul Pasha, the Ataturk Kemal Pasha and others, whose labours have borne fruit. We think also of that great figure whose labours and whose inspiration have brought India to the threshold of her independence — Mahatma Gandhi. We miss him at this Conference and I yet hope that he may visit us before our labours end. He is engrossed in the service of the common man in India, and even this Conference could not drag him away from it.

All over Asia we are passing through trials and tribulations. In India also you will see conflict and trouble. Let us not be disheartened by this: this is inevitable in an age of mighty transition. There is a new vitality and powerful creative impulse in all the peoples of Asia. The masses are awake and demand their heritage. Strong winds are blowing all over Asia. Let us not be afraid of them but rather welcome them for only with their help can we build the new Asia of our dreams. Let us have faith in these great new forces and the things which are taking shape. Above all let us have faith in the human spirit which Asia symbolised for these long ages past.

Promise of Reason

[Jawaharlal Nehru's broadcast to the nation on August 15, 1948 is noteworthy because the words he uttered then hold considerable importance for our contemporary political life. Excerpts from that address are being reproduced here. Better late than never].

Let us not forget where we have failed or where we have erred. For our failures and errors have been many. Some of these are obvious enough, but the real failure has been a failure of the spirit and a falling away from the high standards set by the Father of our Nation, under whose wise guidance we had struggled and marched for over a quarter of a century. He taught us that worthy ends could only be achieved through worthy means, that ideals and objectives could never be divorced from the methods adopted to realise them. He had told us to cast out fear, for fear is not only ignoble but is also the parent of hatred and violence.

Many of us forgot this lesson and fear gripped us, fear not of some distant adversary, but fear of one another, and evil deeds followed in its train.

The Master who guided us and inspired us is no more. We have to shoulder the burden ourselves now and the first question that we have to put ourselves is this: Do we stand by his teaching and message or do we stray into new paths? I want to tell you that this year of hard trial has convinced me more than ever that if India is to prosper and grow in stature, as she must and will, it will be through adherence to that message and teaching. I know I am feeble and have often proved unworthy of India to whose service I had pledged myself so often. But however unworthy we may be of India, we have still something of the strength that the Master gave us. That strength comes not only from him, but from his message, and so today I pledge myself anew to the service of the motherland and of the ideals that Gandhiji placed before us.

All of us talk of India and all of us demand many things from India. What do we give her in return? We can take nothing from her beyond what we give her. India will ultimately give us what we give her of love and service and productive and creative work. India will be what we are: our thoughts and action will shape her. Born of her fruitful womb, we are children of hers, little bits of the India of today, and yet we are also the parents of the India of tomorrow. If we are big, so will India be, and if we grow little-minded and narrow in outlook, so also will India be.

Our troubles during the past year were largely the result of this narrowness in outlook and pettiness in action which is so foreign to India's great cultural inheritance. Communalism threatened to crush the free spirit in us, the communalism of the Muslim, of the Hindu and of the Sikh. Provincialism came in the way of that larger unity which is so essential to India's greatness and progress. The spirit of faction spread and made us forget the big things that we had stood for.

We have to find ourselves again and go back to the free India of our dreams. We have to rediscover the old values and place them in the new setting of a free India. For freedom brings responsibility and can only be sustained by self-discipline, hard work, and the spirit of a free people.

So let us be rid of everything that limits us and degrades us. Let us cast out fear and communalism and provincialism. Let us build up a free and democratic India, where the interest of the masses of our people has always the first place to which all other interests must submit.

Freedom has no meaning unless it brings relief to these masses from their many burdens. Democracy means tolerance, tolerance not merely of those who agree with us, but of those who do not agree with us. With the coming of freedom our patterns of behaviour must change also so as to fit in with this freedom.

There is conflict and there are rumours of greater conflict in India and all over the world. We have to be ready for every emergency and contingency. When the nation is in peril, the first duty of every citizen is to give his or her service to the nation without fear or expectation of reward. But today, I do not wish to speak of conflicts and wars but rather of peace and cooperation and I want say to all the nations of the world, including our neighbour country, that we stand for peace and friendship with them. The only war that we want to fight with all our might is the war against poverty and all its unhappy brood.

A Voyage of Discovery

[Prime Minister Jawaharlal Nehru's speech in the US House of Representatives and the Senate].

Washington D.C.
October 13, 1949

I have come to this country to learn something of your great achievements. I have come also to convey the greetings of my people and in the hope that my visit may help to create a greater understanding between our respective peoples and those strong and sometimes invisible links, stronger even than physical links, that bind countries together. The President referred the day before yesterday, in language of significance, to my visit as a voyage of discovery of America. The United States of America is not an unknown country even in far off India and many of us have grown up in admiration of the ideals and objectives which have made this country great.

Yet, though we may know the history and something of the culture of our respective countries, what is required is a true understanding and appreciation of each other even where we differ. Out of that understanding grows fruitful cooperation in the pursuit of common ideals. What the world today lacks most is, perhaps, understanding and appreciation of one another among nations and people. I have come here, therefore, on a voyage of discovery of the mind and heart of America and to place before you our own mind and heart. Thus, we may promote that understanding and cooperation which, I feel sure, both our countries earnestly desire. Already I have received a welcome here, the generous warmth of which has created a deep impression on my mind and, indeed, somewhat overwhelmed me.

During the last two days that I have been in Washington, I have paid visits to the memorials of the great builders of this nation. I have done so not for the sake of mere formality but because they have long been enshrined in my heart and their example has inspired me as it has inspired innumerable countrymen of mine. These memorials are the real temples to which each generation must pay tribute and, in doing so, must catch something of the fire that burned in the hearts of those who were the torchbearers of freedom, not only for this country but for the world; for those who arc truly great have a message that cannot be confined within a particular country but is for all the world.

In India there came a man in our own generation who inspired us to great endeavour, ever reminding us that thought and action should never be divorced from moral principle, that the true path of man is the path of truth and peace. Under his guidance, we laboured for the freedom of our country, with ill-will to none and achieved that freedom. We called him reverently and affectionately the Father of our Nation. Yet he was too great for the circumscribed borders of any one country and the message he gave may well help us in considering the wider problems of the world.

The United States of America has struggled to freedom and unparalleled prosperity during the past century and a half and today it is a great and powerful nation. It has an amazing record of growth in material well-being and scientific and technological advance. It could not have accomplished this unless America had been anchored in the great principles laid down in the early days of her history, for material progress cannot go far or last long unless it has its foundations in moral principles and high ideals.

Those principles and ideals are enshrined in your Declaration of Independence, which lays down as a self-evident truth that all men are created equal, that they are endowed by their Creator with certain inalienable rights, that among these are life, liberty and the pursuit of happiness. It may interest you to know that, in drafting the Constitution of the Republic of India, we have been greatly influenced by your own Constitution. The preamble of our Constitution states:

> We, the people of India, having solemnly resolved to constitute India into a Sovereign Democratic Republic and to secure to all its citizens:
>
> Justice, social, economic and political;
>
> Liberty of thought, expression, belief, faith and worship;
>
> Equality of status and of opportunity; and to promote among them all Fraternity assuring the dignity of the individual and the unity of the Nation;
>
> In our Constituent Assembly do hereby adopt, enact and give to ourselves this Constitution.

You will recognise in these words that I have quoted an echo of the great voices of the founders of your Republic. You will see that though India may speak to you in a voice that you may not immediately recognise or that may perhaps appear somewhat alien to you, yet that voice somewhat strongly resembles what you have often heard before.

Yet, it is true that India's voice is somewhat different; it is not the voice of the old world of Europe but of the older world of Asia. It is the voice of an ancient civilization, distinctive, vital, which, at the same time, has renewed itself and learned much from you and the other countries of the West. It is, therefore, both old and new. It has its roots deep in the past but it also has the dynamic urge of today.

But however the voices of India and the United States may appear to differ, there is much in common between them. Like you, we have achieved our freedom through a revolution, though our methods were different from yours. Like you we shall be a republic based on the federal principle, which is an outstanding contribution of the founders of this great Republic. In a vast country like India, as in this great Republic of the United States, it becomes necessary to have a delicate balance between central control and State autonomy. We have placed in the forefront of our Constitution those fundamental human rights to which all men who love liberty, equality and progress aspire-the freedom of the individual, the equality of men and the rule of law. We enter, therefore, the community of free nations with the roots of democracy deeply embedded in our institutions as well as in the thoughts of our people.

We have achieved political freedom but our revolution is not yet complete and is still in progress, for political freedom without the assurance of the right to live and to pursue happiness, which economic progress alone can bring, can never satisfy a people. Therefore, our immediate task is to raise the living standards of our people, to remove all that comes in the way of the economic growth of the nation. We have tackled the major problem of India, as it is today the major problem of Asia, the agrarian problem. Much that was feudal in our system of land tenure is being changed so that the fruits of cultivation should go to the tiller of the soil and that he may be secure in the possession of the land he cultivates. In a country of which agriculture is still the principal industry, this reform is essential not only for the well-being and contentment of the individual but also for the stability of society.

One of the main causes of social instability in many parts of the world, more especially in Asia, is agrarian discontent due to the continuance of systems of land tenure which are completely out of place in the modem world. Another-and one which is also true of the greater part of Asia and Africa-is the low standard of living of the masses.

India is industrially more developed than many less fortunate countries and is reckoned as the seventh or eighth among the world's industrial nations. But this arithmetical distinction cannot conceal the poverty of the great majority of our people. To remove this poverty by greater production, more equitable distribution, better education and better health, is the paramount need and the most pressing task before us and we are determined to accomplish this task. We realise that self-help is the first condition of success for a nation, no less than for an individual. We are conscious that ours must be the primary effort and we shall seek succour from none to escape from any part of our own responsibility. But though our economic potential is great, its conversion into finished wealth will need much mechanical and technological aid. We shall, therefore, gladly welcome such aid and cooperation on terms that are of mutual benefit. We believe that this may well help in the solution of the larger problems that confront the world. But we do not seek any material advantage in exchange for any part of our hard-won freedom.

The objectives of our foreign policy are the preservation of world peace and enlargement of human freedom. Two tragic wars have demonstrated the futility of warfare. Victory without the will to peace achieves no lasting result and victor and vanquished alike suffer from deep and grievous wounds and a common fear of the future. May I venture to say that this is not an incorrect description of the world of today? It is not flattering either to man's reason or to our common humanity. Must this unhappy state persist and the power of science and wealth continue to be harnessed to the service of destruction? Every nation, great or small, has to answer this question and the greater a nation, the greater is its responsibility to find and to work for the right answer.

India may be new to world politics and her military strength insignificant in comparison with that of the giants of our epoch.

But India is old in thought and experience and has travelled through trackless centuries in the adventure of life. Throughout her long history she has stood for peace and every prayer that an Indian raises, ends with an invocation to peace. It was out of this ancient and yet young India that Mahatma Gandhi arose and he taught us a technique of action that was peaceful; yet it was effective and yielded results that led us not only to freedom but to friendship with those with whom we were, till yesterday, in conflict. How far can that principle be applied to wider spheres of action? I do not know, for circumstances differ and the means to prevent evil have to be shaped and set to the nature of the evil. Yet I have no doubt that the basic approach which lay behind that technique of action was the right approach in human affairs and the only approach that ultimately solves a problem satisfactorily. We have to achieve freedom and to defend it. We have to meet aggression and to resist it and the force employed must be adequate to the purpose. But even when preparing to resist aggression, the ultimate objective, the objective of peace and reconciliation, must never be lost sight of and heart and mind must be attuned to this supreme aim and not swayed or clouded by hatred or fear.

This is the basis and the goal of our foreign policy. We are neither blind to reality nor do we propose to acquiesce in any challenge to man's freedom from whatever quarter it may come. Where freedom is menaced or justice threatened or where aggression takes place, we cannot be and shall not be neutral. What we plead for and endeavour to practice in our own imperfect way is a binding faith in peace and an unfailing endeavour of thought and action to ensure it. The great democracy of the United States of America will, I feel sure, understand and appreciate our approach to life's problems because it could not have any other aim or a different ideal. Friendship and cooperation between our two countries are, therefore, natural. I stand here to offer both in the pursuit of justice, liberty and peace.

On Religion and Secularism

> "Communalism, of course has to be fought ruthlessly and suppressed. But I really do not think it is such a power as it is made out to be. It may be a giant today

> but it has feet of clay. It is the outcome largely of anger and passion and when we regain our tempers it will fade into nothingness. It is a myth with no connection with reality and it cannot endure. It is really the creation of our educated classes in search of office and employment."

The above quote exemplifies Jawaharlal Nehru's thinking on the challenge of accommodating religion within modern politics as will be seen from the following overview of his early writings and speeches. To begin with however, a system of coding is applied in order to assess the causal assertions inherent in the above statement and to extract a cognitive map for this particular theme of the role of religion in society.

On the topic of religion, Nehru propounded various arguments portraying its negative effects on society and politics. His earliest published volume, *Letters from a Father to his Daughter*, is extremely negative about the role of religion. Describing the origin of religion which, 'first came as fear....But however, much it may have grown, we see even today that people fight and break each other's heads in the name of religion. And for many people it is still something to be afraid of. They spend their time in trying to please some imaginary beings by making presents in temples and even sacrifices of animals'. Nor did Nehru change his tone depending on the audience. For example, speaking in Varanasi in Uttar Pradesh, one of Hinduism's holiest cities, and presumably therefore to an audience amongst which there were people who held religion dear, Nehru had the following to say: 'It is strange that for the most trivial things, for childish superstition or silly prejudice people take risks and lose their reason in a sea of anger. The vital things, the real things that matter pass unnoticed. Ignorance and bigotry put an end to all rational thought. It is almost useless to argue or convince. Religion is degraded and in its name are done the most shameful things. Indeed religion has become the excuse for many sins. It has little sanctity left and it is trotted out in season and out of season and all argument naturally ends.'

Another common attack against religion was that it was partly to blame for India's weaknesses and a reason why the region had succumbed to imperial rule. With independence, the country was to wipe the slate clean and start anew by embracing modernity. The radicalism of the early Jawaharlal Nehru shows through particularly in speeches aimed at rousing the young. For example in his presidential address to the Bombay Presidency Youth Conference in 1928, Nehru proclaimed:

> 'We must aim, therefore, at the destruction of all imperialism and the reconstruction of society on another basis.....Our national ideal must, therefore, be the establishment of a cooperative socialist commonwealth and our international ideal, a world federation of socialist states. Before we approach our ideal, we have to combat two sets of opponents - political and social. We have to overcome our alien rulers as well as the social reactionaries of India....... Religion has in the past often been used as an opiate to dull men's desire for freedom....Religion has been the fountain-head of authoritarianism and meek submission.'

Similarly, in a Presidential address at the Punjab Provincial Conference in April 1928, Nehru reminded his audience:

> 'We forget that our ancient civilizations, great as they are, were meant for different ages and different conditions. We cannot have today, in an industrial age, an early agrarian economy, such as we had in Vedic times; much less can we have in our country a civilization meant for a desert country more than 1,300 years ago. And many of our traditions and habits and customs, our social laws, our caste system, the position we give to women, and the dogmas which religion has imposed on us, are the relics of a past, suitable in those far-off days but utterly out of joint with modern conditions'.

At numerous occasions Nehru expressed his firm conviction that religion and religious categories would lose their relevance. For example this crops up during a series of articles written between 1933 and 1934, published in various newspapers. In response to Muhammad Iqbal who had accused Gandhi of preventing Muslims and the 'Harijans' from making common cause at the Round Table Conference, Nehru stated 'Personally, I am not interested in religious labels and I am sure that they will soon disappear, or, at any rate, cease to have any political significance'. Such statements, of course with the benefit of hindsight, imply a deep misjudgement of his people and their socio-cultural conditions. Nehru went on to define his outlook which 'is not religious and I find it difficult to think of groups in terms of religion. Sir Muhammad evidently does so to the exclusion of other and more modern ways of thinking, and I am afraid he confuses religion with race and culture.'

The unity of India was a central concern for Nehru during this period and almost all his books deal with this theme either from a historical, cultural angle or in terms of the success of a national freedom movement. Though it is not mentioned explicitly, secularism does begin to appear within Nehru's vision as the glue for holding a state such as India together and providing the basis for a national consciousness, overcoming 'numerous superficial differences'. The early Nehru did demonstrate an awareness for the challenges in establishing a level-playing field where the majority community makes compromises and the minority community feels protected and not disadvantaged. However, as Nehru himself pointed out in his retort to Iqbal, 'What are these minimum safeguards (for the protection of a minority) and who is to decide them? The minority itself?...... How are we to know what the minority community really desires? Are we to take the opinion of any small group claiming to represent the community? And when there are several such groups, what are we to do?' Precisely these questions were to return in the 1950s when Nehru attempted to create the institutional foundations for a secular state although, as will be seen later on, the impasse created by the Hindu Code Bill reflected some serious miss-calculations.

Much later on, Nehru's writings in prison reflected a deepening faith in modernisation and a 'scientific rationalism'. Hence, the scientific approach was described by Nehru as 'the refusal to accept anything without testing and trial, the capacity to change previous conclusions in the face of new evidence, the reliance on observed fact and not on pre-conceived theory, the hard discipline of the mind – all this is necessary, not merely for the application of science but for life itself and the solution of its many problems." Whilst in contrast, the methods employed by religion were seen as compounding society's problems, "Concerned as it is principally with the regions beyond the reach of objective enquiry, it relies on emotion and intuition. And then it applies this method to everything in life, even to those things which are capable of intellectual enquiry and observation. Organised religion, allying itself to theology and often more concerned with vested interests than with things of the spirit, encourages a temper which is the very opposite to that of science. It produces narrowness and intolerance, credulity and superstition, emotionalism and irrationalism. It tends to close and limit the mind of man, and to produce a temper of a dependent, unfree person."

Although Nehru had his differences with Gandhi he chose not to publicise them too much. One such occasion when he did articulate his disagreement with Gandhi's goals and methods occurred in September 1932 when Gandhi went on a "fast unto death" on the subject of separate electorates for India's "depressed classes" which Gandhi considered to be a British attempt to divide and undermine Indians along further cleavages. Nehru, on the other hand, considered this to be a 'side issue', writing in his *Autobiography*, that he 'felt angry with Bapu at his religious and sentimental approach to a political question..... And his frequent references to God – God has made him do this – God even indicated the date of the fast.... What a terrible example to set!'

Despite this deeply-held view of religion producing obfuscation, and something which must inevitably fade away with modernisation, there are strong inconsistencies in Nehru's thinking on the subject of religion, religiosity and the need for reform. This comes out most clearly in the different assumptions underlying his diagnoses and recommendations for India's Muslim and Hindu communities. Hence, he posited that, "a special responsibility does attach to the Hindus in India both because they are the majority community and because economically and educationally they are more advanced." However, while Hindus are berated for having fallen behind the rest of the world because of inherently retrograde social customs like the caste system and unnecessary mystification, the particular Muslim trauma had to be treated differently given that it suffered from exogenous shocks. The following needs to be quoted at length as it captures this sentiment:

> "Moslems have produced few outstanding figures of the modern type. They have produced some remarkable men but, as a rule, these represented the continuation of the old culture and tradition and did not easily fit in with modern developments. This incapacity to march with the changing times and adapt themselves culturally and otherwise to a new environment was not of course due to any innate failing. It derived from certain historical causes, from the delay in the development of a new industrial middle class, and the excessively feudal background of the Moslems, which blocked up avenues of development and prevented the release of talent. In Bengal the backwardness of the Moslems was most marked, but this was obviously due to two causes: the destruction of their upper classes during the early days of British rule, and the fact that the vast majority were converts from the lowest class of Hindus, who had long been denied opportunities or growth and progress."

As a result, the narratives Nehru constructed to explain the weaknesses of religious communities to cope with modernity rest on different explanatory variables. On the one hand Hinduism is portrayed as inherently backward whilst the fate of Islam is to be empathised with because of the negative outcomes resulting from its encounter with British rule. This lopsidedness persists through most of Nehru's writings and into his years of policy-making as Prime Minister. For example, although communalism was condemned by Nehru both in its Hindu and Muslim variants, the harsher criticism was always maintained for the Hindu Mahasabha.

Another instance of bias arises in his book, *The Discovery of India*, where Nehru devotes quite a few pages to 'secular' thinkers and movements like that of Vivekananda, Rabindranath Tagore and Annie Besant, but hardly acknowledges the important reform movements of the *Brahmo Swaraj* and *Arya Samaj* which were more explicitly based on Hindu philosophy, Hindu practices and ideals. On the Muslim front however, Nehru lauds the more religious reform movements like Sir Syed Ahmad Khan, leader of the Aligarh Movement as well as more secular Muslim leaders like Abdul Kalam Azad. Recognising the psychological dilemmas that Indian Muslims faced over matters of history and questions of allegiance, Nehru wrote with compassion for the challenges they must have faced. For, "to begin with, the new middle classes were almost absent among the Moslems. Their avoidance of western education, their keeping away from trade and industry, and their adherence to feudal ways, gave a start to the Hindus which they profited by and retained. ....The Revolt of 1857 was a joint affair, but in its suppression Moslems felt strongly, and to some extent rightly, that they were the greater sufferers. This Revolt also put an end finally to any dreams or fantasies of the revival of the Delhi Empire."

Underlying this analysis was his deep conviction that, if it were not for opportunist trouble-makers and reactionary stakeholders, people would respond automatically and primarily to universal economic incentives. Living under modern conditions, Nehru appeared to grant no intrinsic need for spiritual, non-material beliefs. In challenging the Hindu Mahasabha leader, Bhai Parmanandji, Nehru asked the following: 'In the modern world, trains, cars and aeroplanes have almost abolished boundaries and built world unity. Books, newspapers, the telegraphy, radio and cinema influence us and gradually change our ideas....I want to know from Bhaiji what is the stand of our old Hinduism on all these matters? He talks about religion and caste civilizations. But the civilization of the modern world is that of mighty machinery and gigantic workshops. What have they to do with religions?"

To summarise, the central concept within Nehru's assessment and understanding of religion is that of rationality. The scientifically rational person, is epistemologically speaking, someone whose relation to knowledge and reality is primarily positivist and material. Hence, religion is portrayed in various negative ways as (a) a veneer, (b) an instrument for power politics and, (c) a source of dogmatism and debilitation. In each case the implication is that religion contributes to irrational behaviour and this applied to both Muslims and Hindus. At the same time Nehru was committed to the argument that material not spiritual factors ultimately account for people's behaviour. In a series of articles on The Unity of India, Nehru writes that the Muslims are only technically a minority: 'They are vast in numbers and powerful in other ways, and it is patent that they cannot be coerced against their will, just as the Hindus cannot be coerced against their will.... But let us always remember that in political and economic matters people do not function as religious groups. The lines of cleavage are different'.

Translating such a stance into concrete policy recommendations is problematic since in Nehru's ideal state of the world, religion would simply cease to play a role. In the quote with which this section began, Nehru portrays Communalism as 'a giant with feet of clay and when we regain our tempers it will fade into nothingness'. How to convince a population of this, for whom religion had long been a central institution and an important mechanism facilitating exchange and providing social organisation? However, rather than focusing upon this as a key policy concern and the need to develop mechanisms and strategies to bring about a gradual process of change, Nehru appears to have regarded 'social' change to be, by and large, a by-product of 'economic' change. Thus, Nehru could claim that the caste system, which had withstood centuries of challenges, was facing an existential threat: "That is not chiefly because of some powerful urge to reform itself which has arisen in Hindu society...nor is it because of ideas from the west...The change that is taking place before our eyes is due essentially to basic economic changes which have shaken up the whole fabric of Indian society and are likely to upset it completely."

However, in one of his later pieces of writing, The Unity of India, Nehru simply states that "There is no religious or cultural conflict in India. What is called the religious or communal problem is really a dispute among upper-class people for a division of the spoils of office or of representation in a legislature." Given that he saw this essentially as a problem of elites and resources, the envisioned solution, presumably, would not need to deal with intangibles and imponderables such as identity and values. In other words, Nehru could quite comfortably and confidently say, that 'This will surely be settled amicably wherever it arises'. This is markedly different from his approach towards economic planning which foresaw the possible objections, hurdles, and the need for consensus-building. Strangely, in the area of social reform, Nehru seemed to revert most closely to policies initiated by the British, an indication, this thesis proposes, of the limited expertise and understanding that Nehru had for the problem. This leads to the controversial proposition that despite being hailed as founder of a secular state, Nehru contributed very little in terms of actually institutionalising secularism.

For instance on the topic of reforming Hindu Law he presents the following criticism of the British strategy that codified customary law: "customs change and are forced to adapt themselves to some extent to a changing environment. Hindu law was largely custom, and as custom changed the law also was applied in a different way. Indeed, there was no provision of Hindu law which could not be changed by custom. The British replaced this elastic customary law by judicial decisions based on the old texts and Brahmanic interpretations, and these decisions became precedents which had to be rigidly followed. That was, in theory, an advantage, as it produced greater uniformity and certainty, But, in the manner it was done, it resulted in the perpetuation of ancient law unmodified by subsequent customs.......Change could only come by positive legislation, but the British Government, which was the legislating authority, had no wish to antagonise the conservative elements on whose support it counted."

Nehru was aware of the shortcomings of a project, where codification had drastically restricted the capacity for change and adaptation. In his efforts later to introduce the Hindu code bills in the mid to late-50s, Nehru was so convinced of the rational righteousness of his judgement that he forgot these two important lessons that the British experience should have provided: (1) codification as a form of petrification and, (2) legislation as a product of lobbying that is bound to skew original reformist intentions. Furthermore, since Nehru did not initiate any process of consensus-building or fact-finding (as he did in the case of planning), the Hindu code bill was quickly framed within a highly polarised debate pitting 'modernists' and 'reformists' against 'reactionaries' and 'revivalists'. Nehru's attempts to reform Hinduism and the application of Hindu law, fell far short of his expectations.

On Economic Development and Socialism

Encountering the fashionable creed of Fabianism during his student days in London through people like Harold Laski at the London School of Economics, the young Jawaharlal Nehru was full of radical ideas. Visiting Russia in 1928 together with his father, Motilal Nehru, a series of articles by Jawaharlal Nehru were published in various Indian newspapers and then compiled into a book titled, Soviet Russia. Some Random Sketches and Impressions. Admitting a 'fascination for Russia', he wrote that the conditions in Russia have not been and continued to be not very dissimilar to those in India: 'Both are vast agricultural countries with only the beginnings of industrialisation, and both have to face poverty and illiteracy.

If Russia finds a satisfactory solution for these, our work in India is made easier'. The 'economic interpretation of history', or 'historic materialism' appealed greatly to the young Nehru and his later works often allude to the need to explore the economic as well as political roots of problems. For instance in an essay titled, Whither India, written in 1934 there are numerous references to class interests and the inevitable conflict over what freedom meant to "feudal India of the princes, the India of the big zamindars, of small zamindars, of the professional classes, of the agriculturalists, of the industrialists, of the bankers, of the lower middles class, of the workers."

Not much time is spent in Nehru's writings discussing details or grappling with theoretical works either by Laski or Marx (who presumably had an impact on him) and instead he propounded a more personal and rather vague interpretation of socialism. Hence, in the same article mentioned above, Whither India, Jawaharlal analyses the world situation in the following terms, 'capitalism, having solved the problem of production, helplessly faces the allied problem of distribution and is unable to solve it... To find a solution for distributing wealth and purchasing power evenly is to put an end to the basic inequalities of the capitalist system and to replace capitalism itself by a more scientific system.' (italics added).

Similarly, in his 1936 presidential address to the INC, Nehru claimed:

> "I am convinced that the only key to the solution of the world's problem and of India's problems lies in socialism, and when I use this word I do so not in a vague humanitarian way but in the scientific, economic sense. Socialism is, however, something even more than an economic doctrine; it is a philosophy of life and as such also appeals to me. I see no way of ending the poverty, the vast unemployment, the degradation and the subjection of the Indian people except through socialism. That involves vast and revolutionary changes in our political and social structure, the ending of vested interests in land and industry, the ending of private property, except in a restricted sense, and the replacement of the present profit system by a higher ideal of cooperative service. It means ultimately a change in our instincts and habits and desires. In short, it means a new civilization, radically different from the present capitalist order."

Since this is a representative quotation of the young Nehru it is used as a template for analysing his belief system in the area of economic policy. It is nevertheless noteworthy that the term socialism remained under-specified in Nehru's speeches and public pronouncements through the 1930s and 40s for although Jawaharlal Nehru believed that the freedom struggle was, in addition to being a political challenge, also an economic battle against special class privileges and vested interests, he was careful not to rattle Congress party members with too much talk of radicalism.

In 1934, for instance when Subhash Chandra Bose formed the Congress Socialist Party, Nehru pointedly chose to remain outside it, unwilling to isolate himself from the main centre of power politics, the INC and power-holders like Gandhi. Statements such as the following made to the press in 1936 were rare: "What I seek is an elimination of the profit motive in society and its replacement by a spirit of social service, cooperation taking the place of competition, production for consumption instead of for profit." While the concepts underpinning Nehru's vision of Socialism remain relatively under-developed, it is interesting to note that his thoughts on how to formulate and apply a socialist outlook to economic policy are extensive. What are striking are the institutional requirements and the need for consensus-building which Nehru recognised to be important early on in his consideration of the challenges to and conditions necessary for economic development.

Contributing in 1937 to a book on India's envisioned federal structure, he made the following comments about the need for a National Economic Council: "A modern government has to face difficult economic problems and to undertake complicated tasks which require careful thought and expert guidance....The national economic council could also be entrusted with the task of planning the economic life of the community under the general direction and supervision of the federal government. This task is a stupendous one and it may be necessary to create a special planning commission for the purpose." Most importantly he went on to emphasise the need for a broad base of representatives, reflecting interests across the board, including "representatives of the federating units and also representatives of special interests, such as chambers of commerce or industry, agriculture, trade unions of industrial workers, peasant organisations, professional and technical associations, and scientific experts."

And, this was not merely empty rhetoric. In December 1938 a National Planning Committee was formed. Already after its first meeting a questionnaire was issued to all participants for feedback on the general line of action and the type of planning. Aware of the possible backlash against radical ideas Nehru realised there was a need to convince people first and thus plotted his steps accordingly: "If we start with the dictum that only under socialism there can be planning, we frighten people and irritate the ignorant. If, on the other hand, we think in terms of planning apart from socialism and thus inevitably arrive at some form of socialism, that is a logical process which will convert many who are weary of words and slogans." A year later, Nehru was still committed to the task of gradually laying the foundations and the seeds for a planned economy in India of the future. Thus, "the super-structure will inevitably come later. But if even the foundation is laid in men's minds a great national task will have been done... Ultimately it is not the Committee that will decide the future of India or of its political or economic organisation but the people of India who will take the final decision. It is for them, therefore, to pay attention to what this Committee is doing. Perhaps one of the most important and desirable consequences of our work is to make people think of planned work and cooperative society.'

The extent of thought and analysis that is reflected in Nehru's writing on the issue of economic planning is truly remarkable in comparison with the highly opinionated and categorical statements made concerning the role of religion and the need for social reform. In a section of *The Discovery of India* entirely devoted to the National Planning Committee, Nehru makes four essential discoveries about the process of consensus-building. In the first place he recognised the complexity of the issue at stake.

Thinking about how to solve economic problems required a multi-dimensional view with an understanding of how poverty, unemployment, economic regeneration, even national defence needed an all-encompassing approach providing for the development of heavy, key industries, medium scale industries, and cottage industries, as well as agriculture and in addition, social services. He writes how 'one thing led to another and it was impossible to isolate anything or to progress in one direction without corresponding progress in another. The more we thought of this planning business, the vaster it grew in its sweep and range till it seemed to embrace almost every activity.'

The second critical realisation related to the problem of managing a body that represented so many different interests and perspectives. The way out that Nehru identified was one that envisioned the possibility of synergy emerging from conflict and discussion:

> 'We decided to consider the general problem of planning as well as each individual problem concretely

and not in the abstract, and allow principles to develop out of such considerations.'

Thirdly, Nehru recognised the value of fact-finding for 'It did not very much matter even if there were two or more reports, provided that all the available facts were collected and coordinated, the common ground mapped out, and the divergences indicated.' And finally, despite the conflict in opinions and approaches, the Committee would have played an invaluable role for, 'When the time came for giving effect to the Plan, the then existing democratic government would have to choose what basic policy to adopt. Meanwhile a great deal of essential preparation would have been made and the various aspects of the problem placed before the public and the various provincial and state governments'.

In addition, a distinctive approach to the question of economic development seems to have been Nehru's willingness to accept a degree of flexibility and experimentation. This is different compared to the dogmatic instructions that characterise his writing on reforming Hindu institutions, and the rather passionate conviction of his reflections on the world situation and India's place in it. For example the essence of planning being 'a large measure of regulation and coordination......no special rule was laid down but it was made clear that the very nature of planning required control in some measure, which might vary with the industry'. And, on land policy, 'Cooperative farming could be combined either with individual or joint ownership. A certain latitude was allowed for various types to develop so that, with greater experience, particular types might be encouraged more than others.'

As a result of this comparatively flexible approach, it is possible to imagine that in the process of policy implementation, if one method failed, there were alternatives to fall back on without the overall goals of the entire project having to be abandoned. Furthermore, because of the efforts at consensus-building there was less risk of reaching a dead-lock.

On Foreign Policy and Internationalism

Since, in his early writings Nehru did not explicitly discuss the foreign policy aspirations and tools that an independent India might implement, it is necessary to examine his more general appraisal of world politics. For instance, the extensive quotation below offers an insight into his perception of international affairs at the time and the global dynamics driving, hindering and determining world politics. A cognitive map derived from this enables a partial construction of Nehru's worldview. Written during his time in prison in 1934 in the form of letters to his daughter, *Glimpses of World History* reveals Nehru's approach to history, which he regarded as the 'story of man's struggle with living'. In the penultimate chapter of the book, Nehru purveyed the state of affairs in Europe:

> "The whole past tendency has been towards greater interdependence between nations, a greater internationalism. Even though separate independent national States remained, an enormous and intricate structure of international relations and trade grew up. This process went so far as to conflict with the national States and with nationalism itself. The next natural step was a socialised international structure. Capitalism, having had its day, had reached the stage when it was time for it to retire in favour of socialism. But unhappily such a voluntary retirement never takes place. Because crisis and collapse threatened it, it has withdrawn into its shell and tried to reverse the past tendency towards interdependence. Hence, economic nationalism,"

Given that the major cause for conflict was the psychosis of fear, Nehru envisioned the major goal of diplomacy to be to persuade states of the world to cease their practice of mutual condemnation and recrimination. In his view, any state that based its foreign policy on the traditional conception of power politics was destined to work against its true national interests. Hence, Nehru was staunchly against the realists of his time such as Sir Halford McKinder, the British geopolitician, Nicholas J. Spykman, the American geopolitician, Walter Lippmann, the American journalist. Nehru did not think foreign policy should only be about power and, that values such as justice, fairness, tolerance should not only serve the power objective. Lippmann's geopolitical conception of alliances was also dismissed by Nehru: 'Such a proposal looks very clever and realistic' he wrote, 'yet is supremely foolish, for it is based on the old policy of expansion and Empire and the balance of power which inevitably leads to conflict and war'. The traditional effort of states practicing power politics through encircling their rivals did not seem like a realistic practice to Nehru either. Since the world was round, every country was inevitably encircled by others and there was always a potential danger of encirclement. This was seen by Nehru to be a 'continuation of old tradition' in the style of European power politics, leading him to critique Realist thinkers and policy-makers for sticking to the 'empty shell of the past' and refusing to 'understand the hard facts of the present'.

Anticipating the 'English School' of the 1950s which proclaimed the need for a *via media* between realism and liberalism or utopianism, Nehru's writing on international relations contained both pragmatic and radical, revolutionary elements. While he did not at aim at overhauling the Westphalian system of states, or herald the end of conflict altogether, he emphasised the need for international society. This was to be achieved through a transformation of the psychological atmosphere from being one permeated by hostility, suspicion and fear to one infused with rationalism, tolerance, friendliness and cooperation. The 'habit of being moderate in language' as cultivated by Gandhi during the freedom struggle, ought to become characteristic of diplomacy he wrote in his book, *Unity of India*.

What is interesting and which also echoes the amalgam that the English School sought to provide, was the fact that Nehru and his contemporaries, such as Subhash Chandra Bose, did not necessarily see a conflict between nationalism and internationalism. On the one hand fervent nationalists, fighting for the freedom of their nation, these individuals criticised the nation-state system founded on national interests. Emerging perhaps from the collective experience of colonialism and liberation, the most important manifestation of this nascent internationalism came in the form of advocating Asian unity and regionalism. Nehru was the most articulate early post-war advocate of Asian unity, which he saw as the inevitable restoration of cultural and commercial links across Asia that had been violently disrupted by colonialism. A strong theme in his books, he organised the Asian Relations Conferences of 1947 and 1949, the latter being specifically aimed at putting international pressure on the Dutch to grant independence to Indonesia. Interestingly, although Non-alignment was to become a core pillar of his foreign policy later on, it does not feature at all in his books or in his articles of the 1920s, 30s and early-40s.

Using the British Empire as a point of reference, Nehru tried to draw lessons for example from British India's frontier policy: 'the frontier of India and the lands beyond are regarded by the government as a probable theatre of war, and all their policy is directed to strengthening themselves for war purposes....The military mind, ignoring political and psychological factors, thinks only in terms of extending the bounds of an Empire and thus making it safer from attack. As a matter of fact this process often ends in weakening a country or an Empire....... All this has led to the so-called "Forward policy" at the frontier and because of this every excuse is good enough to be utilised for a forward move...... This forward policy becomes an intense preparation for war, for the great war that is prophesied for the not distant future..... The forward policy has another aspect, a communal one. Just as the canker of communalism, fostered by imperialism, weakens and injures public life and our struggle for freedom so also the forward policy introduces that canker at the frontier and creates trouble between India and her neighbours.' It is of course puzzling or perhaps ironic that much later on, it was Nehru's own 'forward policy' on the Sino-Indian border that was seen by the Chinese as provocative and used as a reason to launch the 1962 war.

Living through tumultuous times it is understandable that Nehru's views were to be affected by his perception of the injustices witnessed and the events leading up to World War Two. A strong streak of internationalism pervades a lot of his analysis of foreign policy in general and in particular with regards his ideals for India's standing in the world. Developing an internationalist outlook was considered by Nehru to be vital in order to avoid a narrow nationalism which threatened to be 'an escape sought in dreams of the past...the golden age of past times, of Rama Raj.

However, at the same time there are occasions when the internationalism was given unnecessary emphasis. For example the 'Quit India' resolution adopted by the All-India Congress Committee on 8th August 1942 bore the imprint of Nehru's thinking: 'The Committee approves of and endorses the resolution...and have made it clear that the immediate ending of British rule in India is an urgent necessity, both for the sake of India and for the success of the cause of the United Nations. The continuation of that rule is degrading and enfeebling India and making her progressively less capable of defending herself and of contributing to the cause of world freedom.' Why, it was thought necessary to invoke internationalism alongside the most normal of desires and natural rights to be free, is odd and ran the risk of confusing the most basic of national interests with grand internationalist rhetoric.

A sense of camaraderie with China is another strong theme in Nehru's writing which again seems to fit the great importance given to internationalism. The relationship with China was founded upon a feeling of solidarity with a nation and people also engaged in an anti-imperialist struggle: 'Like China, India is aspiring and fighting for national freedom. The forces of national freedom in both countries extend to each other the hand of sympathy and support. They must band themselves together against the urge of imperialism for exploitation and conquest....The ancient friendship of the two peoples of China and India must now be reinforced by the new camaraderie of the two freedom-loving nations.' Nehru nurtured an interest in Chinese history and a number of chapters in his book, Glimpses of World History focus on China's development. Discussing the rise and fall of dynasties Nehru proposes various explanations for the process of change, the impetus for which he perceived to be largely endogenous. Hence, decline and decay were seen as stemming from inner weaknesses such as corrupt government, decadent elites or even 'too much parental government' which weakened the people.

On a number of occasions China is referred to as India's 'great sister in the East'. However, although Nehru accorded great respect for the achievements and resilience of Chinese culture and in particular admired the secular nature of Chinese society and government, there is an implicit sense of superiority when it comes to the development of political institutions. This is evident for example in the way he treats the founding of the first Chinese Republic under Dr. Sun Yat Sen. Describing the internal tensions within the Kuomintang party Nehru observed how the rivalries and different factions eventually led to the party breaking up, plunging the country into civil war. What is noteworthy is that Nehru drew no parallels with the case of India and the Congress party. He reveals no anxiety about similar developments afflicting the Indian freedom struggle nor does he mention any lessons to be learned from the experiences of upheaval in China.

In other words while waxing eloquent about ancient China and a misty past of sisterhood shared by these two ancient civilizations, there is little about modern China, apart from its size, that Nehru explicitly refers to as the basis for a future partnership of equality and friendship with India. One possible explanation for this is an inherent sense of superiority about India's political development. China, in Nehru's writings is usually lauded for its artistic and cultural achievements but not for its great political and organisational abilities for instance its ability to establish and maintain control over such a large Empire. Nehru's interpretation of Chinese history bears the same attitude prevalent in the West at the time, that China out of its weakness and decadence had succumbed to superior Western power.

On Kashmir

Who is Responsible?

[A talk broadcast from New Delhi, November 2, 1947].

I want to speak to you tonight about Kashmir, not about the beauty of that famous valley, but about the horror which it has had to face recently. We have passed through very critical days and the burden of taking vital and far-reaching decisions has fallen upon us. We have taken those decisions and I want to tell you about them.

The neighbouring Government, using language which is not the language of Governments or even of responsible people, has accused the Government of India of fraud in regard to the accession of Kashmir to the Indian Union. I cannot emulate that language nor have I any desire to do so, for I speak for a responsible Government and a responsible people. I agree that there has been fraud and violence in Kashmir but the question is: Who is responsible for it? Already considerable parts of the Jammu and Kashmir State have been overrun by raiders from outside, well-armed and well-equipped, and they have sacked and looted the towns and villages and put many of the inhabitants to the sword. Frightfulness suddenly descended upon this lovely and peaceful country and the beautiful city of Srinagar was on the verge of destruction.

I want to say at once that every step that we have taken in regard to Kashmir has been taken after the fullest thought and consideration of the consequences and I am convinced that what we have done was the right thing. Not to have taken those steps would have been a betrayal of a trust and cowardly submission to the law of the sword with its accompaniment of arson, rape and slaughter.

For some weeks past we had received reports of infiltration of raiding bands into the State territory of Jammu province. Also of a concentration of armed men near the border of Kashmir with the North West Frontier Province. We were naturally concerned about this not only because of our close ties with Kashmir and her people but also because Kashmir is a frontier territory adjoining great nations and therefore we were bound to take an interest in the developments there. But we were anxious not to interfere and we took no step whatever to intervene even though a part of the Jammu province was overrun by these raiders.

It has been stated that there were raids from the Jammu side across the Pakistan border and that there was communal trouble in Jammu, and Muslims were killed and driven away. In the past we have not hesitated to condemn evil whoever might have committed it, whether Hindus or Sikhs or Muslims, and so if Hindus or Sikhs or any functionaries of the State misbehaved in the Jammu province, certainly we condemn them and regret their deeds.

But I have before me a detailed list of 95 villages in the Jammu province which have been destroyed by the raiders from Pakistan.

Bhimbar, a considerable town, had also been sacked and destroyed. Other towns are besieged and a considerable part of Poonch and Mirpur areas is in the possession of the raiders. Does this indicate that aggression took place from the Kashmir side on to West Punjab or does it not show that there has been continuous organised aggression from West Punjab into the Kashmir State? These raiders possess the latest type of modern arms. It is reported that they have used flame-throwers, and a disabled tank has been discovered with them.

About this time we were asked by the Kashmir State to provide them with arms. We took no urgent steps about it and although sanction was given by our States and Defence Ministries, actually no arms were sent.

On the night of the 24th October I learnt of another raid, this time from the Abbottabad-Mansara Road which enters Kashmir near Muzzafarabad. We were told that armed and well equipped persons in over one hundred lorries had broken in, had sacked Muzzafarabad and killed many persons there, including the District Magistrate, and were proceeding along the Jhelum Valley road towards Srinagar. The State forces were spread out in small numbers all over the State and they could not stop this armed and well-organised raid. The civil population, Hindu and Muslim, fled before the raiders.

It was on the night of the 24th that for the first time a request was made to us or behalf of the Kashmir State for accession and military help On the morning of the 25th we considered this in the Defence Committee but no decision was taken about sending troops in view of the obvious difficulties of the undertaking. On the morning of the 26th we again considered this matter. The situation was even more critical then. The raiders had sacked several towns and had destroyed the great power house at Mahora which supplies electricity to the whole of Kashmir. They were on the point of entering the valley. The fate of Srinagar and the whole of Kashmir hung in the balance.

We received urgent messages for aid not only from the Maharaja's Government but from representatives of the people, notably that great leader of Kashmir, Sheikh Mohammed Abdullah, the President of the National Conference. Both the Kashmir

Government and the National Conference pressed us to accept the accession of Kashmir to the Indian Union. We decided to accept this accession and to send troops by air, but we made a condition that the accession would have to be considered by the people of Kashmir later when peace and order were established. We were anxious not to finalise anything in a moment of crisis and without the fullest opportunity being given to the people of Kashmir to have their say. It was for them ultimately to decide.

And here let me make clear that it has been our policy all along that where there is a dispute about the accession of a State to either Dominion, the decision must be made by the people of that State. It was in accordance with this policy that we added a proviso to the Instrument of Accession of Kashmir.

We decided to send troops on the afternoon of the 26th October. Srinagar was in peril and the situation was urgent arid critical. Our staff worked hard day and night and at daybreak on the 27th our troops went by air. They were small in numbers to begin with but immediately on arrival they rushed into action to stop the invader. Their gallant Commander, a brave officer of our Army, was killed the next day.

Since then troops and equipment have been flown over daily, and I should like to express my high appreciation and the appreciation of my Government for the fine work which our staff have done, as well as the pilots and the air crews who have thrown themselves into this adventure heart and soul. The air lines have cooperated with us fully and to them also I am grateful. Our young men have shown how they can rise to the occasion in a moment of crisis to serve their country.

Srinagar was in peril and the invader was almost on its doorstep. There was no administration left there, no troops, no police. Light and power had failed and there were a vast number of refugees there and yet Srinagar functioned without obvious panic and the shops were opened and people went about the streets. To what was this miracle due? Sheikh Abdullah and his colleagues of the National Conference and their unarmed volunteers, Muslim and Hindu and Sikh, took charge of the situation, kept order and prevented panic. It was a wonderful piece of work that they did at a moment when the nerves of most people might have failed them. They did so because of the strength of the organisation, but even more so, because they were determined to protect their country from the ruthless invader who was destroying their country and trying to compel them by terrorism to join Pakistan. Whatever the future may hold, the people of the valley of Kashmir have exhibited during these past few days remarkable courage, capacity for organisation and unity.

It would be well if this lesson were understood by the whole of India which has been poisoned by communal strife. Under the inspiration of a great leader, Sheikh Abdullah, the people of the valley, Muslim and Hindu and Sikh, were brought together for the defence of their common country against the invader. Our troops could have done little without this popular support and cooperation.

The Maharaja of Kashmir deserves to be congratulated on his decision to make Sheikh Abdullah the head of the administration at this critical juncture. That was a wise step which other rulers might well follow, making their people trustees and defenders of freedom.

It must be remembered, therefore, that the struggle in Kashmir is a struggle of the people of Kashmir under popular leadership against the invader. Our troops are there to help in this struggle, and as soon as Kashmir is free from the invader our troops will have no further necessity to remain there and the fate of Kashmir will be left in the hands of the people of Kashmir. We have passed through days of peril not only for Kashmir but for the whole of India. That peril is less now but it is by no means over and many other dangers confront us. We have to be very vigilant and well prepared for whatever may happen. The first step in this preparation is to put an end completely to ever': manner of communal strife in India and to stand up as a united nation to face every danger which might threaten our freedom. External danger can only be faced effectively when there is internal peace and order and an organised nation.

We talk about the invaders and raiders in Kashmir and yet these men are fully armed and well-trained and have competent leadership. All of these have come across from Pakistan territory. We have a right to ask the Pakistan Government how and why these people could come across the Frontier Province or West Punjab and how they have been armed so effectively. Is this not a violation of International Law and an unfriendly act towards a neighbour country? Is the Pakistan Government too weak to prevent armies marching across its territory to invade another country or is it willing that this should happen? There is no other alternative.

We have asked the Pakistan Government repeatedly to stop these raiders from coming and to withdraw those who have come. It should be easy for them to stop them, for the roads into Kashmir are very few and have to pass over bridges. We on our part have no intention of using our troops in Kashmir when the danger of invasion is passed.

We have declared that the fate of Kashmir is ultimately to be decided by the people. That pledge we have given, and the Maharaja has supported it, not only to the people of Kashmir but to the world. We will not and cannot back out of it. We are prepared when peace and law and order have been established to have a referendum held under international auspices like the United Nations. We want it to be a fair and just reference to the people and we shall accept their verdict. I can imagine no fairer and juster offer.

Meanwhile, we have given our word to the people of Kashmir to protect them against the invader and we shall keep our pledge.

Kashmir has Gone through Fire

[A statement made in the Constituent Assembly (Legislative), New Delhi, November 25, 1947].

I am glad to have this opportunity of explaining to the House the course of events that have led to our intervention in Kashmir' with the aid of armed forces, and the attitude of the Government of India to the grave problems that have arisen in that State.

The House is aware that on the lapse of Grown Paramountcy on the 15th August, this year, Kashmir did not accede to either Dominion. We were of course vitally interested in the decision that the State would take. Kashmir, because of her geographical position with her frontiers with three countries, namely, the Soviet

Union, China and Afghanistan, is intimately connected with the security and international contacts of India. Economically also Kashmir is intimately related to India. The caravan trade routes from Central Asia to India pass through the Kashmir State.

Nevertheless, we did not put the slightest pressure on the State to accede to the Indian Dominion, because e realised that Kashmir was in a very difficult position. We did not want a mere accession from the top but an association in accordance with the will of her people. Indeed, we did not encourage any rapid decision. Eyen in regard to a standstill agreement, no speedy steps were taken by us, although Kashmir had entered into a standstill agreement with Pakistan soon after the 15th August.

We learnt later that serious external pressure was being applied on Kashmir by the Pakistan authorities refusing to send to Kashmir supplies vital to the needs of the people, such as foodgrains, salt, sugar and petrol. Thus, an attempt was being made to strangle Kashmir economically and force her to accede to Pakistan. This pressure was serious, because it was not easy for Kashmir to obtain these essential supplies from, India an account of the difficulty of communications.

In September, news reached us that tribesmen of the North West Frontier Province were being collected and sent to the Kashmir border. In the beginning of October events took a grave turn. Armed bands moved into the Jammu province from the neighbouring districts of West Punjab, committed serious acts of depredation on the local inhabitants, burnt villages and towns and put a large number of people to death. Refugees from these areas poured into Jammu.

On the Jammu side of the border the local inhabitants, who are chiefly Hindu and Rajput, took retaliatory measures and drove out the Muslims living in those border villages. In these border conflicts a very large number of villages were destroyed or burnt by both parties on either side of the frontier.

The raiders from West Punjab into the Jammu province increased in number and spread out over that province. The Kashmir State Army which had to meet these raids at numerous points soon found itself broken into small fragments and gradually ceased to be a fighting force. The raiders were highly organised, had competent officers and modern arms. They succeeded in occupying a considerable part of the Jammu province, more especially in the Poonch area. The town of Poonch, Mirpur, Kotli and some other places held out.

About this time the State authorities asked us to supply them with arms and ammunition. We agreed to do so in the normal course. But in fact no supply was made till events took a more serious turn. Even at this stage no mention was made of accession to India.

The leader of the popular organisation in Kashmir, Sheikh Mohammed Abdullah, President of the Kashmir National Conference, was released from prison during this period and we discussed the situation in Kashmir with him as well as with the representatives of the Maharaja of Kashmir. We made it clear to both of them that while we would welcome the accession of Kashmir we did not want any hurried or forced accession and we would rather wait for the people to decide. Sheikh Abdullah was himself of this opinion.

On the 24th October we heard that large armed bands consisting both of tribesmen from the Frontier and ex-servicemen had broken through Muzzafarabad and were marching to Srinagar. These raiders had crossed Pakistan territory and they were equipped with Bren guns, machine guns, mortars and flamethrowers and had at their disposal a large number of transport vehicles. They moved rapidly down the valley, sacking and burning and looting all along the way. We gave earnest consideration to this situation in our Defence Committee on the 25th and 26th October. The position on the morning of the 26th was that the raiders were marching towards Srinagar and there was no military detachment capable of stopping them. They had been stopped for two days near Uri by the State forces under a gallant commander who resisted this advance to the point of death. These two days thus gained were very valuable.

We were asked at this stage both on behalf of the Maharaja and Sheikh Abdullah to accept the accession of the State to the Indian Union and to intervene with the armed forces of the Union.

An immediate decision was necessary, and in fact it is now clear that if we had delayed the decision even by 24 hours, Srinagar would have fallen and would have suffered the tragic fate that befell Muzzafarabad, Baramula and other places. It was clear to us that we could not possibly accept under any circumstances the ruin of Kashmir by brutal and irresponsible raiders. This would have been a surrender to frightfulness and fanaticism of the worst type and it would have had the most serious consequences all over India. To intervene at this stage was no easy matter and was full of risks and danger. Yet we decided to face this risk and intervene because any other course would have meant ruin to Kashmir and greater danger to India.

In accepting the accession, however, we made it perfectly clear to the Maharaja that his Government must be carried on in future according to the popular will and that Sheikh Abdullah should be charged with the formation of an interim government on the new model adapted in Mysore. Sheikh Abdullah, in our opinion, had undoubtedly the support of the large majority of the people of Kashmir, Muslims, Hindus and Sikhs. Further, we made it clear that as soon as law and order had been restored in Kashmir and her soil cleared of the invaders, the question of the State's accession should be settled by reference to the people.

I shall not detain the House by dealing with the course of the military campaign that followed. The facts are well-known and redound to the credit of our military organisation, our troops and our airmen. It must be remembered also that our operations have been very largely based on air transport in difficult circumstances. Our civil airlines and their aircrews functioned with remarkable success. One fact, however, which contributed to our success, at least as much as the military operations, was the maintenance, under the leadership of Sheikh Abdullah, of the civil administration and the morale of the civilian population. The civilian population, completely unarmed, with the enemy within a few miles of the city behaved in a manner which showed extraordinary courage and coolness. They did so, because they had a great leader and because Hindus, Muslims and Sikhs all joined together under him to throw back the enemy and to save Kashmir, their common heritage. This fact is one of the most remarkable events of recent times in India and one from which the rest of the country may well take a profitable lesson. It was certainly a factor of the most vital importance in the saving of Srinagar.

The present position is that our troops have relieved Poonch and are within 8 miles of Kotli. The terrain in which they are fighting is difficult and mountainous and the roads and approaches have been destroyed by the raiders. Progress is, therefore, slow. In the Poonch area occupied by the raiders several massacres of the non-Muslim inhabitants have taken place involving large numbers of persons.

I should like to say here that certain events happened near Jammu early in November which I regret very deeply. The Muslim convoys of evacuees were being taken away from Jammu when they were attacked by non-Muslim refugees and others and a large number of casualties were inflicted. The troops escorting them did not play a creditable role. I might add that none of our troops were present or had anything to do with this. We have issued the most stringent orders to our troops to protect the people, to act with impartiality and indeed to make friends with the local population. I am glad to say that they have carried out these instructions.

The House is aware that the Pakistan Government have protested emphatically against our action in Kashmir. In doing so they have used language which is not becoming in any government and have alleged fraud and conspiracy on our part. I need only say that I am completely convinced that every action that the Government of India have taken in regard to Kashmir has been straight and above board and I can defend it at any time before the world. We have indeed been over-scrupulous in this matter so that nothing may be done in the passion of the moment which might be wrong. The behaviour of our army has all along been good and worthy of our traditions.

I cannot say this of the Pakistan Government. Their case is that the genesis of the trouble was the extensive killing of Muslims in Eastern Punjab and Kashmir and that the raid on Kashmir was a spontaneous reaction to this on the part of the tribesmen. I think this is completely untrue. I regret deeply that in parts of the

Jammu province Muslims were killed and driven out. This of course has had nothing to do with our Government or our forces. But this mutual killing has been a very tragic feature during these past months in the Punjab, and Jammu was powerfully affected by this. We have sufficient evidence in our possession to demonstrate that the whole business of the Kashmir raids both in the Jammu province and in Kashmir proper was deliberately organised by high officials of the Pakistan Government. They helped the tribesmen and ex-servicemen to collect, they supplied them with the implements of war, with lorries, with petrol and with officers. They are continuing to do so. Indeed, their high officials openly declare so. It is obvious that no large body of men could cross Pakistan territory in armed groups without the goodwill, connivance and active help of the authorities there.

It is impossible to escape the conclusion that the raids on Kashmir were carefully planned and well organised by the Pakistan authorities with the deliberate object of seizing the State by force and then declaring accession to Pakistan. This was an act of hostility not only to Kashmir but to the Indian Union. It is only necessary to see the semi-official organs of the Muslim League and the Pakistan Government to find out the attitude of that Government. If we had allowed this scheme to succeed, we would have been guilty of the betrayal of the people of Kashmir and of a grave dereliction of duty to India. The results of these on the communal and political situation all over India would have been disastrous.

The Pakistan government have proposed a simultaneous withdrawal of our forces and the raiders from Kashmir. This was a strange proposal and could only mean that the raiders were there at the instance of the Pakistan Government. We cannot treat with freebooters who have murdered large numbers of people and tried to ruin Kashmir. They are not a State, although a State may be behind them. We have gone to Kashmir to protect the people and as soon as this duty is discharged our forces need not remain there and we shall withdraw our forces. We cannot desert the people of Kashmir till the danger is passed. If the Pakistan Government are sincere, they can stop the entry of these raiders and thus accelerate the return of peace and order. After that let the people of Kashmir decide and we shall accept their decision.

But if this armed conflict continues, no opportunity is given to the people to decide by peaceful means, and the decision gradually takes shape through the sacrifice and power of the people in this conflict.

In order to establish our bona fides, we have suggested that when the people are given the chance to decide their future, this should be done under the supervision of an impartial tribunal such as the United Nations Organisation.

The issue in Kashmir is whether violence and naked force should decide the future or the will of the people. The raiders, encouraged by Pakistan have sought to enforce by the sword accession to Pakistan against the obvious wishes of large numbers of the people in Kashmir. We cannot permit the success of this method to achieve political ends. It is a tragedy that Pakistan should ally itself to such methods instead of devoting itself to the urgent tasks of economic and social reconstruction.

Kashmir has gone through fire and I am sure that the House would like me to communicate their sympathy to the people of Kashmir for the tribulations they have been going through in recent weeks. This fair land, which Nature has made so lovely, has been desecrated by people who have indulged in murder, arson, loot and foul attacks on women and children. The people have suffered greatly from shortage of the most vital necessities of life and yet, under the inspiring lead of Sheikh Abdullah, they have stood together in the hour of calamity and showed to the rest of India an example of what communal unity can achieve. Whatever the future may hold, this chapter in the history of Kashmir will be worth reading and we shall never regret that in their hour of distress we have been able to be of assistance to this gallant people. Kashmir and India have been bound together in many ways from ages past. These last few weeks have forged a new link which no one can sunder.

Facts Relating to Kashmir

[A statement made at a Press Conference, New Delhi, January 2, 1948].

As is well known now, the Government of India has made a reference to the Security Council of the UNO in regard to the invasion of Kashmir by persons coming from or through Pakistan.

The Government desires to take the Press and the public into full confidence in so far as it can, having regard to diplomatic decorum and propriety. It has waited thus far because it would have been proper for the Security Council to consider the matter first before any publicity was given to it, but, in view of references being made to this subject by the Foreign Minister of Pakistan and by others, it is desirable to state the facts briefly.

I have previously, on several occasions, placed before the country the facts relating to Kashmir ever since we sent our troops there on October 27, 1947. Our troops succeeded in saving the valley of Kashmir and the city of Srinagar and drove back the enemy to Uri along the Jhelum Valley road.

Since then, fighting has taken place on a large front along almost the entire border of the Kashmir State and Pakistan. Very large numbers of armed men, in battle formation and fully equipped with modern arms, have entered Kashmir State territory at many places, and still larger concentrations of these men have been made along the border on the Pakistan side.

These border areas of Pakistan hate become the base of operations for these invaders and, from the security of these bases, large numbers come across and raid, burn and loot on Kashmir State territory which is Indian Dominion territory.

The Government of India would have been justified, in self defence, to strike at these bases, and thus put an end to the sources of supply of these invaders. It has however, scrupulously avoided doing so, so as to limit the field of operations and in the hope that the Pakistan Government will cease aiding and abetting these invaders.

During the last two months, repeated requests have been made to the Pakistan Government to prevent the use of its territory for aggression on India. It has not only not done so, but it is an established fact that these invaders, among whom are a large number of Pakistan nationals, have been helped in every way by the Pakistan Government.

They are allowed transit through Pakistan territory by motor transport and railway trains, supplied petrol, food and accommodation and the arms they possess are manifestly the arms of the Pakistan Army. Pakistan Army personnel have also been captured by our troops in the operations in Kashmir.

Not only has the Pakistan Government not taken effective steps to prevent this invasion, but it has refused even to call upon the invaders to desist from their active aggression.

The Government of India cannot tolerate the use of a friendly and neighbouring country as a base for the invasion of Indian territory but in its desire to avoid any action, unless it is compelled by circumstances to take it, it has decided to refer this matter to the Security Council of the UNO.

On December 22, 1947, a formal request was made in writing to the Prime Minister of Pakistan. In this letter, the acts of aggression of Pakistan and the forms of aid given by Pakistan to the invaders were briefly stated and the Government of Pakistan was asked to call upon Pakistan nationals to cease participating in the attack on the Jammu and Kashmir State and to deny to the invaders: (1) all access to and use of Pakistan territory for operations against the Kashmir State; (2) all military and other supplies; (3) all other kinds of aid that might tend to prolong the present struggle.

The Government of India expressed its earnest desire again to live on terms of friendship with Pakistan and hoped that its request would be acceded to promptly and without reserve. It pointed out, however, that, failing such response, it would be compelled to take such action, with due regard to its rights and obligations as a member of the UNO, as it might consider necessary to protect its own interests and those of the Government and people of Jammu and Kashmir State.

As no reply was received to this formal request, two reminders were sent. Ultimately, on December 30, a formal reference was made to the Security Council of the UNO through the representative of the Government of India with UNO. On December 31, a copy of this reference was sent by telegram to the Pakistan Government.

This reference stated the facts of the case and pointed out that they indisputably pointed to the following conclusions:

- that the invaders are allowed transit across Pakistan territory;

- that they are allowed to use Pakistan territory as a base of operations;
- that they include Pakistan nationals;
- that they draw much of their military equipment, transport and supplies (including petrol) from Pakistan; and
- that Pakistan officers are training, guiding and otherwise helping them.

There was no source other than Pakistan from which such quantities of modern military equipment, training and guidance could have been obtained. The Government of India requested the Security Council, therefore, to ask the Government of Pakistan:

- to prevent Pakistan Government personnel, military and civil, participating in or assisting the invasion of the Jammu and Kashmir State;
- to call upon other Pakistan nationals to desist from taking any part in the fighting in the Jammu and Kashmir State;
- to deny to the invaders: (a) access to and use of its territory for operations against Kashmir; (b) military and other supplies; (c) all other kinds of aid that might tend to prolong the present struggle.

The reference to the Security Council is thus limited to the matters mentioned above. There is an urgency about these matters, for the first step that must be taken is to put a stop to the fighting and this can only be done if the invaders withdraw. It must be remembered that all the fighting has taken place on Indian Union territory and it is the inherent right of the Government of India to drive back any invaders on its territory. Till the Kashmir State is free of the invaders, no other matter can be considered.

The Government of India deeply regrets that this serious crisis has arisen. It is not of its seeking, and it has been thrust upon it by invading armies from outside who have committed acts of barbarism against the inhabitants of the Kashmir State and destroyed and burnt a large number of villages and some towns. No Government can tolerate such an invasion. In its desire, however, to avoid any act which might lead to further complications, it has shown the greatest forbearance and made repeated appeals to the Pakistan Government. Those appeals have been in vain, and hence it decided to refer this particular question to the Security Council. It has naturally reserved to itself freedom to take such action in self-defence as the situation may require.

The Foreign Minister of Pakistan, in a recent Press interview, has brought a large number of charges against the Government of India. I shall not go into these charges except to repudiate them utterly. What has happened during the past year is well known and we are prepared to stand the test of the closest scrutiny. Apparently all this variety of charges has been brought to cover up the Kashmir issue in a forest of other matters which have nothing to do with it.

It is completely untrue, to say that the Government of India has tried to undo the partition or to strangle Pakistan. The mere fact of our agreeing to what everybody recognises to be very generous financial terms is evidence of our desire to help Pakistan and to have friendly relations with it.

It is completely untrue that we have repudiated these financial agreements; we stand by them and shall honour them, but it is true that we have pointed out to Pakistan that we cannot make these payments at present when the money we give might be utilised for warlike operations against India.

The Kashmir issue stands by itself. If the methods of invasion of friendly territory by a barbarous foe are encouraged and submitted to, there is no future either for India or for Pakistan and therefore this has to be and will be resisted by us to the utmost and the Kashmir State will have to be freed completely. Even from the narrowest viewpoint of self interest, the Government of Pakistan should realise that the encouragement of such an invasion is perilous to its own future, because, once the forces of unbridled violence are let loose, they endanger the whole security of any State.

It must be remembered that in Kashmir there is no communal issue as such. Large numbers of Kashmiris, Muslims, Hindus and Sikhs are fighting the invaders. It is a national issue for them to preserve their freedom, and we have gone there to support them. We have pledged our honour to them and we shall stand by our pledge.

I would appeal to the Press for restraint in dealing with this issue at this critical stage and to avoid publishing unauthorised matter. We shall try to give full information to the Press whenever it is possible. The publication of unauthorised stories is likely to do harm to the State and to the cause we represent.

Pledge to Kashmir

[A statement from New Delhi, January 15, 1948.

India very generously agreed to allocate Rs. 75 crores to Pakistan out of the cash balances to help the latter to make a start. It was felt that the Arbitral Tribunal should not have allocated so big an amount to Pakistan, and it was hoped that this generosity on the part of the Indian Union would have reciprocal response. The Deputy Prime Minister, Sardar Patel, made it clear that this financial deal was linked with the overall settlement of all outstanding issues. But in the meantime, in Kashmir Pakistan waged virtually an undeclared war against India; and lest the Rs. 55 crores (Rs. 20 crores having already been paid out of the 75 crores) should be spent against India in Kashmir, it was withheld pending the settlement of the Kashmir issue. It became another cause of bitterness between India and Pakistan. When Mahatmaji began his fast an January 13 and appealed to the nation to remove ill-will, prejudice, and passion which poisoned the relations between India and Pakistan, the Government of India decided to pay the amount due, namely, Rs. 55 crores to Pakistan immediately as a gesture of goodwill to that State and as their contribution "to the non-violent and noble effort made by Gandhiji." On January 18, Mahatma Gandhi terminated his fast in response to the pledge given by the citizens of Delhi through the peace committees that they would banish communalism from their hearts and from the country].

The Government's decision in regard to the payment of the cash balances to Pakistan has been taken after the most careful thought and after consultation with Gandhiji. I should like to make it clear that this does not mean any change in our unanimous view about the strength and validity of the Government's position as set out in various statements made by distinguished colleagues of mine. Nor do we accept the facts or arguments advanced in the latest statement of the Finance Minister of Pakistan.

We have come to this decision in the hope that this generous gesture, in accord with India's high ideals and Gandhiji's noble standards, will convince the world of our earnest desire for peace and goodwill. We earnestly trust also that this will go a long way towards producing a situation which will induce Gandhiji to break his fast. That fast, of course, had nothing to do with this particular matter, and we have thought of it because of our desire to help in every way in easing the present tension.

Six months ago we witnessed a miracle in Calcutta where ill-will changed overnight into goodwill, through the alchemy of a similar fast. The alchemist who worked this change was described by our Governor-General as the one-man boundary force which succeeded when the boundary force of 50,000 men in West Punjab did not succeed in keeping the peace. This unarmed knight of non-violence is functioning again. May the same alchemy work again in India and elsewhere! We have sought to remove one major cause of dispute an argument between India and Pakistan and we hope that other problems will also be resolved. But let it be remembered that the people of Kashmir are suffering from a brutal and unprovoked invasion, and we have pledged ourselves to help them to gain their freedom. To that pledge we shall hold and we shall do our utmost to redeem it. We seek their freedom not for any gain to us, but to prevent the ravishing of a fair country and a peaceful people.

The Sweep of History

[A statement made in the Constituent Assembly (Legislative), New Delhi, March 5, 1948].

Sir, I crave your leave and the indulgence of the House to make a statement on Kashmir. I would beg the House to bear with me for a while, because there is a great deal to say, however briefly I might say I, — not that I am going to make any sensational disclosures, there is nothing very secret about what I am going to say and the facts have appeared in the public Press and in other places frequently enough during the last few months. Nevertheless, it is right that I should place before the House some kind of a consecutive account of what has happened. In order to lessen my task and to help Members of the House, we have prepared a White Paper on Kashmir which will be distributed to members. This White Paper does not bring matters right up-to-date. It is practically up to the period of the reference to the Security Council.

It is not an absolutely complete paper in the sense that every telegram, and every letter is included, but, on the whole, most of the messages that passed between us and the Government of Pakistan, or connected messages have been given in this White Paper.

Now, before I speak on this particular Kashmir issue, I should like by your leave to say a few words on a wider issue of which the Kashmir issue is a part. We have been living through strenuous days; we have been passing through a period of dynamic history in India. Much has happened during the past six months, much that was good and much that was very bad. But, perhaps, when the history of India comes to be written, when much of the horror of today has been forgotten, one of the biggest things that mill be mentioned will be the change that has come over India and that is coming over India in regard to the Indian States. We see something very remarkable happening. It is perhaps difficult for us who live in the middle of this change to appreciate the bigness of what has happened. But it is the upsetting in a very curious way — a peaceful way — of a structure that has endured in India for the past 130 or 140 years, more or less ever since the beginning of the nineteenth century.

We see the sweep of history suddenly coming, the big broom of history, and changing this 130 year old structure and putting something else in its place. We cannot definitely and absolutely say what the final and precise outcome of all this will be, though the picture is clearing up fairly rapidly. It would almost appear that there is the hand of destiny at work. What is happening is nothing that we did not expect. In fact, many of us for many years past have had certain objectives in regard to the Indian States and we have worked for them both through our political and other organisations in India; through the people of the States, through the people of the provinces and otherwise. And, on the whole, what is happening today is in line with the objectives we had laid down. So it is not surprising. Yet, may I confess to you, Sir, that even I who have been rather intimately connected with the States peoples' movement for many years, if I had been asked six months ago what the course of developments would be in the next six months since then, I would have hesitated to say that such rapid changes would take place. Many factors have gone to bring about these rapid changes. Ultimately, I suppose, they are the forces of history working, — the unleashing of all manner of forces which had been repressed for so long. For we had during these 130 years a strange phenomenon. The British Government had constructed a State structure in the course of a quarter of a century in the early days of the nineteenth century. Whether it fitted in, in reality, with conditions then existing in India or not, it is a little difficult to say what would have happened minus the British Government. Anyhow, the dominant power of the British created this system, no doubt for their own advantage as they thought fit.

That system continued, not because of any inherent strength, as is obvious today, but because of the continuance of that dominant power, of the paramount power as it was called. All manner of changes were going on in India and in the outside world and yet the Indian States structure continued. Many of us said that it was rather archaic, it was out of date, it had to change and must change and so on. But now that the protecting hand of a foreign Government has been removed, the repressions also are removed. The forces that had been kept in check suddenly began to function and we see them in action, in rapid action. The forces are there of course; they have not been curbed by any of us, but I think in the manner of dealing with this situation, an intricate and difficult situation — this House will agree with me that we owe a debt of gratitude to my friend and colleague, the Deputy Prime Minister.

So it is in this mighty context of a changing India in regard to the States that we have to view any particular aspect of it. We saw unfortunately six months back the partition of India, the splitting up of India, a part of India going out of India. Immediately after that process of cutting off, another process started, or rather we have always had these two processes the process — of integrating India. We have seen this process of integrating India going one in regard to the States, and not only in regard to the States but, to some extent, even in regard to the provinces, but much more so in regard to the States. So these two things have gone on together — a process of cutting away and a process of integration and in the balance it is difficult to say how far we have gained and how far we have lost. It is difficult to say also how far this process of integration will go and whither it will take us ultimately. Nevertheless, it is interesting for us living through this rather strange and dynamic period of India's history, to look at it in some perspective, not as actors in the drama but rather as historians looking back on what has happened. The historian who looks back will no doubt consider this integration of the States into India as one of the dominant phases of India's history.

Well, Sir, the process is taking various shapes. There has been an actual merger of a large number of small States with India there has been a bringing together of a number of States into Unions of States which form units of the Union of India and a certain number of major States remain as separate entities. But what is equally important — and if I may say so, even more important — is not this integration externally but the inner integration; that is, the growth of democratic institutions and responsible government in the States, because that brings about a real integration; not at the top lever of government but at the level of the people. Both these processes have gone on and both these processes, may I remind the House, are in line with the objectives far which we have laboured for many years.

Now, it is in this context of changes in the States system that this House to consider the particular case of Kashmir, and it stands apart and many other factors come into play. Today India two States stand quite apart from the rest in regard to these processes. These States are Hyderabad and Kashmir. I am not going at this moment to say anything about Hyderabad. In regard to Kashmir, it stands apart for many reasons, partly because it has got entangled in external politics, that is to say, it has got entangled in the relations between India and Pakistan and so the two essentially State issues there are somewhat submerged. It is an odd thing that it should get so entangled. That it got entangled is not odd, but the manner of its entanglement, because the Government of Pakistan have assured us time and again that they have nothing to do with the recent events in Kashmir, raids and invasions, etc. — they go on repeating that; nevertheless, they seek to profit by those events. They seek political advantages out of those events, so that while disclaiming all responsibility for what has happened they do want to share in whatever they might get out of it. Anyhow, the Kashmir problem stands apart.

But for the moment, leaving out this external implication of the Kashmir problem, if you consider it, it is essentially the same problem, that is to say, a problem of the growth of the freedom of the people and the growth also of a new integration. Now, we have been aiming, the Government of India and the States Ministry, at the growth of this inner freedom of the people of all the States. If many of the States have agreed to merge with India or come into closer contact with her, it is not because the States Ministry took a big stick and threatened them with consequences. It is because of those forces, arising from the people, and other forces, and fundamentally the sudden withdrawal of an external force which had kept the States together, or rather the States system together, the might of the British Government and the sanctions behind it. That disappearing, immediately the structure began to collapse and it is an astonishing thing — this sudden collapse of a structure which seemed so solid just a few months or a year ago — not surprising to those who knew the facts, but undoubtedly surprising to those people who take a superficial view of things. So essentially we have been aiming at the freedom of the people, knowing and realising that ultimately it will be for the people of the States to decide what their future will be.

We are not going to compel them. We do not propose to compel them, and indeed we cannot compel them in the context of the world today in any State. There are other compulsions, the compulsions of geography. That is true; one cannot ignore it. There are many other compulsions. And naturally in considering the problem, we, that is, the Government of India, have always to consider the interests of India as a whole, the interests of India in regard to security, defence, etc., but apart from that, we do not wish to exercise any other compulsion in the slightest, over the growth of freedom. In fact, we want to encourage it in the people of the States. We know well that if there is that growth of freedom and freedom of decision by the people of the States, then it will be a powerful factor in bringing them nearer to our people, because we hope that whatever Constitution we may adopt in India, it will be based completely on the will of the people.

Now, may I say a few words before I go on to the Kashmir issue and that is this: in this matter I feel a slight difficulty, because the matter is being or going to be discussed again in the Security Council of the United Nations and I would not like to say anything which might be construed, shall I say, into putting difficulties in the way of coming to a settlement either in the Security Council or elsewhere. Because we earnestly desire a settlement, we earnestly desire that these great forces should be allowed to function normally and to achieve their results; any other result will be an artificial result. We cannot impose a result — certainly Pakistan cannot impose a result. Ultimately there is no doubt in my mind that in Kashmir as elsewhere, the people of Kashmir will decide finally, and all that we wish is that they should have freedom of decision without any external compulsion.

Now, there is one other factor which I should like to put before the House in regard to Kashmir. We have become too used in India, unfortunately, to thinking of every problem or many problems in terms of communalism, of Hindu versus Muslim or Hindu and Sikh versus Muslim and so on. That has been an unfortunate legacy of ours, and the extent to which it took us cannot be forgotten by us nor the tragedies that it has led to. We are trying, I hope, to get rid of the spirit of communal India at least. We hope to put an end to it, not suddenly perhaps, but certainly fairly rapidly.

Now, in this context of communal conflict the case of Kashmir stands apart because Kashmir is not a case of communal conflict; it may be a case of political conflict, if you like; it may be a case of any other conflict, but it is essentially not a case of communal conflict. Therefore, this struggle in Kashmir, although it has brought great suffering in its train to the people of Kashmir and placed a burden on the Government of India and the people of India, nevertheless it stands out as a sign of hope that there we see a certain cooperation, combination and coordination of certain elements, Hindu and Muslim and Sikh and others on an equal level, and for a political fight for their own freedom. I wish to stress this because it is continually being said by our opponents and critics on the other side that this is a communal affair and that we are there to support the Hindus or the Sikh minorities as against the Muslim masses of Kashmir. Nothing can be more fantastically untrue. We could not for an instant send our armies and we would not be there if we were not supported by very large sections of the population, which means the Muslims of Kashmir. We would not have gone there in spite of the invitation of the Maharaja of Kashmir, if that invitation had not been backed by the representatives of the people of Kashmir and may I say to the House that in spite of our armies having functioned with great gallantry, even our armies could not have succeeded except with the help and cooperation of the people of Kashmir. Now, we are blamed by people outside, beyond the borders of India; for going to Kashmir to support an autocratic monarch.

The House will remember that one of the conditions that we made at that critical moment, when we had to decide whether to send the Indian Army or not, whether to accept accession or not, one of the conditions was that there must be a popular government there, not as a goal — and an ideal, but immediately. It was an immediate thing and it was given effect to immediately in so far as it could be given effect to. So it is strange that this charge should be brought against us: Look at this charge in another context. Those people, men and women of Kashmir, who are with us and who are fighting for their freedom and liberty there, they are not newcomers in the struggle for freedom for the greater part of a generation, they have fought for the freedom of Kashmir, in Kashmir; they have suffered for it and some of us have deemed it a privilege to be associated with them in this fight for the freedom of Kashmir against autocratic rule.

These people are with us today. Who are their opponents, who are against them in Kashmir or elsewhere? What has been their record in the past ten, twenty years in regard to the freedom of Kashmir? It is an interesting speculation and an interesting enquiry, because these gentlemen who talk about the autocracy of the Ruler of Kashmir, who talk about autocracy there, what did they do during these last ten, twenty years? They never fought for the freedom of the people of Kashmir; most of is them supported that autocracy; most of them opposed the freedom movement in Kashmir. Now, because of entirely different reasons, they have become the champions of the freedom of Kashmir. And what is the type of freedom they have brought into Kashmir today? The freedom so called that they have brought into Kashmir is the license to loot and murder and burn that lovely country and to abduct and carry away the beautiful women of the Jammu and Kashmir State; and not only carry them away, but place some of them in the open market place for sale! So let us have this background before us when we consider this Kashmir story. It is a stirring background of events and many of us have been distressed at the strangely narrow view that people in the Security Council have taken on this matter.

I do not desire to enter into the details of what happened or did not happen in the Security Council, but I do feel that this background must be appreciated. It is not a Hindu-Muslim question in Kashmir; it is not a question certainly of our standing for any autocracy or anything. We have already, during the last fifteen or twenty years, shown where we stand in regard to the States people and their rulers. In regard to Kashmir, more particularly, we have shown by our actions from the very first day we went there, from October last until today, and I shall have something more to say about it before I finish as to how we feel about the freedom of Kashmir. Now, Sir, I shall go into some slight detail about the events in Kashmir. The House will recall the statement I made on Kashmir on the 25th November, 1947. In that statement I recounted briefly the course of events in the Jammu and Kashmir State up to that day, the part played by the Government of Pakistan in these events, and our own objectives.

Our complaint against Pakistan was that it had incited and aid from outside and its own nationals to wage war on Jammu and Kashmir State. The month of December showed an intensification of military pressure on the State. Nearly 19,000 had been reinforced in the Uri area. 15,000 raiders were operating against the western and southwestern borders of the State. Incursions by the raiders into the State territory, involving murder, loot and the abduction of women were continuing. The booty was being collected and carried to tribal areas to serve as an inducement to the tribesmen to swell the ranks of the raiders. In addition actively participating in the raids, a large number of tribesmen and others, estimated at 100,000, had been collected in different places in the districts of West Punjab bordering upon the Jammu and Kashmir State, and many of them were receiving military training under Pakistan nationals, including officers of the Pakistan Army. They were being looked after in Pakistan territory, fed, clothed, armed and otherwise equipped and transported to the territory of the Jammu and Kashmir State with the help, direct and indirect, of Pakistan officials, both military and civil. The equipment of the invaders included modern weapons, such as mortars and medium machine guns; the men wore the battle dress of regular soldiers, fought in regular battle formation and used the tactics of modern warfare. Man-packed wireless sets were in regular use and even Mark 'V' mines were being employed.

More than once, the Government of India had asked the Pakistan Government to deny facilities to the invaders, facilities which constituted an act of aggression and hostility against India, but without any satisfactory response. On the 22nd December, I handed personally to the Prime Minister of Pakistan in New Delhi, a letter in which the various forms of aid were briefly recited, and his Government were asked to put an end to such aid, promptly and without reservation.

As no reply to this letter was received for some days I sent a reminder by telegram on the 26th December. On the 31st December the Government of India instructed their Ambassador in Washington to convey a message to the Chairman of the Security Council of the United Nations. This message was a reference to the Security Council under Article 35 of the Charter of the United Nations. On that same day, the full text of the message was sent to the Prime Minister of Pakistan by telegram.

On the 1st January, I received a reply from the Prime Minister of Pakistan to my letter, dated 22nd December. The contents of this letter revealed no helpful approach to a solution of the Kashmir problem. They consisted only of a series of fantastic charges against India, e.g. a determination to crush Pakistan, organised genocide of Muslims in India, and the procurement of the accession of Kashmir by force and fraud. This letter, even if it had been received earlier, could not have modified our decision to request the Security Council of the United Nations to ask the Government of Pakistan:

- to prevent Pakistan Government, personnel, military or civil, from participating and assisting the invasion of the Jammu and Kashmir State;

- to call upon other Pakistan nationals to desist from taking in the fighting in the Jammu and Kashmir State;
- to deny to the raiders (a) access to and use of its territory for operations against Kashmir; (b) military and other supplies; (c) all other kinds of aid that might tend to prolong the present struggle.

The House will remember the circumstances in which we had sent our forces to Kashmir. Kashmir State territory, that is, after accession, Indian Dominion territory, was being invaded to the accompaniment of murder, arson, loot and the abduction of women. The whole countryside was being ruined. Fresh raiders were continually coming from Pakistan territory into the Kashmir vale. All the fighting was taking place in Indian Dominion territory. The invaders had their principal bases across the border Pakistan, received supplies and reinforcements from them, and could go back there to rest and recuperate in safety.

Our troops had strict orders not to enter Pakistan territory. The normal course to prevent raids on Indian territory would have been to deny the use of any bases to them in Pakistan. Since Pakistan was unwilling to cooperate thus in this manner, the alternatives left to us were to send our armed forces across Pakistan territory to deal effectively with the invaders, or to request the United Nations to ask Pakistan to do so. Any resort to the first course would have involved armed conflict with Pakistan. We were anxious to avoid this and to try every available method to find a peaceful solution. Therefore, the only course left open to us was to make a reference to the Security Council.

I shall not take up the time of the House with a detailed account of the proceedings of the Security Council; these have reported in the Press. I must confess that I have been surprised and distressed at the fact that the reference we made has not even been properly considered thus far and other matters have been given precedence. If the facts we stated in our reference were correct, as we claim they were, then certain consequences naturally followed from them, both in law and from the point of view of establishing peace and order.

On behalf of Pakistan, there was a repetition of the fantastic chargers against India which had been made previously in the letter of the Prime Minister of Pakistan to which I have referred. Pakistan refused to act at once, to deny assistance in men and material to our enemies in Jammu and Kashmir, to prevent further incursions through Pakistan into the State, and to ask the tribesmen and Pakistanis now in the State to withdraw unless a previous agreement had been reached and announced to the effect that the Indian Armed Forces would be withdrawn completely from the Jammu and Kashmir State, and the administration of the State would be replaced by another administration. There were some other matters in dispute also but the principal ones were the two I have mentioned above.

In effect, Pakistan not only admitted that they were aiding the raiders but made it clear that they would continue to do so till certain political objectives of theirs were achieved by them. This was a proposal to which the Government of India could not agree. For such an agreement would have been a betrayal not only of the people of Kashmir to whom they had pledged their word, but also a surrender to methods of violence and aggression which would have had disastrous consequences both for India and Pakistan. It was impossible for us to withdraw our forces without grave danger to the State and without handing over the people of the State who trusted in us to an unscrupulous and cruel invader who had already brought so much misery to the State and its people. Nor could we share the responsibility of protecting the people of Kashmir with any other outside force.

It was equally impossible for us to agree to the replacement of Sheikh Abdullah's administration by any other. The Government of Jammu and Kashmir is now no longer an autocratic government; it is a government representing the largest popular party in the State and is under a leader who, during these many months of unparalleled stress; has sustained the morale of his people, maintained an effective administration over the greater part of the State, and, generally, has inspired effective resistance to the brutal attempts of the invaders to overrun and destroy Kashmir. There is no alternative administration possible in Kashmir, unless that administration rested on coercion. If Sheikh Abdullah was not there by the will of the people, he could not have survived, much less could he have accomplished what he has done during these difficult months. It is for him to choose any national of Kashmir to assist him in his Government and it would be improper for us to interfere with his discretion in this matter.

I regret greatly that the representative of Pakistan before the Security Council should have made many statements and charges against India which have no foundation to fact. A great deal has happened in India and Pakistan during the last such months or more which has brought shame on all of us and I am prepared to admit at any stage and at any time the errors of our own people, for I do not think that it is good for the individual or the nation to lapse from truth. That is the lesson our Master taught us and we shall hold on to it to the best of our ability. Many horrible things have happened in India and Pakistan during these past months and while we hold strong views as to the initial responsibility for all the frightfulness that has occurred, all of us, in a greater or lesser degree, have a certain responsibility for it. But so far as the events in Kashmir are concerned, I am convinced in my mind than every action that the Government of India has taken has been straight and above board and inevitable in the circumstances.

Our going there at the end of October was thrust upon us by the course of events. Not to have rushed to the rescue of the people Kashmir, when they were in dire peril, would have been an eternal disgrace, a gross betrayal and a deep injury. We feel deeply about this matter and it is not merely a question of political advantage or disadvantage. It has been and is a moral issue with us, apart from other aspects of the case, and because of this, at every stage and at every step, I consulted Mahatma Gandhi and had his approval. In the confusion of a welter of charges and exaggerated statements, the basic facts are apt to be forgotten. I should like to know from anyone who studies our record in Kashmir since that fateful day when the raiders swooped down at Muzzafarabad and started their career of rapine and arson, I should like to know what major step we took that was morally wrong.

The role of the Indian Army in this conflict, which I repeat was not of our own seeking, has been conspicuous for its discipline, impartiality, endurance and gallantry. They have extended their protection to every section of the people of the State. To suggest that should be withdrawn before complete order is restored is to suggest something which is neither practicable nor reasonable and which is further a reflection on the exemplary record of our forces in Kashmir. We are in Kashmir and our forces there because, legally, we are on unassailable ground. But even from law, the moral case of the Indian Union in Kashmir is equally unassailable. If we had not gone there and if our armed forces had not been rushed at great peril into Kashmir, that lovely country would now have been sacked, destroyed and ruined and its men and women who have been noted for ages past for their intelligence and their cultural traditions would have been crushed under the heel of a barbarian invader. No Government in India could tolerate such a happening so long as it had the strength to resist it with all its might, and if such a fate befell Kashmir, what freedom or security would we have in the rest of Indian

We have only two objectives in the Jammu and Kashmir State; to ensure the freedom and the progress of the people there, and to prevent anything happening that might endanger the security of India. We have nothing else to gain from Kashmir, though Kashmir may profit much by our assistance. If those two objectives are assured to us, we are content.

Our making a reference on this issue to the Security Council of the United Nations was an act of faith, because we believe in the progressive realisation of world order and a world government. In spite of many shocks, we have adhered to the ideals represented by the United Nations and its Charter. But those very ideals teach us also certain duties and responsibilities to our own people and to those who put their trust in us. To betray these people would be to betray the basic ideals for which the United Nations stand or should stand. Even at the moment of accession we went out of our way to make a unilateral declaration that we world abide by the will of the people of Kashmir as declared in a plebiscite or referendum.

We insisted further that the Government of Kashmir must immediately become a popular government. We have adhered to that position throughout and we are prepared to have a plebiscite, with every protection for fair voting, and to abide by the decision of the people of Kashmir.

Our delegation has gone back to Lake Success after full discussions with us. They have gone back with a clear appreciation of the position of the Government of India and of Indian opinion and fortified with the knowledge that they have our full support. I should like to express my gratitude to Shri Gopalaswamy Ayyangar and his colleagues for the ability and firmness with which they presented our case before the Security Council. Sheikh Abdullah has not gone back because his work lies with his people at this grave juncture. He has to assume a heavier responsibility. I feel confident that he will discharge this new responsibility with that strength and vision which have endeared him to Muslims, Hindus and Sikhs in Kashmir. His place in the delegation has been taken by Shri Girja Shankar Bajpai, Secretary-General of the Ministry of External Affairs, who has been a tower of strength to me during these difficult months.

I shall not say much about the military situation in Jammu and Kashmir. We have had our moments of anxiety but at no time have I had any doubt about our capacity to meet the enemy and defeat him. Our officers and men are in high spirit, ready to meet any challenge. We have good reason to be proud of our officers and men, both of the Army and the Air Force. In particular I should like to pay a tribute to Brigadier Usman, whose leadership and success have been in keeping with the highest traditions of India's army.

The representative of Pakistan before the Security Council has brought in many charges against us which have little bearing on the Kashmir issue. He has talked of what he called our aggression in Junagarh and genocide and of much else. I do not wish to take the time of the House in dealing with these matters. We wish to conceal nothing and if the Security Council desires an investigation we shall welcome it.

Now, I should like to inform the House that today the Maharaja of Kashmir is issuing a proclamation and I shall briefly place the contents of that proclamation before the House, or I might as well read the whole proclamation:

> Proclamation of his Highness Maharaja Hari Singh Indar Mahindra Bahadur of Jammu and Kashmir, This Fifth Day of March, One Thousand Nine Hundred and Forty-eight.

In accordance with the traditions of my dynasty I have, from time to time, provided for increasing the association of my people with the administration of the State with the object of realising the goal of full responsible government. In pursuance of that object I have, by the Jammu and Kashmir Constitution Act of 1896 (XIV of 1896), established a constitutional government with a Council of Ministers, a legislature with a majority of elected members and an independent judiciary;

I have noted with gratification and pride the progress so far made the legitimate desire of my people for the immediate establishment of a fully democratic Constitution based on adult franchise with a hereditary Ruler from by dynasty as the constitutional head of an executive responsible to the legislature;

I have already appointed the popular leader of my people, Sheikh Mohammed Abdullah, as the Head of the Emergency Administration;

It is now my desire to replace the Emergency Administration by a popular Interim Government and to provide for, its powers, duties and functions, pending the framing of a fully democratic Constitution;

I accordingly hereby ordain as follows:

- My Council of Ministers shall consist of the Prime Minister and such other Ministers as may be appointed on the advice of the Prime Minister. I have by Royal Warrant appointed Sheikh Mohammed Abdullah as the Prime Minister with effect from the 1st day of March, 1948.
- The Prime Minister and other Ministers shall function as a Cabinet and act on the principle of joint responsibility. A Dewan appointed by me shall also be a member of the Cabinet.
- I take this opportunity of giving once again a solemn assurance that all sections of my people will have opportunities of service, both civil and military, solely on the basis of their merits and irrespective of creed or community.
- My Council of Ministers shall take appropriate steps, as soon as the restoration of normal conditions has been completed, to convene a National Assembly based upon

adult suffrage, having due regard to the principle that the number of representatives from each voting area should, as far as practicable, be proportionate to the population of that area.

- The Constitution to be framed by the National Assembly shall provide adequate safeguards for the minorities and contain appropriate provisions guaranteeing freedom of conscience, freedom of speech and freedom of assembly.
- The National Assembly shall, as soon as the work of framing the new Constitution is completed, submit it through the Council of Ministers for my acceptance.
- In conclusion I repeat, the hope that the formation of a popular Interim Government and the inauguration, in the near future, of a fully democratic Constitution will ensure the contentment, happiness and the moral and material advancement of my beloved people.

I am placing this Proclamation on the table of the House.

I should like to congratulate His Highness the Maharaja of Jammu and Kashmir on the decision that he has taken. But the burden now lies on Sheikh Abdullah and his colleagues and the people of Kashmir. I have no doubt as to how they will discharge their burden, because they are not newcomers and we have seen them functioning in the face of all manner of difficulties during the last few months. So I look forward with a certain measure of assurance to the future of Kashmir in spite of all difficulties.

I am, Sir, also placing, a copy of the White Paper on the table of the House.

India has Nothing to Conceal

[A statement from New Delhi, June 10, 1948].

We have seen in the Press reports of a statement said to have been made by the Prime Minister of Pakistan, Mr. Liaqat Ali Khan, on my letter to the President of the Security Council, dated 5th June, 1948. I do not propose to enter into the merits of Pakistan's charges against India of genocide and non-implementation of agreements with Pakistan or against the accession of Junagarh to

India. Our views have been repeatedly stated before the Security Council and also in statements made by me and some of my colleagues. We regard the accusations of genocide and non-implementation of agreements as baseless. That we have protested against the Security Council's decision to include these charges within the scope of the functions of the Council's Commission is certainly not due, as alleged by the Prime Minister of Pakistan, to a desire to conceal anything. Because India has nothing to conceal is no reason why India should acquiesce in an investigation by an outside body in something which, in our view, is outside the competence of that body and which has no foundation in fact.

The Prime Minister of Pakistan has also attributed India's decision to refer the Kashmir dispute to the Security Council to a desire to gain time in which to force a military decision. A reference to India's complaint to the Security Council will show that, contrary to what Mr. Liaqat Ali Khan has suggested, India has all along insisted on the urgency of action by the Council on her complaint against Pakistan. If such action has not been taken, the fault is not India's.

In referring the Kashmir dispute to the India never intended to sacrifice her freedom of military action to rid the State of Jammu and Kashmir of all invaders and to restore peace. She has both the right and obligation to do so in respect of a State which has acceded to her. It is strange that Mr. Liaqat Ali Khan should complain of India's action in using her resources to achieve this legitimate and humane object.

Once more allegations have been made of atrocities by Indian troops against "defenceless old men, women and children in areas occupied by them." I most emphatically repudiate this unfounded charge. The purpose of these accusations, often repeated but without any vestige of truth, can only be to divert the attention of the world from the barbarous atrocities which the raiders whom Pakistan has so actively been aiding and abetting have been committing on innocent civilians, regardless of creed, sex or age, in the areas which they have occupied or into which they have penetrated. Such crimes against humanity can never be concealed. Baramula, Bhimbar, Mirpur and Rajauri, to cite only a few instances, will always proclaim the infamy of their cruel assailants.

Mr. Liaqat Ali Khan has complained of Indian troops violating Pakistan's frontiers and Indian airmen bombing villages well within Pakistan's boundaries. Every complaint of the violation by our troops of Pakistan's frontiers that could be investigated has been enquired into. Most of these complaints have, on enquiry, proved to be baseless. As is well known, the raiders, when forced to retire from State territory, often flee into Pakistan. Our troops chase them up to the frontier of the State; this is their duty as well as their right. As regards our airmen also, every complaint of Pakistan has been carefully investigated. In the particular case of Garhi Habibullah, which the Pakistan Prime Minister has quoted, a double investigation was made to establish the facts and the regret of the Government of India has already been communicated to the Government of Pakistan for the incident. The history of two world wars shows how impossible it is to avoid damage to neutrals through bona fide mistakes of observation. No aggression against Pakistan was intended.

Mr. Liaqat Ali Khan has referred to "the exemplary patience" shown by the Government of Pakistan "in the face of provocations." He has conveniently forgotten the continuous and continuing provocation to which the Government of India have been subjected ever since the invasion, last October, by tribesmen of the valley of Kashmir, itself inspired by Pakistan, in the shape of every kind of aid given by Pakistan to the aggressor. More recently, Pakistan troops have been opposing Indian troops on the Uri front in strength. It is idle, in the circumstances, either to speak of the Pakistan Government's "anxiety to maintain peaceful and friendly relations with India" or to suggest that Indian action in Kashmir constitutes "grave threat to the security of Pakistan" or a campaign of "murder and destruction" against the Muslims of Jammu and Kashmir.

Far from seeking to murder and destroy Muslims in the State, Indian forces have been used to protect them against ruthless marauders whom Pakistan has let loose. An Interim Government, representative of the people, headed by a Muslim who has for years been the most outstanding leader of popular and progressive forces in Jammu and Kashmir, and composed of a majority of Muslims, has been foamed in the State. On the question of accession, India has repeatedly affirmed that the declared will of the people of Jammu and Kashmir shall prevail. Though, short of a declaration of war, Pakistan has done everything to help the invaders of and the insurgents within the State, the Government of India have acted with unexampled restraint in the interests of peace. They still desire to live on the friendliest possible terms with the neighbour State of Pakistan. The fulfilment of that desire, however, is more likely to be defeated than achieved by the kind of statement which Mr. Liaqat Ali Khan is reported to have made yesterday.

The Story of Kashmir Goes On

[A speech delivered at the Constituent Assembly (Legislative), New Delhi, September 7, 1948].

Sir, I crave your leave to place certain papers on the table of the House and to make a statement thereon. These papers relate to the United Nations Commission on Kashmir which has been in India and in Pakistan for about two months now. The Honourable Members of the House must have read in this morning's papers some correspondence which has passed between this Commission and the Government of India; a Resolution passed by the Commission some three weeks ago; the Government of India's reply thereto and some indication of Pakistan's reply. The full set of papers has not been published in the Press yet and in fact, we received them only this morning by special courier from Karachi. No doubt these papers will be published in the newspapers. Meanwhile, I shall place on the table of the House some of these papers, and the rest I hope to place there in the course of the day, as soon as they are typed.

Now, the House knows that this Commission has been here for the last two months or more and the House will have seen from this published correspondence what their resolution was and our response to it. In fact they will have seen that we accepted certain conditions for a truce and ceasefire. Pakistan, however, has rejected them. Now, I do not wish at this stage to say very much more about this matter, partly because I should like to go through those papers more carefully than I have had time to do this morning when they came, partly because the Commission is considering what further steps they may or may not take and it will not perhaps be quite proper for me to say anything which might embarrass the Commission.

As the House perhaps knows, it was the desire of the Commission that we postpone the publication of papers and any statements in this House till today. We have been anxious right from the beginning of these consultations with the Commission to take this House and the country into our confidence, because we wished to take no steps in such a vital and important matter without the full knowledge and consent of this House, but inevitably in the circumstances, it became difficult for us, much as we wanted to do so, to make statements in this House when the Commission was engaged in these delicate negotiations, and so at their request we had to postpone such publication from time to time. Ultimately, they issued their statement yesterday at 4 p.m. in Karachi. Now, although I do not wish to say much on this subject, there are certain facts to which I should like to draw the attention of the House. The facts themselves are very well known not only in this House, but all over the country. Nevertheless, sometimes known and established facts are denied and it does make a difference when those facts are admitted.

The present story and tragedy of Kashmir began over ten months ago. Late in October last year there was an invasion of Kashmir by people coming across or from Pakistan territory, and the Government of India were faced with a very difficult problem, calling for a decision as difficult as any Government to make, and we had to make that decision within a few hours. We made that decision and since then we have followed that decision. It became clear to us then, and that fact has become clear to all the world that wants to know it that this invasion was not only encouraged and patronised but actively supported by the Pakistan Government. Later it became clear that apart from supporting others, there was active participation of the Pakistan army in it. Now, throughout these ten months the Pakistan Government have denied that fact, they denied it aggressively, loudly and persistently. We stated it before the Security Council of the United Nations.

In fact, we went to the Security Council with the very simple plea that the peace of Kashmir had been disturbed by these raiders coming across the Pakistan territory and we stated our case as moderately as possible, although we could have stated it much more forcefully. We said that it was inevitable that people from Pakistan could only come with the assistance and of Pakistan and, therefore, we requested the Security Pakistan not to assist them and not to permit them to come in this way. It was, if I may say so, a very moderate request, couched in moderate language. Pakistan denied that fact and during the long discussions before the Security Council they not only went on denying it, but expressed a great deal of irritation and anger that anyone should have made such a charge against them. Well, I do not want to go into this long history of denial by them, but the point is that today, on their own admission, their denial was false. Now, that is an important matter.

It is important from the point of view not only of practical polities and the situation we have to face today, it is important also from the point of view of the standards of morality, good behaviour and decency that should subsist between nations. Now, I know very well that the standard of public morality and international morality is unfortunately not very high in this world. Nevertheless, certain appearances have to be kept up, certain decencies have to be maintained and some standards have to be observed. I do submit to this House and to the country that the story, of these ten months and more and the way the Pakistan Government have reacted to all that has been said about them in the course of these ten months is so extraordinary as to be hardly creditable for a nation.

Even till yesterday, as far as the world is concerned, even till 4 p.m. yesterday, there was no admission by Pakistan that they were participating in any way in those Kashmir operations. Of course, we knew. We have the most definite and positive evidence to that effect and ultimately you cannot hide large armies. Nevertheless, till 4 p.m. yesterday, when those papers were issued to the public, there was no public admission. In fact, there was a continual denial in the course of the last few weeks, while this large Pakistan Army was active in Kashmir, battling with the Indian forces in Indian Union territory.

Please remember that all the fighting that has taken place in the last ten months has been in Kashmir, has been in Indian territory; there has been no fighting; there has been no incursion, there has been no Indian Army anywhere on Pakistan territory. That is a fundamental and basic fact, which apart from any other enquiry and any other facts would lead one to the conclusion that if any outsiders are fighting in Indian Union territory, those outsiders are the aggressors. Why are they there? During the last six weeks or so, again we pointed out in the most explicit language to the Pakistan Government and to the Prime Minister of Pakistan this presence of Pakistan troops in the Kashmir State.

Again, there was either a denial or an evasion of the issue. It was an extraordinary thing to me. I do not claim to be in any way different from others of my kind. My standards, I hope, are not lower than those of others. It has been a shock to me that any country, any responsible Minister of a Government should make statements which are patently and obviously false and try to mislead the world by that means You will remember that before the Security Council at Lake Success, there were prolonged arguments on this issue. The Foreign Minister of the Pakistan Government, who was the Chief Delegate of their Government there, placed the case for Pakistan before the Security Council.

How does that case stand now, I would beg you and the country and the world to consider, because the whole case was one fundamental fact, that is, the denial of Pakistan's complicity in Kashmir. They denied throughout that they had actively participated in it. If this fact is proved, as it has proved out of their very mouths today, to have been false, then what happens to that whole case so labouriously built up by the Pakistan Government before the Security Council? What happens to the charge that we brought against them which was never considered by the Security Council at all, much to our regret and amazement? So the fundamental thing for us to remember is this, that fact which was denied for ten months and more has at last been publicly admitted by the Pakistan Government. They have of course, admitted in their own way. I shall now read out some passages from their letter to the Commission. They say:

> "India was steadily building its armed forces in Jammu and Kashmir. This building up process did not cease on the 21st April, 1948, but was continued and intensified. The Indian Army mounted a big offensive in the beginning of April, thereby causing a material change in the situation. This offensive action has

> continued ever since. The publicly declared intention of the Government of India was to secure a military decision in Jammu and Kashmir, thus presenting the United Nations Organisation with a fiat accompli. This situation not only put in jeopardy the entire population of the areas under the Azad Kashmir Government, and led to a big influx of refugees into Pakistan, but also constituted a direct threat to Pakistan's security. It was this which compelled the Government of Pakistan to move their troops into certain defensive positions."

Observe here, too, they do not say clearly that the defensive positions happened to be in another country.

Quite apart from their decision in regard to ceasefire and other proposals, the country which participates in aggression against the neighbouring country, maybe in the name of defence or its own security, denies it for many months and then, in fact, when it finds that its guilt is proved, when it cannot hide it any more, then grudgingly admits it and gives some reason for it — how shall we consider the politics of that country from any international or national or moral point of view? Observe that, according to this statement, they took this action in April last, four months or four and a half months ago. If they felt that their security was imperilled, or that something was happening which endangered them and that they had to send their troops, what then should they have done? Obviously, they should have informed the Government of India, and informed the United Nations Organisation that this was happening and that there had been, as they say, a material change in the situation, and therefore they were compelled to take this or that action.

I cannot conceive of any country in the wide world which would not have done so. Quite apart from motives, this is the obvious and inevitable thing to do. They sent this army, according to them, in April last or thereabout and there is no intimation to us into whose territory they were coming, and there was no intimation to the United Nations Organisation which was seized of this question, and was, as a matter of fact, then thinking of sending out a Commission to India. You will remember that in the very early stages of the Security Council's activities, an appeal was made to India and Pakistan in regard to these military operations and in regard to avoiding any situation arising between India and Pakistan. That appeal was repeated. In the few lines I have read to you from Pakistan's reply, they accused India of mounting an offensive. We are trying to push out the invader from Indian Union territory. It has been our declared policy, which we have repeated before the United Nations Security Council, which in fact was inevitable for us and would have been for any other country with any grain of self-respect.

On the other hand, what did the Pakistan Government do? We have, right from the beginning taken whatever step we have taken, in the limelight; there has been no hiding about it. The House has been greatly interested in this matter of Kashmir. The Indian public has taken the greatest interest in it and, rightly, the burden of it has fallen on our Government. It has been a heavy burden. I shall be frank and tell you why it has been heavy on me and more especially on my Government: not because military operations were involved, although that is always a burden, but rather it has best a burden since we wanted to be sure that at no time we acted against the principles we had so long proclaimed.

May I take the House into my confidence? In the early stages, towards the end of October and in November, and indeed sequentially, I was so exercised over Kashmir and if anything would or was likely to have happened to Kashmir, which according to me, might have been disastrous for Kashmir, I would have been heart-broken. I was intensely interested, apart the larger reasons which the Government have, for emotional and personal reasons; I do not want to hide this. I am interested in Kashmir. Nevertheless, I tried to keep down the personal and emotional aspect and consider it from the larger viewpoint of India's good and Kashmir's good. I tried to consider the question from the point of view of not straying or drifting from the high principles which we had proclaimed in the past.

When this question first came up, I sought guidance, as I do in other matters, from Mahatmaji and I went to him and put to him my difficulties. The House knows that apostle of non-violence was not a suitable guide in military matters — and he said so —

but he undoubtedly always was a guide on the moral issue. And so I put my difficulties and my Government's difficulties before him and though it is not proper for me to drag in his name at this juncture in order to lessen my responsibility or my Government's responsibility on this which is complete, I, nevertheless, mention this matter merely to show how the moral aspect of this question has always troubled me. And more especially, when I saw in India all manner of things happening, which had happened in previous months and had brought India's name into disrepute, I was greatly troubled and worried and was anxious that we should keep straight or as straight as we possibly could.

Now, this has been my attitude and on several occasions I had claimed it publicly. And apart from rhetoric and vague insinuations, I should like to know from anybody — friend or enemy, from that day in the last week of October, when we took the fateful decision to send our troops by air to Kashmir till today, what is it we have done in Kashmir which from any point of view and from any standard is wrong.

I want an answer to that question. Individuals may have erred here and there; but I say that the Government of India and the Indian army as a whole have done something which was inevitable, and each step that we have taken has been an inevitable step which, if we had not taken it, would have brought disgrace to us. That is how I have ventured to look at this question of Kashmir: And when I find that on the other side the whole case that has been built up on what I venture to say — using strong language — is falsehood and deceit, am I wrong? That is what I ask this House and the country and the world to consider.

Now, therefore, this is the first fact to remember; that all this case built up by Pakistan before the Security Council crumbles by this admission of theirs and by the proven fact that large armies of theirs are active in Kashmir, and no doubt similar armies — if you like — and others connected with them have operated in Kashmir on Indian Union territory during these ten months or so. Every subsequent proceeding should be viewed from that aspect.

Now, we come to the present, and I must add one more thing. This has been an aggression; and if it is called — as according to their own admission it must be called — an aggression, then certain consequences ought to follow. Now, my difficulty has been that in considering any question if you lose yourself in a forest of intricate detail sometimes you lose sight of the wood for the trees. There have been long discussions over the Kashmir issue and every aspect and phase and the past and present history have been considered. But what has been the major point? I repeat that, because I think the fundamental factor is the aggression of Pakistan on Indian Union territory; secondly, the denial of the fact of that aggression; thirdly, the present admission of the fact. These are the governing factors of that situation. And the argument has gone on for so long, because these governing factors were slurred over and were not emphasised. We emphasised them, of course, and the problem was discussed in intimate detail.

Now, if you start from a wrong premise in an argument, obviously your whole argument goes wrong and you land yourself in difficulties. If you try to solve a problem without analysing or stating the nature of the problem, how are you to solve it? And that has been the fundamental difficulty in this Kashmir business: the fundamental issue has been slurred over and by-passed and passed over. Therefore, we have been dealing with other matters which cannot yield a solution. Now, the basic factor is revealed by the very admission of the Pakistan Government.

Now, coming to this proposal of the United Nations Commission in India in regard to ceasefire and truce, etc., I shall not discuss it much, because I do not wish at this moment to say anything which might embarrass that Commission. But certain papers are before you. I need hardly say that the proposal they made was not welcomed by us with joy and enthusiasm; there were many matters in it which went against the grain.

But we tried to look at the matter as coolly and dispassionately as possible with the view to establishing peace in the harried State of Kashmir, to avoiding needless suffering and shedding of blood; and we agreed to that ceasefire proposal after the Commission had been good enough to elucidate certain points which we had placed before them: We did not place too many points before them but only certain simple obvious points relating to the security of Kashmir. We placed these before them and they were enough to tell us that was their meaning. Thereupon we accepted the ceasefire proposal, accepted many things in it which we did not like, because we felt that both in the interest of peace and of international order, it was a good thing for us to go a few steps forward even though some of the steps might be unwilling ones. We did so in order to bring about this peace and to show that we were prepared to go as far as possible to meet the wishes of an international organisation like the United Nations.

The original proposal of the United Nations was given to us on the 14th August. The 15th was our Independence Day. Immediately after, on the 16th, we met the members of the Commission and discussed the matter with them to find out exactly what they meant and told them exactly what we meant to; and within four days, i.e. on the 20th August we sent them our reply. We did not want to delay matters as they were anxious that they should not be delayed.

The Pakistan Government had also received these proposals at the same time, on the 14th August, at 3 or 4 p.m. They also had the same amount of time. But even after the return of the Commission to Pakistan — and some members of the Commission went in between to Karachi — they were not ready with their reply. And, in fact, it was by the pressure of events or the pressure of the pressure the Commission that ultimately they gave some kind of a reply yesterday. Meanwhile, they sent long letters seeking elucidation. I am sorry I have not yet read the reply wholly because I received it just a little before coming here. But I have read the significant parts of it, and in effect it is a rejection of those proposals.

Now, the Commission told us that these proposals stood as a whole and while they were prepared to discuss any matter gladly it was difficult — in fact, it was not possible for them to accept conditional acceptances, because if we made some conditions and Pakistan naturally made other conditions, what exactly was accepted and by whom? So they said that these proposals were to be accepted as they were, and if there were conditions attached to them, it was not an acceptance but a rejection. Now, therefore, what the Pakistan Government have done is tantamount to rejection. It is for the Commission to decide and to say what they are going to do. It is not for me to advise them. So we have at a curious state of affairs that the country which was the aggressor nation according to its own showing, now even rejects and refuses a proposal for a ceasefire, or puts forward conditions which are tantamount to such a refusal.

Now, certain international consequences should follow from all this. What consequences follow? In a somewhat narrow sphere, all those officers and individuals who are participating in this aggressive war against India in Kashmir territory — there are of course Pakistani nationals and others there too — are participating not only in an aggressive war, but in a war after the refusal of a United Nations Commission proposal or a ceasefire. Their position is worthy of consideration.

That is all that I wish to say on the Kashmir issue. Naturally the story of Kashmir goes on. It has been a saga during these ten months or so, and there has been a great deal of suffering and blood and tears involved in it. There have been high moments also. But for us in India, and for the Government of India, it has been a period of trial and difficulty from many points of view; still, at no time have we considered that we were wrong or that we had taken a step which we could not fully justify. It is in that faith that we are going to continue, and may I say that in all these consultations with the United Nations Commission and in other matters affecting Kashmir, we have kept in close touch with the Kashmir Government under Sheikh Abdullah and consulted him in all the steps that we have taken? That was natural and it is inevitable in the circumstances that we should march together in full consultation with each other. Proceeding on that basis, we shall go ahead, whether in the military sphere other spheres, and I am quite convinced that, if we adhere the right course and do not stray from it, even from the opportunist point of view of some present advantage, we shall win through, and any country that bases its case on an essential falsehood cannot gain its ends.

10

Views on Nehru

Abdul Karim Qasim

It will be observed that the seventy years of Nehru's life represent an extremely important period in the history of the modern world. In many respects, especially in the fields of science and the liberation of the human mind, this period is unique in its achievements.

Although Nehru was born in the last century, he reached maturity during the years following the First World War and was, therefore, influenced by the emerging political and social forces which were at work during the nineteenth century and which later culminated in the outbreak of an armed conflict on a scale unprecedented in history,. The forces which were unleashed as a consequence of the acceleration in industrial and commercial development during the preceding two centuries brought most parts of the world under the physical domination and material exploitation of the industrially advanced countries of Europe and subjected them to the patterns of the European civilization.

The predominance of the West was maintained by its scientific progress and achievements which entailed, *inter alia*, a rise in the standard of living, the subjugation of the underdeveloped areas and the accentuation of conflict in the world. At the same time,

European colonisation had given impetus to the political and cultural awakening of the people of the colonial and other areas of the world and it kindled the flames of nationalism. Thus, the period between the two world wars witnessed a rapid ascent in the forces striving for freedom and independence — a trend accelerated by the dissemination of knowledge and literacy, and by the introduction and utilisation of science and technology in these areas.

It could, therefore, be said that Nehru's seventy years of life had coincided with a period in history which was primarily dominated by forces generated by science in its application to the material and human resources of the world on a scale then unknown.

This advance in the control of nature had set the stage for the emergence of a new world with its many problems, the effects of which have not yet been properly weighed. Among these problems mention should be made of the struggle for higher living standards, for national, political and intellectual freedom, for better social existence, and for the promotion of peaceful and harmonious relations between nations. Nehru did not only live in but was the product of this material and cultural turmoil which dominated the world in general and his own country in particular; and, because of his genius, he was destined to play a major part. Nehru inherited the leadership of the Indian national movement and the responsibility of guiding it, by stages, to its goal, and thereby laid down the foundations of an independent India.

The task was colossal, no doubt, and the challenge was great; but Nehru never hesitated to undertake the task or to meet the challenge. He had done so with a mind and determination which revealed the greatness of his spirit and the depth of his genius. And above all, he has been carrying out his life's mission with marked success.

In my opinion, the secret of his success lies in the fact that he had properly absorbed the spirit of his age and endeavoured to abide by the fundamental laws of development as revealed by the progress of science and by the history of society. This intellectual attitude enabled Nehru to respond to the exigencies of the revolutionary forces of our era, namely, science, nationalism and the struggle for peace and security.

Knowing Nehru from his numerous writings and having followed his long struggle for the liberation of the Indian and other subjugated peoples, I have always been impressed by his great ability to mould the ideals for which he has always stood into the framework of everyday political, social and international life. He is, perhaps, one of those rare historical figures who mastered the art of turning their philosophical concepts into social, economic and political institutions. This may have been the outcome of the intrinsic harmony between his realistic world outlook and his philosophical approach to existence. Because he is endowed with an alert and profound mind, Nehru was able to absorb the spirit which moves the world at large both materially and spiritually.

He was able, in other words, to grasp clearly the working of the main forces which join human history to the existence of the universe. Within such a philosophical framework, Nehru was able to follow a policy which helped India to emerge peacefully from her long and ancient history into the modern stage of existence. The influence of Nehru on Indian renaissance cannot be measured in terms of day-to-day achievement. The whole future of India seems to be in the process of being formulated by Nehru.

On the other hand, Nehru remains the product of his age, revealing in his philosophy and in his political activities the main currents running through the present era in the history of civilization. Although he struggled for India, he was greatly inspired by the history of man. Thus, he moves with the conviction that the world is one and that the fate of men anywhere is influenced by what others do everywhere. His political and other activities reveal the fact that he is moved by a profound sense of responsibility to the world at large.

Any statement made, about Nehru is bound to do him and his complex personality little justice. He is not only a statesman and an ardent fighter for freedom and democracy, but a historian, a philosopher, a distinguished literary figure, a social architect and an internationalist. Hence, his activities have not been confined to the boundaries of the Indian subcontinent but taken him into a number of international fields. His influence on the trends of world development stems from the fact that his approach to the present national and international problems is based on a determination to meet the forces of our time and to utilise them in a constructive manner. He enriched, for example, the Indian national independence movement by-giving it an economic, social and cultural content; by the gradual introduction of planned reforms on a national scale; and by the utilisation of science and technology. Moreover, he realised, perhaps more than others, the necessity for international action to avert the dangers of war, and responded in particular to the call of small nations for peace and security. Thus, he evolved a policy of positive neutrality to alleviate the ever-growing tension between the two contending Powers and to break the trend of polarisation of the lesser powers, by creating what may be called a third force in the world.

The impact of Nehru's contribution to the various fields of his activity will remain for the future historian to evaluate. For the present, we can only say that Nehru is a blessing to all the forces striving for peace, progress and democracy.

Adlai E. Stevenson

We live in an age swept by tides of history so powerful that they shatter human understanding. Only a tiny handful of men have influenced the implacable forces of our time. To this small company of the truly great, Nehru belongs.

The nation is safe in his hands: Those were Mahatma. Gandhi's concluding words when he publicly chose Nehru as his heir and successor — because of his bravery, his prudence and discipline, his vision and practicality, his humility and purity.

A quarter of his life Nehru has spent in prison for the same cause our revolutionary ancestors in America pledged their lives, their fortunes and their sacred honour — freedom. Born to exalted station he knows the "art of being a King", yet he has a common touch that excites the devotion and understanding of all kinds and conditions of people, and he has a pen and tongue that stir the hearts of hundreds of millions.

A man in public office can find no surer guide than Nehru. "Personal integrity, love of country, lofty idealism, faith in the people and a passion to serve them well, far-ranging vision, these are the qualities by which he commands our respect.

Eleanor Roosevelt

I am not really close enough to Nehru to write what I feel would be an adequate appraisal of his achievements but here is something that I would like to say from my heart.

Jawaharlal Nehru's wisdom, his patience, his far-sightedness will be needed in the next ten years as much as they have been in the past. His personal courage as well as his moral courage and his integrity deserve special recognition. He has stood for the things he believed in. We may not always agree with him but it is a wonderful thing to know that the man will stand for the things that he feels are important to his own country and to the world.

Nehru has tried to educate his people in the ways of democracy. This is a tremendous undertaking with a population as great as India's and with a background of illiteracy to start with. His success is already being proved, I think, and not only the Indians but much of the rest of the world owes Nehru a debt of gratitude for his leadership, for his integrity and his courage.

Gamal Abdel Nasser

To write on Jawaharlal Nehru is a source of great joy to one who does it. It provides him with an opportunity to contemplate on a life which in its length — 70 years — has not reached the same extent as it has in its depth and breadth.

Jawaharlal Nehru's life, in its various aspects, has indeed been a full and rich one.

In its depth, it has reached the limit where he has been able, through the residue of centuries and the vicissitudes of history, to touch upon the very soul of India.

In its breadth, it has been able, despite colonialism and its legacies, to respond to his closer world — Asia and Africa — and to show moreover a comprehensive understanding of the other peoples who live beyond Asia and Africa.

I have had many an opportunity of meeting Jawaharlal Nehru. Regardless of the friendship which it was my good fortune to forge with him and whose threads are now closely knit, any meeting I have had with him was a great and productive adventure.

Our first long meeting was on board a steamer in the Nile. Mostly we talked about planning. Nehru's understanding of the subject and the role which planning played in modern times reflected a genuine consciousness on his part of the nature of the delicate and intricate phase through which the nations of Asia and Africa were passing.

He believed that their peoples who had been compelled, under the influence of many historical forces and circumstances, to remain backward in comparison with others and were later touched by the influence of the great revolutionary awakening which pushed them forward towards emancipation, have no other course open to them in order to catch up with those who had gone ahead but to "plan" their path. To them planning is not only a means; it is a necessity.

Nor is the purpose of planning merely to accumulate figures about production. The training of human beings is the most important part of it. I remember Nehru's words to me at that time: "Remember, the future of any country is closely bound up with the type of people who live in that country."

On one occasion, I had the opportunity of attending a meeting addressed by Nehru at a mass rally which was held in the spacious Ram Lila grounds in Delhi. The masses who had waited to hear Nehru's speech were composed of a heterogeneous group of people: young men and young women, squatting on the ground along with children on the threshold of life; close to them sat elderly men, advanced in age, almost on the threshold of the other world. To this mixed gathering, Nehru began to talk.

I know how easy it is always for a speaker who wishes to keep his audience spellbound to stir up their emotions; but Nehru did nothing of the kind. His voice never rose. He never got into a passion. Nor did the enthusiasm of his audience run high or their feelings get stirred up. They merely listened to what he said, albeit eagerly. At times they would all laugh, both men and women, children as well as the aged.

Despite their diverse nature, they all understood what this man said, this man who had spent the years of his youth in the remote universities of the West and yet had never detached himself from his people until destiny placed upon his shoulders the task of leading them during an important transitory period through which their country was passing.

I was sitting on the dais behind Nehru trying to grasp the significance of the occasion. I did not understand the language he spoke, but I could see that his thoughts and words had a great reaction on the heterogeneous masses who listened to him. I pondered over his words about Gandhi, whom he had described as one of those leaders who had gone into history not because they brought new things to their people but because they could fathom their innermost recesses and bring up what was there to the surface, clean it and brighten it by removing the moss that enveloped it.

As I sat on the dais behind Nehru watching him speak to his people I was moved and felt how much what he said about Gandhi applied to himself.

The truth is Nehru is not only the exponent of the dreams deeply nestled in the hearts of the people of India. He is also the expression of human conscience itself particularly for people who lived more or less through the same experiences and faced the same problems as the Indians did.

If Nehru has interpreted, and indeed interpreted well, the urges and aspirations of his people as well as those of Asia and Africa, he has also made another contribution no less significant.

He has also interpreted both to his people as well as to the peoples of Asia and Africa, the dreams and aspirations of other peoples in the rest of the world.

Those who had the opportunity of attending the meetings of the Afro-Asian Conference at Bandung will realise the full meaning of what I say. At the meetings of the Political Committee of the Conference, which may be regarded as a turning point in our history, Jawaharlal Nehru, the man who never forgets to give that touch of beauty which lies in the rose that always rests in his buttonhole, gave to it many a beautiful touch of thought and ideal, understanding and experience, art and culture, even of philosophy and history.

He interpreted others to Asia and Africa, and interpreted Asia and Africa to others. He was the finest example of mutual interpretation that I have seen.

They say a real artist never gets lost in his art or thought. As a matter of fact, Nehru is as much capable of action, of fighting for his thoughts and ideals as he is in expressing them.

Talking of my association with him I shall always remember the message which I received from him at the time of the British-French-Israeli aggression on Egypt, in which he said:

"If colonialism succeeds in coming back to Egypt, it will reverse the entire course of history and return to every other country from which it had been forced to go. Therefore, ... colonialism should not be allowed to succeed in Egypt. Otherwise, it will signal a new and long fight for the whole of Asia and Africa."

What a quick comprehension of a complicated situation! And with what scintillating and brave words he conveyed it! It gave us courage and stirred us to fight back.

Josip Broz Tito

The personality of Jawaharlal Nehru and his activity as a political worker and statesman during the period between the two World Wars, the Second World War and the years following it, were already known to me when I first met him at the end of 1954. Therefore, my first personal contact with him seemed to me like a meeting with a man to whom I had been linked with bonds of long-standing personal acquaintance. There is no doubt that the fact that I also got to know him and his activity through his written works greatly contributed to such a feeling. I have always considered him, side by side with Gandhi, the most important person in the struggle for India's independence and her significant and beneficial performance in international life. I highly esteem particularly his great role in the struggle for peace. My opinion was fully confirmed by the impressions I gained during my two visits to his great country and in the course of our other meetings.

Since our first meeting in New Delhi in December 1954, I have had the opportunity to meet Nehru several times on different occasions in India and Yugoslavia and to exchange with him views both directly and through correspondence on a number of current problems relating to international policy and the relations between our two countries. I became convinced, through these contacts and exchanges of views, that he is a great man sincerely devoted to the welfare of his nation and the cause of peace, international understanding and cooperation. It was very easy for us to find a common language during our talks, since the aspirations and the policies of our peoples were in conformity. So were our views on international issues and this found its full expression in more than one document, out of which I would particularly point out the New Delhi declaration issued on December 22, 1954 and our joint statement with President Nasser signed at Brioni on July 19, 1956.

The greatness of a man and a political leader is reflected, above all, in his ability to symbolise the positive strivings of his people for freedom, prosperity and peace — the fundamental values of contemporary society. In my opinion, precisely in this lies the greatness of Nehru, who made a tremendous contribution to the struggle of the people of India for their independence and for the achievement of the unity of the Indian nation.

He, also, initiated and became the directing soul of India's economic and social development, under her specific conditions, towards progress and socialism, and the champion of a consistent policy of peace and co-existence in the international field. It is because of this that I especially esteem Nehru as a person who has succeeded in rallying around himself the majority of the great Indian nation on the policy of internal progress, and as a fighter for peace and peaceful international policy.

Whenever I met Nehru, I was strongly impressed by the strength of his character, the vivacity of his spirit, his great energy, his insight into approaching problems, his attractive manner and directness in personal contacts. I saw in him a brave man who boldly faces the realities of life and is not daunted by difficulties, a man who does not indulge in illusions or has a dogmatic approach to problems, but is ready, boldly and realistically, to tackle and overcome difficulties. I was also greatly impressed by his love of nature, his humanism and his devotion to his family.

I had also an opportunity to see Nehru engaged in political action in his own country, at the annual conference of the Congress at Avadi, in January 1955, when he heralded the new programme of India's development after a socialist pattern of society. I know this to be the result of Nehru's long years of effort and he could rightly be satisfied with it. On that occasion I was convinced that among the great mass of delegates and people who were assembled, he enjoyed unchallenged authority and deep loyalty, which makes it possible for him to play, under the difficult and complex conditions of the struggle for the development of his country and for the safeguarding of peace, such an important role which transcends far beyond the frontiers of his great country.

India can be proud of having such an outstanding leader, who, through his efforts and farsightedness, is paving the way towards a better future for India, and who, through his untiring activity in the struggle for peace, devotion to the policy 6f co-existence and the strengthening of peaceful international cooperation, has become one of the most outstanding statesmen of the contemporary world.

Today, I wish him many more years of happy life and fruitful activity in the service of his people — and, thus, in the service of peace and international cooperation.

Kwame Nkrumah

A fighter for colonial freedom, I followed avidly the progress of the revolution which was taking place in India prior to her independence. When the time came for me to do something about gaining the political independence of my own country, it was a natural thing that I should take inspiration from India and her leaders who had so recently had to face and overcome problems similar to those then facing my own countrymen. There was no doubt whatever in my mind that Gandhi's policy of non-violence was the only effective means of dealing with the colonial problem.

I have had for many years the greatest admiration for Jawaharlal Nehru, not only on account of the great work that he, in company with other Indian leaders, was doing for his country, but also, and probably more so, because I respected him as a man of purpose, of courage and determination, and one genuinely dedicated to the cause of India. Owing to one reason or another, I did not actually meet Nehru until the summer of 1957 when we both attended the Conference of Commonwealth Prime Ministers in London. He invited me to have breakfast with him shortly after he arrived in England.

More often than not, a person whom you think you know so well through his writings, his personal letters and "from details given by his intimate friends falls sadly short of your expectations when eventually you come face to face with him. I am a realist. I looked forward to this meeting with him more than I can say, but two thoughts were uppermost in my mind that morning as my car sped through the London traffic to Kensington Palace Gardens, where Nehru was staying. Would he, I wondered, measure up to the degree of greatness in which I had always held him? Would I, on the other hand, fail to make a good impression on him?

Nehru was all that I had imagined he would be — and more. I could not, of course, answer the second question, but of one thing I am certain: at that moment of our meeting — of our first handclasp — a firm friendship was forged.

It was my first attendance at the Commonwealth Prime Ministers' Conference and I was feeling very much the new boy, in spite of the very warm welcome that was accorded to me by everyone I met. As a newcomer I decided to observe things at the meetings rather than take part in them — at any rate for the first few days — so that by watching how the older members conducted themselves at the meetings, my "newness" would not be so apparent when the time came for me to participate actively.

At each meeting my admiration for Nehru increased. Some days he barely uttered a word, but with a mere gesture, a nod of his head or by some other sign, he indicated his understanding of or agreement with the matter under discussion. When he spoke, it was always worth listening to, whether you agreed with what he said or not. What he had to say was said with the minimum of words and in the minimum of time, and expressed his views clearly and firmly. It was, I felt, the mark of a wise man.

However, my happiest association with Nehru was in India during my recent visit to that country. I cannot enumerate the many acts of generosity and kindness that he displayed to me, but one stands out particularly in my memory. It was the night that I was leaving by train for the north. I had been warned that it would be pretty cold there and had borrowed an Air Force overcoat for the journey. Shortly before we were due to leave, Nehru unexpectedly arrived at the station looking rather extraordinary in an oversized overcoat. I could not disguise the look of astonishment on my face when I greeted him.

"Come on, come on!" he said, as he hurriedly pushed me into the railway compartment. "I know it is too big for me, but I think it. should be just right for you, and just what you will need in Nangal. Try it on."

I tried it on and it was, as, he had said, just right. I put my hands proudly in the pockets and discovered fresh surprises. In one there was a warm wool scarf and in the other a pair of warm gloves.

Again, I felt particularly honoured to be invited on so many occasions during my brief stay in Delhi into the intimacy of Nehru's home. Here, I discovered the family man, the softer and more relaxed Nehru, surrounded by the things he loved most — his daughter, his grandsons, his dogs and his home.

It is most difficult in so few words to write a real appreciation of Jawaharlal Nehru. All I can say is that I myself feel a better, wiser and richer man for having known him.

Lee Kuan Yew

In the English-speaking colonial world Jawaharlal Nehru is a legend. There is no nationalist in the British Colonial Empire, determined to fight for freedom from British imperialism, who has not heard of Nehru. Few might not have read his early writings, but of those who have there is no one who has not been moved by India's struggle for freedom, as he told it.

Great revolutionaries often die soon after achieving the overthrow of the old order. This is perhaps because had they lived on to see the failure of fulfilment that was expected after the revolution they would not continue to be classified among the great. Nehru is one exception. He has had to stand the test of two judgements: first, how well he succeeded in over-throwing the old order and second, whether he has succeeded in establishing a new order which is better than the old.

Almost thirteen years after independence nobody can say that his reputation has been tarnished as a result of attaining power. That is the highest tribute that one can pay to a revolutionary. For, we should never forget that despite the "respectability" which he has achieved since India became independent and he her first Prime Minister, Nehru was, and still is, one of Asia's great revolutionaries.

Lord Attlee

When a nation achieves independence not infrequently the years that follow are years of disillusion. The leaders in a struggle of this kind are often better at criticism than constructive thinking. Sometimes they are embittered and filled with old resentments and they seek to root out every vestige of the previous regime. Unaccustomed to administration on achieving independence, they empty out, in trying to get rid of their past, the baby with the bath water; rarely is found a man with sufficient breadth of mind and statesmanship to effect a successful transition from the old to a new order.

India, however, was fortunate in finding in Jawaharlal Nehru a man of exceptional character and wisdom.

Several years of imprisonment by the British Government in India had not soured or embittered him. He had the greatness of mind to rise above any pettiness. Understanding both East and West and realising what each tradition could contribute to the future of India he has led his country for nearly twelve years. He understood the vast problems of administering a huge subcontinent. He recognised that Indians who served the old regime as civil servants were as good lovers of their country as those who worked for change. He availed himself fully of their abilities; nor did he rashly smash to pieces a machine of government built up over many decades.

Moreover, there is a great temptation for the leader of a nation emerging from dependence to make himself a dictator. He may through a desire to make rapid progress ignore the principles of democracy and seek a short-cut. Nehru was too wise to do this.

He realised that reforms worked out with the consent of the people are more lasting than those imposed on them by a government from above. He has, therefore, always resisted the temptation to follow totalitarian methods.

As the spiritual heir of Gandhi and with immense personal prestige, he has nevertheless pursued the democratic road. Nationalism is a good servant but a bad master. Carried to extremes it may lead to the fragmentation of a world which needs unity if civilization is to win through the perils with which it is faced. There was, it seems to me, a danger that India might be fragmented if extreme claims for linguistic reorganisation were conceded.

Nehru has had to go some way in the creation of linguistic provinces. Indeed, some alteration of boundaries set up by the British for administrative convenience was desirable, but Nehru has not hesitated to check extremist tendencies. He has faced with courage the difficulties inherent in a multilingual community. Nor has he failed to recognise the danger inherent in any attempt to sweep away entirely the use of English which is in fact the *lingua franca* of democratic Asia.

His domestic policy in India has been in tune with his stand in the international sphere. This was particularly noticeable in his act of wise statesmanship by which he gave the lead for the continuance of India's membership in the British Commonwealth; for, this association with its complete freedom to all its members forms a most valuable link between peoples of different races living in different continents yet united by certain ideals.

I have welcomed the recognition by the peoples of European descent of the claims of the peoples of Asia and Africa to equality in the world, but I have always resisted the idea of self-contained continents looking askance at each other. Nehru has, I think, always recognised this danger. He wants world unity combined with freedom, not just a union of Asia. His attitude has sometimes been misunderstood, particularly in America.

His distaste for lining up with the Western bloc has, I feel, been misunderstood as being due to sympathy with Soviet Russia. Nehru is far too civilized a human being to fall for the arid doctrines of Marxism-Leninism and far too respectful of human dignity, to desire the introduction throughout the world of the totalitarian practices of the Russians.

As early as in 1936, when he was much more enamoured of Soviet Russia and much more hostile, owing to his anti-colonialism, to the West than he is today he wrote in his *Autobiography:* "I am very far from being a Communist, My roots are still perhaps partly in the nineteenth century, and I have been too much influenced by the humanist liberal tradition to get out of it completely. This bourgeois background follows me about and is naturally a source of irritation to many communists. I dislike dogmatism, and the treatment of Karl Marx's writings or any other books as revealed scripture which cannot be challenged, and the regimentation and heresy hunts which seem to be a feature of modern communism. I dislike also much that has happened in Russia, and especially the excessive use of violence in normal times.'

As far as I can see, Nehru desires that the uncommitted nations, by their non-alignment with one group or the other, should develop enough influence in the world to prevent a world catastrophe and towards that end he is anxious that India should play a useful part. That, in effect, is the kernel of his foreign policy.

Nehru is today the doyen of the Prime Ministers of the free world. As leader of a great nation what he says and does is of supreme importance to others. He has, of course, made mistakes. No one who does great things does not make them.

I myself have not always agreed with his policies and I have no doubt he would say the same of me, but I have great admiration for his achievements, and respect and affection for him as a great man.

It seems to me that Nehru is a synthesis of the ideas of the East and the West. He understands both. He is a product of the West; and he is also today the leader of the greatest democracy in Asia. It is my profound hope that the contest between the democratic and the authoritarian world will be fought out not in warfare but in the minds of men and in the ideological sphere. Asia is a battleground of these ideas; and we are lucky that, thanks very largely to Nehru, India stands out in this combat as the champion of freedom, democracy and the rule of law.

Lord Mountbatten

I first met Jawaharlal Nehru on the 18th March, 1946 when he came for a week's visit to Malaya at the time I was Supreme Commander, South-East Asia. He dined alone with my wife and me the first night and our friendship dates from that occasion.

When I went out to India as Viceroy a year later to arrange the transfer of power, his statesmanlike approach, untinged by any bitterness over his long imprisonment in British jails, was of the greatest help to me.

When I remained on as the first constitutional Governor-General of India I was particularly struck by the way he handled the overwhelming problems with which India was faced; what was more, his friendly feeling for Britain and his desire that India should remain within the Commonwealth were evident.

Although we have had no official connection with him since we left India in June, 1948, his friendship with my wife and me has enabled us to see quite a lot of one another and to keep touch by correspondence.

For our part both of us have a sincere sympathy and affection for him, and I feel certain that history will accord him an even greater place than contemporary world opinion gives him today.

Lord Pethick-Lawrence

When I as appointed Secretary of State for India and Burma in 1945 I realised that some 400 million people were being entrusted to my care — a greater number than that controlled by any other human being except the ruler of China in days gone by. Of course my responsibility was not absolute. I was myself a servant of the Grown and under the authority of the British Prime Minister-, and it was the Viceroy who was at the head of the Government of India. All the same, to the extent that it was true it was a solemn and sobering thought. For, the task was immense and bewilderingly complicated.

When I was in India in 1946, conducting with my colleagues the negotiations for the transference of power, Nehru said to me on one occasion, "Do not forget that if you and I come to an agreement, you are laying down a burden and I am picking it up." Today his words have become literally true. The mantle has fallen upon him and, in a much more real sense than it ever was of myself, he is in charge of the destinies of the Indian people who constitute more than half the population of the whole British Commonwealth spread over the five continents of the world.

Moreover, not only is Nehru India's Prime Minister, but he is today by far the most outstanding personality in his country, and is esteemed, obeyed and loved by the vast masses of its people. Nevertheless, powerful as he is, he remains in theory, in practice and, as I am convinced, at heart a democrat.

It has been my privilege and good fortune in the course of a long life to come into close and even intimate contact with several members of the Nehru family. In my early days as a Member of Parliament, I entertained Jawaharlal's father, Motilal, in the House of Commons. Jawaharlal's sister Mrs. Pandit who is the present High Commissioner in London has honoured me by many a personal talk. His daughter Indira was my charming hostess when I visited India at the end of 1957. She has since been chosen President of the Indian National Congress. I say, without fear of contradiction, of all of them and of the Prime Minister himself that their outstanding quality is single-mindedness. Their selfless devotion to the highest ideals of service places them above personal criticism.

That does not mean, of course, that the policies which the Congress has pursued under Jawaharlal's leadership are free from controversy; it could not be so in the very nature of things. India like all Asian countries has vast problems to contend with, which for centuries have defied solution and which some people even today regard as insoluble. Her poverty, unemployment and underemployment must be seen to be believed. Natural calamities, such as prolonged drought, work havoc with plans for feeding a population increasing ever more rapidly as health conditions improve and the death rate falls. The number and variety of her villages, scattered throughout India, make cooperation and education, urgent as they are, matters of extreme difficulty.

The Congress itself, composed as it is of liberal and conservative elements, is confronted therefore with opposition on both flanks and Nehru standing as I would adjudge somewhat to the left of centre finds himself attacked by communists and socialists for instituting changes too slowly, and by the more privileged classes for moving too fast and for being confiscatory and communistic. Further, the projects of successive Five-Year Plans require vast sums of money which strain the financial resources of the country to the utmost in spite of considerable assistance provided by the Commonwealth and the outside world.

Unshaken by the magnitude of his problems and by the criticisms of his policy from within and outside the Congress Nehru shoulders valiantly his full load of responsibility, and his tenacity of purpose and patience in exposition command universal respect. It is an experience for a Westerner to attend one of his political meetings and hear him address his audience. Unlike a European or American orator he does not commence on a bold and emphatic note or end with a carefully prepared rhetorical peroration. His voice begins quietly, almost imperceptibly like a piece of Indian music, it rises to a height of passionate pleading and fades away at the end into silence. And his listeners are greatly moved alike by his sincerity and his restraint.

But the great majority of my countrymen and countrywomen are not familiar with the details of the internal political and economic condition of India and her people. Their interest in Nehru is mainly concerned with his pronouncements and activities in the field of foreign affairs. They do not belong to any one party in our land. They include, of course, some who have accepted rather grudgingly the metamorphosis of our Empire into the Commonwealth as well as those who, like myself, regard this transformation as the highest expression of British democracy.

It is perhaps not surprising that the former are the more vocal and in consequence it is their criticism, often ill-informed and unjust, which is reproduced in India as the British reaction. But in fact this is not true. The great majority of the British people do not expect or wish India's Prime Minister to be a yes-man dutifully reflecting all the views and actions of the leaders who at any particular moment hold the reins of government in the United Kingdom. They realise that he is the recognised leader of a very important Asian country and that as such it is not only his right but his duty to give expression to the considered opinions of the most enlightened of his fellow countrymen.

Jawaharlal Nehru is fully competent to perform this duty. He has the courage and the tenacity to tell us when he differs from us and the generosity when he agrees with us. We, in our turn, are entitled freely to express our reactions to what he says or does. But in both cases it must be the criticism of friends and not of enemies anxious to score off one against the other. That is the essence of our common tradition and knowing Jawaharlal as I do I am confident that as an Asian democrat and a lover of the British people he will uphold that tradition to the mutual benefit of the Commonwealth and to the greater good of human understanding throughout the world.

Ludwig Erhard

When a man like Nehru reaches the age of seventy, with a long life of statesmanship behind him, it is only fitting that the whole world should take notice of the event and pause for a moment to recall what the work, what the existence of such a man means to it.

India is a country where many of the lines of world policy converge; hence, the destiny of our age will to some extent be decided there. The strength of its population and its geographical situation alone would suffice to give it weight. India is thus leading those countries which have in the last decade set out to find new political and social ways of life. It is a gain and blessing for the whole world that this task should be entrusted to the sure hands of a man who knows how to build a bridge that links the past and the present with the future.

India is a country with an old culture and a colourful history; it has poverty and wealth, an industrial tradition and an agricultural base that dates back to times immemorial. The experience and insight gained from this set of circumstances made India commit herself to the path of non-violence. In choosing this way, India has decided against both the old Western and the new Red imperialism. It has become a world power which will hold its own with this moral attitude, without weapons or enormous armaments.

This corresponds in home affairs to its decision in favour of human freedom, not freedom from something but freedom to do something: to unleash the full potential of the farming population so that the farmer, under the guidance of the State and with the common effort of cooperative societies, may produce enough to banish hunger from India; to encourage the activity of entrepreneurs and the industriousness of craftsmen so that the highest and most balanced production may be reached for the benefit of all, and this in both its spiritual and material sense. All these endeavours have gained for India the sympathy and support of the whole world.

Good men all over the globe hope with India that the moral power of non-violence and freedom will secure the future and the peace of India, and with it, perhaps, of the whole world.

Two names are representative of the India referred to in these lines. The names of Gandhi and Nehru, one designating a great historical figure whose influence is still a live force in his country and the other a man who holds the destiny of his people in his strong and wise hands today.

S. Radhakrishnan

There is a theory that history is made and nations are shaped by deep currents, economic or other, which drive them inexorably into predestined channels. Even outstanding human individuals, whatever they may appear to do, are tossed about in the currents and do not alter anything very much. This view is not altogether correct. There are historical forces beyond the control of men which sway the future course of life but the quality of great men is not altogether irrelevant to a nation's destiny. Whether it is Caesar or Napoleon, Lenin or Gandhi, they do affect their country and its fortunes. Jawaharlal Nehru is a person of exceptional quality who has had an enduring impact on India's recent history.

If we wish to judge revolutionary heroes we must watch them at close range and judge them at great distance. When we watch Nehru at close range, we feel that we are in the presence of a man of extraordinary gifts, of talents that amount to genius, who has given himself to the service of his fellowmen. He could kindle in a whole nation the fire that burned within him and interpret its spirit to itself. Posterity will look upon him as one of the great liberators of humanity.

The greatest title ever offered to human effort is that of liberator. Nehru took a leading part in the struggle for freedom and worked for the great opportunity which he now has of liberating the minds and hearts of the Indian people from enslavement, from superstition, from outworn ideas, and leading them to their destiny. What made us slaves for centuries was not the strength of the invader but our own disunion. Consolidation of the country is the task that is set to our generation. Nehru is addressing himself to this great task with all his faith and valour.

Nehru is essentially a democrat. In his way of thinking, there is no place for intolerance, racial or social condescension or national aggressiveness. Even when he acquiesces in policies that are not quite consistent with the spirit of democracy, he does so with the utmost reluctance. In an infant democracy like ours, he is anxious that we should not set up wrong precedents. He is incapable of ruthless action and some may think that no government can govern unless it is hard on evil-doers, the perpetrators of sharp practices and corrupt dealings. But one need not be ruthless to be vigilant about incompetence, graft, corruption and nepotism.

There is some truth in the general impression that Nehru is aloof, that he does not give himself away in conversation, that he is generally reticent and withdrawn with individuals though he is very happy with people. Nehru is readily accessible and is always open to argument, but there are very few who argue with him. That is his misfortune. He is loyal to his friends and that is a noble quality. Being of an introspective turn of mind and very sensitive even to the inaudible currents of public opinion, he strives his utmost to avoid any partiality to friends or unfairness to the country.

He generally inaugurates the Indian Science Congress meetings and pleads for a scientific outlook on all matters. If we do not expand scientific and technical education, we cannot ensure our future. India cannot survive if ability and inventiveness are not encouraged. The history of dictatorships is a monument to the misery, poverty and insecurity of people. If political stability is to be secured, these require to be removed. Nehru wishes to .find a way between unbridled capitalism and totalitarian systems. He pleads for socialism which means for him a fuller and more satisfying life in which standards of education, health and culture enlarge for everyone. He will not sacrifice the freedom of the human spirit for anything. His is therefore a type of ethical socialism which is the central feature of the Indian tradition.

The compound of old and new makes India the most exciting of all countries. She has had a great tradition and that tradition is kept alive, because we do not shrink from examining afresh, from time to time, every custom and institution that we take for granted simply because they have been there for a long time. We should like to remain Indian and yet be modern.

Toleration and appreciation of other points of view have been with us from the beginning of our history. Every society has its own cultural values. Though they may be different from our own, they carry an underlying likeness to our own. In the present context of the world, Nehru feels that we should develop a new method of settling international disputes. The doctrine of Panchsheel which he advocates requires that force should be reduced to the minimum, and persuasion, which implies understanding, mutual consideration, concession and agreement, should be the dominating factor. He has sought to bridge the chasms that separate races, nations and systems. That is why his name has such a great international appeal and become a legend in his own lifetime.

Jawaharlal Nehru is seventy. He is still amazingly young in spirit. Till recently he used to give way to raw emotions, though he recovered tranquillity in a minute. The Indian people love him so much that they forgive him his few frailties. Perfection lives in realms above. Nehru has vision and courage, fire and intensity. He does not spend much time glorifying the past but is always active meeting the challenge of the future. He is the voice of the Indian people, their hopes and aspirations for political stability, for social change, for democratic planning, for world peace. It is our earnest hope that he may live for many years to guide this country on its onward march to freedom and fulfilment.

S. W. R. D. Bandaranaike

I have known Nehru personally for over 25 years. I first came in contact with him when he visited Ceylon in the early-30s. The first thing that struck me about him was the contrast he presented to his great leader, Mahatma Gandhi who also had visited Ceylon some time earlier. The Mahatma was clearly a son of the people. He was also, although a saint and ascetic, very human with a strong sense of humour. Physically, although he looked frail, he was tough with an almost inexhaustible fund of physical energy. Nehru, on the other hand, is a delicately nurtured aristocrat with high-strung nerves, possessed also of inexhaustible energy, though in his case, it is more nervous energy than physical capacity. It is a fact that he often uses up his nervous energy and that makes him sometimes short-tempered and irritable.

I remember a little incident during one of his visits to Ceylon many years ago. We were lunching at an outstation town, Kurunegala, when an admiring crowd was peeping through the doors and windows as we lunched. Nehru turned to us and said, "I can do many things in public but I just cannot eat in public", or words to that effect, I remember saying to myself with some amusement, "There speaks the sensitive aristocrat". We, of course, asked the crowd to withdraw until lunch was over. I suppose in some ways I am qualified to understand such a temperament as that of Nehru. Although he has his outbursts of temper and irritation, he is a most charming personality, and one for whom the more one gets to know him the greater becomes one's regard and even affection. I look upon him in our personal relations as a friend for whom I have both those feelings.

I wish to say something about another side of Nehru: his position as a public man. He is a great servant of his country and an outstanding statesman of Asia and the world generally. I remember some years ago, at a time when he was not the acknowledged leader of India as he later became, asking a prominent Indian leader who in his opinion was the most outstanding leader after Mahatma Gandhi. He said, 'Jawaharlal Nehru'. When I further questioned him why he chose Nehru in preference to some others whose names I mentioned, he replied, because Nehru is so utterly dependable. I should think that it is this feeling about him that has ensured for him the continuing confidence of the vast majority of his people. Nehru is one of the few statesmen of the world who have a background of culture and learning, and who are thinkers beside being also men of action. Such men are necessary as leaders particularly at a troubled period of world history such as this — men with a background of learning, men who can think clearly, men who can see a problem not merely from one point of view, but in all its aspects and who can come to decisions, sometimes very difficult decisions, with knowledge of factors not only in respect of the past and the present, but also of the future. Nehru has not only a knowledge of history so important for statesmen to have, but something much more than that. He understands the philosophy of history. He therefore has a correct feeling for the trends of the present and the future. At the same time he is a man of courage. As he himself has said, "I may sometimes lose my temper but I never lose my nerve." It is these qualities that make him a valuable servant of India and an important world statesman.

I see that he is sometimes blamed in India for being weak and hesitant on certain occasions. Knowing him as I do, I am inclined to think that this is an entirely undeserved criticism. What to some superficial observers may appear to be weakness or hesitation in him is perhaps really nothing more than the fact that he likes to take into account all sides and aspects of a question and that he is possessed of that fundamental sense of fairness that makes him capable of seeing the other man's point of view as well as his own before coming to a decision.

He has now reached what is generally considered to be the span of an average man's life: Threescore and ten. He has had a full, varied and distinguished career. His place in history is already assured. He is still, however, full of vigour and energy and neither India nor indeed the world can afford to dispense with the services of a man such as he. May he be spared for many years to come in the service of India and of us all.

U Nu

The early decades of the twentieth century were momentous

off her lethargy and

developed herself into a modern nation marching shoulder to shoulder with other nations. India embarked on a mission of rediscovering herself, of regaining the place of pride amongst the civilizations of the world which she had held for thousands of years, and convincing herself that India in the modern world had as much to contribute to humanity as she had done in centuries gone by.

This was the struggle into which Jawaharlal Nehru plunged, fresh from his English education and environment. The first step in India's struggle to rediscover herself was to shake off the yoke of foreign domination. Mahatma Gandhi evolved a peculiarly Indian approach to this struggle, through *Ahimsa.* Jawaharlal Nehru saw at once this was the correct approach, and shaking off the inhibitions he had acquired through long years of residence and education in a foreign land, he threw himself whole-heartedly into the struggle. His contribution to the struggle for Indian independence — and his attitude throughout — was as truly Indian as that of any of Mahatma Gandhi's followers. He thus quickly established himself as the idol of his people, as the quintessence of the spirit of independence and of rediscovering India's ancient heritage that permeated India's struggle for freedom.

Jawaharlal's intellectual approach was, however, different from many of his countrymen's. While drawing deeply from the cultural traditions of the past, he never for a moment let himself and his countrymen forget that history has marched on, and no Indian can be content merely with harking back to his past and failing to equip himself as a citizen of the modern world. He was young in those days and full of vision. He had clear ideas as to what the India of his dream should look like, and the influence he exerted on the younger generation through his numerous writings and personal example created a better realisation of the part India must play in the world. This was his major contribution to India's struggle to rediscover herself.

Secondly, his approach was as highly intellectual as it was emotional. No doubt, Jawaharlal was a man of deep emotions; no one without his emotional appeal could have found a place in the heart of his country that he did many decades ago and retains to this day. But his emotionalism was sobered and guided by his keen intellect, and by his deep study and understanding of the ideas and philosophies which permeated and convulsed the world during the thirty years before the Second World War.

He thus became an early convert to socialism — the most dynamic philosophical force of the time. Jawaharlal's second major contribution to India's struggle for freedom was thus to maintain a balance between high emotionalism and cool-headed intellectualism.

These two characteristics asserted themselves fully after India's independence and placed the destiny of this great nation in his hands. They show themselves clearly in Jawaharlal's attitude to communism and economic development. The idealistic aspects of communism had a great emotional appeal for Jawaharlal, as indeed for many of us in the East.

But the methods employed by communism to achieve its ends, and the acquisitive ambitions that it developed during and after the Second World War, soon disenamoured Jawaharlal and many others in our part of the world. With it also came the growing realisation that the communist creed is alien to our soil and Jawaharlal today is a firm opponent of communism in his country.

In the sphere of economic development, Jawaharlal committed his country to a programme of modernisation which alone can assure it of a worthy place amongst modern communities. The success he has had in this field is well known, but the heart-breaks and disappointments he has endured are known only to his close circle and associates. Nevertheless, Jawaharlal has established a balance between emotion and reason in India's economic programmes, which promises her an era of prosperity never known in history.

In foreign affairs also, Jawaharlal has carefully and deliberately moderated his country's emotions by a stern sense of realism. His long association with the Indian struggle for independence and his deep understanding of history made him keenly aware of the fact that no newly-independent nation can preserve its freedom if it allowed itself to be allied with any power group; hence, his firm policy of neutrality for India. Nevertheless, he realised that India cannot exist alone in this world, that she cannot refuse to take a stand in regard to the major issues that arise in world politics, or play an active and positive role in creating understanding between nations. Hence, his policy of positive neutrality. In individual issues, this fine balance between emotion and intellect was most clearly apparent in his recent handling of the Chinese action in Tibet.

He is keenly aware that though the march of history has brought independence to dependent nations, they have not been immune from the interplay of power politics. Attempts by both power blocs to draw the smaller and newly-independent countries into their orbit have been persistent and some have fallen victims thereto. Jawaharlal has been a staunch champion of resisting all such attempts and has successfully withstood all pressure and stood out boldly, despite the many misinterpretations and misunderstanding of his attitude.

This attitude has been a source of deep inspiration to many other countries in Africa and the East; his example has been a standing assurance for the maintenance of their own independence and their national self-respect and pride.

I have had the good fortune of associating myself closely with Jawaharlal Nehru since the end of the Second World War and watching him react through many moods. The dominant impression left on me is of a man perpetually drawn between emotion and a superbly cool-headed intellectualism. Many a time — both at conferences and in private conversation — Jawaharlal seemed to be on the verge of being carried away by his emotions, but on each occasion his superb sense of realism and his fine intellectual appraisal of the issues under discussion have pulled him back and the final result has invariably been a sound, unshakable balance.

This is his great quality. His undisputed leadership in independent India has enabled Jawaharlal to project this personal characteristic on the sphere of Indian politics; through the world-wide emotional conflict of the post-war years, through the long years of cold war tactics between the two great power blocs, India has stood with her feet firmly on the ground, unswayed and in perfect balance.

The balance between emotion and intellect in Jawaharlal's individuality thus projected itself on the individuality of India as a nation and she has as a result acquired a position in the world today unique amongst all newly-independent nations.

We hope and pray not only that this balance will continue into the future but that it will be a source of inspiration to all independent nations of Africa and Asia.

11

Golden Words of Nehru

- Democracy is good. I say this because other systems are worse.
- Every little thing counts in a crisis.
- Facts are facts and will not disappear on account of your likes.
- Failure comes only when we forget our ideals and objectives and principles.
- Great causes and little men go ill together.
- I have become a queer mixture of the East and the West, out of place everywhere, at home nowhere.
- Ignorance is always afraid of change.
- It is only too easy to make suggestions and later try to escape the consequences of what we say.
- It is the habit of every aggressor nation to claim that it is acting on the defensive.
- Let us be a little humble; let us think that the truth may not perhaps be entirely with us.
- Life is like a game of cards. The hand you are dealt is determinism; the way you play it is free will.

- Loyal and efficient work in a great cause, even though it may not be immediately recognised, ultimately bears fruit.
- Obviously, the highest type of efficiency is that which can utilise existing material to the best advantage.
- Our chief defect is that we are more given to talking about things than to doing them.
- Peace is not a relationship of nations. It is a condition of mind brought about by a serenity of soul. Lasting peace can come only to peaceful people.
- A leader or a man of action in a crisis almost always acts subconsciously and then thinks of the reasons for his action.
- A moment comes, which comes but rarely in history, when we step out from the old to the new; when an age ends; and when the soul of a nation long suppressed finds utterance.
- A theory must be tempered with reality.
- Action itself, so long as I am convinced that it is right action, gives me satisfaction.
- Action to be effective must be directed to clearly conceived ends.
- Citizenship consists in the service of the country.
- Crises and deadlocks when they occur have at least this advantage, that they force us to think.
- Culture is the widening of the mind and of the spirit.
- Democracy and socialism are means to an end, not the end itself.
- Peace is not a relationship of nations. It is a condition of mind brought about by a serenity of soul. Peace is not merely the absence of war. It is also a state of mind. Lasting peace can come only to peaceful people.
- Time is not measured by the passing of years but by what one does, what one feels, and what one achieves.

- To be in good moral condition requires at least as much training as to be in good physical condition.
- We live in a wonderful world that is full of beauty, charm and adventure. There is no end to the adventures that we can have if only we seek them with our eyes open.
- What we really are matters more than what other people think of us.
- Without peace, all other dreams vanish and are reduced to ashes.
- You don't change the course of history by turning the faces of portraits to the wall.
- Socialism is... not only a way of life, but a certain scientific approach to social and economic problems.
- The art of a people is a true mirror to their minds.
- The forces in a capitalist society, if left unchecked, tend to make the rich richer and the poor poorer.
- The man who has gotten everything he wants is all in favour of peace and order.
- The only alternative to coexistence is codestruction.
- The person who runs away exposes himself to that very danger more than a person who sits quietly.
- The person who talks most of his own virtue is often the least virtuous.
- The policy of being too cautious is the greatest risk of all.
- The purely agitational attitude is not good enough for a detailed consideration of a subject.
- There is perhaps nothing so bad and so dangerous in life as fear.

12

Nehru's Life at a Glance

1889: Born 14 November in Allahabad, the son of Motilal and Swaruprani Nehru

1905-07: Harrow School, Harrow-on-the-Hill, Middlesex.

1907-10: Trinity College, Cambridge.

1910-12: Inner Temple, London.

1912: Returned to India. Lawyer, Allahabad High Court.

1913: Joint Secretary, Allahabad branch of St John Ambulance Brigade.

1916: Married, 8 February Kamala Kaul.

1917: Joined Home Rule League. Daughter, Indira, born 19 November.

1918: Secretary, Home Rule League.

1919: Started the newspaper, *Independent*, with Motilal Nehru.

1920: Joined the Non-cooperation Movement.

1921: Arrested 6 December for participating in the Volunteer Movement and urging the boycott of the visit of the Prince of Wales to India.

1922: Released 3 March. Arrested 11 May for picketing cloth shops.

1923: Released 26 January. Elected April Chairman, Allahabad Municipal Board. (Resigned January 1925). Arrested 19 September for defying an order banning entry into Nabha State. (Released 6 October). Presided October over the United Provinces Political Conference, Benares. Founded December the Hindustani Seva Dal. General Secretary, Indian National Congress, 1923-25.

1926-7: Visited Europe and Britain. Attended 10 February 1927 the Congress of Oppressed Nationalities, Brussels. Visited November the Soviet Union. Moved December the 'Independence Resolution' at the Madras session of the Indian National Congress. General Secretary, Indian National Congress, 1927-29.

1928: Presided April over the Punjab Provincial Conference. Founded August the Independence for India League. Presided September over the All Bengal Students Conference. Active in the boycott of the Simon Commission; lathi-charged November, Lucknow.

1929: Presided 30 November over the Nagpur session of the All-India Trade Union Congress. Presided 29 December over the Lahore session of the Indian National Congress.

1930: Participated in the Salt Satyagraha Movement and arrested 14 April. (Released 11 October). Arrested 19 October for speech made in favour of the no-tax campaign.

1931: Released 26 January. Motilal Nehru died 6 February. Arrested 26 December for breach of an internment order prohibiting him from leaving the municipal limits of Allahabad. (Released 30 August 1933).

1934: Organised January relief for the victims of the Bihar earthquake. Arrested 12 February for speeches made in Calcutta. (Released 11 August on parole). Returned 23 August to prison. (Released 4 September 1935).

1936: Kamala Nehru died 28 February in Lausanne, Switzerland. Presided 23 April over the Lucknow session of the Indian National Congress. Travelled April-December round India campaigning on behalf of Congress candidates for the General Elections. Presided 27 December over the Faizpur session of the Indian National Congress.

1938: Swaruprani Nehru died 10 January. Visited Spain, France, Britain and some other European countries. Chairman, National Planning Committee.

1939: Visited Sri Lanka and China. Drafted the Congress re-solution on the war.

1940: Chosen to be the second satyagrahi in the Individual Satyagraha Movement. Arrested 31 October for speeches made in Gorakhpur. (Released 4 December 1941).

1942: Negotiations March-April with Sir Stafford Cripps. Moved 7 August the 'Quit India' resolution at the All-India Congress Committee meeting. Arrested 9 August.

1945: Released 15 June. Represented 25 June - 14 July the Congress at the Shimla Conference. Campaigned for Congress candidates in the elections. Appeared November as a lawyer for the defence at the trial of the Indian National Army Officers. Vice-President, Indian Centre of the P.E.N. Elected December President of the All-India States People's Conference.

1946: Visited March South-east Asia. Held April-June talks with members of the British Cabinet Mission. Elected May President of the Indian National Congress. (Resigned in September). Trip June to Kashmir, arrest and release. Interim government formed 2 September with Nehru as Vice-President of the Viceroy's Executive Council and member for External Affairs and Commonwealth Relations. Moved 13 December the 'Objectives Resolution' in the Constituent Assembly.

1947: Inaugurated 23 March the Asian Relations Conference, New Delhi. Broadcast 3 June to the nation accepting the partition proposals. Became 15 August first Prime Minister of free India.

1948: Mahatma Gandhi died 30 January. Attended October the Commonwealth Prime Ministers' Conference, London. Addressed 3 November the Special Session of the United Nations General Assembly, Paris.

1949: Inaugurated 20 January the conference of eighteen nations to condemn Dutch aggression on Indonesia. First visit October-November to the USA and Canada.

1950: India became a Republic 26 January-. Became March Chairman, Planning Commission. (Held this office till his death).

1951: Elected President, Indian National Congress. (Continued till 1954)

1952: Formed May new government after the first General Elections. Began 2 October Community Development Programme.

1953: Chief Ministers' Conference November, New Delhi. Appointed December States Reorganisation Commission.

1954: Chou En-lai visited India. Issued June joint statement of the Prime Ministers of India and China, listing the five principles (Panchsheel) for the regulation of relations between nations.

1955: Moved January the resolution on a 'Socialistic Pattern of Society' at the Avadi session of the Indian National Congress. Afro-Asian Conference, Bandung, 15-25 April.

1956: Conference 17-18 July with President Nasser of Egypt and President Tito of Yugoslavia, Brioni. Conference November of the Prime Ministers of Indonesia, Burma, Ceylon and India, New Delhi.

1957: Formed April new government after the second General Elections.

1959: Sponsored January resolution on cooperative farming and state trading of food grains at the Nagpur session of the Indian National Congress,

1960: Addressed 3 October the United Nations General Assembly, New York.

1961: Conference of Non-aligned Nations, Belgrade, September.

1962: Formed April new government after the third General Elections. Presided June over the National Integration Council meeting. State of Emergency proclaimed 26 October by the President of India following the Chinese aggression.

1963: 'Kamaraj Plan'—ministers relinquished office to reorganise the Congress Party.

1964: Died 27 May in New Delhi. Cremated at what is now Shanti Vana on the banks of the Yamuna.

Bibliography

Ainslie, Embree, T.: *Encyclopedia of Asian History,* Charles Scribner's Sons, New York, 1988.

Alok Datta: *Indian Non-Alignment and National Interest: From Jawaharlal Nehru to Indira Gandhi,* Sujan Publications, 2005.

Balan, K.: *Mahatma Gandhi and Jawaharlal Nehru: The Two Stalwarts Who Shaped India,* Authors Press, 2002.

Chalapathi M. Rau: *Ministry of Information and Broadcasting,* Publications Division, 1973.

———: *Jawaharlal Nehru: Life and Work,* National Book Club, 1966.

Chopra, P. N.: *Thematic Volumes on Sardar Vallabhbhai Patel: Jawaharlal Nehru, Gandhi and Subhas Chandra Bose,* Konark, 2003.

Cohen, Stephen, P.: *The Indian Army: Its Contribution to the Development of a Nation,* Delhi, 1990.

Dennis Judd: *Jawaharlal Nehru,* University of Wales Press, Cardiff, 1993.

Dhawan, S. K.: *Jawaharlal Nehru and the World of Books,* A Select Study, Wave Publications, 1991.

Fane, Henry: *Five Years in India,* London, 1842.

Gopal, S. and Uma Iyengar: *Jawaharlal Nehru: The Essential Writings of Jawaharlal Nehru,* Oxford University Press, 2003.

Iqbal Singh: *Between Two Fires: Towards an Understanding of Jawaharlal Nehru's Foreign Policy,* Orient Longman, 1998.

Jawaharlal Nehru and Karan Singh: *Jammu and Kashmir 1949-64: Jawaid Alam,* Penguin Books, 2006.

Jawaharlal Nehru: *An Autobiography,* Penguin, 2004.

Joseph Stanislaw and Daniel Yergin, A.: *Commanding Heights,* Simon and Schuster, New York, 1998.

Manisha: *Profiles of Indian Prime Ministers: Pt. Jawaharlal Nehru to Dr. Manmohan Singh,* Mittal, 2004.

Michael Brecher: *Nehru: A Political Biography,* Oxford University Press, London, 1959.

Mridula Mukherjee: *Selected Works of Jawaharlal Nehru: Second Series,* Jawaharlal Nehru Memorial Fund, 2009.

Nand Lal Gupta: *Jawaharlal Nehru on Communalism,* Hope India Publication, 2006.

Nanda, B. R.: *Jawaharlal Nehru: A Pictorial Biography,* Publications Division, 2005.

————: *Three Statesmen Gokhale: Gandhi and Nehru,* Oxford University Press, New Delhi, 2004.

Neerja Maheshwari, Deep: Economic Policy of Jawaharlal Nehru, 1997.

Rakesh Gupta: *Use of Metaphors by Jawaharlal Nehru,* Shubhi Publication, 2007.

Robert Sherrod: *Nehru: The Great Awakening,* Saturday Evening Post, 1963.

Santanu Bagchi: *Ideas on Socialism and Social Justice: A Study of Jawaharlal Nehru,* Rammanohar Lohia and Asoke Mehta, Kanishka, 2002.

Selig, Harrison, S.: *The Challenge to Indian Nationalism,* Foreign Affairs, 1956.

Sharada Prasad H. Y. and Damodaran, A. K.: *Selected Works of Jawaharlal Nehru: Second Series,* Jawaharlal Nehru Mem Fund, 2002.

Shashi Tharoor: *Nehru: The Invention of India,* Arcade Books, 2003.

Sunil Khilnani: *A Bunch of Old Letters: Being Mostly Written to Jawaharlal Nehru and Some Written by Him: Edited by Jawaharlal Nehru,* With an Introduction by Penguin Books, 2005.

Taufiq Nizami, A.: *Jawaharlal Nehru: The Architect of India's Foreign Policy,* ICON Publication, 2006.

Vinod Tagra: *Jawaharlal Nehru and the Status of Women in India: An Analytical Study,* Reliance, 2006.

Welles Hangen: *After Nehru,* Rupert Hart-Davis, London, 1963.

Index

I

J

K

L

M

N

P

Q

R

S

U

W

Y

Z

❑❑❑